Environmental and Public Economics

Essays in Honor of Wallace E. Oates

Edited by
Arvind Panagariya
Professor of Economics and co-Director of the Center for International Economics, University of Maryland at College Park, Maryland, USA

Paul R. Portney
President and Senior Fellow, Resources for the Future, Washington, DC, USA

Robert M. Schwab
Professor of Economics, University of Maryland at College Park, Maryland, USA

Edward Elgar
Cheltenham, UK • Northampton, MA, USA

Published by
Edward Elgar Publishing Limited
Glensanda House
Montpellier Parade
Cheltenham
Glos GL50 1UA
UK

Edward Elgar Publishing, Inc.
136 West Street
Suite 202
Northampton
Massachusetts 01060
USA

A catalogue record for this book is available from the British Library

Library of Congress Cataloging in Publication Data

Environmental and public economics : essays in honor of Wallace E. Oates / edited by Arvind Panagariya, Paul R. Portney, Robert M. Schwab.
1. Environmental economics. 2. Economic policy. 3. Oates, Wallace E. I. Oates, Wallace E. II. Panagariya, Arvind. III. Portney, Paul R. IV. Schwab, Robert M.
HC79.E5E5753 1999
333.7—dc21 98–46623
CIP

ISBN 1 85898 611 7

Printed and bound in Great Britain by Biddles Ltd, Guildford and King's Lynn

Contents

Figures

Tables

Contributors

William J. Baumol is Director C.V. Starr Center for Applied Economics, New York University and Professor Emeritus, Princeton University.

Jan K. Brueckner is Professor at the Department of Economics and Institute of Government and Public Affairs, University of Illinois.

Maureen L. Cropper is Professor at the Department of Economics, University of Maryland and University Fellow at Resources for the Future, Washington, DC.

Paul N. Courant is Professor of Economics and Public Policy, University of Michigan.

Alan V. Deardorff is Professor of Economics and Public Policy, University of Michigan.

Terry M. Dinan is senior Analyst at the Natural Resources and Commerce Division of the Congressional Budget Office, Washington, DC.

Dennis Epple is Thomas Word Professor of Economics at the Graduate School of Industrial Administration, Carnegie Mellon University and Research Associate of the National Bureau of Economic Research.

Don Fullerton is Addison Baker Duncan Centennial Professor at the Department of Economics, University of Texas, Austin and Research Associate of the National Bureau of Economic Research.

Lawrence H. Goulder is Associate Professor in the Department of Economics at Stanford University, a University Fellow at Resources for the Future Washington, DC and a Research Associate of the National Bureau of Economic Research.

David L. Hummels is Assistant Professor of Economics at the University of Chicago Business School.

Robert P. Inman is Professor of Finance and Economics, Wharton School, University of Pennsylvania, Philadelphia and Research Associate at the National Bureau of Economic Research.

Nathaniel O. Keohane is a PhD student in Political Economy and Government at Harvard University.

Carol Mansfield is Assistant Professor of Environmental Economics at the Nicholas School of Environment, Duke University.

Elizabeth Newlon is a PhD student at the Graduate School of Industrial Administration at Carnegie Mellon University.

Arvind Panagariya is Professor at the Department of Economics, University of Maryland.

Paul R. Portney is President of and Senior Fellow at Resources for the Future, Washington, DC.

Richard L. Revesz is Professor of Law at the New York University School of Law.

Richard E. Romano is Professor at the Department of Economics, University of Florida, Gainesville.

Robert M. Schwab is Professor at the Department of Economics, University of Maryland.

Kurt A. Schwabe is Assistant Professor at the Department of Economics, Ohio University.

V. Kerry Smith is Arts and Sciences Professor at the Department of Economics and Nicholas School of the Environment, Duke University and University Fellow at Resources for the Future.

Robert N. Stavins is Professor of Public Policy at the John F. Kennedy School of Government, Harvard University and a University Fellow at Resources for the Future.

John Joseph Wallis is Professor at the Department of Economics, University of Maryland and Research Associate of the National Bureau of Economic Research.

David E. Wildasin is Professor at the Department of Economics, Vanderbilt University, Nashville.

Ann Wolverton is a PhD student at the Department of Economics, University of Texas, Austin.

John Yinger is Professor of Economic and Public Administration at the Maxwell School, Syracuse University.

Introduction

Wallace E. Oates has made fundamental contributions in many areas of economics and beyond. But in two key areas, environmental economics and public economics, his influence is so pronounced that it is difficult to imagine what these fields might have been like without his writings. Wally's contributions in these areas have set the agenda for research and the tone of policy debates. As a scholar, he has exhibited an uncanny ability to anticipate important economic problems before anyone else and to offer solutions that eventually become the conventional wisdom. As a teacher, he has nurtured numerous students who have gone on to form the backbone of public economics and environmental economics in both the research and policy communities. To the three of us, he has been a colleague, mentor and valued friend. It is a great pleasure to assemble this volume to honour Wally and to celebrate his many achievements.

Wally was born in California in 1937 and graduated from Stanford University in 1958. After serving in the US Navy, he entered Stanford's PhD program in economics in 1962. His dissertation *The Economics of Federalism: The Stabilization and Tax Harmonization Problems* forcefully opened an area which remains vibrant today. After gaining his degree in 1965, Wally joined the Princeton faculty. In the late 1960s and early 1970s, together with Edwin Mills, he worked with a group of students who would shape the direction of local public finance for decades. Paul Courant, Dennis Epple, Bill Fischel, Michelle White and Bruce Hamilton all received their degrees during this period. While at Princeton, Wally himself wrote *Fiscal Federalism* and co-authored *The Theory of Environmental Policy* with Will Baumol. Both of these books became essential references for researchers and students.

In 1979, Wally joined the University of Maryland faculty where he has worked with many graduate students in both environmental and public economics. Wally has also been a University Fellow at Resources for the Future (RFF) since 1986. He has collaborated with many of his colleagues at both Maryland and RFF including Maureen Cropper, Bill Evans, Harry Kelejian, Arvind Panagariya, Paul Portney, Bob Schwab, and John Wallis.

Wally's contributions go well beyond the narrow confines of economics. His passions range from classical antiquity to Italian frescoes and the Baltimore Orioles. He is a serious student of ancient Greek and has read in Greek the writings of Homer, Euripedes and Plato. He knows Giotto's work well enough to have once caught an error in a draft of a scholarly article on the Arena Chapel (written by the wife of one of the co-editors of this volume, who thanks him profusely for sparing her great embarrassment). But Wally's love of Homer pales in comparison to his love of homers. He and his wife, Grace Mary, are devoted Orioles fans who feel short changed if they miss batting practice before settling in for a doubleheader. The public economics workshop at Maryland is held on Monday afternoons, but we long ago learned not to schedule the workshop on the first Monday of April – none of us dare come between Wally and a chance to see Cal Ripken on an opening day. Who but Wally and Grace Mary would have written John Lowenstein a three-page poem, begging him to remain with the Os?

Wally is a true superstar of the profession: gracious, warm, modest and generous. He is a model for us all.

ENVIRONMENTAL ECONOMICS

Wally was a pioneer in environmental economics. His papers and books – often written in concert with graduate students, colleagues and others fortunate enough to get the opportunity – have profoundly influenced the field. Consider, for example, Wally's research with Will Baumol on the attractiveness of a hybrid system of politically or scientifically determined environmental quality standards, coupled with the use of pollution taxes designed to ensure attainment of those standards. Until that 1971 paper appeared in the *Swedish Journal of Economics*, it is fair to say that economists were struggling with how they might measure the marginal damages associated with varying levels of pollution. This is because the prevailing view of effluent taxes at that time was that they ought to be set equal to marginal damages at the point at which these damages were exactly offset by the marginal costs of pollution control. If the former could not be measured, how could taxes be set?

Oates and Baumol said, in effect, 'so what if we can't measure damages?' Recognizing the difficulty of the first-best approach, they recommended that environmental quality standards – for instance, the maximum permissible amount of sulfur dioxide in the air, or dissolved solids in water – be set whichever was the regulatory authority desired. Once this standard was set, however, they pointed out that a tax on pollution would ensure that it would be met with least cost to society. This would not result in an overall optimum, to be sure, but it would be much more efficient than using technology-based source discharge standards to meet the environmental quality objective. Simple as this idea seems today, it immediately shifted the debate about incentive-based approaches from the benefit–cost paradigm to the cost-effectiveness paradigm. The latter has always been a much easier case to make.

In subsequent work, Wally helped develop the theory behind marketable permits for pollution control, and (often working with graduate students) assisted in the development of the first models used to estimate the efficiency gains these permits made possible. This empirical work, augmented by the work of researchers elsewhere, provided the evidence necessary to 'sell' the permit approach as a real-world solution when Congress was grappling in the late 1980s with a way to control acid rain. Indeed, without too much exaggeration, this body of work could be said to have contributed to the adoption of an air pollution control program embodied in the amendments to the Clean Air Act that is currently saving electricity consumers in the United States \$1 to \$3 billion annually.

Wally's work on environmental federalism, which integrates neatly his research in public finance and environmental economics, has also influenced both academicians and policy makers. This work is aimed at answering the following question: what is the right level of government in which to invest power for various environmental problems? The principal economic justification for environmental regulation is the presence of externalities, generally in the production of goods and services. In the case of air and water pollution, these external effects can easily spill over state and even national borders thus creating the need for at least some federal regulation.

But not every environmental problem generates such interstate or international spillovers; drinking-water contamination and most solid or hazardous waste disposal sites are notable examples. Although these environmental issues would seem to be best addressed at the state or even local level, when laws were passed in the 1970s to deal with them, they gave the most important standard-setting responsibilities to the federal government. Why? According to those who wrote the environmental laws, if lower levels of government were allowed to set their own environmental standards, they would engage in a kind of reckless competition with one another, constantly weakening environmental standards in an effort to lure industrial facilities to move to their city or state. Environmental quality, in their view, would become a victim of a 'race to the bottom'.

Wally showed that this would not necessarily be the case. His 1988 *Journal of Public Economics* paper with Bob Schwab developed a model of economic competition in which jurisdictions can manipulate both the tax rate they impose on capital as well as the emissions limit they impose on firms. Under fairly reasonable assumptions, jurisdictions select environmental standards that maximize the welfare of their residents, rather than set sub-optimally low standards in a blind effort to attract new business. This work, and a change in the tenor of the political debate, has helped stimulate new thinking on the 'optimal jurisdiction' for environmental policy making. In fact, environmental law journals today feature as much research and debate on this subject as on any other, much of it prompted by the recent work of Richard Revesz whose work, in turn, was stimulated in part by Oates and Schwab. It will be a surprise indeed if environmental policy debates over the next decade do not revolve partly around the 'right' level at which to place standard-setting responsibility.

Wally developed many of the key ideas in his research in environmental economics in his pathbreaking book with Will Baumol, *The Theory of Environmental Policy*, published in 1975 (the second edition was published in 1988). This book educated many of the leading scholars in environmental economics today and helped shape the way they, and a generation of policy makers, viewed environmental policy design. Arguably, this has been *the* most influential book in the thirty or so years during which environmental economics has been a widely recognized field.

As a consequence of *The Theory of Environmental Policy* and the veritable explosion of interest in and research on the subject which it helped trigger, the field has grown into one of the largest and most popular in many graduate programs. Interestingly, this book also presaged the growth in interest in the trade ramifications of environmental regulation, and foreshadowed the interest that currently exists in what has come to be known as environmental federalism. They followed that book in 1979 with the less technical *Economics, Environmental Policy, and the Quality of Life* which complemented environmental economics textbooks used at undergraduate level, and helped also to bring the economic view of policy to those in environmental studies programs.

The wonderful thing about reviewing Wally's contributions to environmental economics is that one cannot do so without the feeling that there are more to come. As this is being written, he is in the middle of a fascinating debate on whether or not a tax on pollution, the revenues from which are used to reduce distorting taxes on labor and capital, will both improve the environment and also improve the efficiency of the tax system. Working with researchers at Resources for the Future, Oates is among those now arguing that we cannot be assured that such a 'double dividend' exists. In fact, as their line of reasoning currently goes, this kind of tax shift – externality taxes replacing labor and capital taxation – may even increase the deadweight loss associated with the tax system. As with most debates, the matter will be settled by careful empirical work. It will be a surprise indeed if Wally Oates's work is not at or near the center of the resolution.

PUBLIC ECONOMICS

Wally's contributions to state and local public economics have been as important as his contributions to environmental economics. Several themes run throughout much of his work. First, Wally has long stressed that mobility is a key issue that drives much of state and local public economics. Consider, for example, Wally's discussion in *Fiscal Federalism* of the division of responsibilities among different levels of government. He argues that the optimal form of government would include a mix of different levels of government. The central government would be responsible for the distribution function, that is, for seeing that there is a proper distribution of income. Mobility is central to this argument:

> The difficulty is that within the highly decentralized fiscal system, local governments working independently to achieve differing redistributional objectives are likely to run into real trouble. Consider, for example, a community that adopts a strong negative income-tax program designed to achieve a significantly more equalitarian distribution of income than exists in the rest of the nation. Such a program, in view of the relatively high degree of individual mobility that characterizes a national economy, would create strong incentives for the wealthy to move out to neighboring municipalities and for the poor to migrate into the community. A more nearly equal distribution of income might well result, but it would be caused largely by an outflow of the rich and an influx of the poor, with a consequent fall in the level of per-capita income in the community under consideration. (*Fiscal Federalism*, p. 7)

Wally has explored the implications of mobility in a number of papers. His 1987 paper with Charles Brown in the *Journal of Public Economics* further develops the *Fiscal Federalism* argument in favor of the central government assuming the responsibility for the distribution function. Wally's 1969 *Journal of Political Economy* article on capitalization, one of his best known papers, focuses on a different aspect of mobility. He argues in this paper that in a Tiebout world where households are free to choose among different communities, the value of public services and taxes will be capitalized into the value of homes. Thus, for example, if Community A provides $100 more public services than Community B and the two communities are identical in all other ways – including equal tax rates on homeowners – then homes in A would cost $1000 more than homes in B (assuming a 10 percent interest rate). If this were not the case, then the markets could not be in equilibrium. If, for example, homes in both communities had the same price then families would move from B to A, driving up the prices of homes in A and driving down the prices of homes in B.

Wally's 1985 *American Economic Review* paper is an empirical test of the Brennan and Buchanan Leviathan model of government. Brennan and Buchanan (1977) envision a monolithic government that systematically seeks to exploit its citizenry through the maximization of tax revenue. They stress that fiscal decentralization and mobility are powerful constraints on Leviathan. As they put it, 'interjurisdictional mobility of persons in pursuit of "fiscal gains" can offer partial or possibly complete substitutes for explicit constraints on taxing power'. Thus, if the government in Community A spends too much, households will move to B. Wally finds little to support the Brennan and Buchanan hypothesis, perhaps because the basic claim that governments are self seeking and likely to spend too much is wrong.

Second, Wally has argued many times that decentralization is important because one size does not fit all. In a highly centralized system, everyone will be provided with the same level of public services; in a decentralized system, public services can be better tailored to meet public demand. Here again, *Fiscal Federalism* offers a clear statement of this point. The notion of a *perfect correspondence* plays a key role in Wally's view of the allocation function, that is, the provision of public goods. He explains that in an ideal world there would be

> a level of government for each subset of the population over which the consumption of a public good is defined. This would be sufficient to internalize the benefits from the provision of each good. Such a structure of governments, in which the jurisdiction that determines the level of provision of each good includes precisely the set of individuals who consume the good, I shall call a case of *perfect correspondence* in the provision of public goods. In the ideal model, each level of government, possessing complete knowledge of the tastes of its constituents and seeking to maximize their welfare would provide the Pareto-efficient level of output ... and would finance this through benefit pricing. (*Fiscal Federalism*, pp. 34–5)

What if a perfect correspondence is not possible? Wally argues in Chapter 3 of *Fiscal Federalism* that in such an imperfect world, public decisions may not be efficient. We can hope that government officials will consider the best interest of the voters who elected them; it is too much to hope that they will worry about the welfare of those living outside their community. Thus we might expect to find that public goods are under provided. He then goes on to explain that grants from higher to lower levels of government could solve this efficiency problem. The logic of these grants is the same as the logic of Pigouvian taxes and subsidies. Suppose a higher level of government agrees to pay a proportion θ of the cost of public goods provided by some community. Assuming that governments always know the preferences of their constituents and act so as to maximize their constituents' welfare, it is not hard to see that the government in this community will choose a level of public goods such that the marginal benefit of the public good in that community equals a proportion $(1 - \theta)$ of the marginal cost. If the higher level of government chooses θ so that it reflects the external benefits of the public good, the grant will lead to an efficient outcome.

Third, Wally has argued in favor of a conceptual model of public goods which is quite different from the traditional model. In an important paper David Bradford, Richard Malt and Wally drew a distinction between the output produced directly by the public sector (termed 'D-output') and the output that is of primary concern to the citizen-consumer (termed 'C-output'). D-output is a function of purchased inputs; C-output is a function of D-output and the community environment.

Consider, for example, public safety. By combining police officers and other police inputs, a local government produces a vector of D-output which might include the number of city blocks patrolled, the number of intersections provided with traffic control, and so on. The citizen, however, is concerned with the level of public safety, that is, C-output, which depends not only on D-output but on the community's characteristics as well. For example, poor communities burdened by high unemployment may need to hire more police officers to provide a given level of public safety than wealthier communities.

Wally has developed this view of public goods in several papers. His 1992 *Journal of Political Economy* paper looks at peer group effects on teenage pregnancy and his 1991 *Journal of Public Economics* article examines equilibrium in a system of communities where public goods production depends on the characteristics of the community.

Many of the ideas discussed above are now central to public economics: mobility as a limit to local redistribution, capitalization, Pigouvian grants, community characteristics as inputs in the production of public goods, and the benefits from the decentralization of public services. Wally has made major contributions to the way we think about all these issues. As such, it is clear that Wally has shaped public economics and has had a profound effect on the field.

SUMMARY OF THE PAPERS

In Chapter 1, William Baumol, a long-time friend and associate of Wally Oates, asks the provocative question, how can we preserve environmental friendly programs from the ongoing onslaught by conservatives? To raise this important question forcefully and to offer some answers to it is an appropriate tribute by one pioneer of environmental economics to another. Baumol advocates a multipronged strategy, invoking every available tool as long as it meets sensible economic criteria.

Baumol's first recommendation is that, in some cases, we must not shy away from forming a battle line, vowing not to retreat as Horatio did at the bridge. In the fight against harmful effects of pollutants, improper disposition of toxic wastes and massive accumulations of nuclear wastes, sufficient public support may exist to defend the environmental agenda without giving any ground to conservatives. In areas where conservatives may be right about waste in environmental programs, however, the right strategy is to eliminate the waste. Doing so will strengthen rather than weaken the liberal agenda.

In other areas, environmentalists can simply use conservative tools to promote their agenda. Baumol offers two examples: privatization and user charges. These instruments conservatives are comfortable can be readily deployed to advance environmental goals. Privatization can overcome the tragedy of the commons by internalizing externalities. Although it is not a cure-all solution and may lead to a suboptimal solution when the market undervalues environmental assets as, for example, in the case of the preservation of species, it can serve a useful purpose in many cases. Similarly, where applicable and workable, user charges can serve to arrest certain kinds of environmental degradation.

Baumol ends the chapter on an optimistic tone. 'The main contention of this paper is that much can be done to save what has so far been achieved by environmental policy. More than that – the conservative reevaluation of environmental programs can in some respects constitute an opportunity to do better than we have done before.'

In Chapter 2, Terry Dinan, Maureen Cropper, and Paul Portney evaluate the case for 'environmental federalism' in drinking water standards. The 1986 amendments of Safe Drinking Water Act, passed originally in 1974, direct the Environmental Protection Agency to regulate 83 contaminants and ensure water filtration and disinfection. These regulations are uniform across states. Dinan, Cropper and Portney ask whether there is room for efficiency gains by letting local jurisdictions set their own standards. The theoretical argument for local autonomy is that costs and benefits of decontaminating, filtering and disinfecting water are fully internalized at the local level. Since the cost per household of purifying water depends on the size of the jurisdiction (that is, the number of households covered by a particular facility), the optimal level of purification varies across jurisdictions.

The current federal standards for water purification are set at extremely high levels. Dinan, Cropper and Portney estimate empirically the net cost of meeting these standards to smaller jurisdictions that would most surely choose much lower standards if left on their own. Applying the methodology introduced by Bradford and Oates (1974) to adjusted gross alpha emitters, they conclude that in the smallest jurisdictions covering less than 100 people, the extra cost per household is at least $651 per year. Total net costs of meeting federal standards for this specific contaminant relative to what local jurisdictions would have chosen is $12 million. Arguing that much larger costs are associated with many other federal regulations, the authors conclude in favor of local autonomy in setting water safety standards.

In Chapter 3, Don Fullerton and Ann Wolverton consider the problem of imposing a Pigouvian tax on a pollutant when the level of its emission cannot be monitored directly. The idea developed in the paper is that a tax on the pollutant can be mimicked by a presumptive tax and environmental subsidies on other activities that can be measured. For instance, suppose the consumption of a good generates waste. A tax on the waste can be duplicated by a tax on the product complemented by a subsidy on proper disposal of the waste. Soda bottles, for example, can be subject to a tax with a partial refund upon return of empty soda bottles for proper disposal. Similarly, it may be difficult to measure the emissions of a certain pollutant into the environment. In this case, a Pigouvian tax on them may be mimicked by a presumptive tax on the sales of a final product complemented by a subsidy at the same rate on all purchased inputs.

Fullerton and Wolverton argue that in some cases, the presumptive tax combined with environmental subsidy is superior to direct Pigouvian tax on grounds of feasibility, administrative costs, policy enforcement and political perceptions. For instance, it may be difficult to enforce a tax on 'midnight dumping'. But a presumptive tax with the option to receive a refund upon proof of proper disposal may be feasible. The authors conclude the paper with a discussion of the available policy experience on deposit-refund systems for bottles, waste oil and car hulks.

In Chapter 4, Lawrence Goulder offers a concise and analytic overview of the rapidly-growing literature on the desirability of pollution taxes under a pre-existing distortion caused by the need to raise revenue. The conventional wisdom, outlined in Oates (1993), is that the presence of a revenue objective makes a pollution tax doubly desirable. On the one hand, it helps lower the damage caused by pollution and, on the other, it generates a 'revenue-dividend' which can be used to lower the (distortionary) rate of taxation.

In a series of articles, Goulder has developed the theme that this analysis misses an important detrimental effect which accompanies the pollution tax. Because the pre-existing revenue tax is itself distortionary, the pollution tax generates what may be called a 'tax interaction' effect. Under plausible assumptions, this effect turns out to be negative. Intuitively, the tax on labor income to raise revenue makes leisure more attractive. Worker choices are distorted with a greater consumption of leisure than in the undistorted equilibrium. The introduction of a tax on the polluting good makes that good more expensive. If the good and leisure are substitutes, workers further increase their consumption of leisure, worsening the pre-existing distortion.

In principle, the negative tax-interaction effect can be sufficiently large to outweigh the direct benefit from the reduction in pollution and the by-product benefit of the reduction, namely, the revenue dividend. Therefore, a cost–benefit analysis becomes essential to determine the desirability of any pollution-reduction measures. It cannot be assumed *a priori* that a small reduction in pollution is necessarily welfare improving.

Drawing on some of his collaborative work, Goulder offers numerical examples to assess the importance of the tax-incentive effect. The 1990 Clean Air Act Amendments call for a 10 million ton reduction in SO_2 emissions. If the direct marginal benefit from this reduction is taken to be \$104 per ton or less and emissions are regulated through grandfathered permits which do not generate any revenue, the harm from the tax-interaction effect outweighs the benefit. But since most estimates of marginal benefits are larger than \$104 per ton, the tax-interaction effect does not make the pollution-reduction measure undesirable. The benefits from pollution reduction are, nevertheless, lower than in the absence of the revenue distortion by $907 million.

Many of the papers in this volume ask normative questions. In Chapter 5 Nathaniel Keohane, Richard Revesz, and Robert Stavins ask an important positive question. They begin by arguing that actual environmental policy differs from that which Wally and others might argue is optimal in a number of important ways. In particular,

- We often choose command-and-control strategies over market-based instruments.
- When command-and-control strategies are used, the required level of pollution abatement has generally been far more stringent for new sources than for existing sources.
- When we have turned to market-based instruments, we have nearly always chosen tradable permits rather than emission taxes.
- There is little in the literature on the normative theory of environmental policy that can explain why incentive-based instruments have begun to gain some acceptance in recent years.

Keohane, Revesz, and Stavins offer intriguing answers to these puzzles that draw on many diverse strands of the political economy literature. They argue, for example, that existing firms might be better off under command-and-control strategies coupled with tougher standards for new sources than without regulation. Consider a simple case where firms are required to reduce pollution by reducing output. As a result, prices rise as we move along the industry demand curve, thus creating rents. If entry were free, new firms would enter this industry until the rents had been dissipated. But if the existing firms hold a significant cost advantage over potential entrants because policy requires new sources to meet much stiffer standards, the existing firms will continue to earn rents even in equilibrium.

Keohane, Revesz, and Stavins offer a similar line of reasoning to explain why, in those cases where we have relied on incentive schemes, we typically turn to tradable permits. Like command-and-control strategies, tradable permits create rents. If we endow existing firms with the permits, we give them those rents. Emissions taxes, in contrast, treat existing firms and new entrants equally harshly.

Kerry Smith, Kurt Schwabe, and Carol Mansfield argue in Chapter 6 that there are important limitations to the devolution of the responsibility for setting environmental policy to state and local governments. They suggest that if we were to seek a perfect correspondence (to use Wally's term) in the provision of environmental quality, in most cases we would ask higher levels of government to set policy – often the federal government, in some cases states, but rarely local governments. To the extent that people outside the region assigned the responsibility for decisions about providing environmental quality have an economic stake in that policy, decentralized policy making will inevitably lead to inefficiency. 'Stake' here is to be interpreted broadly. People who use a national park infrequently, who have not used the park in the past but plan to use the park in the future, and people who receive benefits from knowing that the park exists even if they never plan to use it, all have a stake in a policy that determines the fate of the park but are unlikely to have a voice in the setting of that policy.

Smith, Schwabe, and Mansfield present a case study of the Neuse River in North Carolina to illustrate their basic point. The Neuse flows through a number of North Carolina counties. Their estimates suggest that the aggregate benefits from reducing nitrogen loadings in the Neuse would exceed the costs. This proposed policy would, however, have very different impacts on different counties; some would gain, but some would lose. Suppose we were to assign the responsibility for establishing the quality of the Neuse to the counties. Given the variation in net benefits, the counties would be unable to agree to the efficient policy of reducing nitrogen loading (unless they are able to successfully engage in Coase type bargaining over the costs of the project). The state government, however, could impose the appropriate policy on the counties. Thus the Neuse River is a case where the complicated spatial distribution of the costs and benefits of environmental policy strongly suggests that we vest policy making responsibility with a higher level of government. As Smith, Schwabe, and Mansfield put it, the linkages environmental resources create between activities taking place at different locations must ultimately limit the extent of independence in decision making; nature 'trumps' most of the conventional arguments for devolution.

Jan Brueckner's paper on growth controls in Chapter 7 looks at an interesting extension of Wally's 1969 *Journal of Political Economy* paper on capitalization. Brueckner explains that many public policies – not simply taxes and expenditures – will be capitalized into land values. He looks at the capitalization of the benefits of growth controls and offers two competing models. His amenity-creation model focuses on the demand side of the land market. Households suffer a harmful externality from population growth and are thus better off when the city introduces growth controls. If the city is small and households are mobile, the controls cannot change the welfare of residents; households in other communities will bid up the price of land to the point that current residents are no better off after the controls have been imposed than before. As a result, the amenity created by the lower population is fully capitalized in land rents.

Brueckner's second model looks at the supply side of the market. In his supply-restriction model, controls drive up land prices by restricting the supply of developable land. Land prices rise in all cities. Landowners in this second model benefit from higher rents and households are harmed (since in this model there are by assumption no amenities associated with lower population). As a result, in the context of the supply restriction model, the imposition of controls must be seen as the outcome of a political struggle in which landowners prevail. The paper then extends these models in a number of interesting directions.

In Chapter 8 David Hummels, Paul Courant, and Alan Deardorff examine the welfare economics of congestible amenities in one-good and two-good, general-equilibrium models. Their principal objective is to study how a general-equilibrium context may alter the results obtained in partial equilibrium models. They consider a country with two regions, 1 and 2, and two factors, land and labor. Each region has a fixed amount of land while labor is footloose. Region 1 offers an amenity (for example, superior environment from which workers reap extra utility) which is congestible. Both the average and marginal amenity decline with the number of workers living in the region. After the number of workers reaches a critical level, the marginal amenity becomes negative and total amenity begins to decline.

Assuming a one-good economy for the moment, an equilibrium labor allocation obtains when the wage in region 2 equals the wage in region 1 plus the average level of amenity enjoyed by a typical worker there. With wages and, hence, values of marginal product differing between the regions, GDP is not maximized at the equilibrium. Moreover, since workers respond to average rather than marginal amenity, the market equilibrium also fails to maximize welfare. It is even possible to obtain an equilibrium in which labor mobility leads to a decline in the output as well as the total value of the amenity.

In this situation, a tax on wage income in region 1 can improve national welfare. At the optimum, we must equate the difference in wages paid by regions 2 and 1 to the marginal amenity. Intuitively, at the optimum, the loss in output due to the movement of the last worker from region 2 which has a higher value of marginal product to region 1 must be equated to the gain in amenity. In general, wages between the two regions will be different at the optimum and so also the marginal amenity. As such, neither the GDP nor total amenity will be maximized.

This result can change dramatically when the model is extended to allow for another good. Because the same goods prices must prevail in the two regions, as long as the latter are incompletely specialized, factor prices paid by firms are necessarily equalized. And if it so happens that the optimum is itself characterized by incomplete specialization, both the GDP and total amenity are maximized!

In Chapter 9, Dennis Epple, Elizabeth Newlon, and Richard Romano look at the effects of school vouchers and educational tracking by ability. They develop a model in which the quality of a child's education depends on the child's own ability, the ability of the child's peers, and purchased inputs. Thus their notion of education is an example of C-output in the Bradford, Malt, and Oates framework; it is produced by combing D-output (teachers, books, computers, and so on) and the characteristics of the residents of the community. In the Epple, Newlon, and Romano model, students and their parents choose between public and private schools, public schools decide the extent to which they will track students, government decides whether or not to offer vouchers for private schools, and private schools choose tuition policy. They characterize an equilibrium of their model and present simulations that allow them to look at the effect of different policy decisions.

Epple, Newlon, and Romano find that vouchers would lead both high track and low track public school students to choose private schools. Because relatively higher ability students in each track are the first to exit if offered a voucher, the average quality of students in both tracks falls. Consequently, because of peer group effects, those students who are left behind in public schools are worse off as a result of vouchers. However, if public schools did not track students according to ability, vouchers would cause even further damage to the remaining public school students. This is because tracking allows the public schools to compete more effectively with private schools for the most able students. Vouchers in their model increase private school demand for high ability students and, as a consequence, vouchers lead private schools to offer lower tuition to the most able. Thus low income, high ability students stand to gain the most from a voucher plan.

Bob Inman's paper in Chapter 10 looks at fiscal federalism issues in developing countries and countries making the transition from a centrally planned economy to a market economy. This is a very important issue that has received a great deal of attention in recent years. Central governments play a very large role in most developing countries; the World Bank and other international organizations have encouraged many of those countries to give far more responsibility to sub-national governments. Many of the transition economies are now rethinking the relationship among different levels of government. In some, including the former Soviet Union, newly created countries must now define those relationships in a new constitution; in others, including Mongolia, the move to decentralization in the private sector has been accompanied by calls for decentralization in the public sector as well.

Inman focuses on intergovernmental grants between the tiers of government. He begins by reviewing the theory of such grants, drawing heavily on *Fiscal Federalism.* Inman argues that fiscal decentralization could lead to inefficient outcomes for three reasons. First, fiscal competition may create incentives for the inefficient location of private factors of production. Second, as Wally argued in Chapter 3 of *Fiscal Federalism*, communities may fail to take into account spillover benefits or costs to neighboring communities. Third, sub-national governments in developing and transition countries may lack the administrative structure needed to collect government revenue. He shows how a grant from the central government can be designed to correct these market and administrative failures. Inman then uses this framework to analyse the South Africa constitution adopted on 11 October 1996.

Inman's conclusion to his paper points to the important and enduring role Wally's work plays in public economics:

> Wallace Oates's treatise *Fiscal Federalism* provided us with the first systematic guide to the optimal design of fiscal assignments and intergovernmental grants. This paper has sought to update Oates's original contribution, providing guidance for when and how to use intergovernmental transfers to facilitate efficient and fair public sector allocations. That these ideas, many first articulated in *Fiscal Federalism*, now guide fiscal policies in emerging democracies is just further testimony to Wally Oates's important contribution to the theory and practice of public finance.

In Chapter 11, David Wildasin considers a potentially important problem in the process of ongoing integration of labor markets in the European Union (EU). The conventional analysis of labor mobility focuses on the wage differential. But Wildasin notes that differences in pension benefits can serve as an important motivation for labor mobility. Even if current wages are equal across member countries of EU, differences in pension benefits will matter in the decision of workers.

Using data on public pension contributions and benefits, Wildasin estimates the change in the present value of lifetime wealth that 'representative' workers can achieve in seven EU countries by switching from one pension program to another. He finds that for some origin-destination pairs, migrants may experience changes in net public pension wealth that are as large as 25 percent of their lifetime wealth. This finding suggests that free mobility of labor is likely to be a contentious issue in the EU and also likely to be tied into the issue of harmonization of pension systems across member countries.

In Chapter 12, John Wallis applies many of Wally's insights on fiscal federalism to an interesting issue in US economic history. Wallis argues that perhaps at no time in American history were questions about federalism more pressing than in the early nineteenth century. Relations between the national and state governments – defined initially in the Articles of Confederation and then redefined in the Constitution – were in continuous flux and ultimately broke down in the Civil War. Throughout much of this period, the states took the lead in infrastructure investment. The states, for example, were primarily responsible for developing railroads, canals, roads and banks with the federal government playing a minor, secondary role.

Why did the states have the responsibility to provide these public goods which were so important to national economic development? Wallis's answer has five elements. First, the states had traditionally relied on income from their investments in banks and transportation projects. From their perspective a national system was redundant and a threat to their fiscal interests. Second, infrastructure investments often confer benefits on the few; the extension of a railroad, for example, might lead to a windfall for a handful of landowners. There was a strong sense in the US that government should not follow policies that favored a privileged few at the expense of many. National politicians, Wallis argues, were more susceptible to this kind of public outrage than state governments and politicians.

Third, revenues from federal government infrastructure investments would have raised difficult political issues. Tariffs were a major revenue source for the federal government in the first half of the nineteenth century, and thus it is reasonable to suspect that the federal government might have lowered tariffs if it invested in successful projects. But many – manufacturers, for example – benefited from the protection such tariffs provided and thus had little interest in the federal government's assuming a greater role in infrastructure investment. Fourth, there were few technological reasons in favor of a centrally coordinated transportation system. Railroad lines, for example, were rarely longer than roughly 50 miles. Finally, the future of the Union was in doubt throughout the early part of the century. Under these uncertain circumstances it is difficult to see how the national government could have developed a plan that would have satisfied everyone. As Wallis argues, 'Why pay for someone else's improvements today if they might be out of the Union tomorrow?'

John Yinger explains in the introduction to his paper in Chapter 13 that Wally has a long-standing interest in capitalization and the inefficiency in the provision of public goods. Yinger's paper brings these two strands of Wally's work together and asks if capitalization itself has implications for efficiency. The answer to this question is far from straightforward. As Yinger argues, the answer turns on just how knowledgeable voters are. Do they realize that local expenditures and taxes will change the value of their homes? Do they understand that if taxes and expenditures are capitalized into house values, then their property tax bill will change if they vote for higher services even if tax rates were to remain constant? Different levels of sophistication lead to different answers. Yinger comes to a very interesting (and quite unexpected) conclusion. If voters are entirely unsophisticated (that is, they completely ignore capitalization when they vote) or if they are very sophisticated (they understand all of the ramifications of their vote on property values and taxes), the outcome is efficient. On the other hand, if they understand some of the implications of capitalization but not all, the outcome is likely to be inefficient. The aphorism 'a little knowledge is a dangerous thing' has a place even in local public finance!

The problem, as Yinger explains, is that we have essentially no idea about voters' perceptions. He then goes on to propose two possible empirical projects that could shed some light on this important question. He concludes, however, that both projects present some stiff challenges and are unlikely to be feasible. His work thus opens up an interesting topic for new research.

REFERENCES

Baumol, W. and W.E. Oates (1971), 'The Use of Standards and Prices for Protection of the Environment', *Swedish Journal of Economics*, March, **73**: 42–54.

Bradford, David F. and Wallace Oates (1974), 'Surburban Exploitation of Central Cities and Government Structure', in H. Hochman and G. Peterson (eds), *Redistribution Through Public Choice*, New York: Columbia University Press, 43–90.

Brennan, Geoffrey and James M. Buchanan (1977), 'Towards a Tax Constitution for Leviathan', *Journal of Public Economics*, **8** (3): 255–73.

Oates, W.E. (1972), *Fiscal Federalism*, New York: Harcourt Brace Jovanovich.

Oates, W.E. (1993), 'Pollution Changes as a Source of Public Revenues', in H. Giersch (ed.), *Economic Progress and Environmental Concerns*, Berlin: Springer-Verlag, 135–52.

Oates, W.E., D. Bradford and R. Malt (1969), 'The Rising Cost of Local Public Services: Some Evidence and Reflections', *National Tax Journal*, **22**: 185–202.

PART I

Environmental Economics

1. On environmental policy for a conservative era

William J. Baumol*

To waste, to destroy, our natural resources ... will result in undermining in the days of our children the very prosperity which we ought by right to hand down to them.

Theodore Roosevelt,
Message to Congress,
December 3, 1907

I THE SETTING

This paper reports my ruminations about an issue that should concern all who ascribe importance to protection of the environment. The plain fact is that much of what we have worked for in this arena, and much that has been accomplished, is currently under attack. The resurgence of political conservatism is not confined to the United States alone. It is to be found in France, Italy and elsewhere. And while conservatives are not invariably disposed to give the environment short shrift, the widespread occurrence of substantial government deficits together with a novel spirit of radicalism among the conservatives, have ensured that the rightward political shift this time does constitute a marked threat to environmentalism. It has been imperiled by those who regard preservation of natural resources and protection of endangered species as an obstacle to progress. Protection of the environment has roused the enmity of those who regard regulation of any sort as an impediment to the workings of the market mechanism and, consequently, as a drag upon the economy. It has led to opposition by those who regard any costs entailed in protection of the environment as a handicap to the competitiveness of the American economy on the markets of the world. Perhaps most immediately, it has enlisted the opposition of determined budget

* It was a great delight to be invited to contribute to this volume – so richly deserved – in Wally Oates's honor. It recalls to me the many pleasant hours (I recall no unpleasant ones) that we spent working together on our books and articles. I have long missed the stimulation of his ideas and his presence. The opportunity to prepare this paper brings me back to the subject, the environment, on which our attention was focused then, and that too is a benefit, far from incidental, that I derive from this undertaking.

cutters who are willing to impose large sacrifices upon the public for the sake of fiscal retrenchment.

It should be noted that the resulting threat to environmental programs represents a sharp break with conservative tradition. In the past, when conservatives came to power it could be taken for granted that the new government would work to keep things as they were at that moment, opposing additional programs or expansion of those currently in existence. But there was usually little effort to roll things back to the circumstances of an earlier era. Conservatism generally sought to conserve, not to undo. Existing programs, ranging from social security to environmental regulations, were left largely unmodified. This time things are different. No past program is immune from reconsideration, with emasculation or total elimination not ruled out. In short, the new generation of conservatives has undertaken to break the implicit political compact under which change took the form of stop-and-go evolution, with the conservatives' turn in power serving to hold whatever line was then current, but without any marked retrenchment. Now, rather than 'back to the future' the goal of the new and radical conservatism seems to be 'forward to the past.'

This surely calls for re-evaluation of strategy and perhaps even goals by environmentalists, to consider what is the best that can be done under such ominous conditions. The purpose of this essay is to serve as a step in that direction.

II THE *NO PASSARAN* RESPONSE

An immediate reaction may well be that since the environment is well worth fighting for, the only appropriate response to the conservative threat is that of Horatio at the bridge – to form a battle line, vowing no retreat. Of course, such an emotional reaction may not be the most rational, and it may well prove more productive to consider what can be done to save as much as possible of the achievements of the past. After all, more is better than less, and an empty gesture, however self-satisfying, may conceivably turn out to be the most self-destructive of the available options. Later, I will consider some alternative strategy possibilities. But first I should like to argue that a 'they-shall-not-pass' approach may actually not be entirely irrational.

This may be so even despite the fact that the American public is obviously no longer attuned to the old liberal agenda in its entirety. Many of the public-good objectives that have been achieved in the recent past clearly offer benefits too abstract to recommend them to the public in its current mood. Yet many of the programs including, most notably, educational support, environmental protection measures and social security, offer substantial private benefits, benefits that are widely disseminated, and that appear to be valued substantially by a considerable portion of the public. This suggests that if a *no passaran* strategy is decided upon, its most promising tactic in the current political atmosphere is to play up the private benefits threatened by the conservative agenda.[1] Rather than seeking to stimulate idealism and the stake for the general welfare, it seems more promising to focus attention upon the intensely valued private gains that are endangered.

This will obviously be no easy task, and it is far from clear that *no passaran* is, indeed, the most sensible motto for us to inscribe on our banners. I am suggesting only two things about this approach – first that it is not necessarily hopeless, and second that, if adopted, there seems to be a most promising way to go about it.

The approach is not hopeless because there are portions of the liberal agenda that, to the extent they have been carried out, seem to have become accepted as inalienable rights by a considerable part of the public. The prime example, of course, is social security. It is true that the most radical of the new conservatives have even ventured to propose that social-security benefits are not untouchable, but it is not implausible that the massed body of senior citizens will not soon forget, and will take its revenge at the polls. Health is arguably next in line in the list of such public priorities. While concern over health care was patently insufficient to enable the Clinton administration (like the Nixon administration before it) to secure enactment of its proposed health-care program, it does not follow that anything that poses a markedly visible threat of deterioration from the status quo will be accepted with equanimity. This suggests what I believe to be the most promising instrument available for use in a *no passaran* strategy – a massive campaign designed to educate the public about the health risks posed by a retreat on environmental issues. This is already being attempted, perhaps far too quietly, in discussions of species extinction. Here, one commentator recently remarked

> ... the task for those of us who would convince our fellow citizens of the magnitude of the problem of species loss is to specify in plain language what implications the loss of hundreds of thousands of species actually would have for human existence ... Frankly utilitarian values of species diversity are perhaps easiest to grasp ... we humans rely on at least 40,000 different species in our collectively global daily lives. Medicine and agriculture lead the list of reasons we depend on them, and nearly everyone along the information superhighway has by now heard of the Madagascar periwinkle, an endangered species on an endangered island that has produced a potent remedy against certain especially pernicious cancers. Who knows what else of like utility might be driven to extinction before its beneficial products are discovered? (Niles Eldredge, book review section, *New York Times*, 18 February 1996, p. 12)

Yet, while the connection between species extinction and health is clear to specialists it may well appear farfetched and tenuous to the general public. The health consequences of various types of pollutants, the threat of toxic substances improperly disposed of, the horrors posed by massive accumulations of nuclear wastes are likely to seem far more immediate, and are surely far easier to dramatize. It would seem that they promise to become potent weapons in the hands of an environmental coalition determined to meet the conservative challenge head on.

There is also hope that such agenda topics, carefully pushed, can even attract support from the mass media. They are quite legitimately to be regarded as sensational issues. After all, sex and murder aside, few things are as saleable by the press and the electronic media as a threat to survival of the planet. The fact that the end-of-the-world peril is the consistent mainstay of successful science fiction should not hastily be brushed aside as unworthy or irrelevant. If there is to be all-out war to defend our environmental accomplishments one cannot afford to despise even such weapons.

II DEFENSIBLE ELEMENTS IN THE CONSERVATIVE POSITION

While there is, thus, some possibility that an unyielding defense against conservative attack can succeed, there is at least one good reason for second thought. For it seems clear that there is some element of validity in the conservative contentions about current environmental programs. We have long recognized that political considerations have played an important role in the choice of environmental priorities, that the programs have at least sometimes focused on pollutants that are most readily visible to the public rather than those that are most dangerous, and that cost–benefit considerations have not been given the weight in policy determination that they merit. Thus, conservative critics may have a valid point when they suggest that environmental programs have not been immune from waste, that they have sometimes pursued targets entailing disproportionately heavy costs, and that are innately condemned to slow accomplishment and low effectiveness. In short, their priorities have not always been consistent with efficiency in promotion of the public welfare.

Viewed in this way, portions of the conservative environmental agenda may usefully be regarded as more of an opportunity than a threat. They may serve as an opportunity to improve environmental policy by cleaning up its ill-chosen elements. Of course, environmental programs are probably no more tainted by distorting political influences, no more characterized by waste, no more inconsistent with an appropriate weighing of costs and benefits, than are the bulk of public policies in other arenas. That, however, is beside the point – or, rather, it only means that the same point is pertinent elsewhere as well. The fact is that the environmental literature is replete with examples of well-argued complaints about programs whose design is far from ideal for any or all of the reasons that have just been discussed. It seems at least worth considering whether there are ways to benefit from appropriately-selected elements of the conservative onslaught; whether one can use them as a fulcrum for improvement of environmental policy while doing everything possible to prevent gutting of the programs. These two aims need not prove inconsistent, for it is at least possible that effective steps to carry out some of the conservative objectives can serve to blunt some of their other attacking forays.

III COMPATIBILITY OF MARKET INSTRUMENTS WITH THE CONSERVATIVE AGENDA

The conservative aversion to direct controls and to governmental giveaways both fit in well with the economists' preferred approaches to environmental protection. Conservative resistance to direct governmental intervention in decision making by private enterprise hardly needs documentation. Every recent administration that labeled itself 'conservative' has organized commissions to investigate how such intervention could most effectively and expeditiously be reduced. And while critics of those administrations contend that they have been all too prone to give away rights to exploitation of natural resources, replaceable and irreplaceable, conservatives also have manifested some opposition to the most notorious of the giveaway programs. They have, for example, (along with the economists) supported auctions of those financially valuable portions of the communications spectrum so avidly sought by private interests and traditionally presented with little or no compensatory payment to those supplicants in a position to exercise the greatest political influence. They have shown a similar inclination to cut back farm subsidies, programs long held to be untouchable politically.

It is clear that such goals are not inconsistent with the environmental measures long advocated by mainstream economists, even those of the most liberal persuasion. I need hardly remind my colleagues of their long record of support of market-mechanism-based instruments of environmental protection, Pigouvian charges and subsidies, markets in licenses and the like. Nor is it necessary to recall their traditional and consistent support of auctions as the best means for the allocation of scarce public resources among competing candidates for their use. Indeed, ironically, perhaps the strongest source of opposition to the economists' approaches to environmental protection has come, not from those upon whom the financial burden would fall, but from the most dedicated environmentalists, who felt that mere money is hardly a suitable compensation to society for destruction of its natural heritage. The characterization of the economists' device as the sale of 'licenses to pollute' surely played an effective role in the earlier disposition of legislatures throughout the industrial world to favor direct controls and the imposition of detailed regulation over resort to market incentives. My point in the discussion that follows is that a conservative era is a time when it is urgent for dedicated environmentalists to reassess their opposition to the economists' remedial measures, for there is reason to suspect that they constitute one promising means to avoid gutting of the nation's environmental programs.

But it is not only the environmentalists who will have to rethink matters. The economists, too, are likely to find it necessary to take another careful look at the armory of weapons that they have tended to favor. Their market-based approaches have emphasized taxation of emitters, but new taxes, surely, are absolute anathema to conservatives. Even if it were not an article of faith for them, bitter election experience would surely rouse their unyielding resistance. Here we need only recall President Bush's failure to hold to his pledge of 'no new taxes (read my lips)' and the widely-held view that it played a substantial role in his electoral defeat by President Clinton. With such a lesson engraved in memory one can hardly count on conservatives to flock to support of Pigouvian taxes, even though they bear the 'market-approach' label. Economists will have to think through rather carefully which of the approaches they have been advocating can be hoped to prove attractive to conservatives while retaining (or even increasing) the effectiveness of environmental programs.

IV ON EFFECTIVE MARKET INSTRUMENTS TAILORED TO CONSERVATIVE PREDISPOSITIONS – TWO ILLUSTRATIONS

a. Privatization

The environmentalist instrument most likely to appeal to conservative predispositions is privatization. While to economists the workings of this tool may be obvious, to others the notion that it may be a useful way to defend natural resources may be somewhat surprising, if not more than a little suspect. There is, as a matter of fact, something pertinent to be said on both sides of this issue.

What favors the privatization approach is the old adage that a resource that belongs to everyone really belongs to no one. The continuing tragedy of the commons is that it is an institution that by its very nature invites massive overuse, as is dramatically demonstrated by destructive overuse of fisheries which threatens species destruction and undermining of the fishing industry itself. The commons is an institution that is usefully characterized as pure detrimental externality. Overuse by myself comes at the expense of everyone else, and so, unless I am guided by quixotic altruism, I will have every incentive to exploit any common resource to the hilt, and so will everyone else. Altruism here is quixotic, at least unless it is effectively organized on a massive scale, because the social benefit of my abstemiousness is but a drop in the bucket, a negligible offset to the probable massive resource exploitation activity by everyone else. Since, with the best of intentions, my behavior is apt to make little difference, one way or the other, to the rate of resource destruction that the commons invites, even rational altruism provides no reason for me to abstain from full participation in the exploitation process.

There are three clear ways out of this problem: an effective social contract, rules enforced by the state, or privatization. A social contract enforced by means such as ostracism of malefactors has sometimes proven effective in preventing destruction of the commons. For example, it kept the streets of the Dutch Republic clean in the dirty world of the sixteenth and seventeenth centuries, to the amazement of travelers from other countries. The trouble with social contracts is that they are vulnerable. As in the case of a cartel, it may take only a few egregious violators of the contract to raise everyone's doubts about its viability, and once such skepticism spreads the contract does indeed become honored only in the breach.

The imposition and enforcement of rules by government can also work – but not always. We know too many cases in which such rules are flouted to have full confidence in this approach. Enforcement mechanisms are patently imperfect as well as being costly and likely to be oppressive to the innocent. In too many cases the objectionable behavior of individuals is difficult if not impossible to monitor systematically and extensively, as in the case of littering of nature preserves or overfishing. Thus, while intervention by government can help to alleviate the problem of exploitation of commonly-held environmental resources, except in special cases well adapted to this approach, it is hardly the entire answer.

This is not meant to suggest that privatization, by itself, does solve the problem. Rather, I am only claiming, in accord with much earlier literature, that this instrument too, can make a useful contribution. Privatization can help because it internalizes the externalities of the commons. When the commons are enclosed and become the property of a single individual then any destruction of its valuable resources clearly comes at the proprietor's expense rather than at the expense of others. The owner will therefore have every self-interest incentive to protect and preserve those valuable resources, to ensure that they are not subjected to wanton destruction. In other words, the single proprietor becomes society's effective guardian of its natural resources. This role is imposed automatically and enforced by the profit motive that never lets up its conservation pressures.

Nevertheless, there is good reason to proceed slowly and carefully with privatization of natural resources. There is an abundance of unfortunate experience indicating that private interests do not always do very well as defenders of the interests of the future. Owners of forests have often enough cut them down with little thought about the consequences. Agricultural soils have been permitted to erode and rich land has been transformed into a dust bowl. Mines have been exhausted and abandoned leaving the landscape permanently scarred. Fully conscious of such distressing examples environmentalists can hardly be blamed for treating the privatization route with suspicion or outright hostility.

The economic literature provides a profusion of discussions of the reasons for this form of market failure. Already, at the beginning of the century, A.C. Pigou discussed the problem and suggested that investors are generally endowed with 'a defective telescopic faculty,' valuing the future insufficiently. The argument is not really persuasive, because if the rate of interest does accurately reflect the public's rate of discount of the future, then an investor who destroys a property that is likely to have twice its current value one decade hence can be expected to have harmed himself as much as he has harmed society. Moreover, that harm is immediate, at least if markets function efficiently, because then the current market value of the damaged property will have fallen by an amount commensurate with the damage. Of course, markets are imperfect, so there is something to the Pigouvian explanation, but there must be more than that. One can, of course, turn to Frank Ramsey's view that any non-zero rate of discount shortchanges the future, and that the proper social discount should therefore be zero, but for reasons that need not be gone into here, this is also not fully persuasive. My own conjecture is that the sort of damage private owners inflict on the future value of their own properties has three explanations: the imperfections of markets, the imperfect knowledge and rationality of the proprietors, and the fact that a considerable portion of the threatened future benefits take the form of externalities which do not enter into the current market value of the property and which therefore are not pertinent to the proprietor's private financial calculus. This is clearly true, for example, if important components of the loss from destruction of a forest are deprivation of future aesthetic amenity value and extinction of valuable species.

The point here is not to provide a summary of the reasons for marked imperfection of the privatization device as an instrument for environmental protection. Rather, my purpose is to argue that, with all its warts and blemishes, it can be a valuable tool for the purpose. What is needed is careful analysis of the circumstances in which it is likely to be effective and beneficial in guarding the interests of the future, and when it is more likely to prove a threat to those interests. Only when the issue has been explored and is understood more thoroughly can one risk advocacy of the privatization tool. Yet, in the circumstances, the fact that it may be one of the few instruments that are politically saleable in a conservative era makes this task of exploration an urgent matter.

b. User Charges

Another tool for environmental protection that is probably not in conflict with a conservative orientation is the user charge. Unlike privatization, there seems to be no reason to doubt the benefits that this instrument promises for the environment where it is applicable and workable. Moreover, it constitutes a direct recourse to the price mechanism, one that can serve as an immediate substitute for Pigouvian taxation, but one that avoids the political perils of adoption of a new tax levy. User charges extend the market mechanism directly into arenas from which misguided government intervention had previously excluded it. A user charge simply means that users are required to pay for all or at least for more of the resources they utilize, as they would have to do if those resources were provided to them by private enterprise. It constitutes a reduction in the set of governmental giveaways of the resources that belong to the nation as a whole, by extension of the range of utilization of the price mechanism.

Besides the political saleability of user charges as a market-oriented approach that is consistent with conservative goals, it has the added attraction of helping to reduce governmental deficits, one that does so without the need to cut public services or to adopt new taxes. Budget balancing, too, is an item that is clearly high on the list of conservative agenda, so that this attribute of the user charge device, carefully explained, can add materially to its political attractiveness.

For environmentalists, the main feature recommending the user charge is the fact that the benefits it promises are quite unambiguous. An increase in their cost to the user of society's resources should normally serve as an effective disincentive to their use. That, of course, is no new observation; rather, it is nothing more than the logic of the Pigouvian prescription.[2] What is new here is only the observation about the possible political palatability of the instrument, and the urgency of attention to this aspect of the different instruments of environmental protection.

V CONCLUDING COMMENT

This chapter seeks to invite systematic consideration of alternatives to anticipatory surrender to the threatened conservative onslaught on environmental programs. It makes no pretense to have gone beyond mere prologue to such an examination. The hope is that it has shown that such alternatives are possible and that it has illustrated some promising directions for such a project. The main contention of this paper is that much can be done to save what has so far been achieved by environmental policy. More than that – the conservative re-evaluation of environmental programs can in some respects constitute an opportunity to do better than we have done before. Cost–benefit analysis, carefully and intelligently utilized can certainly help society get more for its expenditures on environmental protection. The current state of affairs may also provide an opportunity to promote the fiscal-incentive measures which economists have advocated for so long, but with very mixed success. In sum, it is the contention of this paper that we cannot afford simply to ignore the conservative threat, hoping it will just go away. Rather, it is essential that a determined effort based on systematic analysis be undertaken, not just to contain the damage, but to see what benefits for the environment can be extracted.

NOTES

1. Here it may be useful to remind the politicians of the evidence that environmental concerns are, characteristically, a middle-class value. It may also be apropos to recall that the ex-president who is most noted as an environmental activist is one of the most remembered of the Republican occupants of the office.
2. Elsewhere, Wally Oates and I have argued that there are circumstances in which fiscal incentives are likely not to be the most effective or most appropriate instrument for environmental protection (see Baumol and Oates [1988, Chapter 3]). This is clearly true, in particular, of user charges. Thus, I am surely not suggesting that they constitute a magic formula capable of dealing with all environmental concerns. Rather, they are only one item in the armory of weapons that should be made use of in a full and effective environmental program.

REFERENCE

Baumol, William and Wallace Oates (1988), *The Theory of Environmental Policy*, Second Edition, New York: Cambridge University Press.

2. Environmental federalism: welfare losses from uniform national drinking water standards

Terry M. Dinan, Maureen L. Cropper, and Paul R. Portney[1]

1 INTRODUCTION

Wallace Oates's prodigious contributions to economics span two rather distinct fields – public finance and environmental economics. Much of his work, however, has combined elements of both in creative and enlightening ways. This paper is very much in the spirit of Oates's integrative work. It draws on insights in his classic book, *Fiscal Federalism*, and on the important paper, written jointly with David Bradford, on the estimation of welfare losses that might result from mandatory uniform per-capita spending on public schools (Bradford and Oates, 1974, pp.43–90). It extends that same line of reasoning to an environmental issue of current interest – namely, how should standards be set for contaminants that frequently appear in drinking water systems around the United States?

In several respects, this is an appropriate time to be considering such a question. The 104th Congress, which took office in January 1995, was wholly controlled by the Republican Party for the first time in 40 years. The new majorities in the House and Senate set about attempting to make many changes. These included some to environmental statutes that had remained more or less constant for two decades. One issue frequently raised when environmental laws come up for reauthorization is the appropriate role for the federal government *vis à vis* state or even local governments. Discussion centers on whether there is a rationale for federal government involvement in the environmental issue being addressed, or whether the problem might be addressed more appropriately at a lower level of government.

In many instances, the case for federal regulation is very strong, if not unassailable. For example, most air and water pollutants migrate across state and local boundaries. This makes it difficult for any state acting alone to take the interests of all affected parties into account when it sets standards. In fact, for some common air pollution problems, supranational agreements would appear necessary. This would be the case for problems relating to stratospheric ozone depletion and greenhouse gas accumulation in the atmosphere.

There are some environmental problems where the rationale for an overwhelming federal presence is less strong. These include cases where there is currently a strong federal role. A good example is the Safe Drinking Water Act (SDWA) which spells out the way in which maximum permissible levels for drinking water contaminants are to be set.

Unlike traditional air or water pollution problems, the choice of drinking water standards by one state (or even one community) impose few 'externalities' on other jurisdictions.

Because the regular users of a water system are the primary or sole beneficiaries of measures protecting drinking water, one might argue that lower levels of government should set their own drinking water standards. They could base those standards on their own trade-offs between larger risk reductions and higher control costs.

The 104th Congress amended the SDWA in 1996. Despite making several important changes in the law described below, Congress never deliberated shifting the standard-setting authority under the SDWA from Washington to the 50 state capitals, much less to city halls. There are many possible explanations for that reluctance to consider devolution of standard-setting authority. One may be the absence of any evidence on the welfare losses that attend uniform national drinking water standards. The purpose of this paper is similar to that of the Bradford and Oates (1974) paper mentioned above. Bradford and Oates attempted to measure how much better off citizens would be if local communities were allowed to choose their own level of per-capita spending on public schools. We attempt to measure how much better off citizens would be if state or local governments were allowed to set drinking water standards. Currently those standards are dictated by federal government.

We provide a brief overview of the SDWA in the next section of this chapter. We describe its history and standard-setting provisions as well as highlighting the changes to it which Congress made in 1996. In Section 3 we estimate the welfare losses that households might incur under a proposed federal standard for a particular class of pollutant namely *adjusted gross alpha emitters*. Such a uniform standard precludes localities from choosing the standards that best fit their local circumstances, that is, the level that balances the marginal benefits against the marginal costs associated with tighter standards. We present a conceptual framework for measuring the welfare losses under the proposed standard, describe the data on the costs and benefits of meeting alternative standards for adjusted gross alpha emitters and present the empirical results of our welfare analysis. A final section presents our conclusions. There we speculate about the welfare losses from uniform standard-setting for other drinking water contaminants. In addition, we discuss how the recent revisions to the SDWA could affect welfare losses.

2 OVERVIEW OF THE SDWA

Congress passed the Safe Drinking Water Act (SDWA) in 1974 and mandated the establishment of the first set of federally enforceable standards for drinking water. The SDWA was amended and considerably strengthened in 1986 when the Environmental Protection Agency (EPA) was directed to regulate 83 contaminants as well as to require water filtration (for those sources supplied by surface water) and disinfection.[2] Congress amended the SDWA again in 1996.

The SDWA directs the EPA to establish maximum contaminant level goals (MCLGs). These are 'nonenforceable health-based goals which are set at the level at which no known or anticipated adverse effects on the health of persons occur and which allows for an adequate margin of safety.' For contaminants regulated as carcinogens, the EPA's policy is to set the MCLG at zero. Next, the SDWA directs the EPA to set an enforceable standard, called a maximum contaminant level (MCL), as close to the MCLG as is feasible 'taking costs into consideration.' The legislative history of the SDWA directs the EPA to interpret feasibility based on what types of controls would be affordable to metropolitan and regional water systems (that is, large systems) with relatively clean source water (EPA, 1993, p. 16–22).

Historically, the EPA was not allowed to weigh costs against anticipated benefits when setting an MCL. The 1996 amendments, however, changed that and now specify that if the benefits of a proposed MCL which is found to be 'feasible' (that is, affordable to large systems) do not justify the cost, then the EPA may adjust the MCL. In that case, the EPA may establish an MCL that 'maximizes health risk reduction benefits at a cost that is justified by the benefits.' Although this seems to ensure that standards are set efficiently, the uniform nature of the MCLs prevents this. MCLs are uniform federal standards that apply to all public water systems in the United States, regardless of size or ownership type (public or private). Jurisdictions may elect to meet a standard more stringent than the MCL set by the EPA but they may not, however, opt for a less stringent standard unless granted an exception by the EPA (see below).[3]

What are the consequences of that provision? The EPA is directed to set the MCL at a feasible level provided that the benefits would justify the costs for large systems and systems that are unlikely to receive variances.[4] However, large system impacts will dominate aggregate analyses of costs and benefits because most of the population receives its water from large systems.[5] Standards that are efficient for large systems, however, may not be efficient for small ones. The per household cost of treatment is typically much higher for small systems than for large, while the per household benefit is invariant to system size. Hence, small systems typically bear a much greater financial burden in meeting national standards and experience a far less favorable benefit/cost ratio for any given standard.

As alluded to above, both the 1986 and the 1996 amendments to the SDWA specify conditions under which smaller drinking water systems may adopt a standard less stringent than the MCL. Under the 1986 amendments, the EPA could grant variances to systems whose drinking water originates from particularly contaminated sources. In addition, the EPA could grant exemptions to systems too poor to install the treatment technology. Systems receiving either a variance or an exemption would not be required to meet the MCL. For a variety of reasons, however, such 'escape hatches' were seldom allowed.[6] Under the 1996 amendments, Congress defined 'variance technologies' which should expand the EPA's opportunities for granting latitude to small systems when they cannot afford to meet an MCL. Again, however, these are contingent upon certain conditions being met (House of Representatives Report 104–741, 1996, Section 116). If such conditions are more easily met, smaller drinking water systems may have more success adopting less stringent standards than the uniform national MCLs. If those conditions are not more easily met, the situation will remain much as it has been since 1974.

We should say a word or two here about the benefits and costs of drinking water standards. The former fall into three categories: fewer cancers, reductions in chronic health effects (such as liver or kidney toxicity), and prevention of acute health effects (such as gastrointestinal disorders) (EPA, 1990, p. 29). An interesting feature of drinking water regulations is that their benefits accrue primarily to the customers served by the drinking water system. This is the same population that bears the cost. Individuals outside a particular drinking water system are unlikely to benefit from its control of contaminants which reduce the incidence of cancers and chronic health effects. This is because those adverse effects occur only after long term exposure. Individuals outside a water system can benefit from its control of acute health effects if they visit that area. However, the paying customers of the system are the primary beneficiaries of measures to reduce the occurrence of acute health effects.[7] Those individuals use the system on a regular basis and are therefore most likely to experience the acute health effect if controls are inadequate. Furthermore, communities having many visitors have an economic incentive to account for the health benefits that visitors receive and could experience a significant financial loss if an outbreak of waterborne disease discouraged tourism or commerce from their areas.

The costs of drinking water treatment also fall mainly on those living in the area served by the system, usually through quarterly water bills. Typically, compliance with federal drinking water standards requires the installation of a treatment technology such as reverse osmosis or a granular activated carbon filter. The cost of that equipment and any operating and maintenance expenditures are passed on to the customers of the water district.

Because the benefits of controlling drinking water contaminants accrue largely to the same population that bears the cost, local communities have an incentive to choose an efficient level of treatment. The SDWA, however, compels systems to meet uniform federal standards unless they qualify for special exemptions or variances. As we discussed above, the EPA has rarely used those special provisions in the past. Local communities incur welfare losses when a standard is set at a level where the marginal cost of achieving it exceeds the marginal benefit. Uniform federal standards are particularly likely to result in welfare losses to households served by small systems. This is because of the large economies of scale in drinking water treatment, and the fact that per household benefits are invariant to system size (for a given reduction in a contaminant).

3 QUANTIFYING THE WELFARE LOSSES ASSOCIATED WITH A UNIFORM NATIONAL STANDARD

There are 84 existing drinking water standards and four proposed rules, which set forth standards for either individual or multiple contaminants. Ideally, we would like to estimate the welfare losses associated with each of them. To do that, we would need information on the costs and benefits that communities would receive under each existing (or proposed) standard. In addition, we would need information on the costs and benefits that communities would receive under alternative standards. Data on the costs and benefits of existing or proposed standards is sometimes available but frequently not for alternative standards. Information is available, however, for some proposed standards relating to radionuclides and we have analysed the welfare effects associated with the proposed standard for one particular class of radionuclides – adjusted gross alpha emitters.

The proposed standard for adjusted gross alpha emitters makes an interesting case study for several reasons. First, the primary benefit of the standard is a reduction in the number of expected cancer cases. Since there exists extensive literature on the value individuals are willing to attach to the avoidance of a statistical death, the value of the avoided cancer cases due to the adjusted gross alpha standard may be monetized. This allows us to compare benefits with the costs. Second, the level of the standard is set such that households in some drinking water systems will experience positive net benefits by treating to the standard (that is, benefits that outweigh costs) while households in other systems will experience negative net benefits (costs that outweigh benefits).

A limitation of our analysis is that the EPA proposed the standard we are analysing before the passage of the 1996 amendments. In the conclusions we speculate about how those amendments might alter the welfare losses associated with standards proposed in the future.

3.1 Conceptual Framework

The welfare loss that any household experiences due to a uniform standard is equal to the net benefits that it receives under that standard minus the net benefits it would receive if the optimal contaminant level had been selected. Thus, we use two steps to calculate the welfare losses that water systems would incur under the proposed standard for adjusted gross alpha emitters. First, we determine the net benefits they would receive under the standard. Next, we determine the net benefits that they would receive at the optimal level of treatment.

Figure 2.1 demonstrates how the optimal level of treatment for adjusted gross alpha emitters is determined for two communities, each with an initial pollution concentration of P_0. For each community the total per household benefit of moving to lower contaminant levels is represented by the line VP_0. This is the per household reduction in cancer risk from reducing the level of contamination monetized using the value of a statistical life. As described in the following section, we assume that the reduction in annual cancer risk from reducing the contaminant is linear in the concentration of the contaminant.

The total cost per household of reducing the contaminant level is given by curve AP_0 for the smaller community and by curve BP_0 for the larger community. The fact that the per household cost of remediation is everywhere higher for the smaller system reflects economies of scale in drinking water treatment. The concave shape of the curves reflects the fact that the cost of reducing the contaminant level increases as remediation increases, but at a decreasing rate. Adjusted gross alpha emitters are removed from water through the process of reverse osmosis which will remove up to 99 percent of the contaminant in all water treated. Treatment efficiencies below 99 percent can be achieved by treating only some of the water that passes through the system and mixing it with untreated water. Curves AP_0 and BP_0 reflect the fact that the cost of a 50 percent removal efficiency is less than twice the cost of a 25 percent removal efficiency.[8]

The shapes of the benefit and cost curves in Figure 2.1 have an immediate implication for setting optimal contaminant levels. For curves with the shapes pictured in Figure 2.1, the optimal contaminant level will be a corner solution: It is optimal either to do nothing (to remain at P_0) as is optimal for the smaller system, or to remediate as much as possible, as is optimal for the larger system.

We may also use Figure 2.1 to measure the welfare losses associated with setting uniform standards. Suppose that the EPA sets an MCL of P_1 for both cities. The standard is clearly suboptimal for the small system, which optimally should keep its contaminant level at P_0. The welfare loss associated with the standard is the net benefits of the standard (the negative of the distance *XY*) minus the net benefits of an optimal standard (zero). The benefits and costs of the standard just balance for the larger system. Although the optimal solution for the large system is maximum treatment (distance *VB*), the standard does not impose any welfare loss because the system is free under the SDWA to exceed the standard.

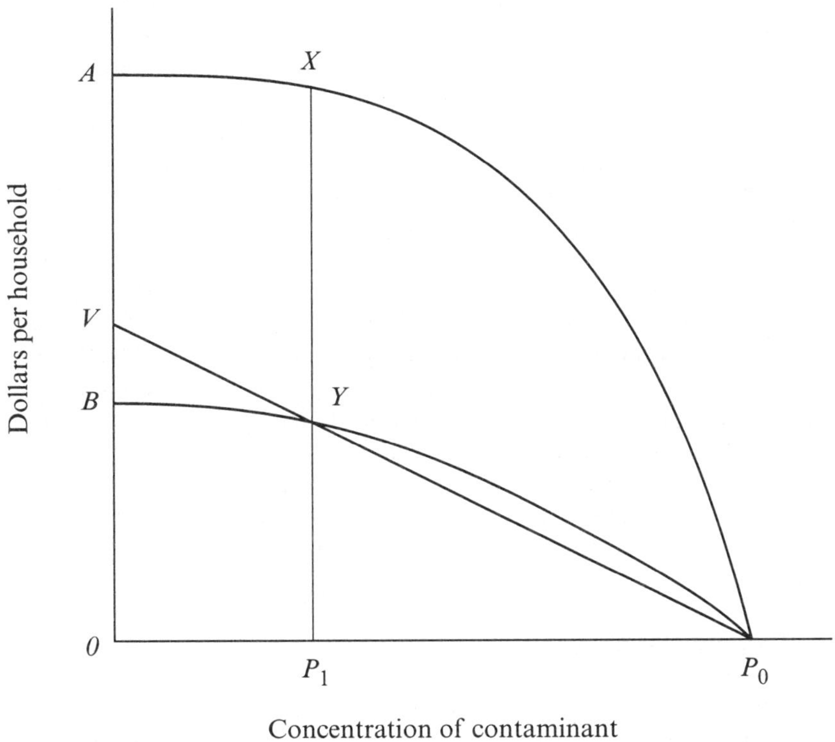

Figure 2.1 Determination of optimal treatment for two sample communities, one large and one small

Because the shapes of the per household total cost and benefit curves associated with remediation of adjusted gross alpha emitters lead to corner solutions, negative net benefits at the level of the proposed standard measure welfare losses. Systems that have a negative net benefit at the standard will have no treatment as an optimal solution (with a corresponding optimal net benefit of 0). Since welfare losses are calculated as net benefits at the standard minus net benefits at the optimum, negative net benefits at the standard are equal to welfare losses here.

Positive net benefits at the standard, however, cannot be interpreted as welfare gains that result from the standard.[9] As indicated in Figure 2.1, systems that have positive net benefits at the standard would find it optimal to exceed the standard. That is, it is optimal for them to reduce their concentration of adjusted gross alpha emitters further than the standard requires. Since we assume that systems choose the optimum in the absence of the standard, the standard does not make them better off. It is also important to note that the standard does not make them worse off either. This is because the proposed adjusted gross alpha standard specifies a minimum level of protection. Systems that find it in their best interest to reduce their concentration level further than the standard requires are free to do so.

The cost curves in Figure 2.1 were developed using the EPA data on the cost of removing adjusted gross alpha emitters. These cost curves have an unusual shape and reflect declining marginal treatment costs. As discussed above, such shapes lead to corner solutions. Systems will find it most beneficial either to undertake no treatment, or to undertake maximum treatment. It is important to note, however, that the basic conclusions about welfare losses resulting from drinking water standards are not dependent on the unusual shape of these cost curves. Uniform drinking water standards cause welfare losses because they do not account for the variation in water treatment costs across communities which stems from several factors, particularly differences in water system size. Unless a federal standard is set so low that it has no effect, therefore, it will impose welfare losses on communities compelled to undertake more treatment than optimal. The following section describes the data and assumptions used in calculating the net benefits associated with the proposed standard for adjusted gross alpha emitters.

3.2 Data and Assumptions

Our analysis uses conservative assumptions in calculating potential welfare losses resulting from a national standard. Those assumptions provide distinctly upper bound estimates of the possible net benefits and, therefore, minimize estimates of potential welfare losses. If the proposed standard is found to create significant welfare losses under those assumptions, then the case against the standard on efficiency grounds is strong. The first of those assumptions is that the isotope, polonium-210, causes all violations of the adjusted gross alpha standard. Adjusted gross alpha emitters include several radioactive isotopes, of which polonium-210 poses the greatest cancer risk. The proposed standard requires that all the isotopes combined should not exceed the level of 15 picocuries/liter (piC/L). Attributing all violations to polonium-210 means that we estimate the maximum cancer reductions for a given decrease in adjusted gross alpha emitters.

A second conservative assumption concerns the value assigned to cancer cases avoided. We use $10 million for that purpose, although most recent studies of the value of a statistical life arrive at a value closer to $5 million. Further, not all cancers result in premature mortality. Finally, fatal cancers usually claim fewer life-years than the occupational fatalities that produce the value-of-life estimates (Viscusi, 1993, pp. 1924–9).

A third conservative assumption is that systems remove only as much of the contaminant as is necessary to meet the proposed standard. When the EPA estimated the cost of meeting the proposed standard, it assumed that each system would remove as much of the contaminant as is technically possible. If we had used the EPA's assumption, we would have obtained a correspondingly higher estimate of welfare losses, as discussed below.

Higher initial concentrations of polonium-210 require greater removal to meet the adjusted gross alpha emitter standard and, therefore, result in greater reductions in household risk (see Table 2.1). The EPA estimated the individual lifetime risk associated with five alternative concentrations of polonium-210 (ranging from 2.6 piC/L to 20 piC/L). These data suggest a linear relationship between concentration levels and risk. We used this linear relationship to calculate the risk associated with concentration levels outside the range considered by the EPA. We converted lifetime risks to annual risks by dividing by 70. Finally, we calculated household risks by assuming that households consisted of 2.7 people.[10] As described above, the reductions in households' cancer risks were valued at $10 million.

The EPA has designated reverse osmosis as the 'best available technology' (BAT) for treating adjusted gross alpha exceedences (Code of Federal Regulations (CFR) Title 40, 1991, p. 33102). The per household cost of utilizing reverse osmosis varies based on system size and removal efficiency. Higher initial concentrations require greater removal efficiencies to meet the standard and, therefore, greater cost. Based on the EPA data, we estimated the cost of the removal efficiencies necessary to meet the adjusted gross alpha standard (15 piC/L). That calculation was made for five different initial concentrations of polonium-210 (see Table 2.2).[11] For any given removal efficiency, per household costs increase sharply as system size decreases.

Table 2.1 Removal efficiencies necessary to meet the proposed standard for adjusted gross alpha emitters (15 piC/L) and resulting benefits

Initial concentration (piC/L)	Necessary removal efficiency	Reduction in polonium-210 (piC/L)	Value of household annual risk reduction (dollars)
20	0.25	5	13.79
25	0.4	10	27.58
30	0.5	15	41.36
35	0.57	20	55.15
50	0.7	35	96.52

Table 2.2 Cost of installing reverse osmosis by system size and required removal efficiency (dollars/household/year)

		Initial concentration (piC/L)				
		20	25	30	35	50
System size		Required removal efficiency				
Category	Population served	25%	40%	50%	57%	70%
1	25–100	664.77	733.47	779.27	811.33	870.87
2	101–500	279.32	340.17	380.74	396.38	425.43
3	501–1K	108.64	199.97	260.86	282.26	322.01
4	1K–3.3K	98.31	155.81	194.15	211.57	243.92
5	3.3K–10K	80.57	112.79	134.28	145.92	167.55
6	10K–25K	69.03	90.61	104.99	115.35	134.58
7	25K–50K	60.71	76.02	86.24	95.17	111.77
8	50K–75K	58.82	72.94	82.35	91.41	108.24
9	75K–100K	10.35	12.86	14.53	16.34	19.71
10	100K 500K	11.71	15.23	17.57	19.62	23.42
11	500K–1 000K	3.84	5.33	6.32	7.13	8.63
12	>1 000K	0.25	0.49	0.60	0.67	0.80

Note: Household costs constructed from estimates of cents/Kgal. EPA estimates of cents/Kgal used for 70% and 50% removal efficiencies. EPA parameter estimates used to develop costs for 25% removal efficiency. Costs for 57% and 40% removal efficiencies are based on linear interpolation.

3.3 The Results

Table 2.3 presents the net benefits associated with the EPA's proposed standard on a per household basis. Those net benefits are presented for alternative system sizes with different initial concentration levels of polonium-210. As described above, negative net benefits serve as measures of welfare losses. This is because no treatment is the optimum for all systems that experience negative net benefits under the proposed standard. However, positive net benefits cannot be interpreted as welfare gains which result from the proposed standard.

Table 2.3 Net benefits per household from remediating polonium-210 using the lowest removal efficiency necessary to meet the standard of 15 piC/L (dollars/year)

		Initial concentration (piC/L)				
		20	25	30	35	50
System size		Required removal efficiency				
Category	Population served	25%	40%	50%	57%	70%
1	25–100	(651)	(706)	(738)	(756)	(774)
2	101–500	(266)	(313)	(339)	(341)	(329)
3	501–1K	(95)	(172)	(219)	(227)	(225)
4	1K–3.3K	(85)	(128)	(153)	(156)	(147)
5	3.3K–10K	(67)	(85)	(93)	(91)	(71)
6	10K–25K	(55)	(63)	(64)	(60)	(38)
7	25K–50K	(47)	(48)	(45)	n.a.	n.a.
8	50K–75K	(45)	n.a.	n.a.	n.a.	n.a.
9	75K–100K	n.a.	n.a.	n.a.	n.a.	n.a.
10	100K–500K	2	n.a.	n.a.	n.a.	n.a.
11	500K–1000K	n.a.	n.a.	n.a.	n.a.	n a.
12	>1000K	n.a.	n.a.	n.a.	n.a.	n.a.

Notes:
Net benefits equal value of household risk reduction (Table 2.1) minus household cost of treatment (from Table 2.2).
Numbers in parentheses are negative.
n.a.: Not applicable because no systems fall into this size category/initial concentration combination.

The results in Table 2.3 are striking in two respects. First, welfare losses vary greatly across system size categories, with households served by small systems incurring large negative net benefits. Households served by systems in the smallest size category (25–100 people) may incur losses of $651 per year or more, depending on their initial level of contamination. For example, households in size category 1 with an initial concentration of 20 piC/L will need to achieve a 25 percent removal efficiency to meet the proposed standard. This will result in a per household benefit of $13.79 (see Table 2.1) but a per household cost of $664.77 (see Table 2.2). The resulting negative net benefit, therefore, is $651. Welfare losses drop rapidly as system size increases. For example, households in system size category 4 with the same initial concentration (20 piC/L) incur annual losses of $85.[12]

The second striking result of our analysis is the preponderance of negative net benefits. Only one system size category has positive net benefits as a result of the proposed standard. Households served by systems serving 100000 to 500000 people experience very small but positive net benefits of $2 annually as a result of meeting the proposed standard. As noted above, however, they could achieve those same net benefits without the standard through their community's decision to undertake treatment in the absence of federal standards.

The preponderance of negative net benefits under the proposed standard is not surprising, given the instructions on setting standards with which the SDWA provides the EPA. As discussed above, the SDWA directs the EPA to set standards as close to a zero risk level as is considered affordable to large systems. Given the economics of scale in drinking water treatment, standards that are affordable for large systems are often not affordable for smaller systems. Furthermore, the adjusted gross alpha emitters standard was proposed before the 1996 amendments. Thus, the EPA was not allowed to use a cost–benefit criterion when establishing it. As discussed below, the consideration of costs and benefits allowed under the 1996 amendments should reduce welfare losses which large systems incur under standards proposed in the future. It is not expected, however, to eliminate welfare losses for small systems.

Although annual losses per household are large for households served by small systems requiring treatment, relatively few households are expected to incur such losses. This is because occurrences of initial contamination levels above the proposed standard of 15 piC/L are expected to be rare. Based on EPA data, only 123 systems (out of a total of over 60000 community water systems) are expected to exceed the proposed standard (see Table 2.4).[13] Of these, the vast majority are small systems serving relatively few households. A total of 100345 households are expected to incur minor positive annual net benefits as a result of meeting the proposed standard. These households are served by systems in size category 10 (see Table 2.5). A total of 178991 households are expected to incur negative net benefits. Those negative net benefits range from $38 to $774 per year.

The total welfare losses associated with the proposed standard are estimated to be $12 million annually.[14] We estimate the total annual compliance cost of the proposed standard to be $19 million (that is the out-of-pocket cost associated with installing and operating the requisite control equipment). Welfare losses, therefore, are 63 percent of the total compliance cost.

Table 2.4 Number of systems exceeding concentration levels for adjusted gross alpha emitters

System size		Concentration levels (piC/L)						
Category	Population served	>15	>20	>25	>30	>35	>40	>45
1	25–100	42	21	11	7	5	3	2
2	101–500	26	14	7	4	3	2	1
3	501–1K	21	12	7	4	3	2	2
4	1K–3.3K	19	10	6	4	3	2	1
5	3.3K–10K	5	3	2	1	1	1	0
6	10K–25K	6	3	3	2	1	1	1
7	25K–50K	2	1	1	0	0	0	0
8	50K–75K	1	0	0	0	0	0	0
9	75K–100K	0	0	0	0	0	0	0
10	100K–500K	1	0	0	0	0	0	0
11	500K–1000K	0	0	0	0	0	0	0
12	>1000K	0	0	0	0	0	0	0

Note: Based on occurrence data in US EPA Regulatory Impact Analysis of Proposed National Primary Drinking Water Regulations for Radionuclides (April, 1991) and extrapolation from the National Inorganics and Radionuclides Survey to the population of community water systems.

The EPA has estimated the total annual compliance cost to be $37 million (CFR Title 40, 1991, p. 33101). Our cost estimate is substantially lower than the EPA's because we assume that systems will remove only as much of the contaminant as required to meet the proposed standard. The EPA's estimate of the cost of the rule is based on the assumption that each system will treat all of its water. Each system, therefore, removes more of the contaminant than is required to meet the standard. Thirty-two million dollars of the EPA's $37 million cost estimate is incurred by systems having a cost per cancer case avoided in excess of $10 million (that is, those that we assume would not meet the standard in the absence of federal requirements). The benefits incurred by those same systems total $6 million.[15] The welfare losses resulting from the EPA's assumptions, therefore, are $24 million.

Table 2.5 Number of households exceeding concentration levels for adjusted gross alpha emitters

System size		Concentration levels (piC/L)						
Category	Population served	>15	>20	>25	>30	>35	>40	>45
1	25–100	873	436	229	145	94	64	45
2	101–500	2348	1264	632	397	258	175	124
3	501–1K	6596	3628	2309	1339	912	648	476
4	1K–3.3K	16345	8172	4903	3395	2312	1644	1208
5	3.3K–10K	15198	7599	5066	3396	2273	1592	1155
6	10K–25K	49632	28361	21271	15224	11277	8640	6801
7	25K–50K	52230	34820	34820	0	0	0	0
8	50K–75K	35769	0	0	0	0	0	0
9	75K–100K	0	0	0	0	0	0	0
10	100K–500K	100345	0	0	0	0	0	0
11	500K–1000K	0	0	0	0	0	0	0
12	>1000K	0	0	0	0	0	0	0

Note: Based on system occurrence data (Table 2.4), EPA data on average population per system and assumption of 2.7 people per household.

3.4 Limitations

Economic theory indicates that federal standard-setting may be more efficient than local standard-setting when externalities are present. Because the costs and health benefits of drinking water treatment generally fall on the local population, our analysis does not reveal any efficiency gains from federal drinking water standards. Further, because the costs of treatment vary greatly across communities, we find that the proposed standard imposes large welfare losses on some communities.

Ideally, we would calculate the welfare losses that would result from an 'optimal' federal standard. Without externalities, the optimal federal standard would vary with local circumstances and would correspond to each optimal local standard. However, given information constraints, and possibly political constraints, the federal government typically sets a single uniform standard.[16] In that case, the optimal minimum federal standard would not compel any system to undertake more treatment than it would choose on its own (providing it attempts to maximize welfare). Given large economies of scale in the removal of adjusted gross alpha emitters, small systems will find it optimal to undertake no treatment. If the EPA had set a lower standard for adjusted gross alpha emitters, therefore, the resulting welfare losses would have been less.

It is important to consider a potential justification for federal standards which is not reflected in our analysis. We base our analysis on the assumption that state or local governments would undertake optimal drinking water treatment in the absence of federal standards. If some lower levels of government were to choose standards that are less stringent than optimal, federal standards have the potential to result in efficiency improvements.[17] Federal standards may result in welfare gains for communities whose governments choose overly lax local standards. Simultaneously, federal standards will impose welfare losses on communities forced to comply with standards that are higher than justified by their unique circumstances. Whether federal standards are more efficient than state or local standards will depend on that trade-off. This issue is not important for the particular standard that we analysed because 'no treatment' is the most efficient course of action for nearly all communities. For other contaminants, however, the issue of whether lower levels of government would choose efficient local standards may be a key factor in determining whether federal standards are warranted.

It is not easy to determine whether lower levels of government would choose efficient standards in the absence of federal requirements. State and local governments made significant strides in protecting drinking water before the passage of the SDWA in 1974. Those actions resulted in a dramatic decrease in waterborne disease and the adoption of voluntary federal guidelines in all 50 states (Oleckno, 1982, p. 237). However, Congress established the SDWA, in part, because of concern that the protection efforts by state and local governments were not adequate (Fri, 1973, p. 74).

A more difficult question is whether state and local governments would ensure sufficient protection in the absence of federal standards today. Protecting drinking water requires accurate information about the contaminants in the water and the risks that they pose, technical knowledge about treatment options, adequate resources for monitoring and installing treatment technologies, and sufficient political will. Drinking water safety may suffer if any of those ingredients are absent, no matter which level of government is responsible for setting standards.

4 CONCLUSIONS

Our analysis of the EPA's proposed standard for adjusted gross alpha emitters shows that this standard may impose large welfare losses on some households. The aggregate value of those welfare losses is limited by the fact that the proposed standard affects few systems and is a relatively inexpensive standard. While individual households could incur losses as much as $774 per year, we estimate total welfare losses at $12 million annually. However, the factors that lead to welfare losses under the proposed standard for adjusted gross alpha emitters are not unique to that standard. The cost of meeting virtually all drinking water standards is much higher for small systems than for large systems. This is due to economies of scale in the treatment of drinking water. Meanwhile, per household benefits of meeting a given standard are invariant to system size.

Regulations that affect many systems may result in larger, more widespread, welfare losses. For example, the EPA estimates that the annual cost of meeting its proposed standard for disinfectants and disinfection by-products is $2.6 billion.[18] The EPA expects that annual household cost of complying with that rule to range from less than $10 (primarily for those served by large surface water systems) to as much as $350 (for those served by small ground water systems) (EPA, 1994, exhibit 5-3 and 5-4). There is a tremendous amount of uncertainty about the magnitude of the benefits that might result from that rule. The EPA currently estimates that the average cost per cancer case avoided under the proposed standard could be as low as $512000 or as high as $12.8 billion (EPA, 1994, p. 5–7). In addition, the 1996 amendments explicitly prohibit the benefit/cost criterion from being applied to that standard (House of Representatives Report 104-741, 1996, Section 104).

The 1996 amendments to the SDWA could considerably reduce, but not eliminate, the welfare losses associated with uniform national drinking water standards. These amendments allow the EPA to consider costs and benefits when setting an MCL. That consideration, however, is likely to be dominated by the effects of large systems. The amendments should reduce the likelihood that standards will be proposed that are feasible (that is, affordable to large systems), but under which all systems (or nearly all) have negative net benefits. The cost–benefit criterion may reduce the welfare losses for large systems. As described above, however, small systems may still incur substantial welfare losses. Owing to the scale economies in drinking water treatment, standards that are efficient for large systems will often be too stringent for small systems.

Widespread use of the variance technologies defined in the 1996 amendments could reduce, but not eliminate, welfare losses for small systems. They would not eliminate welfare losses because an affordability criterion is used in defining the variance technologies, not a cost–benefit criterion. Treatments deemed affordable to small systems may not be justified on the grounds of costs and benefits. In some cases, no treatment, rather than use of a variance technology, may be the efficient solution for small systems. In addition, the EPA and the states must overcome many hurdles to facilitate the widespread use of variance technologies. Those hurdles include developing accepted definitions of what is 'affordable' and what is adequately 'protective of public health'.[19]

Economic theory suggests that uniform federal standards are inefficient for two reasons. First, local governments have an incentive to choose efficient standards. Second, the cost of meeting virtually all drinking water standards is typically much higher for small systems than for large systems. Our analysis shows that, at least in some cases, uniform standards could impose large welfare losses on affected households.

Decentralizing the standard-setting process, however, would *not* mean eliminating the federal role in ensuring safe drinking water. For example, sub-national levels of government would need to make informed decisions if they had the power to set their own drinking water standards. Given the public good characteristics of research and development, it would probably be most efficient for the federal government to conduct drinking water research. This would include research on health effects of contaminants and the availability of treatment technologies. The federal government could then provide that information to lower levels of government.[20] Thus, the federal government would need to retain its current responsibility for those tasks.

Decentralizing the standard setting process could allow state or local governments to choose standards that better reflect their individual costs and benefits. However, several factors would need to be given careful consideration. One such consideration is the fact that water system boundaries do not always correspond with political boundaries. They often cross municipal and, sometimes, state boundaries. As Wallace Oates's own work on the principle of 'perfect correspondence' suggests, those circumstances would require some type of interjurisdictional agreement (Oases, 1972, p.34). Furthermore, financial stability may be a consideration if standard-setting responsibility was assigned to local governments. Federal or state intervention would be necessary when financial problems might prevent local governments from making sound decisions about drinking water standards.

NOTES

1. The findings, interpretations and conclusions expressed in this paper are entirely those of the authors. They do not necessarily represent the views of the World Bank, its Executive Directors, or the countries they represent. Nor do they represent the views of the Congressional Budget Office.
2. For a more detailed description of the history of drinking water regulations and existing and proposed regulations (Congressional Budget Office, 1995, pp.3–7).
3. Such exemptions may be granted by a state if the state has primacy – that is, if the EPA has delegated the implementation of the SDWA to the state.
4. The exception is if the standard applies to a contaminant that is found almost exclusively in small systems.
5. Nearly 80 percent of the population receives its water from systems serving over 10000 people.

6. No variances and only 15 exemptions were granted between January 1990 and March 1994. The EPA does not collect information on the number of systems which requested a variance or an exemption. Neither does it collect information on the level of treatment which systems granted exemptions actually undertook (Congressional Budget Office, 1995, p. 36).
7. The EPA has specified treatment requirements (for example, disinfection) under the Surface Water Treatment Rule and the Total Coliform Rule. The EPA issued both of these rules in June 1989.
8. This is reflected in Table 2.2. For example, a system serving 101 to 500 people has a per household cost of $279.32 to remove 25 percent of polonium-210. That cost increases to $380.74 to obtain a 50 percent removal (that is, less than double the 25 percent removal cost) and to $425.43 for 70 percent removal. Thus, cost increases at a decreasing rate.
9. This result would, of course, still hold if there was an interior solution. Systems having an optimal treatment level that corresponds to, or exceeds, that required by the standard may achieve those same welfare gains in the absence of a federal standard.
10. The EPA assumed 2.7 people per household when estimating household costs for treatment.
11. The EPA estimated the cost (in cents/Kgal) by system size for three removal efficiencies: 90 percent (not used in this analysis), 70 percent and 50 percent (EPA, 1991, Appendix C). We estimated the cost (in cents/Kgal) of a 25 percent removal efficiency based on parameters developed by an EPA contractor (Pirnie, 1992, Tables RO3 and RO6) Costs for 57 percent and 40 percent removal efficiencies are based on linear interpolation. The EPA also estimated household costs associated with a 90 percent removal efficiency (EPA, 1991, Appendix A). Proportionate reductions in cents/Kgal for lower removal efficiencies were used to adjust household costs associated with a 90 percent removal efficiency downward to reflect lower removal efficiencies.
12. As the initial concentration level increases, per household welfare losses for this size category first increase (up to a loss of $156 at an initial concentration of 35 piC/L) and then decrease. This is because of the concave shape of the cost function.
13. An EPA contractor used probability distributions derived from the National Inorganics and Radionuclides Survey to estimate the number of systems in various size categories exceeding concentrations of 15, 20, and 25 piC/L (Wade Miller Associates, 1991, pp. 16–22). We used those size category-specific parameter estimates to predict the number of systems exceeding greater concentration levels.
14. This was calculated by multiplying the annual household net benefit estimate for each system size–initial concentration combination by the number of households estimated to fall into that category and then totaling them. Positive net benefits were not included in this total (and, therefore, do not offset negative net benefits).
15. The EPA estimates that a total of 0.6 cancer cases are avoided by systems that have a cost per cancer case avoided of more than $10 million.
16. Perry Shapiro argues that limited information about citizens' preferences and political constraints leads the federal government to choose uniform standards (Shapiro, 1996).
17. Local governments could also create welfare losses by choosing standards that are overly protective. Federal standards would not reduce welfare losses in that case. This is because federal standards define minimum levels of protection. They do not, however, preclude states or localities from choosing higher levels of protection.
18. This is more than the cost of all existing drinking water standards combined (EPA, 1994, pp. 5–7).
19. Those barriers, in part, explain the very limited use of the special treatment provisions for small systems that were defined under the 1986 Amendments the SDWA (Congressional Budget Office, 1995, pp. 36–9).
20. Information is a public good because, once created, it can be simultaneously consumed by multiple groups of people with the consumption of an additional group not diminishing the consumption of the others. In addition, the information can be provided to additional groups at zero marginal cost. No individual state would have an incentive to conduct a socially efficient level of research because they would not have an incentive to account for the benefits that other states would obtain from that research. Furthermore, states may have an incentive to delay research efforts and try to be 'free riders,' that is to let other states do the research first.

REFERENCES

Bradford, David F. and Wallace E. Oates (1974), 'Suburban Exploitation of Central cities and Governmental Structure', in H. Hochman and G. Peterson (eds), *Redistribution Through Public Choice*, New York: Columbia University Press, pp. 43–90.

Code of Federal Regulations (1991), *Title 40 Parts 141 and 142 National Primary Drinking Water Regulations; Radio nuclides: Proposed Rule Vol 56(138).*

Congressional Budget Office (1995), *The Safe Drinking Water Act: A Case Study of an Unfunded Federal Mandate.*

Environmental Protection Agency (1990), *Estimates of the Total Benefits and Total Costs Associated with Implementation of the 1986 Amendments to the Safe Drinking Water Act.*

Environmental Protection Agency (1991), *Regulatory Impact Analysis of Proposed National Primary Drinking Water Regulations for Radionuclides.*

Environmental Protection Agency (1993), *Technical and Economic Capacity of States and Public Water Systems to Implement Drinking Water Regulations: Report to Congress.*

Environmental Protection Agency (1994), *Regulatory Impact Analysis of Proposed National Primary Drinking Water Regulations: Disinfectants/Disinfection By-Products Rule.*

Fri, Robert W. (1973), 'Statement of Hon. Robert W. Fri, Deputy Administrator Environmental Protection Agency before the Subcommittee on Public Health and Environment of the Committee on Interstate and Foreign Commerce of the House of Representatives', Safe Drinking Water Act House Hearings.

House of Representatives Report 104-741 (1996), *Safe Drinking Water Act Amendments of 1996.*

Oates, Wallace E. (1972), *Fiscal Federalism*, New York: Harcourt, Brace and Jovanovich Inc.

Oleckno, William A. (1982), 'The National Interim Primary Drinking Water Regulations', *Journal of Environmental Health*, **4** (5), 236–44.

Pirnie, Malcolm (1992), *Technologies and Costs for the Removal of Radionuclides from Potable Water Supplies*, Report to the Environmental Protection Agency.

Shapiro, Perry (1996), 'Which Level of Government Should be Responsible for Environmental Regulation: The Federalists Versus Calhoun' in John B. Braden, Henk Folmer and Thomas Ulen (eds), *Environmental Policy with Political and Economic Integration: The European Union and the United States*, Aldershot, UK and Brookfield, US: Edward Elgar, pp. 132–44.

Viscusi, W. Kip (1993), 'The Value of Risks to Life and Health' *Journal of Economic Literature*, **31** (4), 1912–46.

Wade Miller Associates, Inc. (1991), *Occurrence and Exposure Assessment for Gross Alpha Particle Activity in Public Drinking Water*, Report to the Environmental Protection Agency.

3. The case for a two-part instrument: presumptive tax and environmental subsidy

Don Fullerton and Ann Wolverton*

I INTRODUCTION

Economists have long noted that many types of pollution can be controlled efficiently by placing a price or tax directly on the polluting activity (Pigou, 1932). This incentive can induce the household or firm to find the cheapest possible way to reduce waste, whether by recycling, installing new equipment, switching fuels, using labor-intensive methods, or perhaps just reducing production of the offending good. Still, few such taxes are ever employed by policy makers. Most environmental policies in the US and other countries are command and control regulations, and most environmental taxes are labeled as environmental only because the resulting revenues are spent on clean-up, not because the tax applies per unit of a polluting activity.[1]

Perhaps the major reason that taxes on polluting activities are rare is that wastes are hard to monitor and the taxes are difficult to enforce. Practical policy requires that the tax apply to an observable market transaction like the purchase of petroleum or chemical inputs, rather than to the 'spilling of oil' or the 'dumping of chemical wastes.' These polluting activities can be prohibited by law, and controlled through the required use of certain technologies, but they are hard to measure for the application of a waste-end tax.

The point of this paper is that the desirable incentive effects of a waste-end tax can be matched exactly, without the measurement and enforcement problems, by the use of a two-part instrument. To see this equivalence, one must first view the generation of waste as an input to production, with its own marginal product, just like labor, capital, and materials.[2] Then the tax does not need to apply directly to the unobservable wastes. Identical changes in relative prices can be achieved with a tax on an observable transaction such as the purchase of the output, in combination with a subsidy to other observable transactions like the purchase of all other inputs to production except waste.

The intuition is fairly simple, and follows from the idea that the waste-end tax has two intended incentive effects. First, it raises production costs and makes the good more expensive, so the output effect reduces production and therefore consumption of the good. Second, it makes the waste more expensive relative to other inputs, so the substitution effect reduces waste per unit of the remaining amount of the output that still gets produced. By analogy, the two-part instrument accomplishes the same effects separately. The first part imposes a tax on the output, reducing production and consumption of the good. This tax on output is equivalent to a tax at the same rate on all inputs to production, including labor, capital, materials, and waste. The second part subsidizes all non-waste inputs, which makes waste relatively more expensive and reduces waste per unit of output.

We refer to the first part of the two-part instrument as a presumptive tax; it is imposed under the presumption that all production uses a dirty technology or that all consumption goods become waste. The second part is an environmental subsidy; it is provided only to the extent that production uses clean technology or that consumption goods are recycled. The obvious practical example of a two-part instrument is a deposit-refund system: the consumer pays a deposit under the presumption that the item will be discarded improperly, and gets a refund only with proper performance (when the item is recycled). When litter or other illegal disposal cannot be taxed directly, the deposit-refund system can accomplish the same goals (Bohm, 1981; Stavins, 1991; Cropper and Oates, 1992). A subsidy to the form of disposal with lower social costs provides the substitution effect, shifting disposal away from socially-costly dumping, but that subsidy implicitly makes consumption cheaper and *encourages* purchase of the good. An output tax corrects this latter effect.

The literature does not use the term presumptive tax to refer exclusively to the first part of a two-part instrument. Gunnar Eskeland (1994) defines it as a tax that exploits the presumed relationship between the good to be taxed and the pollution to be regulated, but he does not require that it be paired with a subsidy.[3] Using this definition, any indirect tax that acts as a proxy for the direct taxation of emissions can be called a presumptive tax. For example, a gasoline tax is a presumptive tax on emissions, because one presumes that gasoline use is related to emissions. The tax on gasoline is more practical than a tax on vehicle emissions, but it is not a perfect proxy because it does not provide incentives to fix a car's broken pollution control equipment or to buy a car with lower emissions per gallon of gasoline.

In this paper, to avoid categorizing any indirect tax as a presumptive tax, we will refer to a presumptive tax only in combination with an environmental subsidy. The above gasoline tax is an indirect tax on emissions, but we refer to it as a presumptive tax only if it is coupled with a subsidy to the repair of all vehicles' broken pollution control equipment, or a subsidy to the purchase of vehicles with lower emissions per gallon of gasoline. The two-part instrument thus improves the aim of policy at the desired behavioral targets.[4]

The main advantage of the two-part instrument is that both parts apply to market transactions with invoices to help ensure compliance. In contrast, a Pigovian tax may apply to the firm's own measure of an input that is not purchased on the market and therefore does not have an invoice. The two-part instrument puts the information requirements where they can be met most cheaply and efficiently. It shifts the burden of proof. The firm must measure its own clean inputs and provide the evidence necessary to receive the subsidy.

Discussions in the literature of the tax-subsidy combination largely have been limited to deposit-refund systems in which the deposit and the refund are explicitly linked, and in which the deposit and the refund are equal to one another.[5] No such restrictions are made here. The refund may be paid to an individual or firm other than the one who paid the deposit, and the optimal refund may be a different amount than the original deposit. The tax and subsidy may even apply to different commodities altogether.

Current deposits and refunds do apply to particular consumer items such as beverage containers, car hulks, oil, and batteries, but we wish to emphasize that this concept has much wider applicability and may provide a promising alternative to widely-used command-and-control (CAC) policies.[6] In a broad sense, the United States income tax system operates on a deposit-refund principle. An individual pays a presumed amount of tax directly out of his or her paycheck each month, and a refund is given at the end of the fiscal year if the individual files a proper tax return with proof of overpayment. The same approach can be used in an environmental context. Thus, instead of limiting ourselves to a discussion of a deposit and refund, we want to think more generally about how a simple excise tax on a given consumption good can be coupled with a subsidy per ton of recycled material used in production. If markets work, this subsidy can be passed on to suppliers of recycled goods.

We begin in section II by outlining two simple general equilibrium models to demonstrate the equivalence between a Pigovian tax on emissions and a presumptive tax–environmental subsidy combination. This equivalence is shown to hold even when one agent pays the tax on a good or factor and a different agent receives the subsidy, possibly on a different good or factor. In the first model, the deposit always equals the refund. In the second model, however, this is not necessarily the case. Section III examines some practical advantages and disadvantages of using a presumptive tax–subsidy combination to elicit the optimal solution. Section IV provides a review of how this idea of a two-part instrument has been used in actual policy implementation. Finally, we conclude in section V that the presumptive tax coupled with a performance subsidy is a broader and more useful policy instrument than commonly thought.

II THEORETICAL EQUIVALENCE TO A PIGOVIAN TAX

A The Simplest Possible Model

To illustrate the equivalence between the Pigovian tax and the two-part instrument, we build a simple general equilibrium model in the tradition of Baumol and Oates (1988).[7] In the simplest possible model, the economy is a closed one with linear production and only one jurisdiction. We also assume perfect information, no transactions costs, and no pre-existing distortions.

In this simple model, the society consists of n identical households. Each household owns one unit of 'resources,' which may include a fixed amount of labor, capital, land or any other resource that can be sold in the market or used at home. The household sells some of this resource and uses the income to buy a clean good c and a dirty good d. It retains some of these resources to produce a household good h, which can be interpreted either as leisure or as household production. We define the units in our model such that the marginal rate of transformation is equal to 1. Thus, given these assumptions, the resource constraint is simply: $h + c + d = 1$. Utility of the household u depends positively on each of these three goods and negatively on the total amount of the dirty good present in society, $D = nd$. Throughout this chapter, lower case letters denote individual household amounts, while upper case letters denote aggregates for the society.

The social planner maximizes the utility of a representative household, subject to the resource constraint, recognizing the effect of each household's consumption of the dirty good d on the total amount of D. Thus, the optimization problem is:

$$\max u(c,d,h,nd) + \lambda(1 - h - c - d) \tag{3.1}$$

with respect to c, d, and h. This yields the first order conditions:

$$u_c = \lambda \tag{3.2a}$$

$$u_d + nu_D = \lambda \tag{3.2b}$$

$$u_h = \lambda \tag{3.2c}$$

where a subscript denotes a partial derivative, and λ is the social marginal value of the resource. These first order conditions state that the marginal utility from an additional unit of c, d, or h equals the marginal social cost, λ.

In the private market with perfect competition, the individual household maximizes utility subject to its budget constraint:

$$\max u(c, d, h, D) + \gamma[(1 - h)(1 - t_r) - c(1 + t_c) - d(1 + t_d)] \qquad (3.3)$$

where prices are normalized to one, t_c is the tax per unit of c, t_d is the tax per unit of d, and t_r is the tax per unit of resources supplied in the market. A household does not take into account the effect of its own use of d on the total amount of the dirty good D in society. Thus, it maximizes utility with respect to c, d, and h but takes D as given. The first order conditions from the individual household's problem are:

$$u_c = \gamma(1 + t_c) \qquad (3.4a)$$

$$u_d = \gamma(1 + t_d) \qquad (3.4b)$$

$$u_h = \gamma(1 - t_r). \qquad (3.4c)$$

The solution strategy is to find tax rate combinations where the market (equations 3.4a–3.4c) is induced to match the social optimum (equations 3.2a–3.2c). We first examine the case where $t_c = t_r = 0$. From (3.2a) and (3.4a), we then find that $\lambda = \gamma$; the social utility from one more unit of income (or time) is equal to its private utility. Using this relationship and combining (3.2b) with (3.4b) reveals that the optimal tax on d is:

$$t_d = -(nu_D/\gamma) \qquad (3.5)$$

This result is a simplified version of the Pigovian tax derived in Baumol and Oates (1988). It is the total, for all n households, of the marginal disutility from another unit of d, converted into dollars when divided by the marginal utility of income. Since n and γ are positive, a negative externality u_D yields a positive tax t_d. The tax discourages consumption of d, inducing households to reach the social optimum.

Suppose, however, that t_d cannot be used as a policy instrument, either because it is difficult to enforce or because d is hard to measure. We can still obtain the same first-best outcome by using the two other instruments: t_c and t_r. With a non-zero tax on c, however, λ is no longer equal to γ. Using (3.2a) and (3.4a), we find that $\lambda = \gamma(1 + t_c)$. Also, from (3.2c) and (3.4c), we have $\lambda = \gamma(1 - t_r)$. Using these two expressions for λ, it must be the case that $t_c = -t_r$. As a consequence, one of these 'taxes' will in fact be a subsidy.

Next, with $t_d = 0$, (3.4b) states that $\gamma = u_d$. If we substitute $\lambda = \gamma(1 - t_r)$ into (3.2b) and solve for t_r, we have:

$$t_r = -(nu_D/\gamma). \qquad (3.6)$$

Given that $\gamma \geq 0$ and $u_D \leq 0$, t_r is a positive tax. This tax applies to all earnings. As previously established, t_c is the negative of this result. This subsidy is a rebate on all spending *except* spending on the dirty good.[8]

Thus, even a very simple model can be used to demonstrate the equivalence of the two-part instrument with the standard Pigovian tax. The deposit still equals the refund, but otherwise this tax-subsidy combination does not resemble the standard deposit-refund system because the tax applies to labor or capital income while the subsidy is on an entirely different commodity.

This presumptive tax can be part of the income tax collected by the government each year, while a separate subsidy applies to c. As a practical matter, this subsidy can appear simply as a sales tax that is lower on c than on all other goods. Thus, the consumer may not even notice the connection between the tax and the subsidy, despite the fact that together they induce the optimal behavior.[9]

B A Model with Production and Emissions

A second general equilibrium model illustrates the usefulness of the two-part instrument for controlling a firm's emissions from production. As in the previous model, we make the standard assumptions of no transaction costs, perfect information, no pre-existing distortions, a closed economy, and perfectly competitive markets. Again, the society consists of n identical households. Each household's utility u is a function of one good d, household production h, and the total amount of waste in the society $W = nw$. Thus,

$$u = u(d,h,W) \tag{3.7}$$

where $u_d \geq 0$, $u_h \geq 0$, and $u_W \leq 0$.

The good d is produced using the following constant returns to scale production function:[10]

$$d = f(r_d, w). \tag{3.8}$$

where r_d is the direct use of resources r in the production of d. Production cannot occur without the generation of waste w. This waste requires the use of some private resources for removal and disposal r_w, in the amount $r_w = \alpha w$. The household good h is produced using only one input r_h, the amount of the resource retained at home. Thus, $h = r_h$. With a fixed total resource r, the resource constraint for the model is $r = r_d + r_h + r_w$.

The social planner maximizes utility subject to production and resource constraints as well as $r_w = \alpha w$. Substituting these constraints into the planner's problem yields:

$$\max \quad u[f(r_d, w), r_h, nw] + \lambda[r - r_d - r_h - \alpha w]. \tag{3.9}$$

The planner maximizes utility by choosing r_d, w, and r_h, explicitly taking into account the effect of production waste on utility. This gives the following first order conditions:

$$u_d f_{r_d} = \lambda \tag{3.10a}$$

$$u_d f_w + n u_W = \alpha\lambda \tag{3.10b}$$

$$u_h = \lambda \tag{3.10c}$$

where f_{r_d} is the partial of f with respect to r_d, and f_w is the partial of f with respect to w. Intuitively, these first order conditions state that the marginal social benefit from a particular use of the resource is equal to the marginal social cost.

In the private market, the consumer maximizes utility with respect to d and r_h subject to a budget constraint:

$$\max \quad u(d, r_h, W) + \gamma[(r - r_h) - d(p_d + t_d)] \tag{3.11}$$

where t_d is a tax on the consumption of d, and the resource r is the numeraire. The individual consumers have no control over the total amount of waste being produced by firms. However, they are still affected by its generation; thus, $u_W \leq 0$. The first order conditions are:

$$u_d = \gamma(p_d + t_d) \tag{3.12a}$$

$$u_h = \gamma. \tag{3.12b}$$

Producers of d maximize profits by their choice of inputs r_d and w. Thus, the firm's problem is:

$$\max \quad p_d f(r_d, w) - (1 + t_r) \cdot r_d - (\alpha w + t_w w) \tag{3.13}$$

where t_r is a tax on the use of resources r_d, and t_w is a possible tax on waste emissions. The first order conditions yield two important relationships:

$$p_d = (1 + t_r)/(f_{r_d}) \tag{3.14a}$$

$$p_d = (\alpha + t_w)/(f_w). \tag{3.14b}$$

In this model, from (3.12b) and (3.10c), we again have $\lambda = \gamma$. When both t_r and t_d are zero, the government has only t_w available to induce the private market to match the social optimum. We set (3.14a) equal to (3.14b) and use the result along with (3.10a) and (3.10b) to find the Pigovian tax:

$$t_w = -(nu_W/\gamma). \tag{3.15}$$

However, this tax on emissions does not apply to a market transaction and may therefore be difficult to monitor. In the case where emissions cannot be taxed directly ($t_w = 0$), both t_r and t_d can be used to arrive at exactly the same first-best socially optimal solution. This combination may be easier to implement, since it involves a tax on the output of a market good *d*, and on the input of a market resource *r*.

We begin by solving for t_d. Substituting (3.14b) into (3.12a) and then into (3.10b), we find that:

$$t_d = -(nu_W/\gamma f_w) \tag{3.16}$$

Since consumers derive negative utility from *W*, and firms have a positive marginal product from *w*, t_d is a positive tax on consumer purchases of *d*. It can be rewritten as the marginal external damage from *w* (the Pigovian tax on firms in (3.15)) divided by the marginal product of *w*. Thus, intuitively, t_d can be interpreted as the increase in the price of *d* that would have occurred with a tax on waste.

Now we solve for t_r by substituting (3.10a), (3.14a) and (3.16) into (3.12a):

$$t_r = (nu_W f_{r_d})/(\gamma f_w). \tag{3.17}$$

Since $u_W \leq 0$, we know t_r is negative. This subsidy is the marginal external damage from *w* multiplied by the ratio of the marginal products. This latter ratio is the slope of the isoquant, the trade-off between units of the dirty input and the clean input. Thus, if the relative price of r_d is high (α low), then the subsidy must also be high to generate the necessary substitution from *w* to r_d. The subsidy would not exceed 100 percent, however. The optimal subsidy per unit of clean input, t_r, can also be interpreted as the damage per unit of dirty input multiplied by the number of dirty inputs per clean input.

The use of t_d with t_r constitutes a two-part instrument that yields the same efficient results as the standard Pigovian tax on waste. Thus, the equivalence between the two tax systems still holds in a model where producers have a choice regarding emissions per unit of output. In this model, the equivalency between the Pigovian tax and the two-part system holds even though the Pigovian tax is placed on the firm, while the presumptive tax is placed on the purchases made by consumers. As in the previous model, the tax and subsidy are not explicitly linked; the tax is on the output while the subsidy is on the clean input. In addition, the deposit is no longer required to equal the refund.[11]

The tax-subsidy combination is useful particularly when a tax directly on emissions is difficult to enforce. Because emissions are not observed in a market transaction, a presumptive tax is placed instead on the output, which is easily observed in the market. Given a presumed relationship between output and emissions, the tax on output is a proxy for a direct tax on emissions. However, if producers can change emissions per unit of output, then this presumptive tax might not be a good proxy by itself. The firm's purchase of clean inputs such as labor or capital are also observed in the market, and can be subsidized by a reduction in other taxes that are normally collected on those inputs. The combination of a tax on output with a subsidy on clean inputs is a perfect proxy for an unenforceable tax on the dirty input.

III BEYOND THE MODEL: TWO-PART INSTRUMENT vs PIGOVIAN TAX

The two models above are simple, and yet they demonstrate cases where the two-part instrument is equivalent to a Pigovian tax. The results cannot be used to choose one such policy over another, however. To make the case for the two-part instrument, we must look outside the models at considerations such as feasibility, administrative costs, policy enforcement, and political perceptions. We also examine the possible effects of relaxing some of our models' assumptions.

A Practical Differences from a Pigovian Tax

First, consider feasibility. A Pigovian tax directly on the dirty input or emissions may not be possible, either because emissions cannot be measured or because the tax is not enforceable. For example, a tax on vehicle emissions is not yet technologically feasible (Harrington et al., 1994), and a tax on 'midnight dumping' is not enforceable. When the Pigovian tax is not viable, the equivalent two-part instrument has an obvious advantage. It still discourages the illegal disposal which is so costly to clean up and so hazardous to health.

Second, even when the Pigovian tax is feasible, the two-part instrument will often have lower total social costs of administration. The Pigovian tax requires one party, the government, to collect data on emissions of a different party, the polluter. In contrast, the two-part instrument places the data requirements on those with information. The shift in the 'burden of proof' leaves the individual consumer or firm to provide proof that proper disposal has taken place in order to obtain the subsidy. As argued by Russell (1988), these monitoring costs must be lower for the firm or consumer than for a government official who has less knowledge of the production or disposal process. Some of the reduced administrative cost of government may be offset by the increased compliance cost of firms and consumers, but the total is likely to be smaller since the firm's cost of monitoring its own amounts of each type of disposal is probably lower than the government's costs of monitoring those behaviors. The government needs only to set the deposit and the refund, and to check for the authenticity of a returned item or clean input (Stavins, 1991).

Third, consider enforcement problems. To enforce the Pigovian tax, the government must try to prevent illegal dumping by properly setting the rate of taxation, the rate of audit or inspection, and the rate of penalty. The Pigovian tax itself provides an incentive to hide taxable emissions. In contrast, the two-part instrument provides incentives to *reveal* data in order to qualify for the subsidy. In fact, the two-part instrument effectively taxes illegal dumping (by not returning the presumptive tax on amounts dumped), and so it can discourage dumping to the proper extent without any additional legal sanctions.[12]

The two-part instrument might provide doubled opportunities for cheating, since the presumptive tax on output is subject to evasion while the subsidies on clean inputs or on 'proper' disposal are subject to overstatement. The potential for cheating is relatively low for these market transactions, however, since each transaction involves an invoice for payment which is difficult to fabricate. In contrast, the single Pigovian tax on emissions or any less-desired type of disposal does not apply to a market transaction. The firm can make up its own records involving emissions, and it can dump illegally without records at all. No other party verifies the transaction. Two simple examples illustrate this risk. A tanker truck carrying liquid waste can enter a truck wash, start the washer sprays, and open the drain on the bottom of the truck effectively rinsing away the waste without paying the tax. Another example is of waste oil, which can be discarded on roadbeds of railroad lines in order to escape detection and the waste-end tax (Fullerton, 1996). The alternative is a simple tax on all purchases of oil, plus a subsidy on its proper disposal.

Any cheating that does occur under incentive-based policies is frequently due to asymmetric information. The firm or consumer often has more and better information than the government and this, while lending itself to the idea of shifting the burden of proof to the party that has better access to the information, also allows for the danger of falsifying the 'proof' (Russell, 1990). This proof does apply to a market transaction, as just discussed, but some degree of enforcement is necessary in order to ensure that this proof accurately reflects the true behavior of the consumer or firm. Thus, to optimize compliance on the part of the individual firm or consumer, the government must implement the proper mix of penalties and audits – not on emissions or dumping, but on properly reported output subject to a tax and on inputs eligible for a subsidy. Even this type of enforcement can be a difficult and rather inefficient task. Russell (1990) notes that auditing in the United States is infrequent and poorly performed, and thus does not act as sufficient inducement for accurate paperwork. Further complicating the ability of the government to audit a firm is the risk of infringing on the firm's constitutional protection against forced entry without reason. Under Pigovian taxation, audits often must be announced prior to arrival, allowing the firm to cover up any illegalities beforehand. Shifting the burden of proof to the firm under a tax-subsidy combination, on the other hand, means the government does not have to force entry. If the firm wishes to receive the subsidy, then it must open its own doors and provide proof to demonstrate eligibility.[13]

A fourth consideration is political appeal. The Pigovian tax may not be a popular action if it raises taxes on consumers or firms. At least in the case where the same individual or firm that pays the deposit has the opportunity to receive a refund, the deposit-refund system may be more popular with voters. If those who properly dispose of an item can receive a refund on the tax originally paid, then taxes increase only for those who refuse to participate. According to a GAO study (US Government Accounting Office, 1990), the bottle bill faces, on average, an 87 percent approval rating in states with a bottle bill, and a national bottle bill has a 70 percent approval rating with American citizens. For more general two-part instruments, political feasibility may be greater in the case where consumers get the rebate and producers pay the tax than in the case where producers get a subsidy and consumers pay the tax.

A second reason for its potential political appeal, according to the literature, is that the deposit-refund system can be self-financing; the refund can be taken directly from funds generated by deposits (Russell, 1988). However, we wish to emphasize that the pairing of a presumptive tax with an environmental subsidy does not require that the funds gathered from the tax be set aside for the accompanying subsidy nor that the tax equal the subsidy. While this eliminates a potential political advantage, it can create another: flexibility in the use of funds. The two-part instrument can also provide the government with a possible source of revenue. This is not an advantage specific to the two-part instrument, however. As we have shown, the two-part instrument is equivalent to the Pigovian tax. Therefore the revenue from the presumptive tax must exceed the cost of the environmental subsidy by exactly the amount of revenue that would have been collected by the Pigovian tax.

Other attributes have been ascribed specifically to various incarnations of the deposit-refund system. For instance, the deposit on a beverage container does not need to be claimed by the original purchaser. In fact, the incentive to return the item is effectively transferred to anyone finding it (Bohm, 1981). Thus, while a busy person with a high time value might throw a bottle out of the car window, another person with a low time value might pick up bottles along the roadside in order to collect the refunds. This combination is efficient, and it helps to prevent litter.[14] Other argued advantages include: health savings due to a decrease in litter-related injuries; a decrease in roadside damage to bicycle tires and farm equipment; job creation due to an increased demand for truck drivers, sorters, and recyclers; and energy savings from the use of recycled rather than virgin materials.

B A Relaxation of the Models' Assumptions

With several simplifying assumptions, the tax-subsidy combination works perfectly in the context of our general equilibrium models. These simplifying assumptions include: no transaction costs, perfect information, no pre-existing distortions, a closed economy, and perfect competition. When each of these assumptions is relaxed, complications may arise. Any of these complications might reduce the effectiveness of the two-part instrument; however, most of these problems apply equally to the usual waste-end or Pigovian tax. Such considerations are important to discuss.

First, transaction costs can contribute to the cost of compliance for the firm or consumer. A two-part instrument requires two collection or payment points: one at the time of purchase and another at the time of return. Also, a firm accepting the returned item often faces additional storage and transportation costs as well as the cost of providing the promised refund. With a large number of small transactions, the act of paying out a refund can be expensive. In fact, many times these transaction costs are so high that other policy instruments can reach the same goal much more cost-effectively. For these reasons, we emphasize that the two-part instrument need not operate as a strict deposit-refund system. The two-part system does not need to collect and return five cents on each aluminum can. Approximately the same incentives can be provided with substantially lower transaction costs by a simple sales tax or excise tax on beverages and a subsidy paid to recycling firms per ton of recycled aluminum. Without making the individual consumer stand in line to get the five cent refund, the subsidy per ton of recycled aluminum will affect market prices in a way that still induces stores to offer efficient service or some other inducement to consumers who bring in aluminum cans.

A second potential complication is the lack of perfect information. With imperfect measures of social costs, the government might set the wrong rate for the presumptive tax or subsidy. If so, then the two-part instrument will not induce the socially efficient mix of 'proper' disposal (such as recycling) and 'improper' disposal (such as litter). This imperfection can mean costly clean-up of improperly disposed waste, if the refund is too low, or it can signify unwarranted social costs from too much proper disposal, if the refund is too high.[15] This complication equally affects the Pigovian waste-end tax, however, since the authorities are required to know *a priori* what size tax is needed to induce optimal behavior. For the Pigovian tax, Baumol and Oates (1971) describe a system of 'standards and prices' that can be used to adjust the tax rate by trial and error, and the exact same argument applies to the two-part instrument. Once the authorities have set a target for quantities to be recycled, they can adjust the deposit and refund periodically until the desired quantity is reached. Thus, the element of trial-and-error is not particularly worse under a tax-subsidy combination.

A third potential pitfall relates to the theory of the second-best. Pre-existing distortions can affect the size of the tax or subsidy needed to balance two major objectives, namely, raising revenue and ensuring the desired amount of proper disposal. Bovenberg and De Mooij (1994) examine the case of a Pigovian tax with a pre-existing labor tax that distorts the consumer's choice between consumption and leisure. Thus, in the second-best world, neither the Pigovian tax nor the equivalent two-part instrument maximizes social welfare because they both exacerbate the labor-leisure distortion. As shown in Fullerton (1997), however, the two-part instrument and the Pigovian tax equally affect the labor-leisure choice. As a consequence, the same second-best correction applies. The properly modified rate of taxation on waste can still be replaced by equally modified rates for the presumptive tax and environmental subsidy.

Fourth, potential complications arise in relation to the assumption of a closed economy. If the two-part instrument operates as a presumptive tax on all output and a subsidy to all clean inputs, then it still serves as an effective tax on domestic pollution, even if the output is exported. For a deposit-refund system, however, the equivalence can be broken if the deposit is paid on goods before export, and subsequent recycling is not re-imported to receive the refund. Conversely, if the foreign firm pays the deposit on goods shipped to the US, and is then responsible for receiving and recycling its own goods, the extra transportation and transaction costs can operate as a type of non-price trade barrier. It may be easier for the foreign firm to arrange with a domestic firm for the collection, storage, and transportation of its disposed products such as bottles or other forms of packaging. Also, it may be easier to offer a refund to the consumer for the proper return of the product through domestic facilities. Otherwise, the foreign firm may have to set up recycling facilities in the US or transport its recycled products back to the originating country. If this is the case, the domestic firm may gain an advantage over the foreign producer. This argument may be important for products such as computers where many producers rely on a take-back system in order to re-use valuable components. However, in cases where the foreign producer is not responsible for recycling its own product, so that a domestic firm can collect the product for recycling, this advantage disappears.

Finally, imperfect competition or monopoly behavior in certain industries can complicate the model significantly. If a firm with market power has already restricted output below the socially optimal level, then a tax on output can induce a further restriction and decrease social welfare even more. In this case, even without the presumptive tax, a subsidy to proper disposal may reduce the overall cost of production and help offset the pre-existing market distortion (Baumol and Oates, 1988). In a simple monopoly model, the tax-subsidy combination is still equivalent to the emissions tax; it raises production costs and exacerbates the monopoly distortion. In a more complicated game-theoretic model of oligopoly, we hesitate to conjecture about this equivalence.

Though the models above are used to show where the two-part instrument is equivalent to the Pigovian tax, considerations beyond the model are reasons enough to give careful thought to the tax-subsidy combination. In many cases, the problems listed here are of a lesser degree for the two-part instrument than for the Pigovian tax, making the case even stronger for the pairing of a presumptive tax with a subsidy.

IV POLICY EXPERIENCES

This section reviews actual experiences with two-part instruments in the United States as well as in other countries. Examples that are discussed include deposit-refund systems on bottles, waste oil, and car hulks. In many cases the relative success or failure of a deposit-refund system appears to be related to the ability of the government to set the appropriate deposit or refund to induce the desired behavior.

A 'Bottle Bills' for Beverage Containers

A two-part instrument has most often appeared as a deposit-refund system. A 'bottle bill' is one of its most common forms. This policy combines a deposit paid by the consumer at the time of purchase and a refund when the beverage container is properly returned.[16] Ten states in the US reportedly have bottle bills.[17] California's bottle bill differs from those in other states in that the distributors pay the deposit, while consumers receive the refund (Container Recycling Institute, 1992). Also, in most states the deposit does not equal the refund because of a handling fee.[18] Indications of the success of such policies are mixed. Evidence that suggests some degree of success includes reports of a high response rate by consumers, a reduction in solid waste, a decrease in litter, and high-quality recyclable inputs. Evidence is somewhat less convincing with respect to energy savings, job creation, and administrative, production, and distributive costs.

Return rates for bottles appear to be high in the US. Table 3.1 presents both the overall return rate and return rates by bottle type, if available, for each of the US states with bottle bills. Overall return rates range from 76.5 percent in New York to 93 percent in Michigan.[19] For specific bottle types, the lowest return rate is 50 percent for plastic containers in California, while the highest return rate is 95 percent for aluminum containers in Iowa. Such high return rates stand in marked contrast to non-bottle-bill items. For instance, Oregon boasts an overall return rate on aluminum, plastic and glass containers of 92.3 percent, whereas the overall return rate for non-bottle-bill containers is less than 30 percent (Wahl, 1995).

Table 3.1 Return rates for containers in bottle-bill states

State	Return rates (%)	
California	Aluminum	88
	Glass	76
	Plastic	50
	Overall	84
Connecticut	Cans	88
	Bottles	94
	Plastic	70–90
Delaware	Not available	
Iowa	Aluminum	95
	Glass	85
	Plastic	70–90
	Overall	91
Maine	Beer/Soda	92
	Wine/Spirits	80
	Juice	75
Massachusetts	Overall	85
Michigan	Overall	93
New York	Soda	66
	Beer	79
	Overall	76.5
Oregon	Aluminum	86.6
	Glass	94.1
	Plastic	92.5
	Overall	92.3
Vermont	Overall	85

Sources: Gupta (1996), NY Department of Environmental Conservation (1994), Wahl (1995), Iowa Department of Natural Resources (1996), and Container Recycling Institute (1992).

Reports also indicate that solid waste has seen a slight decrease due to the bottle bill. The GAO (1990) cites a 6 percent reduction by weight, and an 8 percent reduction by volume of the amount of solid waste being landfilled. However, opponents cite these small figures as a reason for repeal of bottle bills; the benefits are too small to justify the cost of implementing such a system. Bottle bills seem to have had a significant impact on litter, however. A GAO study (1990) finds a decrease in litter between 79 and 83 percent for nine states with bottle bills (excluding California). Because the bottle bills are so effective at decreasing litter, these states have experienced a significant decrease in damages and injuries due to broken bottles and other discarded beverage containers. For instance, injuries to children caused by broken bottles decreased 60 percent after the implementation of the bottle bill in Massachusetts (Friedland and Perry, 1995).

Critics of the bottle bill often argue that it deprives curbside recycling programs of a large potential source of revenue. A GAO study (1990) found the two policies to be complementary, however. While some consumers will return a bottle in order to receive the refund, others will not be willing to take the time to do so; these individuals may still find it easy to throw the bottle in the recycling bin for curbside pick-up. A Rhode Island study demonstrates that, while having both programs in place is more costly, having a bottle bill in addition to a curbside recycling program will divert an additional 17 to 35 percent from the waste stream (Naughton et al, 1990).[20]

Also, bottle bills provide higher-quality material than curbside recycling programs. Containers are more homogenous because they have been sorted; glass is often unbroken and sorted by color. The monetary incentive guarantees a steady supply of recycled beverage containers (Iowa Department of Natural Resources, 1996). For all of these reasons, firms that use recycled materials have demonstrated their preference for recycled glass and plastic from bottle-bill states. Two-thirds of glass and 98 percent of plastic recycled by firms are purchased from the nine bottle-bill states other than California (Friedland and Perry, 1995) whereas these states contain only 17 percent of the US population.

Questions about the cost of a deposit-refund system such as the bottle bill also have countered these seemingly impressive statistics. Production and distribution costs to the beverage industry have reportedly increased as a result of compliance with the bottle bill (GAO, 1990). The increase in cost is especially evident for firms responsible for collecting the bottles, distributing the refund, and storing the bottles after they are returned. The sheer number of small transactions that take place each day also cost the firm a great deal. In a report issued by the GAO (1990), the increase in cost is estimated to lie between 2.4 and 3.2 cents per container. Ackerman et al (1995) report that Massachusetts' firms face a cost increase of 2.3 cents per container.[21] When viewed by the ton, such costs are substantial. For steel cans, 2.3 cents per can translates into a cost of \$320 per ton of waste reduced. For aluminum cans it is even higher: \$1300 per ton.

Landfilling, in most cases, is a much cheaper disposal alternative. In weighing costs against benefits, several studies find that bottle bills – as they are currently run – may not in fact be economically efficient.[22]

According to the Project 88 report (Stavins, 1991), the design of a deposit-refund system is the primary determinant of its success or failure. For instance, a single-tiered system, where the refund is the same for all containers regardless of differences in recycling value, has lower transaction costs than a multi-tiered system, where different containers have refund values that depend on the material from which they are made. However, the single-tiered system is a poorer estimate of the true social cost (Jenkins and Lamech, 1992). Drop-off requirements can also affect the inconvenience costs to the consumer. In Oregon, for instance, a consumer can drop off beverage containers to any store that carries that brand, regardless of where the beverage was originally purchased. Retailers do not have to sort the containers because distributors have an agreement among themselves on collection and credit for containers.

Evidence also indicates that administrative costs decrease significantly for a more consolidated system. In California, for example, the deposit-refund system is run by the state instead of by the retail firms. In a 'standards and prices' approach[23] a minimum return rate of 80 percent is mandated, and the deposit-refund system is adjusted to reach that goal (Naughton et al., 1990). Redemption centers are jointly arranged by retailers within convenience zones of a halfmile radius (for example, at a centrally-located grocery store), so that retailers do not have to be directly involved in redeeming cans and bottles (Mrozek, 1995). The state also pays a handling fee to recycling centers to collect and process cans. Unclaimed deposits are used to pay for administration. Costs are much lower in California than in other states, approximately 0.2 cents per can. For steel cans, this translates into a decreased cost from $320 to $28 per ton of garbage reduced. For aluminum, the costs decrease from $1300 to $120 per ton (Palmer et al., 1997).[24]

B Deposit-Refund Systems for Other Items in the US

Deposit-refund systems in the United States have also been used to promote oil recycling through the return of used motor oil, and lead recycling through the return of lead-acid car batteries.[25] Two states that have battery deposit-refund systems are Rhode Island and Maine. Other states have unlegislated deposit-refund systems run by industry.[26] Most of the benefits as well as the criticisms listed above for bottles also apply here. The fact that both oil and lead are health hazards and costly to clean up means that a deposit-refund system may be more useful than other policy instruments. Sigman (1995b) examines the determinants of the illegal dumping of lubricating oil and finds evidence that a deposit-refund system is a useful method for decreasing illegal disposal; the availability of opportunities for the reuse of oil are found empirically to affect illegal dumping. Several problems specific to the return of car batteries and oil are noted throughout the literature. One such problem is the possibility that a refund that is set too high will induce individuals either to steal car batteries or to bring in a cheaper oil-like substance to get the offered refund. Thus, it is important to set both the deposit and the refund at an appropriate level.[27] Another problem discussed is the fact that refunds are often available only in large urban areas (Jenkins and Lamech, 1992). Rural populations (which may be significant, depending on the country) may not recycle oil or return car batteries if they have to drive into the city to return the product.

Evidence of other deposit-refund systems in the US is scattered. Idaho has a deposit-refund system in place for old tires (Dinan, 1993). In that state, a $1 up-front user fee is assessed on each new motor vehicle tire purchased. From these fees, retreaders are paid a $1 subsidy for each retreaded tire, and other end-users of old tires are paid $20 per ton (Idaho Department of Health and Welfare, 1996).[28] Also, Maine reportedly has a deposit-refund system in place for commercial pesticide containers (Stavins, 1991).

C Experiences with Deposit-Refund Systems Outside the US

Deposit-refund systems have also been used outside the United States. Within the OECD, the number of deposit-refund systems in each country has grown 35 percent to 100 percent between 1987 and 1993; this growth is mainly caused by a concern for packaging waste (Barde and Opschoor, 1994). Table 3.2 provides the number of deposit-refund systems in existence in mainly OECD countries, and it shows the types of items covered under these systems. Sweden and the United States are reported to have four different types of deposit-refund systems in place. Norway, Austria, Germany, Canada, and Australia all have three deposit-refund systems in operation; the remaining countries have only one or two systems. The most commonly covered items under a deposit-refund system are metal cans, plastic and glass containers, and car hulks. Some of the more unusual items covered by a deposit-refund system include fluorescent light bulbs in Austria, and logging in Indonesia.

Japan has its own 'bottle bill' with a return rate of 92 percent (Rhee, 1994). Korea also has two main deposit-refund systems in place: one on glass bottles, and one on solid and toxic waste. The program for solid waste covers items such as televisions, washing machines, tires, and batteries. Evidence suggests that Korea's deposit-refund systems have not been successful. Proper disposal of toxic wastes has been extremely low; only 8 percent of firms paying the initial deposit receive a refund. In total for Korea, approximately US$ 16.9 million has been collected in deposits while only US$ 38 000 has been returned as refunds. Taiwan also has a deposit-refund system for 12 different products. In 1992, the return rate – at least for plastic PET bottles – rose substantially, to just under 80 percent. Before, however, it was 41 percent.

Table 3.2 Deposit-refund systems by country

Country	Number of D-R systems	Items affected
Australia	3	Metal cans, plastic containers, glass bottles
Austria	3	Plastic containers, glass bottles, fluorescent bulbs
Belgium	1	Glass bottles
Canada	3	Metal cans, plastic containers, glass bottles
Denmark	2	Plastic containers, glass bottles
Estonia	1	Glass bottles
Finland	2	Plastic containers, glass bottles
France	1	Glass bottles
Germany	3	Plastic containers, glass bottles, packaging
Grecce	1	Car hulks
Iceland	2	Plastic containers, glass bottles
Indonesia	1	Logging
Japan	1	Beverage containers
Korea	2	Glass bottles, solid and toxic waste items
Netherlands	2	Plastic containers, glass bottles
Norway	3	Car hulks, plastic containers, glass bottles
Portugal	1	Metal cans, plastic containers, glass bottles
Sweden	4	Car hulks, metal cans, plastic and glass bottles
Switzerland	1	Glass bottles
Taiwan	1	12 product items
Turkey	1	Glass bottles
United States	4	Metal cans, plastic and glass bottles, car batteries

Sources: Barde and Opschoor (1994), and OECD (1994b).

One reason listed for Japan's success – and for the relative failure of bottle bills in Taiwan and Korea – is the long history of deposit-refund systems run by private industry in Japan prior to the government program (O'Connor, 1994). Also, in Korea, the government deliberately set the deposit and refund too low because of a concern about inflation (Rhee, 1994).

A more creative use of the two-part instrument has been attempted in Indonesia. This country has experimented with a deposit-refund system in order to try to slow deforestation. Loggers pay an up-front fee before harvesting trees and then receive a refund when the logged trees are replaced with saplings. However, initial findings show this scheme to be ineffective. Even with the subsidy, the net benefits of replanting are reported to be less than the net benefits from not doing so (O'Connor, 1994). Thus, little replanting actually takes place.

Many instances of deposit-refund systems appear in Europe, mostly on beverage containers.[29] Return rates are between 40 and 100 percent, depending on the country and the type of container. A few of these programs are discussed below in more detail.

Sweden has deposit-refund systems for items such as aluminum cans, other beverage containers, and car hulks. The Swedish government has attempted to enforce a mandatory return rate of 75 percent. Evidence regarding car hulks, however, is not encouraging. Due to a small refund of SEK 300, and 12 years without adjusting for inflation (at which point the refund was the equivalent of SEK 120), returns of car hulks have been low (OECD, 1994a). The promised refund cannot compete with alternatives to returning the car hulks, such as storing or selling the parts and then dumping the remaining hulk (OECD, 1989).

Norway also has a deposit-refund for car hulks. Contrary to its Swedish counterpart, Norway's deposit-refund system works quite well, mainly due to a higher refund. The return rate is estimated to be between 90 and 99 percent. The deposit is paid when a new car is purchased, and the refund is given when a car is taken to a scrapping facility. One criticism of the Norwegian deposit-refund system, however, is a lack of scrapping facilities in convenient locations (OECD, 1989).[30]

The Netherlands has private deposit-refund systems in place for PET and glass bottles. The 1992 government budget also provided for the obligatory return of batteries, refrigerators, aluminum cans, and oil in the event that the current industry system fails (OECD, 1994a). Failure is defined by the government as less than a 30 percent return rate (OECD, 1989).[31] Also, the Dutch literature has discussed the feasibility of a deposit-refund system for controlling polluting substances such as cadmium and nitrates. Any domestic or imported product containing the polluting substance would be subject to a deposit upon sale. Refunds would be provided once the item was properly disposed of or exported.[32]

So far, almost all of the policies reviewed here still relate to explicit deposit-refund systems with a particular link from the deposit to the refund. A major point of this paper, however, is that the two-part instrument can be defined more broadly and employed more widely. Indeed, virtually all governments already employ implicit two-part tax-subsidy combinations. For example, a sales tax or value-added tax is collected on the purchase of all items, while the collection of household waste is subsidized through the provision of free municipal garbage services. 'Proper' household disposal is subsidized by this curbside collection, since the city pays for the trucks, work force, and tipping fees. The alternative is a Pigovian waste-end tax that would collect the marginal social cost per bag of garbage put on the curb for collection. This Pigovian tax might work well in suburbs and small towns where illegal dumping is not prevalent, but it would not work well in rural or urban areas where the fee can easily be avoided by dumping garbage on deserted roads, vacant lots, or in commercial dumpsters (Fullerton and Kinnaman, 1995). This improper disposal is avoided by the free collection of garbage, and municipal solid waste budgets are often financed by a local sales tax. The resulting combination is a two-part instrument, whether intended or not.

V CONCLUSION

This paper builds two relatively simple general equilibrium models to demonstrate the equivalence between the Pigovian tax and the combination of a presumptive tax and performance subsidy. These models also help demonstrate the flexibility of this two-part instrument. To analyse the usefulness of the tax-subsidy combination, we review conceptual problems with its implementation and practical problems with the actual use of the tax-subsidy combination throughout the world. While the tax-subsidy combination is increasingly being used, in the form of a deposit-refund system, we argue that more flexible interpretations are important to explore. The two parts of such a policy do not have to apply to the same side of the market. Enactment might be easier, for example, if firms pay the tax while consumers receive the subsidy. The tax and subsidy do not have to equal one another, and they can apply to different goods altogether. Compared to a Pigovian tax, a two-part instrument may be easier to enforce, may be easier to enact, and can still force the market to recognize the social cost of disposal.

NOTES

* We are grateful for financial assistance provided by EPA grant R824740-01-0. A special thanks to Gunnar Eskeland, Gib Metcalf, Arvind Panagariya, Bob Schwab, Hilary Sigman, Rob Stavins, Margaret Walls and Sarah West for helpful comments and suggestions. This paper is part of the NBER's research program in Public Economics. Any opinions expressed are those of the authors and not those of the Environmental Protection Agency or the National Bureau of Economic Research.

1. The US Internal Revenue Service identifies four 'environmental taxes': (1) petroleum, for the Oil Spill Liability Trust Fund and for Superfund; (2) chemical feedstocks, for Superfund; (3) ozone-depleting chemicals, for the general fund; and (4) motor fuels, for the Leaking Underground Storage Tank (LUST) fund. These taxes apply to useful petroleum and chemical inputs, not to waste by-products or emissions (Fullerton, 1996).
2. One can think of labor, capital, and materials as inputs to the production of a good output and a bad output (such as waste). Then the production function can be rearranged algebraically

by moving waste to the other side of the equation, so that the good output is a function of capital, labor, materials, and waste.

3. The presumptive tax-subsidy combination is not excluded from his analysis, but it is not his primary focus. Eskeland simply defines presumptive taxation more broadly to include taxes unaccompanied by subsidies. Eskeland and Devarajan (1996) show how different combinations of instruments can be used to approach the effect of an ideal Pigovian tax.
4. Actually, the two-part instrument might be difficult to implement perfectly for vehicle emissions because driving is not a market commodity which can be taxed in a way that will mirror the subsidy for clean inputs to driving. Certain kinds of heterogeneity also can be a problem for the two-part instrument, as discussed below.
5. Several papers compare this restricted deposit-refund system to other policies such as an advanced disposal fee or a virgin materials tax. Sigman (1995a) uses a partial equilibrium framework to analyse lead recycling, while Miedema (1983) uses a general equilibrium context to compare solid waste policy options. Dinan (1993) finds that, since a deposit-refund system is equivalent to a waste-end tax, it is more efficient than a virgin materials tax. Palmer et al. (1997) build a partial equilibrium model and run simulations in which the deposit is assumed to equal the refund, but where the deposit is paid by producers while the refund is given to recyclers. Swierzbinski (1994) uses a partial equilibrium, game-theoretic approach that allows the deposit to differ from the refund, but he requires that they apply to the same firm.
6. The two-part instrument may not be such a promising alternative, however, in cases where emissions are already being measured cheaply and effectively. Air emissions such as SO_2, for instance, are already monitored effectively by the EPA with installed continuous emissions monitoring (CEM) systems; firms are fined at the end of the year if actual emissions exceed the amount allowed. The two-part instrument may be more important in cases with many small polluters, where expensive emission monitoring equipment would be required for each.
7. Another model, similar to this one, is applied to the specific problem of household disposal in Fullerton and Kinnaman (1995).
8. We can generalize this result to an n good model in which a Pigovian tax on one good can be mimicked by taxes and subsidies on the remaining $n - 1$ goods. This follows from the fact that supply functions are homogenous of degree zero in prices, and demand functions are homogenous of degree zero in prices and income.
9. A simple modification to the model can introduce the idea of a 'bottle bill' explicitly by making utility a function of $q(c,d)$ where q is the quantity of drinks consumed, c is the clean disposal of those bottles through recycling and d is the dirty disposal alternative. The two-part instrument would then be to tax q and subsidize c, which effectively taxes the use of d without actually applying a direct tax to this disposal alternative.
10. Because of constant returns to scale, all of these variables can be expressed in amounts per household.
11. Note that if two or more unobservable pollutants are used as inputs to production, this scheme will not work unless the Pigovian solution were to tax these pollutants at the same rate.
12. In fact, this argument suggests that any further legal sanctions on dumping are not only unnecessary, but also undesirable. If the firm pays a presumptive tax on all output that is equal to the social external cost of dumping, and then receives a subsidy on all activities except dumping, it already pays the marginal social cost of that dumping. Then the chosen amount of dumping is the socially optimal amount of dumping, and any additional legal sanction would overcorrect the externality and reduce social welfare!
13. See Swierzbinski (1994) for a partial equilibrium game-theoretic approach to this problem. His model allows the firm the opportunity to request an audit, in order to get refunds, but such an audit still requires the government officials to measure the emissions.
14. The waste-end tax might be just as efficient, if high-time-value individuals can get their trash sorted by paying low-time-value individuals, but the waste-end tax would not directly subsidize low-time-value individuals to pick up litter along the roadway. Also, the refund provides some incentive to clean up the existing stock of litter, while the waste-end tax applies only to new litter (Lee et al., 1992).

15. In the case where the refund level is too high, individuals may even try to bring in a stolen or substitute item in order to receive the refund.
16. A beverage container is usually defined as 'any sealable bottle, can, jar, or carton which is primarily composed of glass, metal, plastic, or any combination of those materials and is produced for the purpose of containing a beverage' (Massachusetts Executive Office of Environmental Affairs, 1989).
17. These ten states include California, Connecticut, Delaware, Iowa, Maine, Massachusetts, Michigan, New York, Oregon, and Vermont. The system in California is sometimes called a deposit-refund system and is sometimes referred to as an advanced disposal fee.
18. According to Jenkins and Lamech (1992), the handling fee in most states is 20 percent of the deposit.
19. Porter (1983) finds a slightly higher return rate for Michigan of 95 percent.
20. A Massachusetts study also finds that the bottle bill actually helps the recycling programs in that state, since a bottle bill is often a cheaper option in locations where curbside collection is expensive to implement. Also, restaurants and businesses are usually excluded from curbside recycling and can use a bottle bill to recycle containers. This can mean a substantial increase in a state's total recycling; 80 percent of the beverage containers collected in Massachusetts come from commercial sources (Friedland and Perry, 1995).
21. These costs do not include administrative costs to government or political rent-seeking costs to firms.
22. Porter (1978) concludes that in Michigan, for a five cents per container average time cost, the average benefit received from proper disposal must be greater than $12.48 per person annually (in 1974 dollars) in order for the deposit-refund system to be considered economically worthwhile. Using Porter's framework, Naughton et al. (1990) estimate the average inconvenience costs in California of returning aluminum, non-refillable glass and plastic containers. Per container, estimates ranged from 29 to 57 cents.
23. See Baumol and Oates (1971) for more on the 'standards and prices' approach.
24. Technology can also play an important role in making the deposit-refund system more efficient. One such technology is the reverse vending machine. It can be installed in a grocery store where consumers then load their beverage containers into the machine. The items are placed on a conveyor belt where each is scanned to distinguish valid containers from invalid ones, as well as type (if the refund differs by type) of container. The machine then either prints out a voucher or pays the proper refund to the consumer. Thus, the store need not dedicate extra personnel to the task of refunding money or sorting containers (Pang, 1996).
25. Nationally, 'do-it-yourselfers' apparently account for 50 percent of the illegal dumping of oil, while they only account for 5 percent of the recycling of oil (Stavins 1991). Thus, a deposit-refund system that creates incentives to discourage littering and illegal dumping is a promising policy tool. Also, reportedly 80 percent of lead consumption in the United States is attributable to lead-acid batteries (Sigman, 1995a). Therefore, concentrating on lead-acid batteries when formulating policy seems justified.
26. Such lead-acid battery deposit-refund systems reportedly exist in Arizona, Arkansas, Connecticut, Idaho, Michigan, Minnesota, New York, and Washington (Sigman, 1995a).
27. Analogous rebates are offered in programs that buy up old cars. Alberini et al. (1994) note several potential problems with this type of program. Individuals might be induced to let their cars deteriorate more than otherwise, or they may bring old cars into the jurisdiction in order to get the rebate.
28. Waste tires are principally used as a fuel supplement. The Idaho tax-subsidy combination for tires was scheduled to end by 1 July 1996.
29. Andersen (1994) states that a system of fees coupled with subsidies is appealing relative to an emissions tax for the countries he focuses on – Denmark, France, Germany, and the Netherlands – for reasons of political acceptability.
30. The Estonian deposit-refund system on glass bottles also functions poorly due to a lack of return locations (OECD, 1994b).
31. Again, the 'standards and prices' approach in Baumol and Oates (1971) is being used; a standard of 30 percent is set, and then a pricing mechanism, in the form of the deposit-refund system, is adjusted to attain the standard.

32. Tax-subsidy combinations are also suggested in the literature for the recovery of CFCs from refrigerators and air conditioners (Fisher et al., 1995), as well as for the recovery of sulfur dioxide from the air (Bohm, 1981).

REFERENCES

Ackerman, Frank, Dmitri Cavander, John Stutz and Brian Zuckerman (1995), *Preliminary Analysis: The Costs and Benefits of Bottle Bills*, Draft Report to USEPA/Office of Solid Waste and Emergency Response, Boston: Tellus Institute.

Alberini, Anna, David Edelstein, Winston Harrington and Virginia D. McConnell (1994), 'Reducing Emissions from Old Cars: The Economics of the Delaware Vehicle Retirement Program', Discussion Paper, no. 94-27, Washington, DC: Resources for the Future.

Andersen, Mikael Skou (1994), *Governance by Green Taxes: Making Pollution Prevention Pay*, Manchester: Manchester University Press.

Barde, Jean-Phillippe and Johanes Baptist Opschoor (1994), 'From Stick to Carrot in the Environment', *OECD Observer*, **186**, 23–7.

Baumol, William and Wallace Oates (1971), 'The Use of Standards and Prices for Protection of the Environment', *Swedish Journal of Economics*, **73**, 42–54.

Baumol, William and Wallace Oates (1988), *The Theory of Environmental Policy*, Second Edition, New York: Cambridge University Press.

Bohm, Peter (1981), *Deposit-Refund Systems*, Washington, DC: Resources for the Future.

Bovenberg, Lans and Ruud de Mooij (1994), 'Environmental Levies and Distortionary Taxation', *American Economic Review*, **84**, 1085–9.

Container Recycling Institute (1992), *Beverage Container Deposit Systems in the United States*, Washington, DC: Container Recycling Institute.

Cropper, Maureen and Wallace Oates (1992), 'Environmental Economics: A Survey', *Journal of Environmental Literature*, **30**, 675–740.

Dinan, Terry (1993), 'Economic Efficiency Effects of Alternative Policies for Reducing Waste Disposal', *Journal of Environmental Economics and Management*, **25**, 242–56.

Eskeland, Gunnar (1994), 'A Presumptive Pigovian Tax: Complementing Regulation to Mimic an Emissions Fee', *The World Bank Economic Review* **8**(3), 373–94.

Eskeland, Gunnar and Shantayanan Devarajan (1996), *Taxing Bads by Taxing Goods: Pollution Control with Presumptive Charges*, Washington, DC: World Bank.

Fisher, Brian, Scott Barrett, Peter Bohm, J.K. Mubazi, Anwar Shah and Robert Stavins (1995), 'An Economic Assessment of Policy Instruments to Combat Climate Change', *Report of Working Group III of the Intergovernmental Panel on Climate Change*, Switzerland.

Friedland, Shelly and Amy Perry (1995), *Many Happy Returns: A Retrospective of the Massachusetts Bottle Bill*, Massachusetts: MASSPIRG.

Fullerton, Don (1996), 'Why Have Separate Environmental Taxes?' in James M. Poterba (ed.), *Tax Policy and the Economy*, **10**, Cambridge: MIT Press for the National Bureau of Economic Research.

Fullerton, Don (1997), 'Environmental Levies and Distortionary Taxation: Comment', *American Economic Review*, **87**, 245–51.

Fullerton, Don and Thomas Kinnaman (1995), 'Garbage, Recycling, and Illicit Burning or Dumping', *Journal of Environmental Economics and Management*, **29**, 78–91.

Gupta, Ashok (1996), Letter, Albany: New York State Department of Environmental Conservation, March.

Harrington, Winston, Margaret Walls and Virginia McConnell (1994), 'Shifting Gears: New Directions for Cars and Clean Air', Discussion Paper, no. 94-26-REV, Washington, DC: Resources for the Future.

Idaho Department of Health and Welfare, Division of Environmental Quality (1996), *Idaho Waste Tire Disposal Annual Report to the Legislature*, Boise.

Iowa Department of Natural Resources (1996), *Beverage Container Law Overview*, Des Moines.

Jenkins, Glenn and Ranjit Lamech (1992), 'Market-Based Incentive Instruments for Pollution Control', *International Bulletin of Fiscal Documentation*, **46** (11), 523–38.

Lee, Dwight, Philip Graves and Robert Sexton (1992), 'Controlling the Abandonment of Automobiles: Mandatory Deposits vs. Fines', *Journal of Urban Economics*, **31**, 14–24.

Massachusetts Executive Office of Environmental Affairs (1989), *Provisions for Recycling of Beverage Containers*, Massachusetts.

Miedema, Allen (1983), 'Fundamental Economic Comparisons of Solid Waste Policy Options', *Resources and Energy*, **5**, 21–43.

Mrozek, Janusz (1995), 'Beverage Container Recycling: Incentives versus Attitudes as Explanations of Behavior', Working Paper, Atlanta: Georgia Institute of Technology.

Naughton, Michael, Frederick Sebold and Thomas Mayer (1990), 'The Impacts of the California Beverage Container Recycling and Litter Reduction Act on Consumers', *The Journal of Consumer Affairs*, **24**(1), 190–220.

New York Department of Environmental Conservation (1994), *Report on Unclaimed Beverage Container Deposits*, New York: Division of Solid Waste.

O'Connor, David (1994), 'The Use of Economic Instruments in Environmental Management: The East Asian Experience', in *Applying Economic Instruments to Environmental Policies in OECD and Dynamic Non-Member Countries*, Paris: OECD.

Organisation for Economic Cooperation and Development (1989), *Economic Instruments for Environmental Protection*, Paris: OECD.

Organisation for Economic Cooperation and Development (1994a), *Environment and Taxation: The Cases of the Netherlands, Sweden and the United States*, Paris: OECD.

Organisation for Economic Cooperation and Development (1994b), *Managing the Environment: The Role of Economic Instruments*, Paris: OECD.

Palmer, Karen, Hilary Sigman and Margaret Walls (1997), 'The Cost of Reducing Municipal Solid Waste', *Journal of Environmental Economics and Management*, **33**, 128–50.

Pang, Tanya (1996), 'Empty Bottles Fill Coffers of Norwegian Firm', *Reuter European Community Report*, 28 April.

Pigou, Arthur (1932), *The Economics of Welfare*, Fourth edition, London: MacMillan and Co.

Porter, Richard (1978), 'A Social Benefit–Cost Analysis of Mandatory Deposits on Beverage Containers', *Journal of Environmental Economics and Management*, **5**, 351–75.

Porter, Richard (1983), 'Michigan's Experience with Mandatory Deposits on Beverage Containers', *Land Economics*, **59** (2), 177–94.

Rhee, Ho-Saeng (1994), 'The Use of Economic Instruments in Environmental Protection in Korea', in *Applying Economic Instruments to Environmental Policies in OECD and Dynamic Non-Member Countries*, Paris: OECD.

Russell, Clifford (1988), 'Economic Incentives in the Management of Hazardous Wastes', *Columbia Journal of Environmental Law*, **13** (2), 257–74.
Russell, Clifford (1990), 'Monitoring and Enforcement' in Paul Portney (ed.), *Public Policies for Environmental Protection*, Washington, DC: Resources for the Future.
Sigman, Hilary (1995a), 'A Comparison of Public Policies for Lead Recycling,' *RAND Journal of Economics* **26** (3), 452–78.
Sigman, Hilary (1995b), 'Midnight Dumping: An Empirical Analysis of Illegal Waste Oil Disposal', Working Paper, University of California, Los Angeles.
Stavins, Robert (1991), *Project 88-Round II: Incentives for Action: Designing Market-Based Environmental Strategies*, Sponsored by Timothy Wirth and John Heinz, Washington, DC: US Senate.
Swierzbinski, Joseph (1994), 'Guilty Until Proven Innocent – Regulation with Costly and Limited Enforcement', *Journal of Environmental Economics and Management*, **27** (2), 127–46.
United States General Accounting Office (1990), *Trade-Offs Involved in Beverage Container Deposit Legislation*, Washington, DC: USGAO.
Wahl, Mary (1995), Letter to State Representative Lisa Naito, Oregon Department of Environmental Quality, Portland.

4. Tax-interactions, revenue-recycling, and the efficiency impacts of pollution-abatement policies

Lawrence H. Goulder*

I INTRODUCTION

At least since Pigou (1938), economists have examined ways in which taxes and other policy instruments can address environmental problems associated with externalities. Economists tend to view taxes (and, to some degree, other policy instruments) as mechanisms for internalizing externalities and thereby 'getting the prices right', that is, bringing prices into alignment with marginal social cost. Pigou launched a tradition in environmental economics in which environmental policies were analysed with an almost exclusive attention to the externality of immediate concern and little attention to other distortions or market failures. There was little attention, for example, to how pre-existing distortions in factor markets (resulting from prior income taxes) might influence the costs of new environmental policy initiatives. Neither was there significant regard to how the impacts of environmental taxes might depend on the way revenues from these taxes are 'recycled' to the private sector.

Increasingly, economists have come to recognize the importance of interactions between environmental policies and other (non-environmental) distortions in the economy, and in particular the interconnections between environmental taxes and the distortions imposed by pre-existing income or commodity taxes. Wally Oates was among the first to recognize the significance of these interactions, and as a result his research has forged important links between environmental economics and public economics. To take one example: Oates (1993) points out that in a world with pre-existing distortionary taxes, the revenues raised by environmental tax reforms take on greater importance than is implied by earlier, first-best analyses. Standard analyses tended to assume that a dollar raised by environmental taxes had a social value of one dollar. Implicitly, these analyses assumed either that there were no prior distortionary taxes in the economy, or that environmental tax revenues were returned to the economy in a lump-sum fashion. Wally's work points out that, in a second-best setting with distortionary taxes, revenues from environmental taxes can be used to finance cuts in pre-existing distortionary taxes, and that the social value of revenues used in this way is more than one dollar. The social value exceeds a dollar because the cut in prior taxes avoids not only a dollar in payment of ordinary taxes but also the excess burden from the distortionary tax. This public finance perspective on environmental policy has important implications for the design of environmental taxes and for the choice between environmental taxes and other instruments for environmental protection.[1]

Perhaps the first to consider closely the interactions between environmental taxes and the rest of the tax system was Sandmo (1975), who analysed the optimal setting of commodity taxes when the production or consumption of one of the commodities generates an externality. Sandmo showed that when the government's need for revenue exceeds the level that can be generated by taxes set according to the 'Pigovian principle' (that is, set equal to the marginal environmental damages), then optimal tax system includes taxes not only on externality-generating goods or services but on other goods and services as well. In Sandmo's analysis, the optimal tax rates on environmentally damaging activities and on ordinary activities are intimately connected.

The interconnections between ordinary and environmental taxes, so central to Sandmo's optimal tax result, also figure importantly in the analysis of the impacts of marginal (that is, less than globally optimizing) environmental reforms. A line of research conducted during this decade shows that one cannot effectively evaluate the impacts of many environmental reforms without paying attention to the magnitudes and types of existing, distortionary taxes such as income, payroll, or sales taxes. There are two important interconnections here. First, as Terkla (1984), Lee and Misiolek (1986), Oates and Schwab (1988), Oates (1993), Repetto et al. (1992), and others have emphasized, the presence of distortionary taxes introduces opportunities to use revenues from new environmental taxes to finance cuts in the marginal rates of the ordinary distortionary taxes. To the extent that revenues from the environmental tax finance marginal rate cuts of this kind, some of the distortions that the ordinary taxes would have generated are avoided. This *revenue-recycling effect* suggests that the overall *gross*[2] costs of environmental taxes will be lower in a second-best world than in a first-best setting.

However, a second interconnection works in the opposite direction. Recent work by Bovenberg and de Mooij (1994a), Bovenberg and van der Ploeg (1994), Bovenberg and Goulder (1996, 1997), Parry (1995, 1997), and others[3] shows that environmental taxes are implicit taxes on factors of production such as labor and capital. By raising the costs of production and the costs of goods in general, environmental taxes (and many other environmental regulations) reduce after-tax factor returns, augmenting the adverse impacts of existing factor taxes on rates of return. Thus, environmental taxes function as increments to existing factor taxes, tending to magnify the factor market distortions already generated by pre-existing factor taxes. The additional efficiency costs of environmental taxes associated with the reduction in factor returns brought about by higher costs and output prices has been called the *tax-interaction effect*.[4] The larger the rates of pre-existing factor taxes, the larger the tax-interaction effect, and thus the higher the gross costs from environmental taxes and other regulations that reduce after-tax returns to factors. The tax-interaction effect implies that, for any given method of recycling the revenues, the gross costs of environmental taxes are higher in a second-best setting with pre-existing factor taxes than they would be if there were no prior taxes on factors. As will be discussed in more detail later in this paper, the tax-interaction effect tends to be of greater magnitude than the revenue-recycling effect; that is, it is only partly offset by the revenue-recycling effect.

The revenue-recycling and tax-interaction effects are highly relevant to the evaluation of currently debated environmental policy alternatives. In discussions of carbon tax policies, for example, there has been great interest in the possibility that judicious recycling of the revenues from carbon taxes could cause the overall gross costs of these policies to be become zero or negative. Proponents of carbon taxes certainly would welcome this result, since it implies that policy makers must only establish that there are non-negative environment-related benefits from the carbon tax policy to justify the policy on efficiency grounds. Given the vast uncertainties about the environment-related benefits from carbon abatement, it would significantly reduce the information burden faced by policy makers if they simply needed to determine the sign, rather than magnitude, of the environmental benefits. If one ignores the tax-interaction effect and concentrates only on revenue-recycling (and the revenue-recycling effect), the prospects for a zero-cost carbon tax will seem quite good. But the tax-interaction effect also has a key role here and, as will be discussed below, this latter effect significantly reduces the scope for the zero-cost result. This does not mean that carbon taxes are a bad idea; it only means that justifying these taxes requires attention to the magnitudes (not just the sign) of the environmental benefits.

A second area where the revenue-recycling and tax-interaction effects are important is in the choice among alternative policy instruments. Consider, for example, the choice between pollution tax policies (or pollution permits policies involving the auctioning of permits by the government) and freely allocated (or 'grandfathered') emissions permits. The former policies raise revenue and thus are capable of taking advantage of the revenue-recycling effect. The latter policies, in contrast, do not raise revenue and therefore cannot exploit this effect. As discussed below, the tax-interaction effect arises under both policies, but only under the revenue-raising policies is the (costly) tax-interaction effect offset by the revenue-recycling effect. Recent work by Parry (1997), Goulder, Parry, and Burtraw (1997), Parry, Williams, and Goulder (1999), and Fullerton and Metcalf (1997) reveals that the presence or absence of the revenue-recycling effect can fundamentally affect the overall efficiency impacts of these policies.[5] In fact, when marginal benefits from pollution abatement fail to exceed a certain threshold value, pollution permit policies which fail to enjoy the revenue-recycling effect may be unable to produce any efficiency improvements, no matter what the level of pollution abatement![6] This analysis shows that the decision to give out pollution permits free rather than to auction them (or, equivalently, to employ a pollution tax) comes at a high price in terms of efficiency, and indeed may affect the sign of the overall efficiency impact. There may be other considerations (such as distributional impacts) that tend to support the use of grandfathered permits rather than auctioned permits or pollution taxes, but this recent literature indicates that the efficiency disadvantage of grandfathered permits is more significant than was previously recognized.

This paper examines the efficiency impacts of pollution taxes and some other pollution-control regulations in a second-best setting, pointing out the contributions of the tax-interaction and revenue-recycling effects to the overall efficiency outcomes. It aims to articulate and pull together some key ideas from recent papers on this subject. The next section provides a simple analytical framework for defining and evaluating the efficiency effects in a second-best setting. Section III then elaborates on and qualifies the central results from the analytical framework. Section IV briefly depicts some results from investigations that apply this second-best framework to assess the efficiency impacts of actual US policies to reduce sulfur dioxide emissions from coal-fired power electric power plants, and of proposed policies to reduce carbon dioxide emissions resulting from the combustion of fossil fuels. The final section offers conclusions.

II AN ANALYTICAL FRAMEWORK

Here we present a simple analytical framework for assessing the impacts of environmental taxes and quotas in a second-best setting with prior distortionary taxes. The framework is based on an analytical model presented in Goulder, Parry and Burtraw (1997), which we hereafter will refer to as GPB.

A The Basic Model

A representative agent model is assumed in which household utility is

$$U(X,Y,\ell) + V(Q) \tag{4.1}$$

where $U(.)$ is quasi-concave, $V(.)$ is concave, and both functions are continuous. X and Y are market goods, l is leisure or non-market time, and Q is the quality of the environment. Separability between environmental and non-environmental goods implies that the demand functions for X, Y and l are independent of Q.

X and Y are produced by competitive firms using labor as the only input.[7] The marginal product of labor in both industries is constant and unaffected by environmental quality. Normalizing units to imply transformation rates of unity, we can write the economy's resource constraint as:

$$T = X + Y + \ell \tag{4.2}$$

where T is the household time endowment ($T - \ell$ is labor supply).

The production of X causes waste emissions that harm the environment; that is:

$$Q = Q(X) \tag{4.3}$$

where $Q_x < 0$.[8] From (4.1) and (4.3), we can define marginal environmental damages from production of X in terms of dollars by

$$D(X) = (1/\lambda)V'Q_X \tag{4.4}$$

where λ is the marginal utility of income. We make the usual assumption that $D'(X) \geq 0$. In the absence of policy intervention, there is assumed to be no internalization of environmental damages by firms or households.

Finally, the government has an exogenous total revenue requirement TR, levies a proportional tax of τ_L on labor income, and regulates X. For our purposes it does not matter what TR is used for; we assume it is returned to households as a lump sum transfer.[9]

B Impacts of Pollution Taxes (with Revenues Used to Cut Marginal Tax Rates)

Now consider a revenue-neutral policy involving a new environmental tax τ_X per unit of output X. The environmental tax is accompanied by a reduction in the labor tax τ_L, where the reduction is such as to make the overall policy revenue-neutral. Normalizing the gross wage to unity, we can express the household budget constraint as:

$$(1 + \tau_X)X + Y = (1 - \tau_L)(T - \ell) + TR \tag{4.5}$$

Households are assumed to maximize utility (4.1) subject to their budget constraint (4.5), taking environmental quality as given. This yields the first order conditions

$$U_X = (1 + \tau_X)\lambda; \quad U_Y = \lambda; \quad U_\ell = (1 - \tau_L)\lambda \tag{4.6}$$

From (4.5) and (4.6) we can implicitly derive the (uncompensated) demand functions

$$X(\tau_X, \tau_L); \quad Y(\tau_X, \tau_L); \quad \ell(\tau_X, \tau_L) \tag{4.7}$$

Government revenues are the sum of labor and pollution tax revenues. Therefore government budget balance requires

$$TR = \tau_L (T - \ell) + \tau_X X \tag{4.8}$$

Since the policy is revenue-neutral, *TR* is kept constant. Substituting (4.7) in (4.8) and totally differentiating the resource constraint (4.2) while holding TR constant gives:

$$\frac{d\tau_L}{d\tau_X} = -\frac{X + \tau_X \dfrac{dX}{d\tau_X} - \tau_L \dfrac{\partial \ell}{\partial \tau_X}}{T - \ell - \tau_L \dfrac{\partial \ell}{\partial \tau_L}} \tag{4.9}$$

This expression can be combined with equations (4.1), (4.2), (4.3), (4.4), and (4.7) (see GPB) to yield:

$$\frac{1}{\lambda}\frac{dU}{d\tau_X} = \underbrace{(D - \tau_X)\left(-\frac{dX}{d\tau_X}\right)}_{dW^P} + \underbrace{M\left(X + \tau_X \frac{dX}{d\tau_X}\right)}_{dW^R} - \underbrace{(1+M)\tau_L \frac{\partial \ell}{\partial \tau_X}}_{\partial W^I} \tag{4.10}$$

where

$$M = \frac{\tau_L \dfrac{\partial \ell}{\partial \tau_L}}{T - \ell - \tau_L \dfrac{\partial \ell}{\partial \tau_L}} \tag{4.11}$$

M represents the marginal welfare cost per dollar of revenue from labor taxation. The numerator in the expression for M is the welfare cost of the policy change. This is the increase in leisure multiplied by τ_L, the wedge between the gross and net wage. The denominator is the overall increase in government revenue from a marginal increase in the labor tax.

Equation (4.10) is the overall efficiency or welfare impact of the policy change. The equation divides this impact into three components. The first is the *Pigovian* (or partial equilibrium) effect ∂W^P. This is the reduction in X from a marginal increase in the environmental tax, multiplied by the wedge between marginal social cost and the demand price, or marginal social benefit. The second is the gain from the (marginal) *revenue-recycling effect*, ∂W^R. This is the product of the efficiency value per dollar of tax revenue (the marginal welfare cost of taxation) and the incremental pollution tax revenue. The third is the (marginal) *tax-interaction effect*, ∂W^I. The pollution tax raises the demand price of the good X. When X and leisure are substitutes, the higher price of X implies a reduction in the real wage, which implies an increase in leisure. This in turn exacerbates the welfare cost of the labor tax by $\tau_L(\partial \ell/\partial \tau_X)$. This also reduces labor tax revenues by $\tau_L(\partial \ell/\partial \tau_X)$. The tax-interaction effect is the welfare loss from these two impacts.

We can use the information in (4.10) to compare the magnitudes of the revenue-recycling and tax-interaction effects. ∂W^I can be manipulated (see GPB) to give the following approximation for the tax-interaction effect:

$$\partial W^I = \phi_X MX; \quad \phi_X = \frac{\eta^c_{Xl} + \eta_{LI}}{\dfrac{X}{X+Y}\eta^c_{XL} + \dfrac{Y}{X+Y}\eta^c_{Yl} + \eta_{LI}} \tag{4.12}$$

where η^c_{Xl} and η^c_{Tl} are the compensated elasticity of demand for X and Y with respect to the price of leisure, and is the income elasticity of labor supply. ϕ_X is a measure of the degree of substitution between X and leisure relative to that between aggregate consumption and leisure. ϕ_X equals unity when X and Y are equal substitutes for leisure (equals) and is greater (less) than unity when X is a relatively strong (weak) substitute for leisure (that is, when is greater (less) than). When η^c_{Xl} equals η^c_{Yl} equation (4.12) reduces to $\partial W^I = MX$. Equation (4.10) indicates that under these circumstances the tax-interaction and revenue-recycling effects exactly cancel each other out if pollution abatement is incremental, that is, if $\tau_X = 0$. However, for more than incremental abatement (that is, for $\tau_X > 0$), the tax-interaction effect is larger than the revenue-recycling effect (by the amount $M\tau_X(dX/d\tau_X)$). The pollution tax affects the relative prices of consumer goods, 'distorting' the household's consumption choice as well as its labor-leisure choice.[10] Recycling the revenues help return the real wage to its original value and thereby mitigates the labor-market distortion, but such recycling does not undo the change in relative consumer good prices and the associated 'distortion' in consumption.[11] For this reason the revenue-recycling effect only partly offsets the tax-interaction effect when the level of abatement is non-incremental.

This means that pre-existing taxes usually imply that the overall efficiency gains from environmental taxes are lower than in a first-best setting, unless the environmentally damaging good is a sufficiently weak substitute for leisure (that is, unless (ϕ_X is sufficiently below unity). This is the first main result.

C Impacts of Non-Auctioned Pollution Quotas (or Pollution Taxes with Revenues Returned Lump-Sum)

Now consider, in contrast with the pollution tax case, the situation where a binding, non-auctioned quota is imposed. The analysis is formally the same for a pollution tax policy where the revenues are returned lump-sum rather than in the form of marginal rate cuts.[12] It is also the same in the case of freely allocated (or grandfathered) emissions permits.[13]

We define this quota by a virtual tax τ_X, that is, by the tax that would induce the equivalent reduction in X as the quota. This quota produces rents of $\pi = \tau_X X$, which are retained by households (who own firms). Here we assume that these rents are not taxes, so that all of π becomes household income.[14] Therefore π appears as an exogenous lump-sum component of income in the household budget constraint. The household demand functions can now be summarized by:

$$X(\tau_X,\tau_L,\pi); \quad Y(\tau_X,\tau_L,\pi); \quad \ell(\tau_X,\tau_Y,\pi) \tag{4.7'}$$

The key difference compared with the previous case is that the quota policy generates no revenue. Therefore the government budget constraint is:

$$TR = \tau_L (T - \ell) \tag{4.8'}$$

Again we consider a revenue neutral incremental increase in τ_X. Following the same procedure as for the pollution tax yields:

$$\frac{d\tau_L}{d\tau_X} = \frac{\tau_L \dfrac{\partial \ell^I}{\partial \tau_X}}{T - \ell - \tau_L \dfrac{\partial \ell}{\partial \tau_L}} \tag{4.9'}$$

Since $\partial\ell^I/\partial\tau_X$ is (in general) positive, the revenue neutral quota induces an overall increase, rather than a decrease, in the labor tax.

Following the analogous procedure as for the pollution tax yields the following expression for the general equilibrium welfare change from the policy:

$$\frac{1}{\lambda}\frac{dU}{d\tau_X} = \underbrace{(D-\tau_X)\left(-\frac{dX}{d\tau_X}\right)}_{dW^P} - \underbrace{(1+M)\tau_L\frac{\partial\ell}{\partial\tau_X}}_{\delta W^I} \qquad (4.10')$$

The quota policy leads to a Pigovian welfare effect and a tax-interaction effect. The key difference between (4.10') and (4.10) is that the quota does not generate a revenue-recycling effect to counteract the tax-interaction effect.

D Welfare Implications of Policy Choice

The presence or absence of the revenue-recycling effect can importantly affect the efficiency outcomes of environmental policies. The above results indicate that given levels of pollution abatement are achieved at lower cost through a pollution tax (with revenues returned through cuts in the labor tax) than through a pollution quota. Under the two policies, the Pigovian gain and tax-interactions are the same, but the revenue-recycling effect applies only under the pollution tax.

In fact, as indicated in the introduction, the presence or absence of the revenue-recycling effect can determine the sign of the overall efficiency impact. An efficiency improvement will occur if and only if the combination of the Pigovian gain and the revenue-recycling effect (if applicable) is larger than the tax-interaction effect. The revenue-recycling effect may be necessary to meet this condition. If the revenue-recycling effect is absent, and the Pigovian gain is less than the tax-interaction effect, then the environmental policy will be efficiency-reducing. Note that the tax-interaction effect is non-incremental, even at the first incremental amount of abatement, as can be seen from equation (4.10) or (4.10'). This means that when the revenue-recycling effect is absent, the Pigovian gain – or the marginal environmental benefits from reducing pollution (net of direct abatement costs) – must exceed a certain positive value to allow an efficiency improvement.

Under traditional Pigovian analysis, the marginal cost of the first units of pollution abatement is zero; hence environmental regulation can increase welfare so long as the marginal environmental benefits are positive. In a second-best setting, if X is an average substitute for leisure, a pollution tax with revenues recycled through income tax cuts also has the property that the marginal cost of pollution abatement is zero at the first unit of abatement. Thus in this case, the overall efficiency impact will be positive if marginal environmental benefits are positive (and the amount of abatement is not too great). However, in the pollution quota case, the absence of the revenue-recycling effect means that the incremental welfare change from regulation is positive only if marginal benefits from abatement exceed a certain threshold value. The threshold value is the tax-interaction effect evaluated at $\tau_X = 0$.[15]

How large is this critical value? With a value of 0.3 assumed for the marginal welfare cost of labor taxation,[16] the analytical framework above implies that the critical value of marginal environmental benefits is 60 percent, 30 percent, or 15 percent of firms' marginal production costs, when the elasticity of demand for the polluting good is 0.5, 1, or 2, respectively.[17] We look more closely at these critical values in section IV, where we consider specific regulatory contexts.

As mentioned at the beginning of this section, the analysis of pollution quotas is formally identical to that for a pollution tax whose revenues are returned lump-sum, or for a set of freely offered or grandfathered pollution permits. Also, the analysis for the pollution tax with revenues financing labor tax cuts is the same as that for a set of auctioned pollution permits. Thus, the revenue-recycling effect accounts for the differences between pollution taxes or auctioned pollution permits (with revenues applied to labor tax cuts), on the one hand, and pollution quotas, grandfathered pollution permits, or pollution taxes with revenues returned lump-sum, on the other.

E A Graphical Illustration of the Main Findings

Some key results from the analytical model are:

1. For incremental pollution abatement through a pollution tax (with revenues devoted to cuts in the labor tax), the marginal tax interaction effect is exactly offset by the revenue-recycling effect (if X and Y are equal substitutes for leisure).
2. For non-incremental pollution abatement through the pollution tax, the marginal tax interaction effect is only partly offset by the revenue-recycling effect.
3. The absence of the revenue-recycling effect puts pollution quotas (as well as grandfathered pollution permits and pollution taxes with lump-sum recycling of revenues) at an efficiency disadvantage relative to pollution taxes with revenues devoted to cuts in the labor tax.
4. The marginal tax interaction effect is strictly positive, even at incremental pollution abatement (that is, even for an incremental pollution tax). The marginal tax-interaction effect at incremental abatement is a critical value

for marginal environmental benefits. If the marginal benefits are below this value, any pollution abatement through a quota policy is efficiency-reducing.

Figure 4.1 illustrates these results. The figure shows the marginal efficiency costs of pollution abatement, at different levels of abatement, where the efficiency costs represented here the benefits from environmental improvement. The lowermost (dashed) line depicts the marginal costs of abatement in a first-best setting, that is, in the absence of pre-existing distortionary taxes. In a first-best setting, the marginal costs of abatement are the same regardless of whether a pollution tax or pollution quota is imposed. The other lines represent

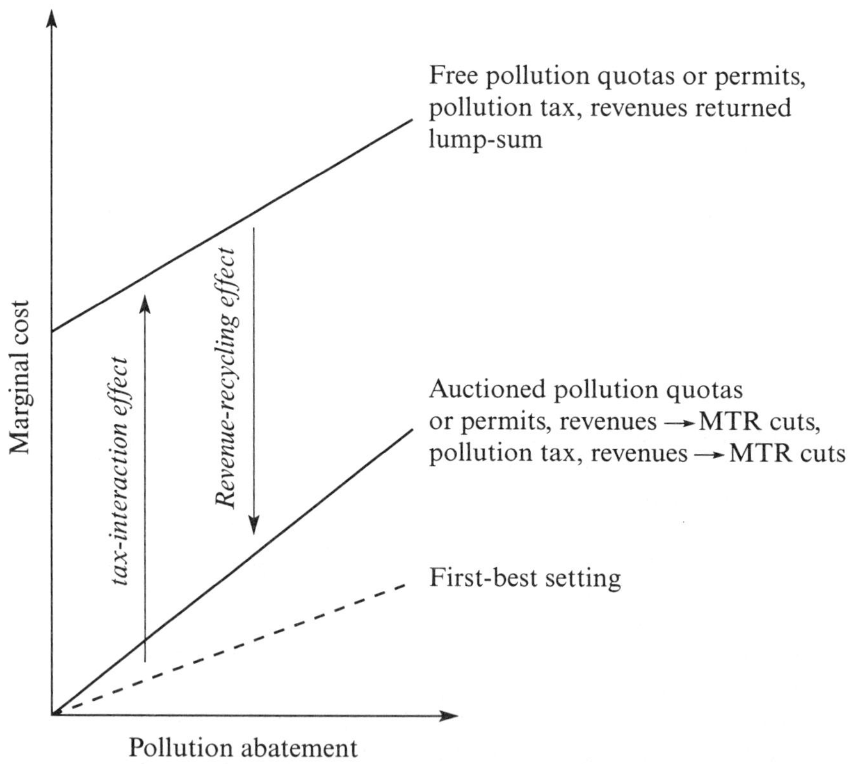

Figure 4.1 Marginal costs of pollution abatement in first-best and second-best settings

the marginal costs in a second-best setting with pre-existing distortionary taxes. The top line depicts the marginal costs of abatement for a pollution quota, grandfathered pollution permits, or pollution tax with lump-sum recycling of revenues. At all levels of abatement, the marginal costs of abatement under a quota are higher than in the first-best case. This is the case even at incremental abatement: the second-best marginal cost curve has a positive intercept, whereas the marginal cost of incremental abatement for the quota is zero (dashed line) in the first-best case. At any level of abatement, the tax-interaction effect is represented by the vertical distance between the top and bottom (dashed) marginal cost curve.

The intercept of the top marginal cost curve represents the critical value for marginal environmental benefits from pollution abatement through quotas or grandfathered permits. If the marginal benefits are (always) below this value, then pollution reductions through one of these policies will always involve costs that exceed the benefits. Thus, these policies will be efficiency-reducing regardless of the level of abatement.

Some efficiency costs can be avoided through policies that raise revenues and devote them to reductions in the labor tax. The middle line in Figure 4.1 represents the marginal costs of abatement for a pollution tax or set of auctioned pollution permits with revenues used in this way. The revenue-recycling effect is represented by the vertical distance between the top and middle marginal cost curves. At incremental abatement, the revenue-recycling effect fully offsets the tax-interaction effect; hence, the marginal cost of abatement is zero at incremental abatement (as in the first-best case). However, for larger amounts of abatement, the revenue-recycling effect only partly offsets the tax-interaction effect (for the reasons given in subsection B above), and thus the costs of abatement exceed the costs of comparable abatement in a first-best setting.

III INTERPRETATIONS, QUALIFICATIONS, AND EXTENSIONS

A Can Pollution Taxes Deliver a 'Double Dividend'?

In recent years there has been considerable debate about the possibilities for 'green tax reform', that is, the substitution of taxes on pollution for ordinary, distortionary taxes. A general argument for such reform is that it makes sense to concentrate taxes on 'bads' like pollution rather than 'goods' like labor effort or capital formation (saving and investment). To buttress the case for green tax reform, some analysts have argued that the revenue-neutral swap of pollution taxes for ordinary taxes will produce a 'double dividend': not only (1) improve the quality of the environment, but also (2) reduce certain costs of the tax system. This argument has occupied a prominent place in the debate about carbon taxes, as mentioned in the introduction. Few analysts deny the first dividend; it is the second dividend that generates controversy.

Can environmental taxes generate the second dividend? Different policy analysts have meant different things by this dividend, and this has led to confusion. Goulder (1995) distinguishes a 'strong' and 'weak' version of the double dividend claim, as follows. Let $C(\tau_E, \Delta\tau_L)$ refer to the gross cost of a revenue-neutral policy involving a new environmental tax τ_E that finances the change (reduction) $\Delta\tau_L$ in pre-existing distortionary taxes.[18] Let $C(\tau_E, \Delta T)$ denote the gross cost of a revenue-neutral policy in which a new environmental tax τ_E finances the lump-sum reduction in taxes, ΔT. The weak double dividend claim is:

$$C(\tau_E, \Delta\tau_L) < C(\tau_E, \Delta T)$$

The above expression asserts that a reform in which revenues from the environmental tax are recycled through cuts in the rates of distortionary tax involves lower gross costs than a policy in which revenues are returned lump-sum. This weak double-dividend claim is easy to justify: environmental taxes, with revenues devoted to cuts in distortionary taxes, do indeed lower the costs of the tax system relative to what the costs would be if the revenues were returned lump-sum. As shown in Goulder (1995), the weak double-dividend claim is upheld so long as the tax τ_L is appropriately labeled as distortionary. That is, the weak claim is upheld if and only if the tax τ_L has a positive marginal excess burden.

In terms of Figure 4.1, the weak double-dividend claim is verified by the fact that the marginal cost curve for the pollution tax with lump-sum revenue-replacement lies above the curve for the pollution tax accompanied by cuts in the distortionary tax. In essence, the weak double-dividend claim amounts to the assertion that, in terms of efficiency, it pays to take advantage of the revenue-recycling effect. Thus it is closely related to the notion that pollution taxes which finance cuts in distortionary taxes are preferable on efficiency grounds to pollution quotas or grandfathered tradable permits.

The stronger double-dividend claim is

$$C(\tau_E, \Delta\tau_L) \leq 0$$

that is, the revenue-neutral swap of an environmental tax for existing distortionary taxes involves zero or negative gross costs. This is equivalent to asserting that the gross distortionary cost directly attributable to the environmental tax is smaller than the avoided gross distortionary cost stemming from the environmental-tax-financed cut in the distortionary tax. If this strong double-dividend claim held for a carbon tax, then, as noted in the introduction, the tax would be justified on efficiency grounds so long as the environment-related gross benefits from the policy were non-negative.

Is the stronger claim justified? Figure 4.1 sheds light on the answer. For the strong claim to be valid, the marginal cost curve for the pollution tax accompanied by cuts in distortionary taxes would have to lie on or below the horizontal axis. Clearly the curve does not fulfill this requirement – except at zero abatement. To support the stronger double-dividend claim, the revenue-recycling effect would not only have to fully offset the tax-interaction effect, but also overcome the usual, first-best abatement costs represented by the dashed line. Thus, the simple theoretical model of section II rejects the strong double-dividend claim. For anything but an infinitesimal amount of abatement (infinitesimal environmental tax) the gross costs of a revenue-neutral environmental tax reform are positive.

Some qualifications are in order. More complex theoretical models can provide more scope for the strong double-dividend claim than is offered here.[19] It may be noted, in particular, that the model of section II considered only one primary factor of production – labor. In theoretical models with both capital and labor, an environmental tax reform can produce a second dividend under certain circumstances. Specifically, if the tax system initially is highly inefficient in the sense that one factor is overtaxed relative to the other,[20] and if the environmental tax reform (the combination of the tax itself and the recycling of the revenues) serves to shift the tax burden from the overtaxed to the undertaxed factor, then the reform will produce a *tax-shifting effect* which works towards a more efficient tax system. If the beneficial tax-shifting effect is large enough, it (combined with the revenue-recycling effect) can entirely compensate for usual 'first-best' abatement costs and the tax-interaction effect.[21] Thus, under these circumstances, the strong double dividend materializes after all.

Most empirical studies indicate that in the US, capital is overtaxed (in efficiency terms) relative to labor.[22] With these initial conditions, an environmental tax reform will produce a favorable tax-shifting effect if it shifts the burden away from capital and towards labor. Bovenberg and Goulder (1997) examine two environmentally motivated, revenue-neutral tax reforms – a BTU tax applied to fossil fuels and an increase in the Federal gasoline tax – and find that the latter policy produces a tax-shifting effect that significantly reduces the gross costs. However, the tax-shifting effect is generally not strong enough to make the gross costs zero or negative, except under extreme values for behavioral parameters. Although the results are somewhat mixed, other simulation studies have tended to support the idea that it is difficult to generate the strong double dividend under plausible parameter values and realistic policy specifications.[23]

The absence of the strong double dividend does not vitiate the case for green tax reform. It only means that the positive *sign* of the environmental benefits is not a sufficient condition for justifying such reform. If there is no (strong) double dividend, policymakers are obliged to consider the magnitudes of the environmental benefits and compare them with the (positive) gross costs. Also, the absence of a double dividend does not repudiate our intuition that it makes sense to orient the tax system, to a degree, on 'bads' (polluting activities) rather than 'goods' (labor and capital). Even if the strong double-dividend claim fails, it is still the case that 'Pigovian considerations' should be part of the design of an efficient tax system: other things equal, the tax on a given good or activity should be higher, the larger the environmental externalities associated with that good or activity. Higher environmental benefits justify higher taxes on polluting activities. It is the larger environmental benefits that justify the greening of the tax system, not the presumption of zero gross costs.

B Instrument Choice and the Scale of Abatement

The theoretical model indicated that the pollution taxes and auctioned pollution permits have an efficiency advantage over pollution quotas and grandfathered pollution permits to the extent that the former policies exploit the revenue-recycling effect. However, the size of the efficiency advantage generally declines with the amount of abatement. In fact, this advantages approaches zero as the extent of abatement approaches 100 percent.

This is illustrated by Figure 4.2, which is borrowed from the GPB study. Marginal costs rise faster for the pollution tax (or auctioned pollution permit) policy. Eventually, when the extent of abatement is substantial, marginal costs under this policy exceed those for the pollution quota (or grandfathered permit) policy. Why is this so? Consider the pollution tax. Because of this policy's negative impact on labor supply and on emissions, marginal tax revenue declines as the emissions tax rate rises. This means that, with greater abatement, the ability to exploit the revenue-recycling effect diminishes. Eventually, the point is reached where, at the margin, additional abatement (via an incrementally higher pollution tax) raises no more revenue than is raised under the quota policy.[24]

That is the point where the pollution tax and pollution quota marginal cost curves cross. To the right of that point, at the margin the tax policy is more costly than the quota policy, because at the margin it has a negative revenue-recycling effect (as compared with the negligible revenue-recycling effect of the quota policy). Indeed, if one pursues emissions reductions to the point of 100 percent abatement, the *total* costs of the two types of policies are identical. This makes sense, since at 100 percent abatement neither policy earns any revenue, and thus there is no effective difference between a tax and a quota at that point. Thus the areas under the marginal cost curves from 0 to 100 percent abatement are the same for both policies.

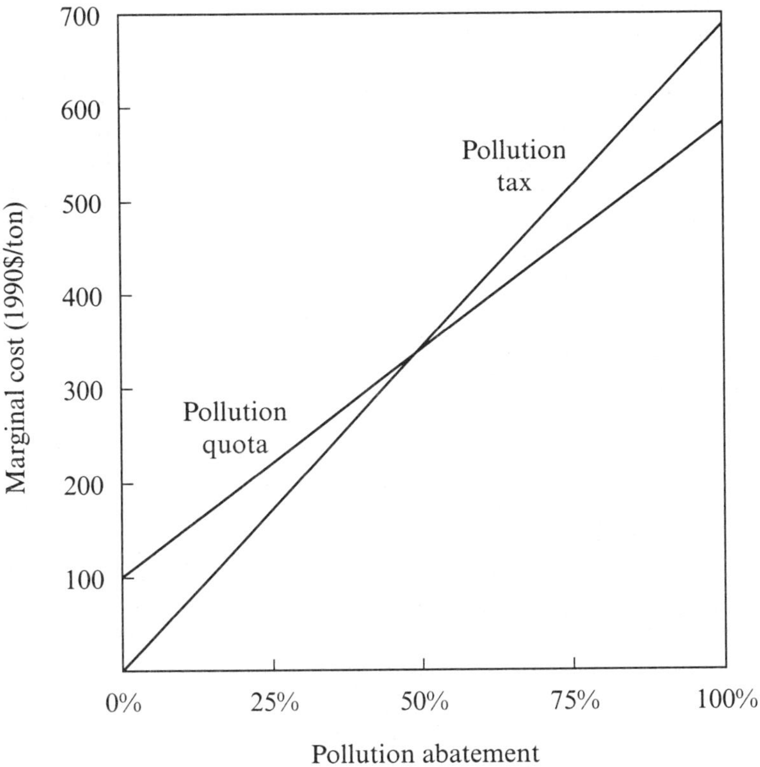

Figure 4.2 Marginal costs over the entire range of possible emissions reductions

These results demonstrate that the relative superiority (in terms of lower cost) of policies that exploit the revenue-recycling effect diminishes with the extent of abatement. At low levels of abatement (as would be appropriate if marginal environmental benefits are low), these policies have a considerable cost advantage. But at high levels of abatement (as would be justified when marginal environmental benefits are high) the advantage of these policies is much smaller. In the limiting case of 100 percent abatement, these policies have no cost advantage.

C Emissions Taxes vs. Output Taxes

The simple theoretical model assumed a constant ratio of pollution to the quantity of output of the pollution-related good, *X*. A constant ratio applies in some circumstances: for example, in the case where *X* is coal and the pollutant is carbon dioxide. However, in many cases firms have opportunities to alter the ratio of pollution to the level of output by changing the input mix or purchasing pollution-abatement equipment. Under a more general formulation, reducing output is not the only channel through which pollution can be reduced.

Some analytical models of second-best environmental taxation or regulation incorporate these expanded opportunities for pollution abatement. Bovenberg and Goulder (1996) and Parry (1995, 1997) develop analytical models in which pollution is associated with the use of a particular intermediate input. By changing the input mix, firms can change the amount of pollution per unit of output. In analytical models by Fullerton and Metcalf (1997) and Goulder, Parry, and Burtraw (1997), firms can lower the pollution-output ratio by purchasing abatement equipment or services.

In general, the qualitative results obtained in section II and illustrated by Figure 4.1 remain when more expanded abatement options are considered. Additional abatement options attenuate the increase in costs to firms associated with a given tax on pollution: firms end up paying less pollution tax per unit of output. But as long as there is any increase in cost to the firm, the output price rises and the real wage falls. Even the slightest reduction in the real wage generates a first-order (that is, non-incremental) efficiency cost in the labor market when the pre-existing labor tax is positive. Hence, as in the simple model, the tax-interaction effect is still strictly positive at the first, incremental amount of abatement. And as before, the revenue-recycling effect does not fully offset the tax-interaction effect. This is the case because (as before) revenue-recycling cannot undo the 'distortion' in relative prices of intermediate inputs or consumer goods brought about by the pollution tax. Thus, the same general results apply when more realistic abatement options are considered. Although the qualitative results do not change when an expanded range of abatement options is considered, the quantitative evaluation of policy impacts can be much affected by the specification of abatement options. Allowing for flexible pollution-output ratios permits one to consider meaningfully the differences between the impacts of taxes on emissions (for example, sulfur dioxide) and taxes on ordinary outputs closely associated with pollution (for example, electricity from coal-fired power plants). The quantitative impacts of these policies may differ significantly, and models that impose fixed pollution-output ratios obscure these differences.

D Impacts of Other Environmental Policies in a Second-Best Setting

Thus far, all of the discussion in this paper has centered on pollution taxes, quotas, and permits. Recent papers by Fullerton and Metcalf (1997) and Goulder, Parry, Williams, and Burtraw (1999) examine the impacts of other policy instruments (in addition to pollution taxes and quotas) in a second-best setting.[25]

Two additional instruments analysed by Fullerton and Metcalf are a subsidy to consumption of a 'clean' good and a mandated technology. The subsidy applies to consumption of a good whose production or use does not involve pollution; it is financed by an increase in the pre-existing distortionary tax (the tax on labor).[26] Additional instruments examined by Goulder, Parry, Williams, and Burtraw are a mandated technology, performance standard, and a tax on fuels (as opposed to a tax on emissions or pollution). In these recent studies the mandated technology is a constraint on the ratio of pollution emissions per unit of output in the production of the good associated with pollution emissions.[27]

These additional instruments give rise to marginal cost schedules that resemble the middle schedule in Figure 4.1 (the schedule that applies to pollution tax or auctioned permits policies the revenues of which finance labor tax cuts) in that the marginal costs of abatement are zero at the first, incremental amount of abatement. However, beyond this first increment of abatement, the new instruments generally involve higher marginal costs than the pollution tax or auctioned permits. As discussed in Goulder, Parry, Williams, and Burtraw, this reflects the inability of these alternative instruments to provide the appropriate prices of inputs and outputs. For all of these policies, the marginal cost curves lie above the curves that would apply under the same policy in a first-best setting: environmental regulation is more costly in a second-best setting than in a first-best world.

It is worth considering further the fact that the marginal cost curves of these alternative instruments emerge from the origin, as in the case of the pollution tax or auctioned quota (with revenues devoted to marginal rate reductions). Since the mandated technology, performance standard, and subsidy to a clean good do not raise revenue, these results make clear that raising revenue *per se* is not necessary for the zero-marginal-cost-at-initial-abatement property to obtain. The effects of all of these policies can be explained in terms of the tax-interaction and revenue-recycling effects. At the first incremental amount of abatement, the mandated technology and performance standard produce neither a tax-interaction effect nor a revenue-recycling effect. Hence the marginal costs of abatement are again zero at initial abatement.[28] The pollution subsidy's impact can be decomposed into a positive (in terms of efficiency) tax-interaction effect and a negative (in efficiency terms) revenue-recycling effect. The positive tax-interaction effect stems from the reduction in the output price (and increase in the real wage) associated with the subsidy to the clean good. The negative revenue-recycling effect reflects the need to raise the explicit tax on labor in order to finance the subsidy. At the first, incremental amount of abatement, the two effects cancel out, and thus the marginal cost of abatement is zero. However, for larger amounts of abatement, the revenue-recycling effect dominates (that is, it involves a cost that is not entirely offset by the tax-interaction effect), so marginal costs of abatement are positive.

Why do the marginal cost curves have a zero intercept under some policies, but a strictly positive intercept in the case of non-auctioned pollution quotas, grandfathered pollution permits, or pollution taxes with revenues recycled in lump-sum fashion? One can explain these differences in terms of whether the tax-interaction and revenue-recycling effects cancel at initial abatement. But the differences can also be linked to the presence or absence of a lump-sum transfer. The government effectuates a lump-sum transfer to individuals when it introduces a pollution tax and returns the revenues lump-sum, when it implements a pollution quota (thus generating quota rents that are not entirely taxed away), or when it introduces a pollution tax and recycles the revenues through cuts in the marginal tax rate on a perfectly inelastically supplied factor of production.[29] In a second-best world, such transfers involve an efficiency cost because they must ultimately be financed through distortionary taxes. In contrast, under the pollution tax or fuels tax (with revenues financing cuts in prior taxes), or under the mandated technology or performance standard, there is no such transfer. Thus the presence or absence of a positive intercept of the marginal cost function corresponds to the presence or absence of this lump-sum transfer.[30]

IV SOME NUMERICAL RESULTS

The analytical results obtained so far are largely qualitative. How much difference do these second-best elements make in real-world settings? To address this question, we will look at results from two explorations with numerical models.[31]

A Sulfur Dioxide Abatement

The GPB study includes an assessment of the costs of reducing emissions of sulfur dioxide (SO_2) from US coal-fired electric power plants. Provisions of the 1990 Clean Air Act Amendments call for such reductions and introduce a system of grandfathered SO_2 emissions permits to achieve them.

Two questions arise. First, how much higher are the costs of reducing SO_2 emissions as a result of pre-existing taxes? And how much of the increase in abatement costs could be avoided if the reductions were achieved through a policy that auctioned the permits (or imposed an SO_2 tax) and exploited the revenue-recycling effect, rather than through a policy that grandfathered the permits? Figure 4.3 gives GPB's best estimates of the answers to these questions. The two solid lines in the figure are the ratios of total costs in a second-best setting

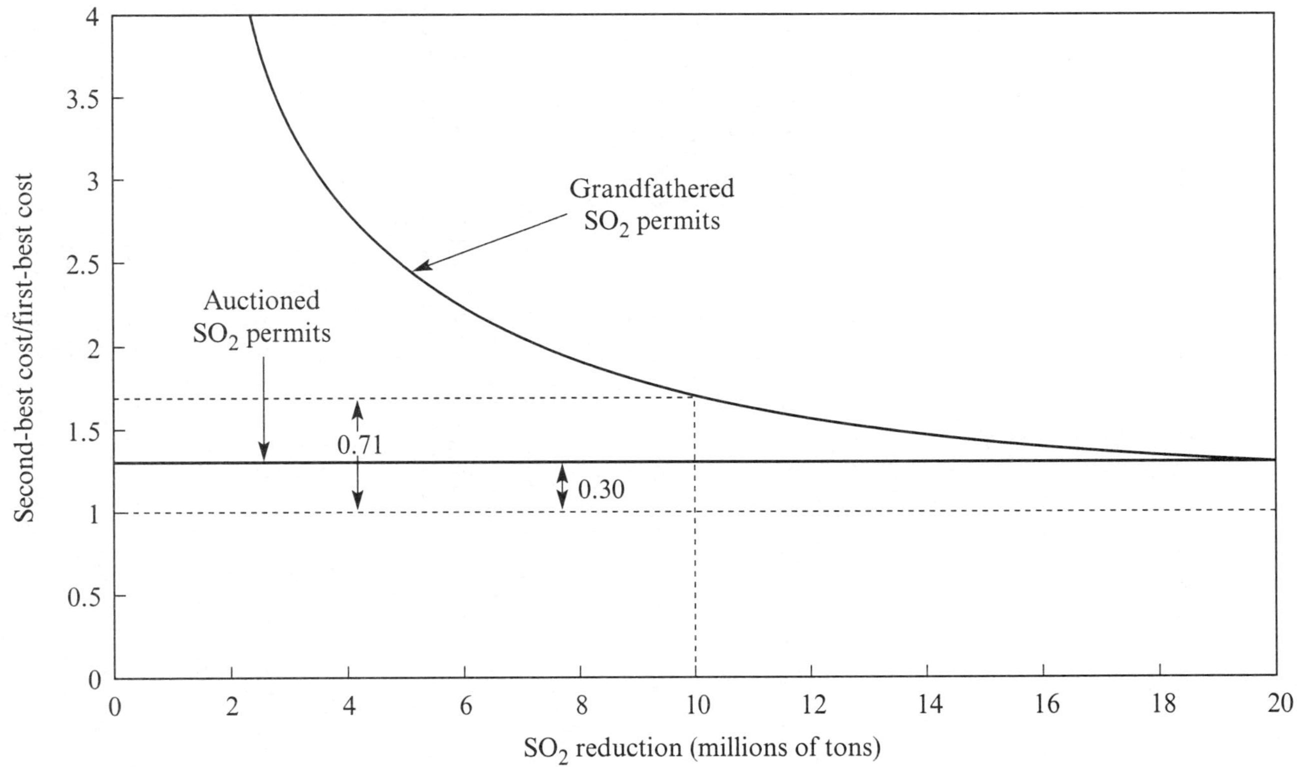

Figure 4.3 Ratio of second-best to first-best total costs, SO_2 case

(with a positive pre-existing tax rate on labor equal to 0.4) to total costs in a first-best setting (with no pre-existing tax on labor). In the case of auctioned permits (or pollution taxes), the line is almost perfectly horizontal: this ratio is approximately constant throughout the entire range of possible emissions reductions (0 to 20 million tons). Second-best considerations raise the costs of auctioned permits by about 30 percent, regardless of the extent of emissions abatement. For the actual policy of grandfathered emissions permits, the ratio of total cost is very sensitive to the extent of abatement. Under this policy the ratio begins at infinity, in keeping with the fact that the intercept of the marginal cost function is positive for this policy in a second-best world and zero in first-best world. As the level of abatement approaches 100 percent, the ratio of total costs approaches the ratio for auctioned permits. This is in keeping with the point made in section III that the efficiency disadvantage of policies that forgo the revenue-recycling effect disappears at 100 percent abatement.

The 1990 Clean Air Act Amendments call for a 10-million-ton (or approximately 50 percent) reduction in SO_2 emissions. There may be significant distributional or political objectives that are served by grandfathering, but Figure 4.3's results indicate that they come at a high price in terms of the social cost of abatement. At 10 million tons of abatement, annual total costs under the actual policy are estimated to be 71 percent (or $907 million) higher than they would be in a first-best world. As indicated in this figure, over half of this extra cost could be avoided by auctioning the permits or employing an SO_2 tax. The difference in cost between the two types of policy is $533 million.[32] These results indicate that pre-existing taxes and the presence or absence of revenue-recycling have a very substantial impact on the costs of environmental policies.

Figure 4.4 brings in the benefit side in considering the overall efficiency gains from SO_2 abatement. The overall gains obviously depend on the marginal benefits from SO_2 reductions, and these are highly uncertain. Most estimates are in the range of $100–600 per ton, but some recent estimates are as high as $1000 per ton. Figure 4.4 displays the net efficiency gains as a function of different values for the marginal benefits, ranging from zero to $750 per ton.[33] The figure shows the efficiency gains that result under optimal levels of abatement, that is, abatement levels that equate marginal benefits with marginal costs. For low and intermediate values of the marginal benefits, the efficiency gains are considerably larger when SO_2 permits are auctioned than when they are grandfathered, in keeping with the lower marginal costs of abatement in the former case. Indeed, net gains under grandfathered permits are zero if marginal benefits are below $104 per ton, because in this circumstance the optimal policy is not to regulate SO_2; that is, the optimal reduction in SO_2 is zero. For very high values of the marginal benefits, there is less difference in the net efficiency gains. In fact, the net efficiency gains are identical for marginal

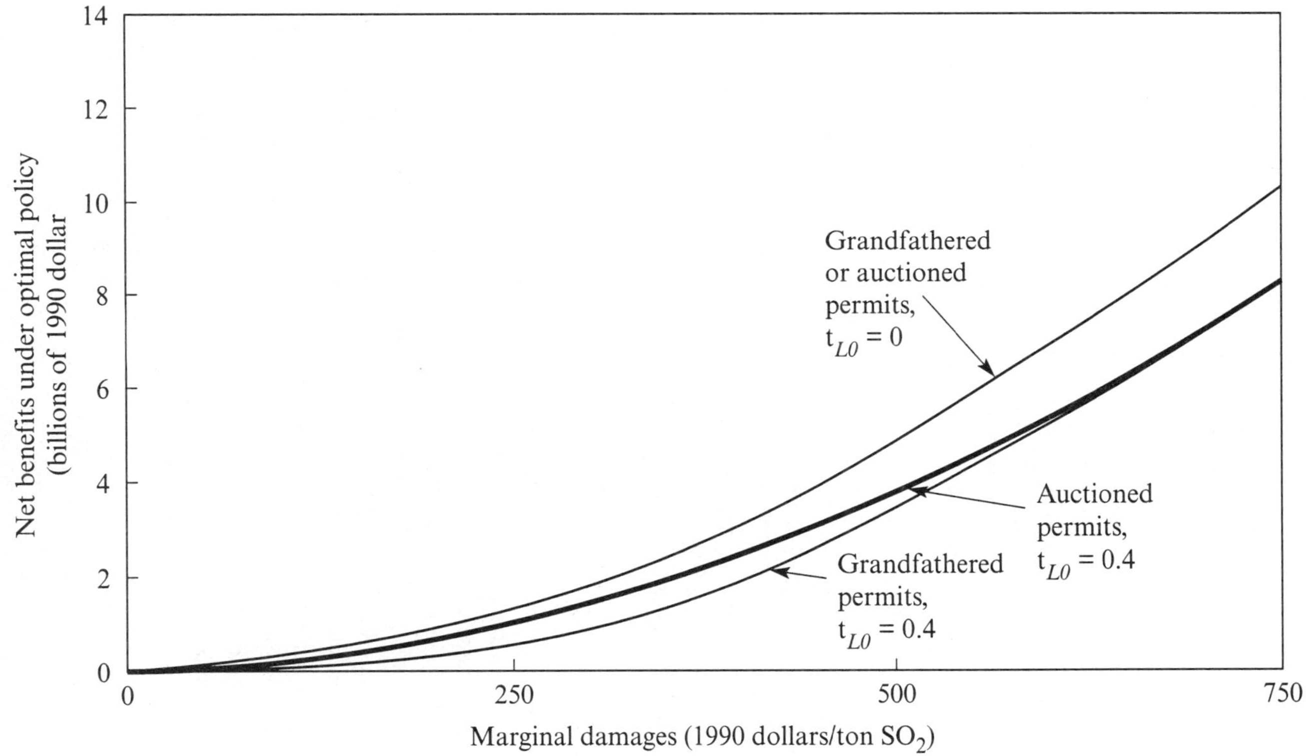

Figure 4.4 Net welfare gain from the optimal level of SO_2 regulation

benefits greater than or equal to about $680 per ton. When marginal benefits exceed this level, the optimal policy is to eliminate SO_2 emissions entirely. At this point it makes no difference whether permits are grandfathered or auctioned, since no permits are actually provided and thus no revenue can be raised in either case.

B Carbon Dioxide Abatement

Recent work by Parry, Williams, and Goulder (1999) examines these issues in the context of carbon dioxide (CO_2) emissions abatement in the US. Figures 4.5 and 4.6, based on results from this study, provide for CO_2 abatement policies the same sort of information as was displayed for SO_2 policies in Figures 4.3 and 4.4.

Figure 4.5 presents the ratio of second-best ($\tau_L = 0.4$) and first-best ($\tau_L = 0$) total costs, under a carbon (CO_2) tax and a carbon (CO_2) quota.[34] The carbon tax policy exploits the revenue-recycling effect: revenues from the tax are devoted to cuts in the pre-existing distortionary (labor) tax. The results are qualitatively similar to the results that were shown in Figure 4.3. For the carbon tax, the ratio of total costs is virtually unaffected by the extent of carbon emissions abatement. For the carbon quota, in contrast, the ratio of total costs is highly sensitive to the amount of abatement, for the same reasons as were discussed earlier.

Figure 4.6 shows Parry, Williams, and Goulder's best estimates for net efficiency gains from carbon abatement policies, for a range of values for the marginal benefits from CO_2 abatement. Efficiency gains are considerably larger under the carbon tax than under the carbon quota. In fact, efficiency gains under the quota are zero (the optimal amount of abatement is zero) if marginal benefits are below $17 per ton. This reflects the fact that the (gross) marginal costs of CO_2 abatement begin at $17 per ton under the quota policy. Thus, any emissions abatement from this type of policy will be efficiency-reducing if the marginal benefits are below this value. Most estimates of the marginal environmental benefits from carbon abatement obtain values below $17 per ton.[35] Thus, these results suggest that any carbon abatement by way of a quota (or freely offered set of carbon permits) will be efficiency reducing![36]

Thus, in the context of regulating SO_2 and CO_2 emissions, second-best interactions have a very substantial effect on the gross costs and net efficiency gains. Pre-existing taxes significantly raise the costs of achieving emissions reductions relative to the costs in a first-best setting. And they put policies involving emissions quotas or grandfathered permits policies at a very significant cost disadvantage relative to policies that raise revenue and finance cuts in pre-existing taxes. Second-best interactions have first-order consequences.

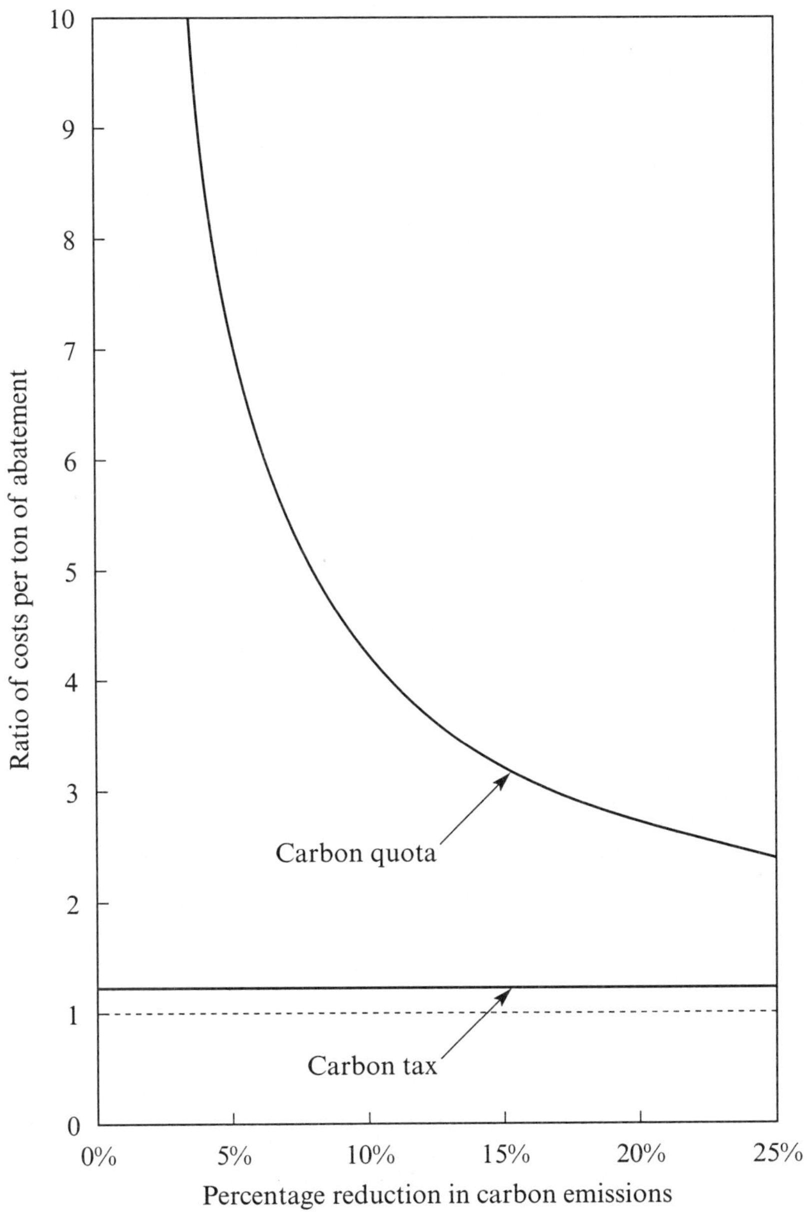

Figure 4.5 Ratio of second-best to first-best costs, CO_2 case

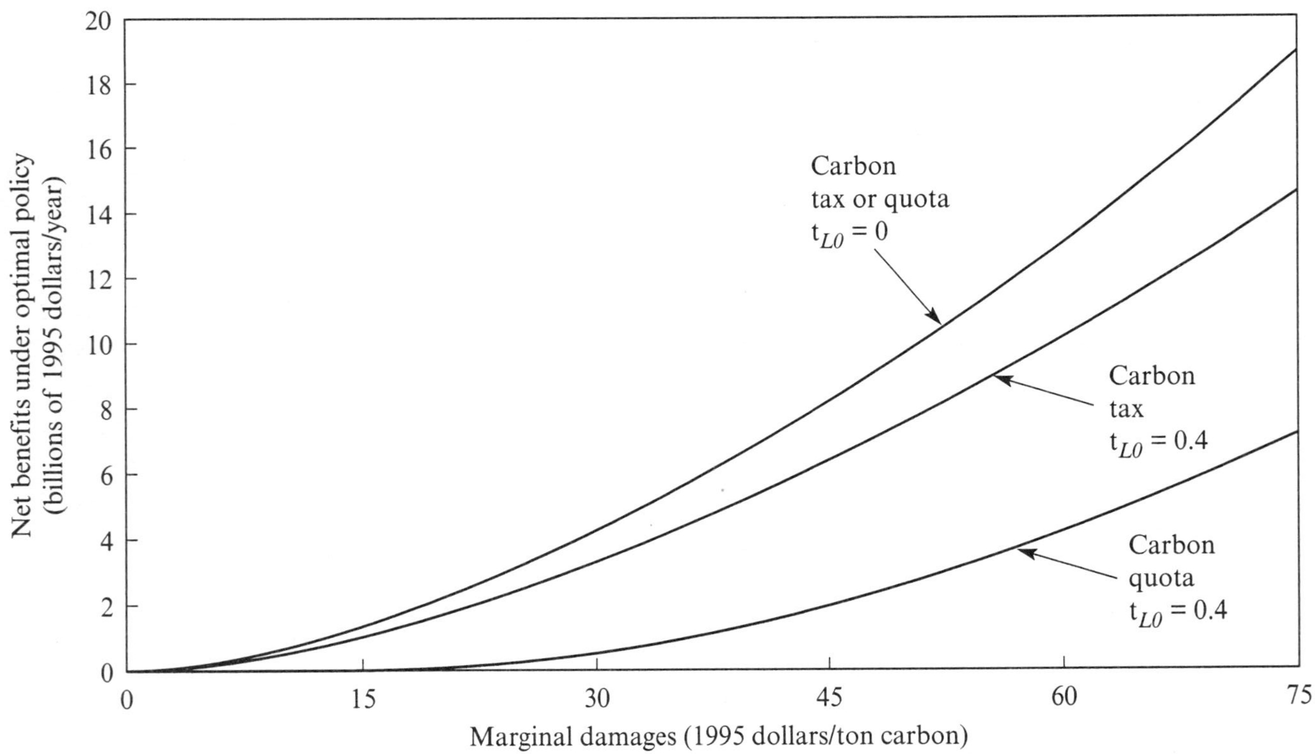

Figure 4.6 Net welfare gain from the optimal level of CO_2 regulation

V CONCLUSIONS

This paper shows that interactions with pre-existing factor taxes can substantially raise the costs of pollution taxes, quotas and permits relative to what they would be in a first-best world. Moreover, these interactions put pollution quotas and grandfathered pollution permits at a serious efficiency disadvantage relative to 'revenue-raising' policies, that is, pollution taxes or auctioned permits whose revenues finance reductions in the marginal rates of existing taxes. Indeed, if the marginal environmental benefits from pollution reductions are below a certain threshold value, then any level of pollution abatement through quotas or grandfathered permits is efficiency-reducing. These results emerge from simple analytical models and are confirmed by numerical investigations in specific regulatory contexts.

Two effects underlie these results. The tax-interaction effect is the adverse impact in factor markets arising from reductions in after-tax returns to factors (labor) brought about by environmental regulation. In a world with prior taxes on factors, this effect leads to significantly higher costs of regulation relative to what would apply in a first-best world with no pre-existing taxes. By generating revenues and using them to reduce pre-existing tax rates, pollution taxes and auctioned pollution permits exploit a revenue-recycling effect that offsets some of the tax-interaction effect. In contrast, pollution quotas and grandfathered permits enjoy no such offset. Thus the costs of achieving given reductions in pollution are higher under these latter policies. The tax-interaction effect is relevant to government regulation outside the environmental area. To the extent that government regulations of international trade or agricultural production raise the costs of output and thereby reduce real factor returns, these regulations exacerbate the labor market distortions from pre-existing taxes and thus involve higher social costs than would be indicated by partial equilibrium analyses.[37]

Even when they take advantage of the revenue-recycling effect, pollution abatement policies through pollution taxes or auctioned permits generally entail positive gross costs. The revenue-recycling effect only partly offsets the gross costs attributable to the tax-interaction effect. This implies that pollution-abatement through these policies is more costly in a second-best setting than it would be in a first-best world, and that the double dividend claim (in its strong form) is not upheld.

In recognizing the efficiency advantages of these pollution-tax and auctioned-permit policies over policies involving pollution quotas or grandfathered permits, one should not lose sight of related equity issues. The decision whether to exploit the revenue-recycling effect fundamentally affects the distribution of wealth between taxpayers, on the one hand, and owners and employees of polluting firms, on the other. Clearly, there are important equity issues associated with the differences in distribution. The second-best considerations raised in this paper do not reduce the importance of the equity issues, but at the same time they do indicate that the efficiency costs of forgoing the redistribution toward taxpayers are greater than that suggested by a first-best analysis.

NOTES

* I am grateful to Ian Parry and Roberton Williams III for many helpful discussions and to the National Science Foundation (Grants SBR-93 10362 and SBR-96 13458) for financial support.

1. Oates and Schwab (1988) also integrate the disciplines of environmental economics and public finance in an analysis of environmental quality and capital taxes at the level of local communities. Here the issue is the level of capital tax and environmental quality that results when communities compete with each other for industry and income. The paper shows that when communities must finance local public goods with capital taxes, the equilibrium levels of environmental quality (and associated environmental tax rates) will generally be suboptimal from an efficiency point of view.
2. The modifier 'gross' indicates that the costs do not net out the policy-generated benefits associated with an improved environment.
3. For reviews of this new literature, see Oates (1995) and Goulder (1995).
4. Parry (1995) was the first to isolate the tax-interaction and revenue-recycling effects in evaluating the second-best welfare impacts of environmental taxes. He termed these the 'interdependency' and 'revenue' effects.
5. Fullerton and Metcalf explain differences in efficiency outcomes in terms of whether policies generate privately-retained scarcity rents, rather than in terms of whether they exploit the revenue-recycling effect. As discussed in section III, the two issues are intimately connected.
6. This result, for pollution permits, was foreshadowed by Bovenberg and Goulder's (1996) finding that a carbon tax with lump-sum replacement of the revenues will be efficiency-reducing if marginal environmental benefits from carbon abatement are below a certain threshold (about \$50 per ton). Parry (1997) recognized that the same formal analysis applies to the case of pollution quotas and grandfathered pollution permits; thus the same 'threshold' issue arises.
7. The focus of the present paper is environmental regulation of competitive enterprises. Oates and Strassman (1984) offered an important examination of the impacts of environmental policies under alternative market structures. That paper included an analysis of the impacts of regulation in a monopoly setting, and showed how in that setting environmental regulation generates costs associated with the reduction in the monopolist's supply of output. Optimal regulation must balance these costs against the benefits from pollution reduction. More recently, Browning (1997) and Fullerton and Metcalf (1997) have examined interactions between new regulations and pre-existing tax distortions in the presence of monopoly.
8. Therefore, reducing waste emissions requires a reduction in output. In a more general formulation, this could also be achieved by substituting waste emissions for other inputs in production.
9. An alternative specification would incorporate *TR* as a public good in the household utility function. This produces the same results as in our model, since *TR* is held constant.
10. The word 'distort' is in quotes to acknowledge that we are ignoring environment-related benefits here. The changes in relative prices of commodities occasioned by the pollution tax may contribute to higher gross costs, but these same relative price changes may bring about an overall efficiency improvement, since overall efficiency incorporates the environment-related benefits that result from the relative price changes.
11. The tax-interaction effect exceeds the revenue-recycling effect to the extent that the revenue-neutral reform causes relative prices to depart from their Ramsey optimum. In this model, if the two consumer goods are equal substitutes for leisure, the Ramsey optimum calls for

uniform taxation of these two goods or, equivalently, simply a tax on labor. If the two consumer goods are not equal substitutes for leisure, the Ramsey optimum will differ. In particular, if the dirty good is a weaker substitute for leisure than the clean good, the Ramsey optimum calls (on non-environmental grounds) for higher taxation of the dirty good than the clean good. Under these conditions, if initially the two goods were equally taxed (or, equivalently, if the only tax in place were the labor tax), then imposing a new tax on the dirty good could produce a tax-interaction effect of smaller magnitude than the revenue-recycling effect. For a more detailed discussion, see Bovenberg and Goulder (1998).

12. See GPB, appendix B.
13. This framework abstracts from the heterogeneity of production or abatement cost functions across firms in a given industry: all producers of a given good are regarded as identical. Considerations of heterogeneity can importantly influence the choice among policy instruments. In particular, heterogeneous abatement cost functions make a policy of tradable pollution permits attractive relative to one of fixed pollution quotas, since trades can be a key mechanism for creating production efficiency (equality of marginal abatement costs). These heterogeneity issues are important, but can largely be examined separately from the issues emphasized in this paper.
14. The taxation of rents does not change the qualitative results, except in the limiting case where 100 percent of the rents are taxes. This limiting case corresponds to the pollution tax case already examined. For further discussion of this issue, see GPB and Fullerton and Metcalf (1997).
15. It is implicitly assumed that marginal environmental benefits are constant or decreasing in the amount of abatement.
16. This value is consistent with values obtained in empirical investigations. See, in particular, Ballard et al. (1985) and Browning (1987).
17. For further discussion, see GPB.
18. In keeping with the analytical model of section II, we use the subscript 'L' to refer to the distortionary factor tax. The points raised here apply to economies in which there are several distortionary taxes, including taxes on capital as well as labor.
19. Bovenberg (1996), Goulder (1995), and Bovenberg and Goulder (1998) analyse a range of complicating issues.
20. In efficiency terms, one factor of production is overtaxed relative to another if the tax on this factor has a larger marginal excess burden per dollar of revenue than the tax on the other factor.
21. For a theoretical treatment of the tax-shifting issue, see Bovenberg and de Mooij (1994b), and Bovenberg and Goulder (1997).
22. See, for example, Ballard et al. (1985), Fullerton and Mackie (1987), Jorgenson and Yun (1990), Lucas (1990), and Goulder and Thalmann (1993).
23. Goulder (1995) surveys these studies.
24. The quota policy does not necessarily raise zero revenue. This policy will tend to raise revenue insofar as quota rents are taxed, and will tend to lose revenue insofar as the policy causes a loss of overall real income and a reduction in the labor tax base.
25. See also Ng (1980), who analysed environmental subsidies in the presence of prior tax distortions.
26. In fact the subsidy to the clean good (financed by an increase in the tax on labor) is equivalent to a pollution tax on the dirty good (financing a decrease in the tax on labor). See Fullerton (1997).
27. Fullerton and Metcalf model this as a constraint on the emissions-labor ratio. In their model, this has the same economic impact as a constraint on the emissions-output ratio.
28. More precisely, the technology mandate produces two tax-interaction effects and two revenue-recycling effects. As indicated by Fullerton and Metcalf, the mandated technology is equivalent to the combination of a subsidy to the use of the clean input and a tax on emissions. The subsidy and tax components respectively account for negative (in efficiency terms) and positive revenue-recycling effects, which cancel out, and positive and negative tax-interaction effects, which also cancel out (at the first unit of abatement).
29. This last case is examined by Bovenberg and de Mooij (1996) and Williams (1999).
30. Fullerton and Metcalf (1997) point out that pollution regulation through grandfathered permits creates scarcity rents that remain in private (that is, the regulated firm's) hands, and indicate

that this accounts for the fact that the marginal costs of incremental abatement are strictly positive. The creation of scarcity rents is an example of the government's bringing about a lump-sum transfer to the private sector.

31. Real-world environmental taxes and other regulations involve 'large,' as opposed to incremental, changes in the level of pollution. Numerical simulation is usually necessary to evaluate the efficiency implications of these changes.
32. The costs of a 10-million-ton reduction are \$2182 and \$1649 million under the grandfathering and auctioning of emissions allowances, respectively. Although this paper points out the efficiency drawbacks of the grandfathering element of SO_2 emissions regulation under the 1990 Clean Air Act Amendments, it is not intended to be a wholesale critique of this legislation. We would note that the 1990 legislation achieved major reforms in environmental regulation by introducing a flexible, incentive-based approach to regulation in the form of emissions allowance trading. This approach has a number of theoretical advantages over the traditional, less flexible methods (see, for example, Tietenberg (1985)), and empirical studies already indicate that this approach will yield a dramatic reduction in overall compliance costs, compared to conventional approaches (see, for example, Burtraw [1996], and Ellerman and Montero (1996)).
33. The marginal benefits are assumed to be constant, that is, independent of the level of abatement.
34. The tax and quota policies actually would be oriented toward the use of carbon-based fuels (oil, coal, and natural gas) rather than emissions of CO_2 itself. Emissions from the combustion of these fuels are strictly proportional to carbon content, so that taxing or regulating the use of these fuels is virtually equivalent to taxing or regulating CO_2 emissions. A complication is posed by non-combustion or feedstock uses of these fuels. In the US, such uses represent a very small share (less than four percent) of total use.
35. See, for example, Nordhaus (1991), Peck and Teisberg (1993), and Fankhauser (1994).
36. Several studies suggest that the marginal climate-related damages increase with CO_2 concentrations. If this is the case, and if CO_2 concentrations increase through time, then marginal damages from CO_2 emissions (or marginal benefits from CO_2 emissions abatement) will increase over time. Under such circumstances the prospects for efficiency gains under a quota policy improve with time.
37. Similarly, Browning (1997) finds that monopoly pricing exacerbates pre-existing distortions in factor markets. Hence the efficiency costs of monopoly pricing increase with the magnitude of pre-existing factor tax rates. Browning estimates that monopoly pricing in the US is ten times more costly than it would be in the absence of prior factor taxes.

REFERENCES

Ballard, Charles, L., John B. Shoven, and John Whalley (1985), 'General Equilibrium Computations of the Marginal Welfare Costs of Taxes in the U.S.', *American Economic Review*, **75**(1), 128–38.

Bovenberg, A. Lans (1996), 'Environmental Policy, Distortionary Labor Taxation, and Employment: Pollution Taxes and the Double Dividend', in Carlo Carraro, Yiannis Katsoulacos, and Anastasios Xepapadeas (eds), *Environmental Policy and Market Structure*, Dordrecht: Kluwer Academic Publishers.

Bovenberg, A. Lans and Ruud A. de Mooij (1994a), 'Environmental Levies and Distortionary Taxation', *American Economic Review*, **84**(4), 1085–9.

Bovenberg, A. Lans and Ruud A. de Mooij (1994b), 'Environmental Taxation and Labor Market Distortions', *European Journal of Political Economy*, **10**(4), 655–83.

Bovenberg, A. Lans and Ruud A. de Mooij (1996), 'Environmental Taxation and the Double-Dividend: The Role of Factor Substitution and Capital Mobility', in

C. Carraro and D. Siniscalco (eds), *Environmental Fiscal Return and Unemployment*, Dordrecht: Kluwer.

Bovenberg, A. Lans and Lawrence H. Goulder (1996), 'Optimal Environmental Taxation in the Presence of Other Taxes: General Equilibrium Analyses', *American Economic Review*, September.

Bovenberg, A. Lans, and Lawrence H. Goulder (1997), 'Costs of Environmentally Motivated Taxes in the Presence of Other Taxes: General Equilibrium Analyses', *National Tax Journal*, **50**(1), March.

Bovenberg, A. Lans and Lawrence H. Goulder (1998), 'Environmental Taxation', in A. Auerbach and M. Feldstein, (eds), *Handbook of Public Economics*, New York: North Holland, forthcoming.

Bovenberg, A. Lans and F. van der Ploeg (1994), 'Environmental Policy, Public Finance and the Labor Market in a Second-Best World', *Journal of Public Economies*, **55**, 349–70.

Browning, E. K. (1987), 'On the Marginal Welfare Cost of Taxation', *American Economic Review*, **77**, 11–23.

Browning, E. K. (1997), 'The Welfare Cost of Monopoly and Other Output Distortions', *Journal of Public Economics*, **66**, 127–44.

Burtraw, Dallas (1996), 'The SO_2 Emissions Trading Program: Cost Savings Without Allowance Trades', *Contemporary Economic Policy*, **XIV**(2), April, 79–94.

Ellerman, A. Denny and Juan Pablo Montero (1996), 'Why Are Allowance Prices So Low? An Analysis of the SO_2 Emissions Trading Program', CEEPR 96-001, Massachusetts Institute of Technology, February.

Fankhauser, Samuel (1994), 'The Social Costs of Greenhouse Gas Emissions: An Expected Value Approach', *The Energy Journal* **15**, 157–84.

Fullerton, Don (1997), 'Environmental Levies and Distortionary Taxation: Comment', *American Economic Review*, **87**.

Fullerton, Don and J. Mackie (1987), 'Investment Allocation and Growth under the Tax Reform Act of 1986', in *Compendium of Tax Research 1987*, Office of Tax Analysis of the US Department of the Treasury, Washington, DC, pp. 131–71.

Fullerton, Don and Gilbert Metcalf (1997), 'Environmental Controls, Scarcity Rents, and Pre-Existing Distortions', NBER Working paper 6091, Cambridge, Mass.; July.

Goulder, Lawrence H. (1995), 'Environmental Taxation and the 'Double Dividend': A Reader's Guide', *International Tax and Public Finance*, **2**(2), 157–83.

Goulder, Lawrence H. and Philippe Thalmann (1993), 'Approaches to Efficient Capital Taxation: Leveling the Playing Field vs. Living by the Golden Rule', *Journal of Public Economics*, **50**, 169–96.

Goulder, Lawrence H., Ian W. H. Parry and Dallas Burtraw (1997), 'Revenue-Raising vs. Other Approaches to Environmental Protection: The Critical Significance of Pre-Existing Tax Distortions', *RAND Journal of Economics*, Winter.

Goulder, Lawrence H., Ian W. H. Parry, Roberton C. Williams III and Dallas Burtraw (1999), 'The Cost-Effectiveness of Alternative Instruments for Environmental Protection in a Second-best Setting', *Journal of Public Economics*, forthcoming.

Jorgenson, Dale and Kun-Young Yun (1990), 'Tax Policy and the Cost of Capital', Oxford: Oxford University Press.

Lee, Dwight R. and Walter S. Misiolek (1986), 'Substituting Pollution Taxation for General Taxation: Some Implications for Efficiency in Pollution Taxation', *Journal of Environmental Economics and Management*, **13**, 338–47.

Lucas, Robert E. (1990), 'Supply-side Economics: An Analytical Review', *Oxford Economic Papers*, **42**, 293–316.

Ng, Y. K. (1980), 'Optimal Corrective Taxes or Subsidies when Revenue-Raising Imposes an Excess Burden', *American Economic Review*, **70**, 744–51.

Nordhaus, William D. (1991), 'To Slow or Not to Slow: The Economics of the Greenhouse Effect', *The Economic Journal*, **101**, 920–37.

Oates, Wallace E. (1993), 'Pollution Charges as a Source of Public Revenues', in Herbert Giersch (ed.), *Economic Progress and Environmental Concerns*, Berlin: Springer-Verlag, pp. 135–52.

Oates, Wallace E. (1995), 'Green Taxes: Can We Protect the Environment and Improve the Tax System at the Same Time?', *Southern Economic Journal*, **61**(4), 914–22.

Oates, Wallace E. and Robert M. Schwab (1988), 'Economic Competition among Jurisdictions: Efficiency Enhancing or Distortion Inducing?', *Journal of Public Economics*, **35**, 333–54, April.

Oates, Wallace E. and Diana L. Strassmann (1984), 'Effluent Fees and Market Structure', *Journal of Public Economics*, **24**: 29–46.

Parry, Ian W. H. (1995), 'Pollution Taxes and Revenue Recycling', *Journal of Environmental Economics and Management*, **29**, S64–S77.

Parry, Ian W. H. (1997), 'Environmental Taxes and Quotas in the Presence of Distorting Taxes in Factor Markets', *Resource and Energy Economics*.

Parry, Ian W. H., Roberton Williams and Lawrence H. Goulder (1999), 'When Can Carbon Abatement Policies Increase Welfare? The Fundamental Role of Distorted Factor Markets', *Journal of Environmental Economic and Management*, **37**, 52–84.

Peck, Stephen C. and Thomas J. Teisberg (1993), 'Global Warming Uncertainties and the Value of Information: An Analysis Using CETA', *Resource and Energy Economics*, **15**, 71–98.

Pigou, A.C. (1938), *The Economics of Welfare* (4th Edition). London: Weidenfeld and Nicolson.

Repetto, Robert, Roger C. Dower, Robin Jenkins and Jacqueline Geoghegan (1992), *Green Fees: How a Tax Shift Can Work for the Environment and the Economy*, World Resources Institute, November.

Sandmo, Agnar (1975), 'Optimal Taxation in the Presence of Externalities', *Swedish Journal of Economics*, **77**.

Terkla, David (1984), 'The Efficiency Value of Effluent Tax Revenues', *Journal of Environmental Economics and Management*, **11**, 107–23.

Tietenberg, T.H. (1985), *Emissions Trading: An Exercise In Reforming Pollution Policy*, Washington, DC: Resources for the Future.

Williams, Roberton C. III (1999), 'Revisiting the Cost of Protectionism: The Role of Tax Distortions in the Labor Market', *Journal of International Economics*, forthcoming.

5. The positive political economy of instrument choice in environmental policy

Nathaniel O. Keohane, Richard L. Revesz, and Robert N. Stavins*

1 INTRODUCTION

The design of environmental policy requires that two central questions be addressed: (1) what is the desired level of environmental protection? and (2) what policy instruments should be used to achieve this level of protection? With respect to the second question, thirty years of positive political reality in the United States have diverged strikingly from the recommendations of normative economic theory. Our purpose in this paper is to explain why.

Four gaps between normative theory and positive reality merit particular attention. First, despite the well-known economic advantages of market-based instruments,[1] command-and-control standards have been used much more frequently (US Congress, Office of Technology Assessment, 1995). Second, when command-and-control standards have been used, the required level of pollution abatement has generally been far more stringent for new sources than for existing sources. This dual system may actually worsen pollution by encouraging firms to keep older, dirtier plants in operation (Stewart, 1981).[2] Third, in the relatively rare instances in which market-based instruments have been adopted, they have nearly always taken the form of tradable permits rather than emission taxes,[3] although economic theory suggests that the optimal choice between the two is dependent upon case-specific factors.[4] Moreover, the initial allocation of such permits has been through 'grandfathering,' or free initial distribution based on existing levels of pollution,[5] rather than through auctions, despite the economic superiority of the latter mechanism.[6] There are four alternative market-based instruments available: taxes, revenue-neutral taxes, auctioned permits, and grandfathered permits. Despite the numerous trade-offs that exist in normative economic terms, the US experience has been dominated by one choice – grandfathered permits. A fourth, conceptually different, gap, between prior and current political practice, is also worthy of attention: in recent years, the political process has been more receptive to market-based instruments,[7] even though they continue to be a small part of the overall portfolio of existing environmental laws and regulations. After being largely ignored for so long, why have incentive-based instruments begun to gain acceptance in recent years?

Commentators have advanced various explanations for the existence of these four gaps between normative theory and positive reality. Some explanations emerge from formal theories. Others take the form of informal hypotheses: they purport to explain certain aspects of environmental policy, but are not part of a formal theory of political behavior. In this paper, we review, evaluate, and extend these explanations. Moreover, we place these disparate explanations within the framework of an equilibrium model of instrument choice in environmental policy, based upon the metaphor of a political market.

The scope of the paper is intentionally limited. Our emphasis is on the control of pollution rather than the management of natural resources. We treat Congress, rather than administrative agencies, as the locus of instrument choice decisions and we view legislators (rather than regulators) as the 'suppliers' of regulation.[8] Moreover, we focus exclusively on the choice among the instruments, such as tradable permits, taxes, and standards, used to achieve a given level of environmental protection. We do not explore the related issues of how the level of protection is chosen or enforced. Nor do we address the issue of why Congress chooses to delegate authority to administrative agencies in the first place (Fiorina, 1982). Finally, our outlook is positive, not normative: we seek to understand why we have the set of tools we do, rather than which tools are desirable.

The next section presents the key features of our market framework. In Part 3, we consider the demand for environmental policy instruments, and in Part 4, we examine the supply side. Part 5 offers concluding remarks.

2 A MARKET FRAMEWORK FOR EXAMINING INSTRUMENT CHOICE

The metaphor of the 'political market' is a fairly common one, especially among economists and public choice theorists interested in the politics of regulation.[9] Some theorists have contemplated the market for votes *within* a legislature – with legislators acting both as demanders and as suppliers of votes. Others have modeled politicians as brokers in a market between those who 'demand' benefits (firms and special interests) and those who 'supply' them (taxpayers). Finally, perhaps the most common approach (and the one we take in this paper) focuses on the exchange between legislators and constituents or interest groups.

We use the market metaphor to provide a framework for synthesizing various theories of instrument choice. In our simplified model of the legislature as a political market, interest groups (the 'demanders') provide 'currency' in the form of political resources in return for legislators' support for a given instrument in a specific policy context. A schematic view of this political market is provided in Figure 5.1. For each instrument, a competitive equilibrium is determined by the interaction of the aggregate supply of political support and the aggregate demand for such support. This equilibrium determines the aggregate support in the legislature for a particular instrument The legislative outcome – the choice of a policy instrument – then depends upon the relative degrees of support generated for alternative policy instruments.

In the following sections we describe the political market's commodity and currency, and then discuss the origins of regulatory demand and supply, respectively. Finally in this part, we discuss the nature of political market equilibria and the legislative outcomes that result.

2.1 The Political Market's Commodity and Currency

We view each legislator as supplying some degree of support for a given regulatory instrument. Interest groups seek to secure support from legislators in the political market. Importantly, we take this commodity to be *homogeneous* among legislators. That is, the support produced by one legislator is equivalent to (a perfect substitute for) support produced by any other legislator. Hence, we think of this commodity as 'effective support.'[10] It is a measure of impact (output), not of effort (input).

To be sure, different legislators require differing amounts of effort to produce a unit of effective support. These variations in productivity are due to such factors as the size and effectiveness of members' staffs, their seniority, their committee assignments, and their leadership positions, including committee chairmanships. Moreover, a legislator's effort (the 'input' into the production of support) may encompass a much larger range of activities than simply voting for a given instrument: among other things, a legislator might hold hearings, attend committee markups, draft or sponsor legislation, insert statements into committee reports, propose amendments, seek to influence colleagues, or make behind-the-scenes deals.[11]

We take the political currency in this market to be resources for the legislator's re-election: not only votes, but also monetary and other contributions.[12] An environmental interest group, for example, may publicly endorse a candidate for office, or may volunteer time and effort to mobilize votes in a legislator's district. Other forms of 'payment' (assistance) to legislators, such as time spent drafting legislation or policy information provided to the legislator, are also valued

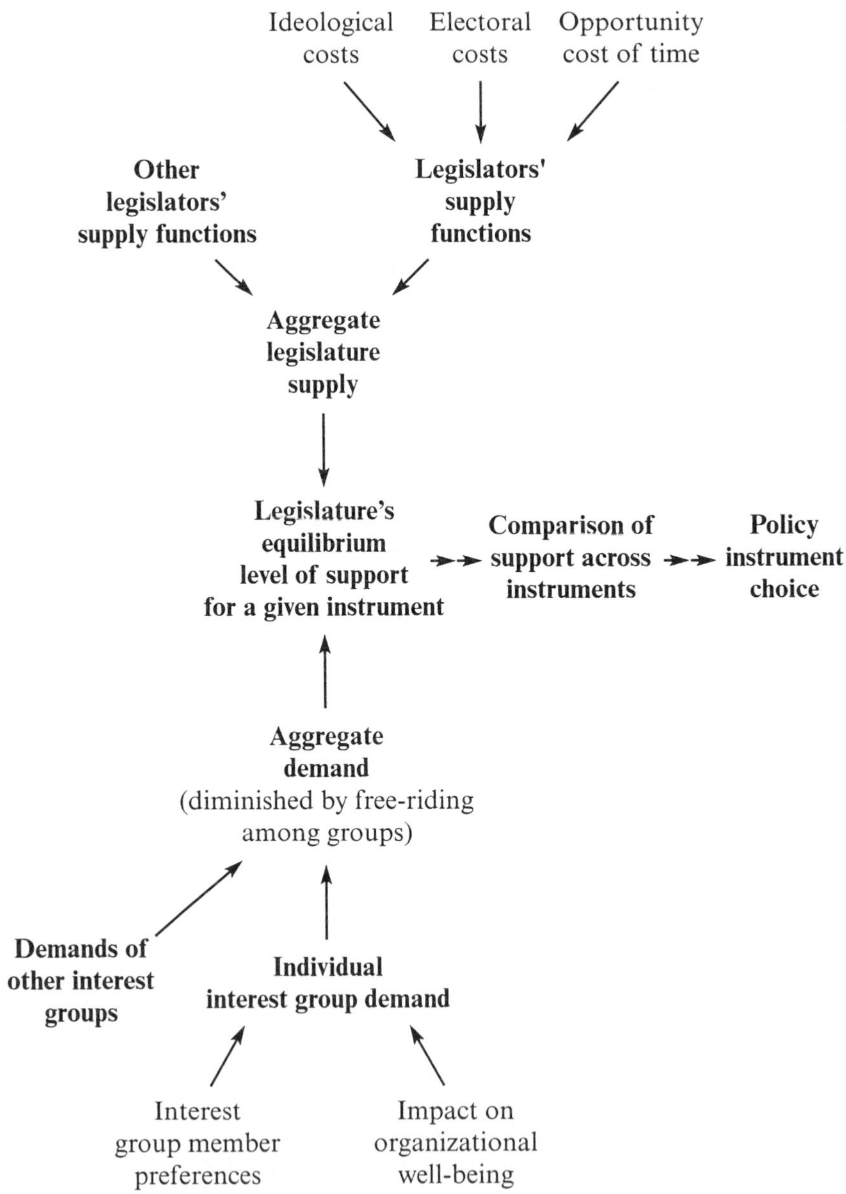

Figure 5.1 An equilibrium framework for examining the political market

by a legislator seeking re-election, since association with the interest group may increase the legislator's support, and the time saved by the legislator may be spent on activities that generate home district votes. We incorporate home district votes, financial contributions, and nonmonetary contributions in the currency of 'resources,' and we adopt a monetary numeraire simply for purposes of convenience.

2.2 Origins of Demand for Environmental Policy Instruments

Demand for the support of legislators comes from diverse interest groups, including environmental advocacy organizations, private firms, and trade associations. Each demander has its own demand function: a decreasing marginal willingness-to-pay for a legislator's policy support. For individuals in particular (as well as for firms), political demands are expressed by interest groups, raising the possibility of free-riding.

2.2.1 Firms and individuals

Firms are affected by environmental regulation through the costs they incur in producing goods and services. Consider a price-taking firm wishing to maximize its profit from producing a single product and that employs a set of factors in its production, each of which has some cost associated with it. One of these factors or inputs is the set of relevant features of the regulatory environment. In seeking to maximize profits, the firm chooses levels of all its inputs, including the efforts it puts into securing its desired regulatory environment. In the simplest model, firms have a decreasing marginal willingness to pay to secure particular policy instruments, producing a downward-sloping factor demand curve for legislative support.[13]

The choice of environmental policy instruments can also have an effect on individuals. For example, individuals can be affected by the level of environmental quality that results from the use of a particular instrument,[14] or by the costs of environmental protection that are reflected in the prices of the goods and services they buy. Individuals might even derive some direct utility from knowing that a particular type of policy instrument was employed. It seems reasonable to assume that individuals will respond to an increase in the 'price of legislative support' relative to other goods by reducing their demand for legislators' services, yielding a downward-sloping demand function for legislative support.[15]

Individuals can be thought of as having attributes of 'consumers,' 'environmentalists,' and 'workers.' These three categories are neither mutually exclusive nor exhaustive. We think of individuals as 'consumers' to the degree that the choice of environmental policy instrument affects them through its impact on the prices of goods and services; as 'environmentalists' to the degree that they are affected by the impact of instrument choice on the level of environmental quality; and as 'workers' to the degree that they are affected by environmental policy through its impact on the demand for labor, and hence their wages.

2.2.2 Interest groups

Because there are significant costs of lobbying and because the target of demand – the public policy – is a public good,[16] an individual and even a firm will receive relatively small rewards for any direct lobbying efforts. For individuals, the marginal costs of lobbying are likely to outweigh the perceived marginal benefits over much of the relevant range of lobbying activity, and individuals will undersupply lobbying, hoping instead to free ride on the efforts of others. Although some large firms maintain offices in Washington, DC to facilitate direct lobbying of the Congress, most of the demand for public policies from both firms and individuals is transmitted through organized interest groups.

The free-riding problem that stands in the way of individual lobbying efforts can also be a significant obstacle to the formation of interest groups (Olson, 1965). For an interest group to organize, it must find a way to overcome the free-riding problem: it must offer its members enough benefits to make the costs of membership worthwhile. For a citizen group, such as an environmental advocacy organization, these benefits are likely to include: 'material incentives,' such as newsletters, workshops, or gifts; 'solidary incentives,' essentially the benefits derived from social interaction; and 'purposive incentives,' the personal satisfaction derived from membership in an organization whose activities one supports (Rothenberg, 1992; Wilson, 1973). Among citizen groups, taxpayer and consumer organizations may face greater free-riding problems than environmental groups: it is likely that environmental groups have more material incentives (calendars, stickers, outdoor trips, and so forth) and more compelling purposive incentives (the moral mission of 'saving the planet') to attract potential members.

In order to overcome their own set of free-rider problems, trade associations can offer a range of benefits to their members that non-members do not enjoy, including: influence over policy goals; information on policy developments; reports on economic trends; and participation in an annual convention (Olson, 1965). Compared with citizen groups, trade associations may have significant advantages in overcoming free-riding: they are usually smaller, making the contributions of each member more significant; and even substantial annual dues may be negligible costs for member firms (Wilson, 1973). Hence, we might expect that private industry interests will be over-represented in the political process compared with citizen groups.

Once organized, an interest group may not simply aggregate the political demands of its members. Rather, the interest group (or more precisely, its staff) has its own self interests, which may diverge from the goals of its members. If members are unable to observe the output or effort of the interest group staff, a principal–agent problem may arise between the members (the principals) and the staff (their agents). The result can be 'slack' between what members want and what the organization actually does. A trade association, for example, may not only want to maximize the profits of its member firms; it may also seek to expand its membership or to increase revenue from member dues. Similarly, the objective function of an environmental group may include not only the level of environmental quality, but also factors such as membership size, budget, and reputation among various constituencies which affect the organization's health and viability.[17]

In seeking to secure as much support as possible in the legislature for its preferred outcome, an interest group must decide how to allocate its scarce resources. The total benefits to an interest group of the legislature's support for an instrument rise with the degree of support offered, but there are decreasing marginal returns. As in the case of individuals and firms, a unit increase in support when the legislature is already very favorably disposed to one's position is worth less than a unit increase in support by a lukewarm or previously unsupportive legislature. This characteristic produces a downward-sloping demand function: an interest group's marginal willingness-to-pay for support decreases as the legislature's total support increases.[18]

2.3 Origins of Supply of Environmental Policy Instruments

We consider a case of a legislator who derives utility from a constellation of factors made possible by being a legislator: making public policy, doing good things for the country or for her district, satisfying ideological beliefs, having prestige and the perquisites of office, and so on. To continue getting utility from these factors, the legislator must be re-elected. We assume that legislators seek to maximize their expected utility. In choosing a policy position (level of support for a proposed instrument), therefore, the legislator takes into account the effort required to provide that support, the inherent satisfaction she derives from providing that level of support, and the effects her position will be likely to have on her chances of re-election.[19]

Thus, our framework allows for the legislator's supply function to consist of three components: (1) the opportunity cost of time (effort) required to provide a given degree of support for a policy instrument; (2) the psychological cost of supporting an instrument *despite* one's ideological beliefs (if supporting the instrument is consistent with one's ideological beliefs, then this is a 'negative cost,' that is, a benefit); and (3) the opportunity cost (in terms of reduced probability of re-election) of supporting an instrument not favored by one's electoral constituency (this is also a 'negative cost' if supporting the instrument is consistent with one's constituents' positions).

The first component emerges from the individual legislator's productivity in providing 'effective support.' Some legislators are more efficient producers of effective support from a given amount of effort than others for a host of reasons, including the size and effectiveness of their staffs, their seniority in the legislature, and – importantly – their membership and leadership on relevant committees. If each legislator experiences decreasing marginal returns to effort in the production of effective support, the generic 'support production function' will be concave. By placing a value on the opportunity cost of time and effort, we derive a convex opportunity cost function. In turn, such a cost function implies an upward sloping marginal opportunity cost of effort, as shown in Figure 5.2.[20]

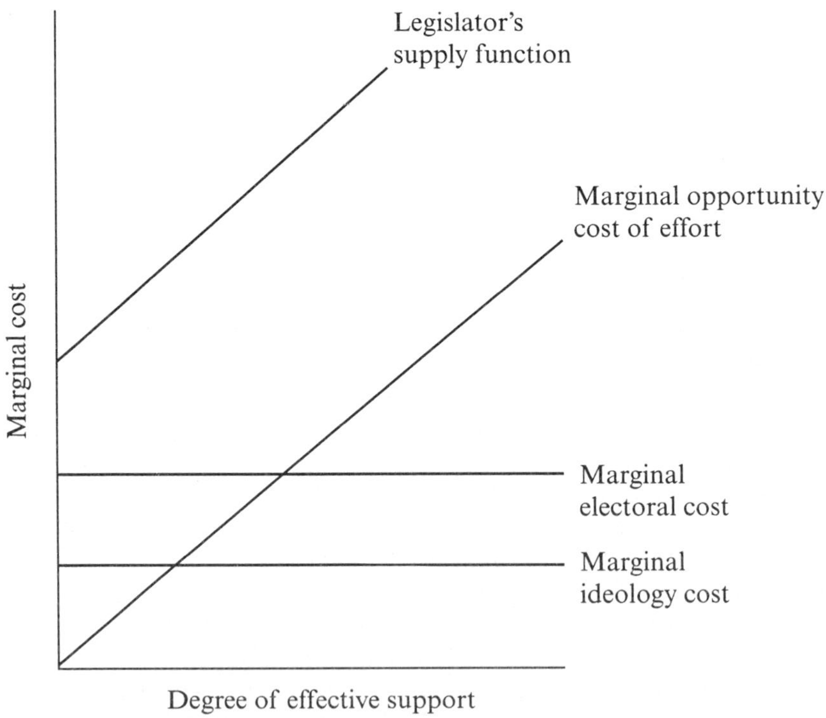

Figure 5.2 Opportunity costs and the supply of political support by an individual legislator

Next, we posit that a legislator derives disutility from acting inconsistently with her ideology. Thus, we introduce the psychological cost of supporting a policy that is inconsistent with one's ideological beliefs. As suggested above, this cost would be negative (a benefit) if one were ideologically predisposed to favor the particular policy. In either case, it is conceivable that these marginal (psychological) costs might be increasing or decreasing (in absolute value) with the degree of support, but for ease of presentation we portray this marginal cost as constant in Figure 5.2. In this case, the legislator's ideology has no effect on the slope of the combined marginal cost function; rather, ideology shifts the function upwards (for inconsistency with ideology) or downwards (for consistency with ideology).

The final component of the legislator's supply function is the marginal 'electoral cost' of support. To the extent that a legislator offers support to an instrument not favored by her electoral constituency, her re-election becomes less likely, forcing the legislator to expend more resources to achieve a given probability of re-election. This effect can be either direct in the form of lost votes from constituents unhappy with the legislator's position, or indirect as a result of the opposition of interest groups unhappy with the legislator's position, which through protest and grassroots mobilization could affect the constituents' assessment of the legislator.[21] Again, this effect is a 'negative cost' if supporting the instrument is consistent with one's constituents' positions. As with ideological costs, these marginal electoral opportunity costs could be increasing or decreasing with the level of the legislator's support, but to keep things simple we draw them as constant (and positive) in Figure 5.2.[22]

The overall (individual) marginal cost function – the legislator's supply-of-support function – is simply the vertical summation of these three components: opportunity costs of effort, ideological costs, and constituency costs (Figure 5.2). The amount of support for a policy instrument that a legislator would supply at zero price, that is, in the absence of any contributions helpful to advancing the member's goals, including her re-election, is represented in Figure 5.3 as the 'preferred point,' the intersection of the supply function with the horizontal axis. In this framework, the legislator can be induced to offer greater degrees of support than this preferred point by offers of 'political compensation' which offset the legislator's opportunity costs arising from such support.

Thus, the legislator has an upward-sloping marginal opportunity-cost or supply function, beginning at her preferred degree of support along the horizontal axis. The intersection of the supply function with the horizontal axis can take place at either a positive or a negative degree of support (see S_1 and S_3, respectively, in Figure 5.3). A politician who is strongly opposed to a given instrument because of a combination of her own ideology and her constituents' preferences will have a supply function with a negative intercept on the horizontal axis (and a positive intercept on the vertical axis). For such a legislator, a positive, nonmarginal shadow price of political compensation is required for any positive degree of support to be forthcoming (see point *A* in Figure 5.3).

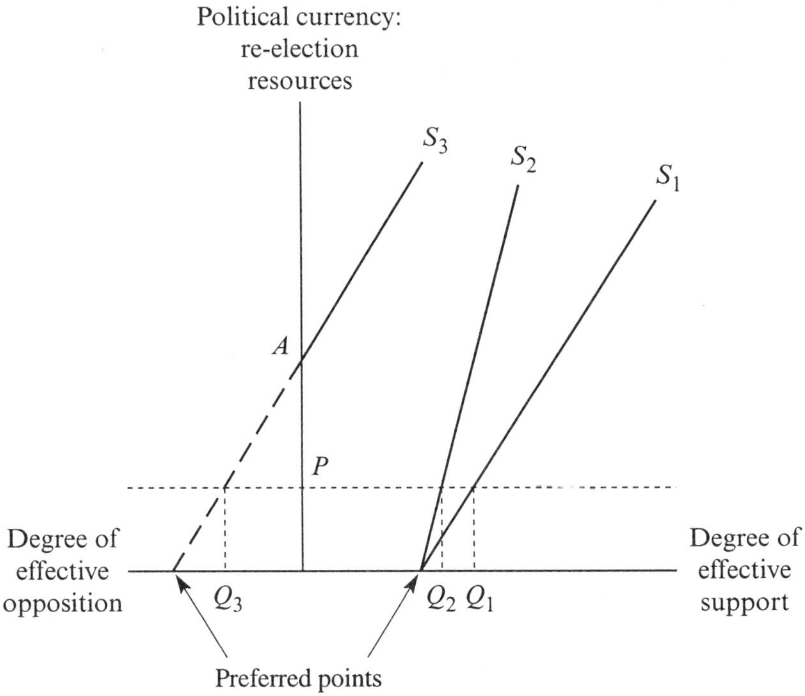

Figure 5.3 Supplies of political support by individual legislators

A legislator's supply function is affected by several exogenous factors. First, an exogenous increase in the negative impact of a given instrument on a legislator's constituents (for example, the construction in the legislator's district of a new factory which would have to pay pollution taxes) would increase the legislator's opportunity costs of supporting that instrument. Conversely, an exogenous increase in the benefits of an instrument to the legislator's constituents (for example, the expansion of a firm in the district which produced a mandated abatement technology) would decrease the legislator's opportunity costs. Second, the position of the legislator's political party is also relevant. Parties supply funds and organizational support in re-election campaigns. Moreover, leadership posts in the party offer opportunities for increased effectiveness in the legislature. Obviously, parties are likely to be more generous with legislators who are loyal.[23] Third, the actions of other legislators will have a bearing on the costs of supplying support because of the possibilities for vote trading. For example, one legislator may care a great deal about the level of environmental protection chosen, while having only a slight preference for standards over taxes; another legislator may care less about the exact level but have a strong preference for taxes over standards, perhaps because of her own market-oriented ideology. In a logroll, both legislators could gain from vote trading, and such a logroll would affect both legislators' costs of supplying support for a given instrument. Fourth and finally, it is both the intent and the consequence of some lobbying activities to shift legislators' supply functions. In other words, in addition to being the primary demanders for alternative forms of regulation, organized interest groups can also play a role in determining the position and shape of legislators' supply functions. Lobbyists might attempt to: affect a legislator's ideologically-based perception of the merits of a proposed policy instrument (Kingdon, 1989); affect a legislator's perceptions of her constituents' policy preferences (Austen-Smith and Wright, 1994); and/or affect a legislator's effort-support production function through, for example, provision of information or technical support (Bauer, Pool, and Dexter, 1963).

2.4 Formation of Equilibria and Legislative Outcomes

Up to this point, we have focused on the origins of supply and demand for a single policy instrument. In many contexts, there will be a *set* of possible instruments considered for achieving a given policy goal: for example, a standard, tax, and a system of tradable permits. In addition, there will exist the possibility of doing nothing, that is, maintaining the status quo. Hence if N alternative instruments are under consideration, then there will be $N + 1$ possible choices of action.[24] We view each option as defining a 'political market' for effective support. On the demand side, each policy instrument may have an associated set of interest groups seeking to secure support for it. On the supply side, each policy instrument gives rise to its own set of legislator supply functions. A single legislator may be more efficient at producing support for one instrument than for another; she may have differing ideological attitudes towards different instruments; and the preferences of her re-election constituency may vary across instruments as well.

The legislative outcome is the choice of one of the $N + 1$ alternatives arising from the interactions of interest groups' demands for and legislators' supplies of support for alternative instruments. The degree of aggregate support for each instrument results from an equilibrium established in the legislature, and the outcome in the legislature favors the policy instrument with the greatest degree of total support.

In the following sections, we examine the component parts of this process. We first consider the nature of the aggregation of demand for a policy instrument across interest groups, and the aggregation of supplies of support for a policy instrument across members of the legislature. Then, we consider the formation of equilibria in the legislature for alternative policy instruments and the consequent choice of political outcome. Finally, we discuss alternative approaches to modeling this political market.

2.4.1 Aggregation of demand for policy instrument support

Typically, more than one interest group will be pressing for support from the legislature. How is such interest group demand to be aggregated?[25] In our framework, the most obvious approach for aggregating interest-group demand functions might be simply to sum, at each level of willingness-to-pay, the degrees of support each group demands at that price. Such demand aggregation makes sense for private goods, but the support the legislature provides is essentially a public good. Hence, an efficient approach might involve taking a given level of support and summing up what each interest group is (marginally) willing to pay for that degree of support; that is, vertical summation rather than horizontal summation of individual demands. Such an (efficient) approach is unlikely to reflect positive reality, however, as long as free-rider problems exist among interest groups. Therefore, the aggregate demand thus calculated represents the upper bound of actual aggregate demand, that is, the demand which would be experienced in the absence of free-riding.

2.4.2 Aggregation of supply of policy instrument options

Since, in this framework, the degree of support by individual legislators is denominated in terms of homogeneous units of 'effective support,' where the differences among legislators are incorporated in the production functions which underlie these individual marginal opportunity cost of effort functions (as well as the individual marginal ideology and electoral cost functions), the appropriate aggregation to derive the supply function for the legislature is the horizontal summation of the supply functions of individual legislators. As noted above, some legislators' supply functions may extend to the left of the vertical axis (for example, S_3 in Figure 5.3), corresponding to opposition to the instrument in question. Therefore, when the individual legislator supply functions are horizontally added, the aggregate supply function for the legislature represents the relevant *net* supply of support. Like the supply function for an individual legislator, the aggregate function for some instruments may intersect the vertical axis at a positive price.

2.4.3 Equilibrium support in the legislature for a policy instrument

We treat the legislature as operating as if it were a competitive market for the support for policy instruments.[26] Given the homogeneity of the commodity that is demanded and supplied, the number of members in the two houses of Congress, and the number of active interest groups, this seems like a reasonable first approximation. Thus, the equilibrium, aggregate level of 'effective support' provided for the policy instrument is that level for which aggregate supply equals aggregate demand (Q^* in Figure 5.4). This level is associated with a shadow price (P in Figure 5.4) representing the aggregate marginal willingness-to-pay for support in the legislature's equilibrium.

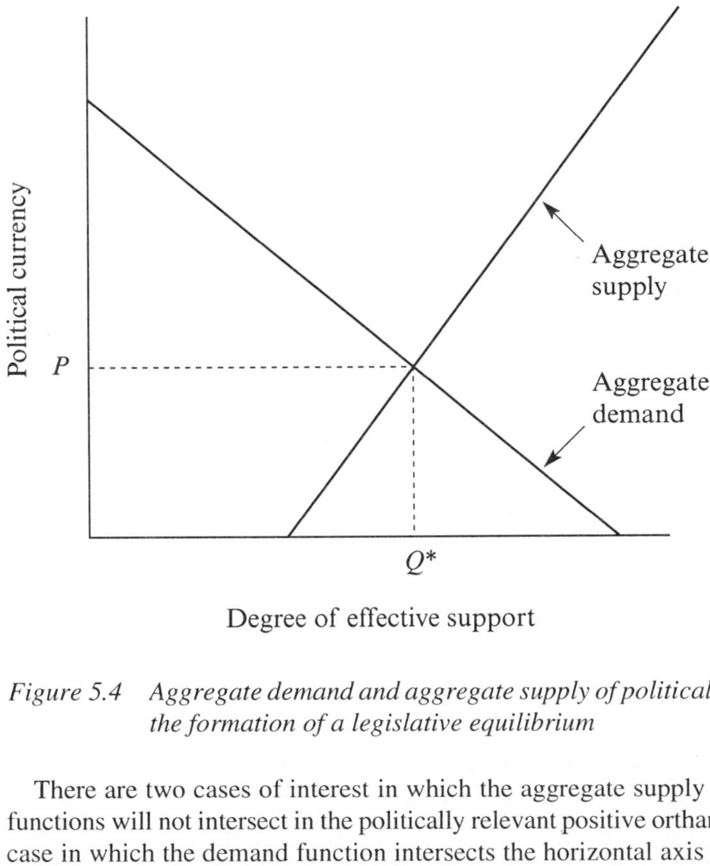

Figure 5.4 Aggregate demand and aggregate supply of political support and the formation of a legislative equilibrium

There are two cases of interest in which the aggregate supply and demand functions will not intersect in the politically relevant positive orthant. One is the case in which the demand function intersects the horizontal axis to the left of the legislature's 'aggregate preferred point' (see the gap between points B and E_A in Figure 5.5); that is, the maximum support demanded in the aggregate by interest groups (at zero price) is less than the legislature would provide on its own. In this case of 'excess supply,' it is reasonable to assume that the legislature will provide support at its preferred point (E_A). Given the likelihood of free-riding among interest groups, it would not be surprising if in certain instances the aggregate demand by interest groups fell short of the support a strongly committed legislature was willing to provide absent any lobbying. In this case the competitive equilibrium price is zero, and so each legislator provides support at her own preferred point.

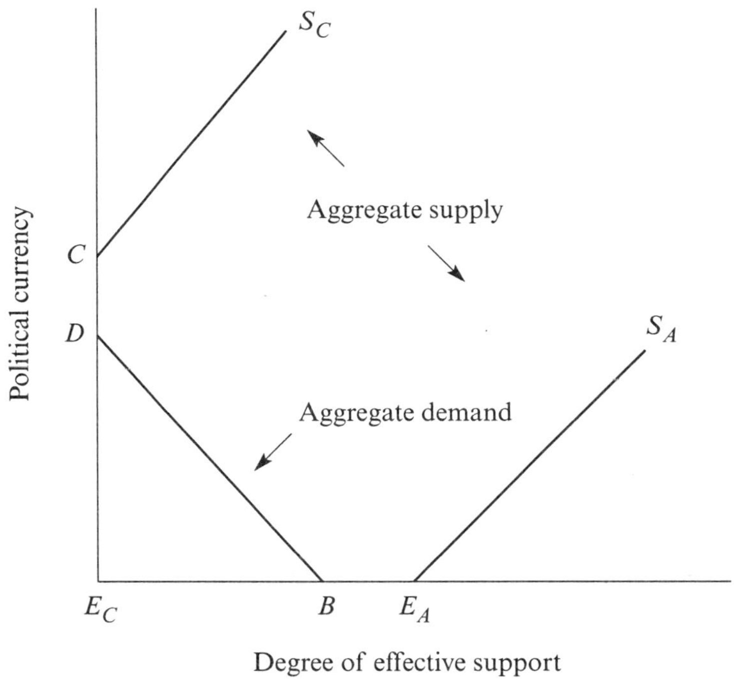

Figure 5.5 Degenerate cases in the political market

The second special case of interest might arise when a legislature so strongly opposes a policy that its upward-sloping aggregate supply function intersects the vertical axis at a positive price (point *C* in Figure 5.5). In this case, the supply function could conceivably lie entirely above the interest groups' aggregate demand function. The political price that such a legislature would require for a positive degree of support is simply greater than the interest groups' overall reservation price for obtaining such support (point *D* in Figure 5.5).

In this competitive political market framework, an individual legislator will tend to supply support for a particular policy instrument up to the point where her marginal opportunity costs of doing so are equivalent to the infinitely elastic demand for support she faces from interest groups, represented by the horizontal line through the point *P* in Figure 5.3 (derived from the equilibrium in Figure 5.4). Thus, a set of legislators with supply functions represented by S_1, S_2, and S_3 (Figure 5.3), would provide effective support of Q_1, Q_2, and Q_3, respectively.

The legislator with supply function S_3 provides a negative level of support, that is, opposition. An interest group might benefit from contributing to this legislator in the hope of reducing her degree of active opposition,[27] just as it can benefit by increasing the support of a 'friendly' legislator. It would take a level of demand (and political compensation) equivalent to point *A* in Figure 5.3 to move this same legislator to a position of inaction or indifference.

On the other hand, legislators such as those represented by S_1, and S_2 in Figure 5.3 derive benefits (negative costs) from supporting an instrument, no matter what the position of relevant interest groups. Not surprisingly, such friendly legislators end up supplying even greater levels of support in response to interest group demand.

2.4.4 Legislative outcomes

How do individual levels of support for policy instruments translate into policy outcomes? If our interest is in aggregate quantity of support (as defined), then total support is simply equal to the sum of the individual levels of equilibrium support, which is identical to the original market equilibrium. On the other hand, institutional processes that translate individual levels of support into a collective decision (for example, various kinds of voting mechanisms) may involve very different sorts of aggregation. In general, institutional features of the legislature will influence the nature of the appropriate aggregation.

First, the committee structure of Congress (especially in the House of Representatives) gives different legislators widely different levels of influence over policy (Shepsle and Weingast, 1987; Weingast and Marshall, 1988). Thus, legislators vary greatly in the effectiveness of the support they can supply for a given instrument. But in our framework, with its focus on degrees of effective support, this reality is already incorporated (through the political support production functions) and has no effect on the appropriate aggregation; it remains one of simple summation of individual equilibria. Second, legislative outcomes are affected by voting rules. The number of votes necessary for passage, taking into account the veto power of the executive, determines the level and distribution of support needed to pass a bill.[28] Furthermore, the order of voting on amendments and the nature of the final vote also affect the outcome.[29] This brings us to the important issue of how support is translated into votes. Whereas our 'degree of support' is a continuous variable, it may produce a binary variable, a vote. Any empirical implementation of this framework would need to address the linkage.[30] For our purposes, however, we can focus on the reality that, in general, the policy instrument chosen will be the alternative that has garnered the greatest aggregate support.

3 DEMAND FOR ENVIRONMENTAL POLICY INSTRUMENTS

Demand-side explanations for the choice among environmental policy instruments can be separated into four sectors of regulatory demand: firms, environmentalists, consumers, and labor.

3.1 Firms

Firms will tend to demand the policy instruments that promise the highest profits (or the least losses) from regulation. While all environmental regulation imposes costs of compliance on firms, not all instruments impose the same costs to achieve a given regulatory goal. Positive political economy explanations of firm demand for environmental regulation can be divided into three principal categories: firm preferences for one instrument over another arising from lower aggregate costs of compliance to industry as a whole; the presence of rents and entry barriers; and differential costs of compliance across firms in a given industry.[31]

3.1.1 Lower aggregate costs to an industry as a whole

All else being equal, firms will naturally tend to prefer regulatory instruments that have lower aggregate costs for the industry as a whole. Because market-based approaches are likely to be more cost-effective than command-and-control instruments, this suggests that private industry, as a whole, would be more supportive of market-based approaches in general. However, there is a crucial distinction between the aggregate costs for society and aggregate costs for private industry. Cost-effective instruments, by definition, minimize costs to society, but they vary in the proportion of that cost they place on polluters. The use of market-based instruments does not guarantee that firms' compliance costs will be less than those under command-and-control.

We can expect that firms will oppose regulatory instruments that shift a greater cost burden on to industry. For example, the virtually unanimous opposition by private industry to pollution taxes can be explained by the fact that under such schemes firms pay not only their private costs of compliance, but also the costs of tax payments to the government for all residual emissions.[32]

Similarly, under tradable permit schemes, firms bear equivalent costs if the initial distribution of the permits is by means of an auction. In contrast, under a tradable permit scheme with grandfathered permits, existing firms do not bear any cost for their residual emissions.[33]

These arguments suggest that private industry, as a whole, will prefer grandfathered permits *and* standards to other instruments. Grandfathered permits are cost-effective and minimize the burden placed on industry – at least on existing firms. Emissions standards may not fare as well on the total-cost criterion, but are likely to be preferred by firms over auctioned permits or taxes.

3.1.2 Generation of rents and erection of entry barriers

Certain types of regulations can actually augment firms' profits through the generation of rents and the erection of entry barriers. Consider an industry made up of identical firms in a long-run competitive equilibrium. If the government imposes a command-and-control standard which sets an allowable level of pollution for each firm, where firms can meet the standard only by reducing their output, the standard will lead to reduced total production and therefore an increase in price along the aggregate demand curve (Buchanan and Tullock, 1975). If the environmental restriction is not exceptionally severe, the new price will be above average cost for all firms, and firms will earn rents. Hence, in this very simple model, firms may prefer standards to no regulation at all, and firms will prefer standards to taxes, since a tax is a charge for a resource which otherwise is free.[34]

Firms, however, are not limited to the single response of cutting output. They can also reduce emissions by adopting a new technology or changing their input mix. In this more general and realistic scenario, depending on the stringency of the standards and other factors, command-and-control standards can still have the effect of providing rents to regulated firms (Maloney and McCormick, 1982). Here, too, under certain conditions, firms may prefer command-and-control standards to no regulation at all.[35]

The enhanced industry profitability that results from rents will be sustainable over the long term only in the presence of entry restrictions. Thus, firms regulated by a rent-generating instrument, such as command-and-control standards, will benefit if that instrument is linked to a mechanism that imposes barriers to entry. In theory, such a mechanism might prohibit new entry outright, but a more politically feasible approach would impose higher costs on new entrants (Stigler, 1971; Rasmusen and Zupan, 1991).

This body of theory helps explain why private firms (and their trade associations) may have strong demands for command-and-control standards, which create rents, and especially for considerably more stringent command-and-control standards for new sources, which create barriers to entry.[36] The theory thereby provides the beginnings of an explanation for the prevalence of such instruments in US environmental laws. Further, theory indicates that under certain conditions the regulated industry will be better off under such a scheme than under no regulation.

Although the theoretical arguments are strong, there are no conclusive empirical validations of these demand-side propositions. Direct empirical tests of firm demand for instruments – such as analyses of resources devoted to lobbying for instruments as a function of firms' stakes in an issue – are virtually non-existent. Instead, most empirical work in this area simply seeks to measure the benefits an industry receives under regulation. Thus, it is not instrument demand that is examined, but an underlying premise for such demand. Maloney and McCormick (1982) employed financial market event analysis in two regulatory cases to test whether the value of regulated firms, as measured by stock market prices, was positively affected by the announcement of regulation, as the economic theory of regulation would suggest. They found that cotton-dust standards promulgated by the US Occupational, Safety, and Health Administration (OSHA) raised the asset value of cotton producers, consistent with the notion that regulation increased firms' profits by creating rents. But a more comprehensive study by Hughes, Magat, and Ricks (1986) reached the opposite conclusion. This discussion also provides a positive political economy explanation for why marketbased instruments have virtually always taken the form of grandfathered tradable permits, or at least of why private firms should be expected to have strong demands for this means of permit allocation. In tradable permit schemes, grandfathering: (1) conveys scarcity rents to firms, since existing polluters are granted valuable economic resources for free; and (2) provides entry barriers, in that new entrants must purchase permits from existing holders. Hahn and McGartland (1989) provide anecdotal evidence for rent-seeking in the decision-making process over the Environmental Protection Agency's (EPA) implementation of the Montreal Protocol restricting the use and production of chlorofluorocarbons (CFCs). They argue that a rent-seeking model explains the positions of large producers, such as DuPont, which supported grandfathered tradable permits and opposed other implementation schemes, including an auction proposal.

The preceding discussion does not provide a compelling explanation for the prevalence of command-and-control standards over grandfathered tradable permits. In principle, either instrument could provide sustainable rents to existing firms. We must search elsewhere for positive political economy explanations of this phenomenon.

3.1.3 Differential costs across firms in an industry

A different explanation for the landscape of environmental policy instruments arises from the existence of differential costs of environmental compliance across firms. Because of this heterogeneity, a firm may support policy instruments that impose costs on it, as long as those costs affect it less than the industry average and thus give it a competitive advantage (Leone and Jackson, 1981; Oster, 1982). For example, firms with large refineries for which lead reduction involved relatively low costs were supportive of the tradable permit system by which the leaded content of gasoline was reduced in the 1980s (Kerr and Mare, 1995), whereas firms with smaller refineries were vehemently opposed.[37]

Similarly, the largest producers of CFCs – DuPont and Imperial Chemical Industries – supported a ban on CFCs in large part because they were best able to develop substitutes (Oye and Maxwell, 1995). Other empirical work, however, has cast doubt on the proposition that firms advocate instruments based on inter-industry or intra-industry transfers. Leone and Jackson (1981) found that legislators with a paper producer in their districts voted against water pollution control legislation, regardless of whether that producer stood to gain or lose relative to its competitors.

Another form of cost differential arises as a result of the erection of barriers to entry. It is important to distinguish here between the entry of new firms and the expansion of existing firms. The entry barriers of environmental regulation generally apply to both situations. Thus, within an industry, firms with no plans to expand would derive a greater benefit from entry barriers, which could discourage further growth by their competitors.

Conversely, firms with ambitious expansion plans relative to their existing operations would benefit from weaker barriers. Such firms might also try to structure barriers in a manner that would give them an advantage over newcomers. For example, the 'bubble' program of the Clean Air Act makes these barriers less onerous for existing firms because they can engage in intra-firm emissions trading. Under this program, a firm can reduce the emissions of an existing source by an amount at least equal to the emissions of the new source, instead of having to take the more costly step of meeting the command-and-control standard otherwise applicable to new sources.[38] The Clean Air Act's 'netting' policies, which allow intra-firm trading across time periods, also make expansion by an incumbent easier than entry by a new firm.

The mechanism for allocating tradable permits might also produce different winners and losers within an industry. Under a grandfathering scheme that allocated permits on the basis of emissions at the time of establishment of the tradable permit scheme, firms that invested in pollution abatement prior to regulation stand to lose, relative to their more heavily polluting competitors (Hahn and Noll, 1990).[39] Such firms might conceivably prefer the allocation of permits by means of an initial auction.[40]

3.2 Environmental Organizations

As noted above, we anticipate that the utility of an environmental advocacy group will be affected by both the organization's well-being and the level of environmental quality. First, organizational well-being may be measured partly by budgetary resources, which are a function of donor contributions. This financial concern can affect an organization's demand for specific policy instruments if such support attracts members, persuades donors to make contributions, or, more broadly, increases the visibility and prestige of the organization. Hence, an organization's demand for a given policy instrument is likely to be affected (*ceteris paribus*) by several factors: the likelihood that the instrument will be chosen by policy makers;[41] the degree to which the organization can be clearly identified with supporting the instrument; the magnitude of potential funding gains due to distinguishing itself from other environmental groups; and the ability to offer donors and members a compelling argument, on environmental-quality grounds, in support of the instrument.

A prominent example is provided by the Environmental Defense Fund's (EDF) enthusiastic and effective support of the SO_2 allowance trading system adopted as part of the Clean Air Act Amendments of 1990. With the Bush administration eager to back up the President's claim of being 'the environmental President,' and with key senior staff in the administration having strong predispositions to the use of market-based approaches, the proposal had a chance of succeeding. EDF had already become a champion of market-based approaches to environmental protection in other, less nationally prominent, domains. Now it faced an opportunity to strengthen that position and solidify its reputation as a pragmatic environmental organization willing to adopt new strategies involving less confrontation with private industry. By supporting tradable permits, EDF could seize a market niche in the environmental movement, distinguishing itself further from other groups. Importantly, EDF was able to make a powerful argument for tradable permits on environmental, as opposed to economic, grounds: the use of a cost-effective instrument would make it politically possible to achieve greater reductions in sulfur dioxide emissions than would otherwise be the case.

EDF is an outlier in this realm. Most environmental advocacy groups have been relatively hostile towards market-based instruments. This should not be terribly surprising. Considering their interest in strengthening environmental protection, environmental organizations might be expected to prefer command-and-control approaches to market-based schemes for three reasons. The first reason is philosophical: environmentalists have portrayed pollution taxes and tradable permits as 'licenses to pollute' (Kelman, 1981),[42] and they have voiced concerns that damages from pollution – to human health and to ecological well-being – are difficult or impossible to quantify and monetize, and thus cannot be summed up in a marginal damage function or captured by a Pigouvian tax rate (Kelman, 1981).

Second, environmental organizations may oppose market-based schemes on strategic grounds. Once implemented, permit levels and tax rates may be more difficult to alter than command-and-control standards. If permits are given the status of 'property rights,' an attempt to reduce pollution levels in the future may meet with 'takings' claims and demands for government compensation (Hahn and Noll, 1990). This concern, however, can be alleviated by an explicit statutory provision (like that contained in the acid rain provisions of the Clean

Air Act Amendments of 1990) stating that permits do not represent property rights, or by 'sunset' provisions that specify a particular period of time during which a permit is valid.

Likewise in the case of pollution taxes, if increased tax rates become desirable in response to new information about a pollutant or about the response of firms to the existing taxes, adjustment may be unlikely because raising tax rates is politically difficult. Furthermore, taxes have long been treated as 'political footballs' in the United States (as in the recent case of calls to reduce gasoline taxes). Hence, environmental organizations might oppose pollution taxes out of fear that they would be reduced or eliminated over time. A related strategic reason for why environmentalists might oppose the use of tax instruments is that a shift from command-and-control to tax-based environmental regulation would shift authority from environment committees in the Congress, frequently dominated by pro-environment legislators, to tax-writing committees, which are generally more conservative (Kelman, 1981).

Third, environmental organizations may object to decentralized instruments on technical grounds. Although market-based instruments are theoretically superior in terms of cost-effectiveness, problems may arise in translating theory into practice (Hahn and Axtell, 1995). For example, an emission tax or tradable permit scheme can lead to localized 'hot spots' with relatively high levels of ambient pollution. While this problem could be addressed through the use of permits or charge systems that are denominated in units of environmental degradation (Revesz, 1996), the design of such systems might be perceived as excessively cumbersome.

3.3 Labor

Since unions seek to protect jobs, they might be expected to oppose instruments likely to lead to plant closings or other large industrial dislocations. Under a tradable permit scheme, for example, firms might close their factories in heavily polluted areas, sell permits, and relocate to less polluted areas (Hahn and Noll 1990). In contrast, command-and-control standards have generally been tailored to protect aging plants. The threat of factory dislocation is a likely explanation of support from northern, urban members of Congress for the 'prevention of significant deterioration' (PSD) policy in clean air regulation, which has discouraged movement of industry from urban areas in the north-east, to high-quality air sheds in the south and west (Crandall, 1983; Pashigian, 1985). Depending on the trade-offs between job creation effects and job preservation effects, labor might support stricter standards for new sources.

There are other examples of labor concern over the choice of environmental policy instruments. In the 1977 debates over amendments to the Clean Air Act, eastern coal miners' unions fought to include a command-and-control standard that effectively required scrubbing, thereby seeking to ensure continued reliance on cheap, high-sulfur coal from the east, over cleaner western coal (Ackerman and Hassler 1981). Likewise, in the debates over the SO_2 allowance trading system in the 1990 amendments to the Clean Air Act, the United Mine Workers opposed the system because it would create incentives for the use of low-sulfur coal from largely non-unionized mines in Wyoming's Powder River Basin instead of high-sulfur coal from eastern, unionized mines.

3.4 Consumers

Consumer groups typically have not expressed strong demands for environmental policies because of obstacles to organizing, arising from free-rider and limited-information problems. To the extent that they do have preferences over instruments, we would expect them to favor those instruments that minimize any increases in the prices of consumer goods and services, and this would seem to suggest cost-effective (hence, market-based) instruments over command-and-control. In practice, however, organized consumer groups have tended to ally themselves with environmental organizations on most issues, pursuing environmental-quality interests, rather than broader consumer interests. The latter concerns have more often been voiced by 'taxpayer organizations,' but these groups usually do not become involved in the relative minutiae of choosing environmental policy instruments. Hence, environmental interest groups have been effectively unopposed by other public interest organizations.

4 SUPPLY OF ENVIRONMENTAL POLICY INSTRUMENTS

There are several plausible positive political economy explanations for the nature of the supply of environmental policy instruments. First, legislators and their staffs are thought to be predisposed by their predominantly legal training to favor command-and-control approaches to regulation (Kneese and Schultze 1975). Similarly, unfamiliar policy instruments may require legislators to spend time learning about them before they can provide substantial support, thereby giving rise to a status quo bias in favor of the current regime of command-and-control regulation.[43] Both these effects may become weaker in the coming years, as a result of the increasing understanding of economics among lawyers as well as among legislators and their staffs (Hahn and Stavins, 1991).[44]

Second, ideology plays a significant role in instrument choice. Kelman (1981), in his survey of congressional staff members, found that support and opposition to effluent charges was based largely on ideological grounds: Republicans who supported the concept of pollution charges, for example, offered as a reason the assertion that 'the free market works,' or 'less government intervention' is desirable, without any real awareness or understanding of the economic arguments for market-based programs. Likewise, Democratic opposition was largely based upon analogously ideological factors (that is, greater faith in the government as opposed to the private sector), with little or no apparent understanding of the real advantages or disadvantages of the various instruments.

Third, constituents react to their perceptions of the costs and benefits to themselves and others of a particular policy, regardless of the real costs and benefits (McCubbins and Sullivan, 1984; Hahn, 1987). The more visible the benefits, the greater the demand for an instrument; the more visible the costs, the greater the opposition and thus the political costs to the legislator. Hence, politicians are likely to prefer command-and-control instruments because they tend to *hide* the costs of regulation in the price increases passed on to consumers (McCubbins and Sullivan, 1984).[45] In contrast, market-based instruments, although they impose lower total costs, generally impose those costs directly, in the form of effluent charges or prices paid for permits. Grandfathered permits fare better on the visibility criterion than auctioned permits or taxes since no money is exchanged at the time of the initial allocation.[46]

Fourth, voters' limited information may also lead politicians to engage in symbolic politics: the use of superficial slogans and symbols to attract constituent support, even when the policies actually implemented are either ineffectual or inconsistent with the symbols employed. Such symbolism offers the legislator political benefits at little opportunity cost. Command-and-control instruments are likely to be well suited to symbolic politics, because strict standards – strong statements of support for environmental protection – can be readily combined with less visible exemptions (Hahn and Noll, 1990). Congress has on several occasions passed environmental laws with strict compliance standards, while simultaneously including lax or insufficient enforcement measures. Tradable permits and taxes offer neither the powerful symbolic benefits of declaring strict standards, nor as convenient a range of options to undermine their practice.

Fifth, if politicians are risk averse, they will prefer instruments that involve more certain effects.[47] Concerning environmental policy instruments, uncertainty is likely to arise with respect to the distribution of costs and benefits among the affected actors and to the implementation of the legislative decision by the bureaucracy. The flexibility inherent in permits and taxes creates uncertainty about distributional effects and local levels of environmental quality (McCubbins and Page, 1986). Typically, legislators are more concerned with the distribution of costs and benefits – in particular their geographic distribution – than with a comparison of total benefits and costs (Hahn and Stavins, 1991). For this reason, aggregate cost-effectiveness – perhaps the major advantage of market-based instruments – is likely to play a less significant role in the legislative calculus than whether a politician is getting the best deal possible for her constituents (Shepsle and Weingast, 1984). Moreover, politicians are likely to oppose instruments (such as tradable permit schemes) that might induce firms to close business and relocate elsewhere, leading to localized unemployment (Hahn and Noll, 1990). Although there will be winners as well as losers from such relocation, potential losers are likely to be more certain of their status than potential gainers. This asymmetry creates a bias in favor of the status quo.[48]

For the same reason, grandfathering of tradable permits is more likely to attract a winning coalition than auctions, since grandfathering allows leeway in rewarding firms and distributing the costs and benefits of regulation among jurisdictions. Allocating permits by grandfathering can produce fairly clear 'winners' and 'losers' among firms and states, as demonstrated by the distribution of sulfur dioxide emissions permits in the 1990 amendments to the Clean Air Act (Joskow and Schmalensee, 1995). An auction, on the other hand, would allow no such political maneuvering.

Sixth, command-and-control instruments offer Congress greater control concerning the implementation of legislative outcomes by administrative agencies. To ensure that the interests of the winning coalition are protected in implementation, Congress may, in effect, prescribe administrative rules and procedures that favor one group over another (McCubbins, Noll, and Weingast, 1987). Such a practice, in theory, protects intended beneficiaries of legislation by constraining the scope of subsequent executive intervention in implementation. If stacking the deck is an important aspect of policy making, it is more likely to be successful in the context of command-and-control legislation. Market-based instruments leave the allocation of costs and benefits up to the market, treating polluters identically (Hahn and Noll, 1990). Standards, on the other hand, allow the administrative agency greater control and therefore open up possibilities for stacking the deck. For example, Congress might place the burden of proof in standard-setting on to the administrative agencies to favor industry; or legislators might include citizen-suit provisions allowing legal action to force the enforcement of standards favoring environmental groups.

Seventh, bureaucrats are less likely to undermine the legislative decision if their preferences over policy instruments are accommodated. Administrative decision makers are likely to oppose decentralized instruments on several grounds: they are familiar with command-and-control approaches; market-based instruments may not require the same kinds of technical skills that agencies have developed under command-and-control regulation; and market-based instruments imply a scaled-down role for the agency by shifting decision making from the bureaucracy to private firms, thereby undermining the prestige of the agency and the job security of its staff (Hahn and Stavins, 1991).

5 CONCLUSIONS

We have attempted to synthesize the seemingly diverse strands of the positive political economy literature by viewing them as relating to component parts of a political market framework. In this framework, interest groups have demands for particular instruments. Legislators, in turn, provide political support for such instruments. The demands of the various interest groups are aggregated, as are the supplies of support from individual legislators. The interaction of such aggregate demand and supply produce a legislature's equilibrium level of aggregate support, with each member simultaneously determining her effective support level. The effective support levels of the various legislators are combined, in an institutional context, to produce the legislature's choice of policy instrument.

This framework is far from complete. We have focused on the decisions of individual legislators, while leaving unanswered questions of how individual (and continuous) legislator support translates into binary votes and how such support or votes are aggregated to the level of the legislature. For example, we do not deal with competition among legislators, only briefly have we considered the role congressional committees and other institutions play in structuring and influencing instrument choice, and we have not explained how instrument choices are framed. Likewise, we have only explored a competitive legislative model as a first approximation, and have commented briefly on alternative approaches. These issues represent promising avenues for extending this framework and building a workable model of instrument choice.

In this chapter, we have taken a modest step toward a unified framework for positive analysis of policy instrument choice. This framework may permit greater understanding than approaches that focus almost exclusively on one component of the problem at a time. Thus, for example, if one considers only the benefits a particular industry derives from a proposed regulatory program, one might be led to conclude that a program will be forthcoming if the benefits are sufficiently high. Attention to questions of supply shows why this might not be the case. If the legislature prefers the status quo to the instrument demanded by the interest group, and if the legislature's aggregate supply function is sufficiently inelastic, there may be no equilibrium under which the legislature provides positive support for the demanded instrument. Indeed, the supply function of such a legislature might be above the industry demand function everywhere in the politically relevant domain. Similarly, whether a large shift in the demand for a particular instrument resulting from exogenous factors causes a comparable shift in the actual support provided by the legislature depends on the elasticity of supply. There will be relatively little change in equilibrium support if supply is inelastic, but a far larger change if supply is elastic.

This framework helps us to organize and, to some degree, synthesize available explorations of the four gaps with which we introduced the paper – three gaps between economic prescription and political reality and one gap between past and current political practices. With respect to the first – the predominance of command-and-control over market-based instruments despite the economic superiority of the latter – firms are likely to prefer command-and-control standards to auctioned permits and taxes. Standards produce rents, which can be sustainable if coupled with sufficiently more stringent requirements for new sources. In contrast, auctioned permits and taxes require firms to pay not only abatement costs to reduce pollution to a specified level, but also costs of polluting up to that level. Environmental interest groups are also likely to prefer command-and-control instruments, for philosophical, strategic, and technical reasons.

On the supply side, command-and-control standards are likely to be supplied more cheaply by legislators for several reasons: the training and experience of legislators may make them more comfortable with a direct standards approach than with market-based approaches; the time needed to learn about market-based instruments may represent significant opportunity costs; standards tend to hide the costs of pollution control while emphasizing the benefits; plus standards may offer greater opportunities for symbolic politics. Finally, at the level of the legislature, command-and-control standards offer legislators a greater degree of control over the distributional effects of environmental regulation. This feature is likely to make majority coalitions easier to assemble, because legislative compromise is easier in the face of less uncertainty, and because the winning coalition can better guarantee that its interests will be served in the implementation of policy.

The second gap – that when command-and-control standards have been used, the standards for new sources have been far more stringent than those for existing sources, despite the potentially perverse incentives of this approach – can also be understood in the context of our market framework. Demand for new source standards comes from existing firms, which seek to erect entry barriers to restrict competition and protect the rents created by command-and-control standards. In turn, environmentalists often support strict standards for new sources because they represent environmental progress, at least symbolically. On the supply side, more stringent standards for new sources allow legislators to protect existing constituents and interests by placing the bulk of the pollution control burden on unbuilt factories.

Many of these same arguments can also be used to explain the third gap: the use of grandfathered tradable permits as the exclusive market-based mechanism in the United States, despite the disadvantages of this allocation scheme. Like command-and-control standards, tradable permits create rents; grandfathering distributes those rents to firms, while auctioning transfers the rents to government. Moreover, like stringent command-and-control standards for new sources, but unlike auctioned permits or taxes, grandfathered permits give rise to entry barriers. Thus, the rents conveyed to the private sector by grandfathered tradable permits are, in effect, sustainable.

Moreover, grandfathered tradable permits are likely to be less costly for legislators to supply. The costs imposed on industry are less visible – and less burdensome – for grandfathered permits than for auctioned permits or taxes. Also, grandfathered permits offer a greater degree of political control over the distributional effects of regulation, facilitating the formation of majority coalitions. In both these respects, grandfathered permits are somewhat analogous to command-and-control standards.

The fourth and final gap – between the recent rise of the use of market-based instruments and the lack of receptiveness such schemes had encountered in the past – can be credited to several factors. These include the increased understanding of and familiarity with market-based instruments; niche-seeking by environmental groups interested in both environmental quality and organizational visibility; increased pollution control costs, which create greater demand for cost-effective instruments; attention to new, unregulated environmental problems without constituencies for a status quo approach; and a general shift of the political center toward a more favorable view of using the market to solve social problems. Overall, the image is one of both demand and supply functions shifting rightward, thus leading, over time, to greater degrees of political support for these market-based instruments.[49]

To the extent that some of the current preference for command-and-control standards reflects simply a desire to maintain the regulatory status quo, the aggregate demand for a market-based instrument is likely to be greatest and the political opportunity costs of legislators providing support is likely to be least when the status quo instrument is essentially non-existent, that is, when the environmental problem has not previously been regulated (Hahn and Stavins 1991). Hence, in the future, we should be more optimistic about introducing such market-based instruments for 'new' problems, such as global climate change, than for existing, regulated problems, such as abandoned hazardous waste sites.

We end with some thoughts about how a market framework can generate empirical work on the positive political economy of instrument choice for environmental regulation. So far, most of the academic work in this area has been theoretical; very few arguments have been subjected to empirical validation. Several of the existing empirical studies have addressed the question of why firms might support particular instruments, rather than whether firms actually provide such support. There have been no empirical studies that have constructed demand functions by determining how much firms actually are willing to pay – for example, in the form of lobbying expenses and campaign contributions – to secure particular outcomes. Similarly, there has been no work seeking to determine the nature of demand by interest groups other than industry. In particular, the motives of environmental organizations merit more consideration. We have discussed the possible self-interested motives of such organizations, and how their demands for particular policy instruments may be motivated by niche seeking. But whether their expenditures in the political process comport with this theory remains essentially untested.

On the supply side, there are substantial impediments to empirical work. The existing studies have primarily attempted to determine the factors that affect legislative votes on particular programs (for example, Hamilton, 1995; Pashigian, 1985). In recent years, however, Congress has enacted a greater proportion of legislation by voice vote, rather than recorded vote. There has also been a shift from votes on comparatively narrow bills to votes on omnibus bills, which make it virtually impossible to determine a legislator's actual position with respect to specific components. Thus, there is now less new data than previously with which to perform studies of legislative voting behavior.

Legislative voting studies also share a substantial problem: distinguishing votes which reflect a legislator's true views about a bill from votes cast as part of an implicit logrolling trade, in which a legislator votes in favor of a program that she otherwise opposes in order to obtain a more valuable *quid pro quo*.[50] Moreover, as we argued above, a vote constitutes only one component of the support that a legislator can extend to a bill. But the other components of support, of course, are less well suited to quantitative analysis.[51] Thus, in some cases, the best way to explore empirically the supply side of the equilibrium framework may be through detailed case studies of the legislative decision making process, such as that undertaken by Ackerman and Hassler (1981).

The metaphor of the market will, in the end, be an imperfect and incomplete description of political behavior. But there are real advantages to considering instrument choice within this framework, and from developing more fully the details of the market metaphor and its implications. The ultimate test of the usefulness of such a framework will be the extent to which it enables reliable predictions of the choices legislatures make, and the extent to which it facilitates the design of policy instruments that are both economically rational and politically successful.

NOTES

* Helpful comments on a previous version of the paper were provided by: David Charny, Cary Coglianese, John Ferejohn, Don Fullerton, Robert Hahn, James Hamilton, Robert Keohane, David King, Lewis Kornhauser, Robert Lowry, Roger Noll, Robert Schwab, Kenneth Shepsle, and Richard Stewart. Financial support was provided by the Dean's Research Fund, John F. Kennedy School of Government, and the Filomen D'Agostino and Max E. Greenberg Research Fund at the New York University School of Law. The authors alone are responsible for remaining errors.

1. 'Market-based' or 'economic incentive' policy instruments – primarily pollution taxes or charges and systems of tradable permits – are those which align private incentives with social objective

to control pollution through direct price mechanisms or the creation of transferable property rights. The seminal work on pollution taxes is Pigou (1920); on tradable permits, see Dales (1968) and Montgomery (1972). At least in theory, pollution taxes and systems of marketable permits, under appropriate conditions, achieve emissions reductions at minimum total cost (Baumol and Oates, 1988). Incentive-based instruments also have dynamic efficiency properties (Milkman and Prince, 1989; Jaffe and Stavins, 1995). Command-and-control standards include design standards, which require the use of a particular technology to control emissions, and (more commonly) performance standards, which prescribe the maximum amount of pollution that a source can emit – usually in proportional terms, as a quantity of allowable emissions per unit of product output or input. In this chapter, we use 'standards' as a generic term for command and control standards; and except where stated otherwise, we refer to proportional performance standards.

2. New plants ought to have somewhat more stringent standards because their abatement costs are lower; however, such standards should be linked with actual abatement costs, not with the proxy of plant vintage. For empirical evidence on this point, see Maloney and Brady (1988); Nelson, Tietenberg, and Donihue (1993).
3. Taxes (so-called unit charges) have been used in some communities for municipal solid waste collection (US Congress, Office of Technology Assessment, 1995). Gasoline taxes serve primarily as revenue-raising instruments, rather than environmental (Pigouvian) taxes *per se*. Interestingly, the European experience is the reverse: environmental taxes are far more prevalent than tradable permits, although the taxes employed have typically been too low to induce pollution abatement (Stewart, 1996). A more comprehensive positive analysis of instrument choice than we provide here would seek to explain this difference between the European and US experiences.
4. For discussion of the relevant conditions, see: Weitzman, 1974; Yohe, 1978; Stavins, 1996.
5. Although the sulfur dioxide allowance program established by the 1990 Clean Air Act Amendments includes annual auctions, these involve less than 3 percent of the total allocation (Bailey, 1996).
6. With perfect information and no transactions costs, the efficient outcome will result regardless of how permits are initially distributed (Montgomery, 1972; Coase, 1960). Under more realistic scenarios, however, auctioning is superior on grounds of cost-effectiveness (Stavins, 1995), 'revenue recycling' (Goulder, Parry and Burtraw, 1996; Fullerton and Metcalf, 1996), and the incentives facing firms to reduce emissions (Dewees, 1983; Hahn and McGartland, 1989).
7. Beginning in the 1970s, the US Environmental Protection Agency (EPA) offered states the option of employing variants of tradable permits for the control of localized, criteria air pollutants (Hahn, 1989). More significantly, tradable-permit systems were used in the 1980s to accomplish the phasedown of lead in gasoline (Kerr and Maré, 1995) and to facilitate the phasedown of ozone-depleting chlorofluorocarbons (CFCs); and in the 1990s to cut nationwide SO_2 emissions by 50 percent by the year 2005 (US Environmental Protection Agency, 1996), to achieve ambient ozone reductions in the northeast, and to implement stricter local air pollution controls in the Los Angeles metropolitan region.
8. We do not intend, however, to deny the importance of executive branch departments and administrative agencies, such as the EPA. For example, the intra-firm emission trading programs of the 1970s were largely the direct creation of EPA.
9. Space does not permit us to review the considerable body of work in the economics and public choice literatures that seek to explain general patterns of economic regulation. This literature is well reviewed in Romer and Rosenthal (1987). A few theoretical works have advanced frameworks other than a market model for considering the choice of policy instrument; see especially Campos (1989), Hahn (1990), and Rasmusen and Zupan (1991).
10. It might be argued that interest groups ultimately care about votes, which at the level of an individual legislator reduces to a binary variable. But there are several reasons to focus on support, rather than on votes alone. First, this approach facilitates comparisons among several instruments, since the outcome of the legislative process is the instrument that garners the most effective support. Second, empirical analysis has largely failed to link campaign contributions with legislators' votes (Hall and Wayman, 1990), while campaign contributions have been found

to be highly correlated with legislators' participation in committees, itself closely linked with the notion of 'effective support' (Grier and Munger, 1993; Silberman and Durden, 1976). Third, committee membership (especially in the House) accords a great deal of power over the fate of legislation, in terms of institutional powers (Shepsle and Weingast, 1987), deference by other members (Weingast and Marshall, 1988), committee expertise (Kingdon, 1989), and other factors. Moreover, votes of committee members are usually less critical than how vigorously members provide support (Hall, 1987; Mayhew, 1974). Hence, interest groups may be primarily interested in securing the support of key members (that is, committee chairs), even though the groups ultimately care about the floor vote.

11. Denzau and Munger (1986) describe the range of services legislators can offer interest groups. Silberman and Durden (1976) analyse a similar measure of legislator participation, which they call 'political support effort.' It is worth noting that these models generally treat as an output what in our framework is an input: namely, the effort exerted by the legislator, used to produce effective support. We have incorporated differences among legislators in effectiveness and productivity into the supply side (production of effective support) rather than the demand side (demand of interest groups for support from different legislators). For further discussion of the ways in which Congressmen can participate in policy making, especially in committee, see: Hall (1987, 1996); and Hall and Wayman (1990).
12. Monetary contributions can be used to finance advertising campaigns, literature production and distribution, and other activities that increase the probability of a legislator being re-elected.
13. The firm's profit maximization problem yields a factor demand function. Given a convex profit function, the demand curve will be downward-sloping. But see note 15, below.
14. We said at the outset that we were restricting our attention to the policy instruments used to achieve a *given* level of protection. As we note below, however, the choice of cost-effective instruments, for example, can lead to the adoption of more stringent environmental standards.
15. A formal treatment would incorporate the choice of policy instrument into individuals' utility functions, as goods with associated prices. In the usual way, optimization subject to the budget constraint will lead to demand functions that are downward sloping in price, as long as the utility function has the usual properties. It is possible, however, that over a certain region the demand function will be *increasing*. For example, a unit of support for an instrument will be virtually worthless at very low levels of support, since adoption of that instrument will be extremely unlikely. We assume, however, that the demand function is decreasing over the *politically relevant* range, in which adoption of the instrument is a realistic possibility. It might also be argued that if a legislature was composed of a single legislator and there was perfect information, demand functions for political support would (in the case of support relevant for voting) be a step function with a single step: interest groups would have no willingness-to-pay below some level of (adequate) support, and no willingness-to-pay above a sufficient level of support. But in a multi-member body, more support from individual legislators can always be worth something, and if there is uncertainty about how much support is sufficient, the demand function is likely to be downward sloping over at least some range.
16. Of course, regulation may not always be non-exclusive. Loopholes, narrowly-applying clauses in statutes, and bureaucratic exemptions can all afford special treatment for some firms or narrowly defined categories of consumers. This possibility may provide enough incentive for some individual firms to lobby.
17. The principal–agent problem is probably far more serious for environmental advocacy groups than for private industry trade associations. An environmental organization may have a hundred thousand members or more scattered across the country, paying scant attention to the operational priorities of the organization (let alone the details of its day-by-day activities). Trade associations, on the other hand, may be dominated by a large producer, with an incentive to monitor the association's activities; and their boards of directors may be made up of executives from member firms. Moreover, trade associations have many fewer members, and therefore the stake of each in the organization is greater, and monitoring is more likely to be worthwhile. On the other hand, trade associations have their own set of problems. Among these is the possible necessity of obtaining an expression of consensus from member firms prior to undertaking specific lobbying efforts. For an extensive treatment of the agency problem in environmental groups, see Lowry (1993).

18. Up to this point, we have examined lobbying activities of interest groups exclusively in terms of their demand-side effects. It can also be argued that some such activities are intended to and may succeed in shifling legislators' supply functions. We examine this possibility below.
19. This notion of legislators' goals is consistent with Fenno's (1973) description of Congressmen as having three basic objectives: re-election, influence within the House, and good public policy. In our framework, 'influence within the House' and 'good public policy' are combined in 'being a legislator.' If the legislator wishes to continue to be a legislator in the future, she will also value re-election.
20. In the face of the overwhelming claims on her time and resources – both in Washington and in her home district – a Congressman's time and effort carries a significant opportunity cost (Bauer, Pool, and Dexter, 1963; Kingdon, 1989; Fenno, 1978). Effort invested in providing support for one bill could have been spent working on other legislation that would satisfy ideological goals, reflect voters' objectives, and/or attract votes, dollars, and other resources; or visiting the home district and supplying constituency services such as help dealing with the bureaucracy (Denzau and Munger, 1986; Grier and Munger, 1993). To keep the explication simple, the marginal cost function is assumed in the figure to be linear.
21. Congressmen tend to take into account the preferences of the people who voted for them, that is, their 'supporting coalition' (Kingdon, 1989) or their 're-election constituency' (Fenno, 1978). A conservative legislator whose re-election constituency is anti-regulatory, for example, will not be affected by a minority group of environmentalists calling for command-and-control regulation.
22. In the figure, we represent both ideological costs and electoral costs as being positive; that is, support for the policy is essentially inconsistent both with the legislator's own ideology and her constituents' preferences. It is not inconceivable that these could be of opposite sign, but in a representative democracy, that would be the exception, not the rule. As stated by Fenno (1978, p. 142): '"If your conscience and your district disagree too often," members like to say, "you're in the wrong business."'
23. Party leaders may conceivably also become effective demanders for policy instrument support by offering various resources to legislators in exchange for support, in which case the parties are essentially functioning as interest groups.
24. We simply take the choice set of instruments as given. Important questions remain regarding how it is determined, but these are beyond the scope of this chapter.
25. This issue of aggregation touches on the more general issue of competition among interest groups for influence. The classic model associated with Stigler (1971) and Peltzman (1976) is essentially a policy auction in which the interest group with the highest bid gains control over regulation. In Becker's (1983) model, one group is taxed, the other subsidized, and each tries to improve its lot at the expense of the other. More recently, Epstein and O'Halloran (1997) model interest group competition as a game in which the legislator's type is private information.
26. Alternatively, we might treat individual legislators as monopoly suppliers of unique services, each one setting her marginal opportunity cost equal to her 'marginal revenue' generated by interest groups' demand for policy. Such an extreme case of monopoly suppliers seems to be a less reasonable approximation of political reality than perfect competition, but it illustrates the potential for considering alternative models of imperfect competition. Various models of co-operative and non-cooperative oligopoly could capture significant elements of legislative relationships. For the purposes of this paper, however, we proceed with the basic competitive framework.
27. Hall and Wayman (1990) examine legislator participation in committees, and argue that interest groups give contributions to 'hostile' legislators in order to reduce their participation, that is, their opposition.
28. In the US Congress, to use a familiar example, a bill needs a bare majority in the House of Representatives, but may have to clear a higher hurdle in the Senate to bring closure to debate. If the President vetoes the bill, of course, two-thirds majorities in both houses are required to enact legislation.
29. In the Congress, a bill, as modified by successful amendments, is considered opposite the status quo in the final vote. This arrangement favors the status quo and requires that each bill be compared ultimately with the status quo rather than with other alternatives.

30. For example, discrete-choice econometric models that have as their theoretical basis the existence of an unobserved latent variable are an obvious candidate.
31. There are other plausible explanations for firms' preferences. Firms' may simply support the continuation of the status quo, which is generally the command-and-control approach, because replacing familiar policies with new instruments can mean that existing expertise within firms becomes less valued (Kelman, 1981; Stewart, 1996). For example, lobbyists – the agents in a principal–agent relationship – may be expected to rationally resist the dissipation of their human capital (Hahn and Stavins, 1991). It has also been suggested that market-based instruments may be opposed simply because they are not well understood (Kelman, 1981; Welch, 1983), and there is at least anecdotal evidence that this has been the case. Such lack of understanding can also affect the supply side, and we discuss this later.
32. On this point, see Kelman (1981); Crandall (1983); Hahn and Noll (1990); and Arnold (1995). Actually, firms pay less than the full amount of the tax; a share is passed on to consumers.
33. Grandfathering distributes the rents from permits to firms that participate in the initial allocation (Dewees, 1983), in contrast with an auction (Yohe, 1976).
34. Even if the restriction is severe enough to impose losses on firms, they will prefer standards to taxes, which impose new costs. In the long run, under a tax scheme, firms will exit the industry until a new zero-profit equilibrium is reached; but in the short term, firms will lose money. The tax reduces each firm's present value of income, whether it remains in the industry or exits. Firms will therefore oppose the introduction of pollution taxes.
35. Pollution restrictions raise both the average and marginal cost curves. Each firm will produce at the level where restricted marginal cost intersects the per-firm demand curve. If the minimum average cost under regulation is to the left of this point, the price (marginal cost) will exceed average cost, and firms will earn rents. Maloney and McCormick (1982) identified three conditions that are sufficient for regulation to enhance producer profits: (1) output under regulation corresponds to some cost-minimizing level of output in the absence of regulation; (2) pollution increases with output; and (3) average costs increase more at higher levels of output under regulation. The necessary and sufficient condition for higher profits is that the intersection of average and marginal cost under regulation lie to the left of the firm's demand curve.
36. Other barriers to entry result, for example, from the permitting requirements for new sources under the prevention of significant deterioration (PSD) and non-attainment programs under the Clean Air Act, as well as by non-attainment programs' offset requirements for new sources. The significance in a positive sense of scarcity rents as a major explanation for the prevalence of particular forms of environmental regulation has important nominative implications, as well. This is because in the presence of pre-existing tax distortions, the distribution of these rents can have efficiency implications (Fullerton and Metcalf, 1996). It is ironic that precisely that mechanism that facilitates political acceptance of some environmental policies (transmission of scarcity rents to the regulated sector) may also undo some or all of the welfare gains that would have been forthcoming.
37. The small refineries' opposition is discussed in the case they brought to stop or delay the program: Small Refiner Lead Phasedown Task Force v. EPA, 705 F.2d 506 (D.C. Cir. 1983). Another example of such intra-industry differentials, and the resulting splintering of lobbying strategy, occurred when the National Coal Association (NCA) divided over the question of scrubber requirements in clean air legislation. A universal scrubber requirement would have preserved demand for eastern coal, which had higher sulfur content than its cleaner western competition. The NCA split between eastern and western coal producers and stayed out of the debates leading up to the 1977 Clean Air Act Amendments (Ackerman and Hassler, 1981).
38. A general system of tradable permits would eliminate this advantage.
39. Also, small firms might be particularly supportive of grandfathering out of concern that auctions will be dominated by larger players (Hahn and McGartland, 1989). Similarly, since the transition to a grandfathered-permits system is likely to involve less uncertainty than an auction, it might receive disproportionate support from risk-averse firms.
40. Anecdotal supporting evidence is provided by the establishment of a market in take-off and landing 'slots' at four of the nation's busiest airports. In 1986, the Federal Aviation Admin-

istration (FAA) replaced the existing system of allocation-by-committee with a system of grandfathered tradable permits. At Congressional hearings concerning the FAA's proposal, large airlines (which already held most of the slots) supported grandfathering. In contrast, smaller airlines looking to expand – such as People's Express and Western – opposed grandfathering, calling for existing slots to be auctioned or distributed by lottery. See: U. S. Congress, House of Representatives (1986).

41. We need to distinguish here between strategic and tactical decisions by advocacy groups. The strategic decision by an environmental organization to express demand for a policy instrument and get it on the agenda for consideration is probably positively related to perceived probability of success; but the tactical decision to allocate resources (express demands) for an instrument already on the agenda may well be negatively related to probability of success.
42. This criticism overlooks the fact that under conventional command-and-control regulations, firms receive these same licenses to pollute for free (Hahn and Stavins, 1991).
43. A legislator may not need to understand an instrument to vote for it, but such understanding is more likely to be a necessary precondition for other forms of support, such as insertion of a statement into the legislative history, efforts to get a bill through committee, or attempts to persuade other legislators. Moreover, a lack of understanding may prove to hurt the legislator if it becomes an issue in her re-election campaign. The greater the prominence of an issue, the more important it will be for a legislator to have a compelling rationale for her position. Responding to this need, interest groups may supply legislators with justifications for supporting given policies (Fenno, 1978; Kingdon, 1989).
44. Thus, outreach efforts by economists and others may be thought to have both demand-side and supply-side effects. On the demand side, increased understanding of market-based instruments may have increased the demand for these instruments by various interest groups. On the supply side, increased understanding reduces learning costs for legislators. Since both effects are rightward shifts of the respective functions, the outcome is unambiguous in terms of increased degrees of support.
45. This point is related to the more general one that legislators will seek to disguise transfers to special interests (Coate and Morris, 1995).
46. Hahn (1987) emphasized the importance of observable costs and benefits in explaining why Wisconsin chose a largely state-funded pollution-credit program over an effluent charge. The instrument offered visible job creation, by favoring the construction of new facilities, at the expense of diffuse, less visible costs to widely distributed third parties. In contrast, the market-based alternative would have appeared to sacrifice jobs while its cost-saving benefits would have been less evident.
47. As McCubbins, Noll, and Weingast argue, 'Legislators are likely to behave as if they are risk averse ... if their constituents punish unpredictable policy choices or their reelection probability is nearly unity' (1989, p. 22).
48. The Clean Air Act Amendments of 1977 provide an example of legislation built upon such compromises (Hahn and Noll, 1990). Stringent standards for urban non-attainment areas were offset by industry-specific exemptions and by measures preventing relocation of urban factories to less polluted areas, the so-called policy of Prevention of Significant Deterioration (PSD). The winning coalition would probably not have held up under a tradable permit scheme, which would have allowed rust belt firms to purchase pollution permits from firms in cleaner areas and thus to relocate. On the other hand, a tradable permit scheme which prevented inter-regional trading could presumably have protected northern factory jobs just as well.
49. It is also possible that changes in some of the institutional features identified above affected individual legislator degrees of support. For example, changes may have occurred which led to particular legislators taking on important committee positions, thus changing their production functions, and hence their opportunity costs.
50. See Kau and Rubin (1979) for an attempt to sort out the importance of logrolling.
51. Silbernman and Durden (1976) attempted to overcome this problem by using patterns of votes on a series of amendments as a proxy for a continuous underlying support variable. Such series of closely related votes, however, are rarely available, particularly in the case of instrument choice. In a different approach, Hall and Wayman (1990) examined the relationship between campaign contributions and degrees of participation in committee activities.

REFERENCES

Ackerman, Bruce A. and William T. Hassler (1981), *Clean Coal/Dirty Air*, New Haven: Yale University Press.

Arnold, Frank S. (1995), 'Environmental Policy in Theory and Practice', *Economic Analysis of Environmental Policy and Regulation*, New York: Wiley and Sons.

Austen-Smith, David and John R. Wright (1994), 'Counteractive Lobbying', *American Journal of Political Science*, **38**(1), 25–44.

Bailey, Elizabeth M. (1996), 'Allowance Trading Activity and State Regulatory Rulings: Evidence from the U.S. Acid Rain Program', MIT-CEEPR 96-002 WP, Center for Energy and Environmental Policy Research, Massachusetts Institute of Technology.

Bauer, Raymond A., Ithel de Sola Pool and Lewis Anthony Dexter. (1963), *American Business and Public Policy*, New York: Atherton.

Baumol, William J. and Wallace E. Oates (1988), *The Theory of Environmental Policy*, second edn, New York: Cambridge University Press.

Becker, Gary S. (1983), 'A Theory of Competition among Pressure Groups for Political Influence', *Quarterly Journal of Economics*, **98**(3), 371–400.

Buchanan, James M. and Gordon Tullock (1975), 'Polluters' Profits and Political Response: Direct Controls Versus Taxes', *American Economic Review*, **65**(1), 139–47.

Campos, J.E.L. (1989), 'Legislative Institutions, Lobbying, and the Endogenous Choice of Regulatory Instruments: a Political Economy Approach to Instrument Choice', *Journal of Law, Economics and Organization*, **5**(1), 333–53.

Coase, Ronald H. (1960), 'The Problem of Social Cost', *Journal of Law and Economics*, **3**, 1–44.

Coate, Stephen and Stephen Morris (1995), 'On the Form of Transfers to Special Interests', *Journal of Political Economy*, **103**(6), 1210–35.

Crandall, Robert W. (1983), *Controlling Industrial Pollution*, Washington: Brookings Institution.

Dales, John H. (1968), 'Pollution, Property, and Prices', Toronto: University of Toronto Press.

Denzau, Arthur T. and Michael C. Munger (1986), 'Legislators and Interest Groups: How Unorganized Interests Get Represented', *American Political Science Review*, **80**(1), 89–106.

Dewees, Donald N. (1983), 'Instrument Choice in Environmental Policy', *Economic Inquiry*, **21**, 53–71.

Epstein, David and Shayn O'Halloran (1997), *Modeling Madison: A Multiple Principals Model of Interest Group Competition*, Unpublished manuscript, Columbia University, 42+ pp.

Fenno, Richard F., Jr (1973), *Congressmen in Committees*, Boston: Little, Brown.

Fenno, Richard F., Jr (1978), *Home Style*, Boston: Little, Brown.

Fiorina, Morris P. (1982), 'Legislative Choice of Regulatory Forms: Legal Process or Administrative Process?', *Public Choice*, **39**, 33–66.

Fullerton, Don and Gilbert Metcalf (1996), 'Environmental Regulation in a Second-Best World', Paper presented at the National Bureau of Economic Research Workshop on Public Policy and the Environment, Cambridge, Massachusetts.

Goulder, Lawrence H., Ian W. H. Parry and Dallas Burtraw (1996), 'Revenue-Raising vs. Other Approaches to Environmental Protection: The Critical Significance of Pre-Existing Tax Distortions', Paper presented at the National Bureau of Economic Research Workshop on Public Policy and the Environment, Cambridge, Massachusetts.

Grier, Kevin B. and Michael C. Munger (1993), 'Comparing Interest Group Pac Contributions to House and Senate Incumbents, 1980–1986', *Journal of Politics*, **55**(3), 615–43.

Hahn, Robert W. (1987), 'Jobs and Environmental Quality: Some Implications for Instrument Choice', *Policy Sciences*, **20**, 289–306.

Hahn, Robert W. (1989), 'Economic Prescriptions for Environmental Problems: How the Patient Followed the Doctor's Orders', *Journal of Economic Perspectives*, **3**(2), 95–114.

Hahn, Robert W. (1990), 'The Political Economy of Environmental Regulation: Towards a Unifying Framework', *Public Choice*, **65**, 21–47.

Hahn, Robert W. and Robert Axtell (1995), 'Reevaluating the Relationship Between Transferable Property Rights and Command-and-Control Regulation', *Journal of Regulatory Economics*, **8**, 125–48.

Hahn, Robert W. and Albert M. McGartland (1989), 'The Political Economy of Instrument Choice: an Examination of the U.S. Role in Implementing the Montreal Protocol', *Northwestern University Law Review*, **83**(3), 592–611.

Hahn, Robert W. and Roger G. Noll (1990), 'Environmental Markets in the Year 2000', *Journal of Risk and Uncertainty*, **3**, 351–67.

Hahn, Robert W. and Robert N. Stavins (1991), 'Incentive-based Environmental Regulation: a New Era from an Old Idea?', *Ecology Law Quarterly*, **18**(1), 1–42.

Hall, Richard L. (1987), 'Participation and Purpose in Committee Decision Making', *American Political Science Review*, **81**(1), 105–27.

Hall, Richard L. (1996), *Participation in Congress*, New Haven: Yale University Press.

Hall, Richard L. and Frank Wayman (1990), 'Buying Time: Moneyed Interests and the Mobilization of Bias in Congressional Committees', *American Political Science Review*, **84**(3), 797–820.

Hamilton, James T. (1995), *Taxes, Torts, and the Toxics Release Inventory: Congressional Voting on Instruments to Control Pollution*, Unpublished manuscript, Duke University, 29 pp.

Hughes, John S., Wesley A. Magat and William E. Ricks (1986), 'The Economic Consequences of the OSHA Cotton Dust Standards: an Analysis of Stock Market Price Behavior', *Journal of Law and Economics*, **29**(4), 29–59.

Jaffe, Adam B. and Robert N. Stavins (1995), 'Dynamic Incentives of Environmental Regulation: The Effects of Alternative Policy Instruments on Technology Diffusion', *Journal of Environmental Economics and Management*, **29**, S43–S63.

Joskow, Paul L. and Richard Schmalensee (1995), *The Political Economy of Market-based Environmental Policy: The 1990 U.S. Acid Rain Program*, Draft manuscript, MIT, 72 pp.

Kau, James B. and Paul H. Rubin (1979), 'Self-interest, Ideology, and Logrolling in Congressional Voting', *Journal of Law and Economics*, **22**(2), 365–84.

Kelman, Steven P. (1981), What Price Incentives?, Boston: Auburn House.

Kerr, Suzi and David Maré (1995), 'Market Efficiency in Tradeable Permit Markets with Transaction Costs: Empirical Evidence from the United States Lead Phasedown' *Contracts and Tradeable Permit Markets in International and Domestic Environmental Protection*, Suzi Kerr, PhD thesis, Department of Economics, Harvard University, pp. 93–167.

Kingdon, John W. (1989), *Congressmen's Voting Decisions*, 3rd edn, Ann Arbor: University of Michigan Press.

Kneese, Allen V. and Charles L. Schultze (1975), *Pollution, Prices, and Public Policy*, Washington, DC: Brookings Institution.

Leone, Robert A. and John E. Jackson (1981), 'The Political Economy of Federal Regulatory Activity: the Case of Water-pollution Controls', in *Studies in Public Regulation*, Gary Fromm (ed.), Cambridge: MIT Press, pp. 231–71.

Lowry, Robert C. (1993), *The Political Economy of Environmental Citizen Groups*, PhD thesis, Harvard University, 313 pp.

Maloney, Michael T. and Gordon L. Brady (1988), 'Capital Turnover and Marketable Pollution Rights', *Journal of Law and Economics*, **31**(4), 203–26.

Maloney, Michael T. and Robert E. McCormick (1982), 'A Positive Theory of Environmental Quality Regulation', *Journal of Law and Economics*, **25**(4), 99–123.

Mayhew, David (1974), *Congress: The Electoral Connection*, New Haven: Yale University Press.

McCubbins, Matthew and Terry Sullivan (1984), 'Constituency Influences on Legislative Policy Choice', *Quality and Quantity*, **18**, 299–319.

McCubbins, Matthew and Talbot Page (1986), 'The Congressional Foundations of Agency Performance', *Public Choice*, **51**, 173–90.

McCubbins, Matthew D., Roger G. Noll and Barry R. Weingast (1987), 'Administrative Procedures as Instruments of Political Control', *Journal of Law, Economics and Organization*, **3**(2), 243–77.

McCubbins, Matthew D., Roger G. Noll and Barry R. Weingast (1989), 'Structure and Process, Politics and Policy: Administrative Arrangements and the Political Control of Agencies', *Virginia Law Review*, **75**: 431–82.

Milliman, Scott R. and Raymond Prince (1989), 'Firm Incentives to Promote Technological Change in Pollution Control', *Journal of Environmental Economics and Management*, **17**, 247–65.

Montgomery, W. David (1972), 'Markets in Licenses and Efficient Pollution Control Programs', *Journal of Economic Theory*, **5**, 395–418.

Nelson, Randy, Tom Tietenberg and Michael Donihue (1993), 'Differential Environmental Regulation: Effects on Electric Utility Capital Turnover and Emissions', *Review of Economies and Statistics*, **75**, 368–73.

Olson, Mancur (1965), *The Logic of Collective Action*, Cambridge: Harvard University Press.

Oster, Sharon (1982), 'The Strategic Use of Regulatory Investment by Industry Subgroups', *Economic Inquiry*, **20**, 604–18.

Oye, Kenneth A. and James H. Maxwell (1995), 'Self-Interest and Environmental Management', in *Local Commons and Global Interdependence: Heterogeneity and Cooperation in Two Domains*, Robert O. Keohane and Elinor Ostrom (eds), London: Sage Publications, pp. 191–221.

Pashigian, B. Peter (1985), 'Environmental Regulation: Whose Self-interests Are Being Protected?', *Economic Inquiry*, **23**: 551–84.

Peltzman, Sam (1976), 'Toward a More General Theory of Regulation', *Journal of Law and Economics* **19**, 211–40.

Pigou, Arthur Cecil (1920), *The Economics of Welfare*, London: Macmillan and Company.

Rasmusen, Eric and Mark Zupan (1991), 'Extending the Economic Theory of Regulation to the Form of Policy', *Public Choice*, **72**(2-3), 275–96.

Revesz, Richard L. (1996), 'Federalism and Interstate Environmental Externalities', *University of Pennsylvania Law Review*, **144**(8), 2341.

Romer, Thomas and Howard Rosenthal (1987), 'Modern Political Economy and the Study of Regulation', in *Public Regulation: New Perspectives on Institutions and Policies*, Elizabeth E. Bailey (ed.), Cambridge: MIT Press, pp. 73–116.

Rothenberg, Lawrence S. (1992), *Linking Citizens to Government: Interest Group Politics at Common Cause*, New York: Cambridge University Press.

Shepsle, Kenneth A. and Barry R. Weingast (1984), 'Political Solutions to Market Problems', *American Political Science Review*, **78**, 417–34.

Shepsle, Kenneth A. and Barry R. Weingast (1987), 'The Institutional Foundations of Committee Power', *American Political Science Review*, **81**, 85–104.

Silberman, Jonathan I. and Garey C. Durden (1976), 'Determining Legislative Preferences on the Minimum Wage: an Economic Approach', *Journal of Political Economy*, **84**(2), 317–29.

Stavins, Robert N. (1995), 'Transaction Costs and Tradeable Permits', *Journal of Environmental Economics and Management*, **29**, 133–48.

Stavins, Robert N. (1996), 'Correlated Uncertainty and Policy Instrument Choice', *Journal of Environmental Economics and Management*, **30**, 218–32.

Stewart, Richard B. (1981), 'Regulation, Innovation, and Administrative Law: a Conceptual Framework', *California Law Review*, **69**, 1256–70.

Stewart, Richard B. (1996), *Economic Incentives for Environmental Protection: Opportunities and Obstacles*, Unpublished manuscript, New York University, 69 pp.

Stigler, George J. (1971), 'The Theory of Economic Regulation', Bell *Journal of Economics*, **2**, 3–21.

U.S. Congress, House of Representatives (1986), 'Government Policies on the Transfer of Operating Rights Granted by the Federal Government' Hearing before the Subcommittee on Aviation, Committee on Public Works and Transportation, 99th Congress, 1st session, 10, 19 September, 22 October, 1985, Supt. Doc. Y4.P6/11, 99–33.

U.S. Congress, Office of Technology Assessment (1995), *Environmental Policy Tools: A User's Guide*. OTA-ENV-634. Washington: U.S. Government Printing Office.

U.S. Environmental Protection Agency (1996), *1995 Compliance Results, Acid Rain Program*, EPA/430R-96-012. Washington, DC: Office of Air and Radiation, U.S. Environmental Protection Agency.

Weingast, Barry R. and William J. Marshall. (1988), 'The Industrial Organization of Congress', *Journal of Political Economy*, **96**(1), 132–63.

Weitzman, Martin (1974), 'Prices vs. Quantities', *Review of Economic Studies*, **41**, 477–91.

Welch, W.P. (1983), 'The Political Feasibility of Full Ownership Property Rights: the Case of Pollution and Fisheries', *Policy Sciences*, **16**, 165–80.

Wilson, James Q. (1973), *Political Organizations*, New York: Basic Books.

Yohe, Gary W. (1976), 'Polluters' Profits and Political Response: Direct Control Versus Taxes: Comment', *American Economic Review*, **66** (5), 981–2.

Yohe, Gary W. (1978), 'Towards a General Comparison of Price Controls and Quantity Controls Under Uncertainty', *Review of Economic Studies*, **45**, 229–38.

6. Does nature limit environmental federalism?

V. Kerry Smith, Kurt A. Schwabe, and Carol Mansfield*

INTRODUCTION

Devolution left the sidelines of public policy and entered center stage with sustained Republican congressional victories. The resulting call for greater attention to shifting responsibility for public services from the federal to state and local levels of government has heightened interest in the economic issues underlying the scope for federalism in public programs. No economist has contributed more to the important theoretical and empirical issues of fiscal federalism than Wallace Oates, whom this volume honors. As he observed in his collected essays on federalism (Oates, 1991), his PhD thesis was motivated by Musgrave's (1959) initial treatment of the subject.[1] More than 30 years have passed since Wally's PhD thesis started defining what most of us now understand about the preference, production, and taxation issues underlying the role of the various levels of government in the provision of different types of public and private goods. Moreover, few analysts would suggest that the conceptual dimensions of his work need to be revisited. Instead, like Gold (1996), they argue it is the set of empirical 'realities' of these choices that need to be periodically updated with new, more specific (to current problems) information.

In a somewhat different context, comparable arguments are being made concerning the organization of responsibilities for regulating activities which affect environmental resources. Schoenbrod (1996), for example, contends that the Environmental Protection Agency (EPA) should be changed in dramatic terms that would remove nearly all its regulatory authority.[2] Under such new rules it '... could retain its leadership role only by convincing states to adopt its regulations by the quality and sensibility of its [proposed] policies.'[3] There is no formal analysis that underlies his conclusion and even less empirical evidence. This absence of attention to the details has not diminished enthusiasm for environmental devolution. The most ardent advocates of applying federalism concepts to environmental regulation suggest that the trends for environmental improvement were underway before the 1970s national legislation establishing a goal of uniform levels of environmental quality.[4]

In contrast to this perspective, we know in principle that the physical and temporal form of a regulatory standard can influence the nature of behavioral response and, ultimately, the resulting pattern of environmental quality. Ambient quality is a reflection of decisions made over a spatial grid. It arises from (a) environmental policies, determined in part by the political boundaries; (b) behavioral responses motivated by the incentives created by policy; *and* (c) the nature of the ecosystems governing how the spatial distribution of actions influence the quality at each receptor location.[5] There is some evidence that federal standards for air quality have been effective in influencing the nature of private responses. Henderson's (1996) analysis of the distribution of ozone reading across monitoring stations from 1977 to 1987 provides a convincing example of how the form of the standard can definitely affect the nature of the response. Evaluated using the statistic that defines the standard (the second highest daily maximum), there is a clear shift down in the estimated mode and a tightening in the estimated spread of the distribution. No change in the approximate mode would have been detected using distributions across stations for the annual mean concentration over the same period. There was a tightening in these distributions, but this change came largely at the expense of reducing air quality in the cleaner areas (measured by averages). Thus, in this case we have evidence that national standards did have an impact on the nature of the temporal patterns of air quality around the US.

Limited attention has been given to using the principles developed to identify the optimal jurisdiction for 'produced' public goods in a different situation where government does not produce the public good. These cases arise where regulations of private activities are the primary means to 'deliver' some types of public goods. We address this issue by considering factors that may limit the devolution of environmental regulations. The framework underlying benefit–cost analysis is used to describe devolution as an issue arising from defining 'the extent of the regulatory market' for such analyses. A case study of nutrient control for the Neuse River in North Carolina illustrates how benefit–cost analysis requires some resolution of the questions that directly parallel those involved in implementing federalism principles.

The next section uses the condition for an efficient allocation of resources in the presence of public goods to describe how strategic separability assumptions underlie most arguments for decentralizing environmental policy. Following that we summarize the estimates of the benefits and the costs for a nutrient control plan for the Neuse River. Our primary focus is on the impact of the regulatory jurisdiction for the net benefits of different nutrient control targets. This discussion illustrates the potential for a mismatch between the political boundaries for policy choices and the spatial distribution of net benefits in a devolved system.

The last section argues that nature 'trumps' most of the conventional arguments for devolution. That is, the linkages environmental resources create between activities taking place at different locations must ultimately limit the extent of independence in decision making. Preference-based considerations can also lead to the need to impose more stringent control (and higher levels of quality) because the impacted environmental resources are important to people beyond a jurisdiction defined by physical linkages alone.

EFFICIENCY AND DEVOLUTION

A key premise of those arguing for decentralization of public sector responsibilities is that most public goods are local, with production processes that do not exhibit appreciable scale economies. As a result, a Tiebout (1956) argument would imply increased variety (across jurisdictions) in the offerings of public goods available to consumers and competition among jurisdictions for citizens. The latter is sometimes argued to provide limits on a central government's monopoly taxation policies (Brennan and Buchanan, 1977). In the case of policies intended to maintain or enhance environmental resources, the ability to reproduce environmental public goods is limited by the spatial distribution of natural assets which generate these services as well as by the spatial interconnections in environmental effects of economic activities. Real world examples of these types of linkages are common (see Kneese and Bower, 1979).

To illustrate how these arguments relate to decisions about the efficient level of a public good, consider a simple specification for the i th individual's preferences with one private good, x, and one public good, q, as in equation (6.1).

$$u^i = u_i(x_i, q) \tag{6.1}$$

An individual's incremental willingness to pay for increases in q is defined by the change in x_i, dx_i, that would be paid for dq so that the individual is indifferent between the initial level of q and $q + dq$. An efficient increase in the public good q would be set where the sum of these marginal payments exactly equals the cost of providing q, as given in equation (6.2).

$$-dx = \sum_i dx_i = dq \sum_i MRS^i_{xq} = dq \cdot MRT_{xq} \tag{6.2}$$

This Samuelsonian condition for an efficient allocation of resources between a private good helps in organizing discussions of fiscal federalism and the selection of a jurisdiction for environmental regulations.[6]

Conventional discussions of federalism assume we can classify the cases where: (a) the technology warrants a federal solution (that is, based on properties of the *MRT* term); (b) the practical financing issues imply a specific level of government based on ease or efficiency in collecting required taxes;[7] or (c) the diversity in preferences warrant variety in public good levels (the *MRS* terms). When we consider changes in q through some form of regulation on private activities, we need to add to this list. Regulations will require modifications in the private goods production activities that are linked to q. These changes will be reflected in the *MRT* term.

Even with this addition there remains an important missing element from the list of federalism issues. Environmental public goods change because of an alteration in production and consumption activities that emit residuals impacting the natural assets responsible for providing these environmental goods. To describe adequately what can be expected requires incorporating into the analysis the linkages outside of markets introduced through the interconnections in ecosystems.[8]

Environmental linkages were the central motivation for Kneese and Bower's (1979) work in developing the Delaware Estuary model.[9] Indeed, the research of Kneese's Environmental Quality Program was organized with an explicit recognition that the regional locus of environmental quality management was a key decision.[10] This regional perspective lead to more than a decade of research describing the economic, environmental, and political dimensions of alternative policy decisions. They began from a spatial premise – the definition of a regional unit of analysis largely based on environmental criteria, with the lower Delaware Valley, their most detailed case. However, the size of the region was never treated as an issue for analysis.

Regulatory federalism makes the definition of the region a part of the problem. If the technical linkages are known then they comprise one component of the constraints conditioning the decisions of private citizens and local governments assigned responsibility for different environmental public goods. Unfortunately, uncertainty over the nature and costs of external effects abounds and is often among the important reasons for questioning the use of economic policies in resolving these types of problems.

These issues are present in varying degrees for other environmental decisions. Air and water quality are not special cases. The principles underlying the establishment of the national park system or the wilderness system were based on the premise that these land areas could be set aside and managed to achieve preservation and recreation objectives largely independent of what happened to the land around them. This view of habitat management would imply that one could assign responsibility for any particular park (or wilderness area) based exclusively on the left side of equation (6.2). There is now growing appreciation that there are zones of influence around these reserves that affect the environmental services that they provide.[11] The specifics differ depending both on the environmental resources involved and the external activities in each location. There is an extended general equilibrium system that connects both sides of equation (6.2). The effects of the economic components of that general equilibrium system have been recognized for some time with the early writings on second-best and optimal taxation. They are largely 'controlled' in analytical work through strategic separability assumptions imposed on preferences or production relationships.[12]

This may be a plausible argument for public goods produced by the government. It is not relevant to those associated with environmental public goods because of the linkages connecting activities outside the conventional boundaries used to define production and preference relationships. As a result, we can expect extended general equilibrium effects in addition to the preference and the production based contributions to the incremental opportunity costs measured in expressions like our equation (6.2).[13]

There is another aspect of the conditions for efficient allocation of resources that is sometimes overlooked. This issue relates to the number of people assumed to 'care about' the level of q. Discussions of this issue in the context of local public goods also follow the logic developed by Oates (1972, 1977). Welfare gains or losses due to centralization of the decisions about the amount of a public good to provide are generally held to depend on the heterogeneity in the levels of individual demand for a given 'price' and the price elasticities of the individuals' demands. This approach assumes that the goods can be reproduced in different locations. For some environmental resources such as clean air or water, this characterization may be adequate. However, national parks and other natural assets give rise to a different type of environmental public good. In these cases, decisions about who counts in computing the benefits of a policy, or analytically, whose MRS_{xq} is included on the left side of equation (6.2), are especially important to the amount of public good that is provided.[14]

This issue is one of the most contentious questions in the current literature associated with non-market valuation of environment resources. While it is described in terms of the 'nonuse values' for environmental resources, the issues extend beyond this question.[15] To the extent people outside the region assigned with responsibility for decisions about increments to q also have an economic stake in what is done, but are not counted, then decentralization inevitably leads to inefficiencies. The nature of their stake can be infrequent patterns of current use, expected future use, or motives attributed to nonuse or existence values. This argument relies on the assumption that fairly close substitutes for the resources are not available in locations where the individuals reside and influence the local allocation decisions. Thus, linkages in the environmental system and extent of the economic market for q are two new dimensions added to the issues affecting the extent of regulatory federalism for environmental resources.

These questions are not simply 'grist' for an academic debate. Equation (6.2) is after all akin to a comparison of incremental benefits with incremental costs for *dq*. Benefit–cost mandates for rules have begun to devolve to the state level. Over twenty states now have such mandates. The issues we have raised are beginning to be acknowledged. Whisnant and Cherry (1996), for example, observed that there are few incentives to confront the external effects that extend across state boundaries regardless of whether these effects arise from environmental linkages or consumer preferences for resources that are outside their state of residence.[16] Moreover, lack of accurate data on the effects at increasing distances from activities within the state, together with a presumption that those impacted are themselves mitigating any impacts, makes the analysis required to determine a prudent assignment of responsibility exceed the limits of most states' analytical capacities.

Most economists, and even advocates of devolution appear to be willing to concede that environmental linkages set limits to devolution.[17] Unfortunately this concession does not extend to linkages due to nonuse values that influence the extent of the market concerned about any proposed regulatory change. In the next section we use the benefit–cost analysis of nutrient control for the Neuse River basin in North Carolina to illustrate the impact of how consideration of the environmental linkages and definition of what 'counts' can influence measures of both the cost and aggregate benefits.

NUTRIENTS IN THE NEUSE RIVER: A CASE STUDY

Most environmental management problems must be treated in a spatial context.[18] To illustrate how nature can set limits to devolution, we use a water quality management issue in North Carolina. It involves different locations within the state and the divergence in uses and consequences for a natural resource – the Neuse River.[19]

The Neuse River basin, with over 3000 stream miles, extends from nearly the north western boundary of North Carolina with Virginia, to the Pamlico Sound in New Bern. Over the past three years, the river has been the subject of much local and national attention due to fish kills attributed to excess nutrients. Considerable evidence indicates toxic dinoflagellates may be involved. A nutrient management strategy for the Neuse River was the first rule subjected to a fiscal note (required by the North Carolina's mandate for economic analysis of regulations). This fiscal note is intended to evaluate the impacts on the state's economy (as well as on those responsible for meeting the control objectives) of proposed policies to reduce nitrogen loadings throughout the Neuse River basin by at least 30 percent.

Analysis of this proposal requires addressing the same issues being posed under the mantel of regulatory federalism. Our case study illustrates the potential importance of any proposal arbitrarily assigning responsibility for environmental regulations to a specific level of government. It is organized in three parts. The first uses a large scale nutrient-balance process model for the Neuse River basin to describe how the activities generating nutrient loadings influence the cost estimates associated with different levels of control. This analysis demonstrates how devolution can influence the opportunity costs attributed to a regulation.

The second uses the model to evaluate a pure incentive based policy for meeting the proposed 30 percent reduction. It focuses on the distribution of costs across the 12 counties included in Schwabe's (1996) model of the river basin. This distribution indicates how environmental linkages, together with the spatial location of activities, influence the cost estimates for nutrient control. The last combines the cost estimates by county with benefit estimates developed based on a telephone-mail-telephone survey of households in North Carolina conducted from November 1995 through January 1996. This survey was designed to evaluate whether households would support policies to reduce nitrogen loadings from swine operations that impact the same coastal areas. Net benefits are measured for each county as well as for the state as a whole to show how the extent and composition of the regulatory market can influence the evaluation offered by the economic analysis.

Nutrient Control Costs

Table 6.1 summarizes the control cost estimates for a 30 percent reduction in nitrogen loadings with four different versions of the Schwabe model. The first includes only cropping activities. This model treats each county as if it were a cost minimizing farm producing one or more field crops (corn, cotton, or soybeans) with different cropping systems and nitrogen control practices (including conservation tillage, controlled drainage, and vegetative filter strips). Land is distinguished by three characteristics relevant to nutrient run-off – erodibility, slope, and transmissivity. Crop land is further separated by region – the Piedmont, Upper Coastal and Lower Coastal Plains to account for yield differences.[20] The production activities are adjusted based on the technical characteristics of the land in each area.

The second model adds to the cropping activities18 wastewater treatment plants (WWTP) located along the Neuse River. The descriptions of these plants allow for primary and secondary treatment of nitrogen where the equipment available suggests the relevant treatment would be feasible. The third model includes nitrogen loadings from swine operations together with the cropping activities sub-model, but does not allow for control options at these locations. This specification increases the baseline estimates for loadings. As a result, in the model with cropping and swine operations, greater effort will be required on the part of the cropping activities to meet a 30 percent reduction. This conclusion follows because the base level of nitrogen emissions changes as the set of activities in the model which are responsible for these nitrogen residuals expands. As more activities are added the baseline level of nitrogen changes. Thus, a 30 percent reduction will lead to a different absolute amount of nitrogen removal across the models with different baseline levels of loadings. This distinction influences comparisons across these four versions of the model. All four cases solved in Table 6.1 consider only the use of command and control (CAC) regulations to meet the 30 percent reduction. In a CAC format the percentage is applied to each source individually so its goals do not change, unless the change introduces background or activities that are assumed incapable of being controlled. This is the situation when loadings from swine operations are included. To meet a 30 percent reduction in total loadings with no control options feasible for these swine farms, the target for cropping activities must be increased to greater than 30 percent so the overall control level is met. Total

Table 6.1 *Costs for 30 percent nutrient reduction in the Neuse River: extent of regulatory market (1994 $)*

	Baseline[b]	Cropping Activities	Cropping and WWTP[c]	Cropping and Swine Operations	Complete Model
Total costs[a]	157273	162449	165264	163665	166479
Control costs[a]	–	5176	7991	6392	9206
Cost per pound removed	–	4.76	5.74	5.37	6.15
Unit control cost as % of complete model's unit cost estimates	–	77	93	87	–

Notes:

[a] These costs are measured in thousands of dollars. They are annual costs and do not include land costs. Reductions in nitrogen loadings in all models are achieved using a command and control policy.

[b] Baseline solution corresponds to cases where only cropping activities are present.

[c] WWTP designated the eighteen major wastewater treatment plants included in the Schwabe model.

control costs increase as more sources are added in a CAC framework because each source (that can exercise some control) is constrained to meet the same percent reduction. However, average control costs may not increase. New sources previously outside the group defined for control may be able to reduce nitrogen loadings at lower cost per pound than those previously subject to control. The overall average will depend on how large this discrepancy is and on how much of the total reduction in loadings is due to these sources. The last model combines all three components.

North Carolina's Division of Water Quality estimates that 8.7 million pounds of nitrogen enter the Pamlico Estuary from the Neuse River each year. About 2.1 million pounds of this total are attributed to point sources, the remaining 6.6 million to non-point sources. By varying the composition of the point and non-point sources included in the Schwabe model, we can see dramatic differences in the estimates of control costs. To some extent, the total control cost estimates may be misleading because, as we noted earlier, what counts as a cost and the actual amount of nitrogen removed from the effluent stream varies across these models. To reflect this effect the third row reports the unit cost per pound removed from the waste stream (measured at the estuary). These average costs range from \$4.76 to \$6.15 depending on the composition of the model. This is nearly a 25 percent difference in unit cost estimates arising from the mix of activities allowed to count as contributing to the nutrient problem in the Neuse River. These cost differences illustrate the types of impacts that can arise in defining a jurisdiction for environmental regulations.

Spatial Disaggregation

Table 6.2 disaggregates the implied costs under a CAC policy with each county's cropping activities and point sources required to reduce loadings by 30 percent (where that goal is technically feasible). The first three columns of data detail the non-point, point, and total costs of realizing the 30 percent reduction. The last column reports the unit costs per pound of nitrogen removed measured at the Pamlico Sound. Clearly there are wide differences in the average costs. As we observed in Table 6.1 for models composed of different types of nitrogen sources (for example, farms versus wastewater treatment plants), small changes in the spatial composition of the regulated area leads to control cost differences. The measured differences in unit costs across counties imply substantial scope for gains from trade (that is, incentive based policies). Part of the reason for these differences stems from the characteristics of the land in each county and its location in relation to the Pamlico Sound. Because nitrogen loadings are measured in equivalent units at New Bern, N.C. (that is, on the coast), control measures in the western counties are not as cost effective as those in the Upper and Middle Coastal Plain.

Table 6.2 Spatial distribution of control costs for a command and control policy (CAC) and 30 percent reduction

County	Annual Cost[a]			Average cost per lb removed
	Non-point sources	Point sources	Total cost	
Orange	121.4	–	121.4	174.5
Durham	8.5	–	8.5	92.6
Wake	207.7	1125.4	1333.1	8.1
Johnston	728.4	202.3	930.7	6.7
Nash	240.0	–	240.0	7.4
Wilson	436.7	255.2	691.9	12.4
Wayne	936.1	15.6	951.7	4.1
Greene	724.4	–	724.4	5.1
Lenoir	936.2	1166.1	2102.3	7.4
Pitt	504.9	–	504.9	2.5
Jones	671.6	–	671.6	11.4
Craven	875.7	50.4	926.1	5.7

Note: [a] These costs are measured in thousands of 1994 dollars. The estimates are developed from results reported in Schwabe (1996).

The cost effects of devolution are illustrated in two ways with the model. Current water pollution policy assigns EPA with responsibility for point sources and excludes agriculture within the same watershed. Thus, the effects of region used for analysis in a devolved system could well arise because point sources were regulated with a federal system and non-point sources in a devolved state or local system. The unit (and incremental) cost of nutrient control for specific river systems can be very different depending upon whether each type source is regulated separately or both are handled in a unified regulatory system. This point is partially illustrated in Table 6.1. Equally important, the region defined as the Neuse River basin and treated as a unit for analysis could be considered a devolution issue. Agricultural activities and point sources have specific locations along the river and the choice of regional borders determines which sources are included. Table 6.2 illustrates that this has clear potential to impact the incremental costs of meeting a standard, especially with incentive based policies.

Limiting the trading areas to a few high or low cost counties treated in isolation such as Wayne, Lenoir, Pitt, or Craven for the lower unit cost case would lead to an underestimate of the potential gains from allowing permit trades. Failure to include some counties as sources of nitrogen affects the estimated levels of

Table 6.3 A comparison of the nitrogen loading responsibilities under CAC versus IB policies[a]

Type of discharge	Source	Baseline solution (pounds)	Loadings under 30% reduction CAC (pounds)	Loadings under 30% reduction IB (pounds)	Change in responsibility (pounds)
Non-point	Orange	2318	1523	2318	–696
	Durham	307	215	307	–92
	Wake	36848	25794	36848	–11055
	Johnston	420738	294517	315964	–21447
	Nash	107891	75524	77714	–2190
	Wilson	125123	87586	94993	–7407
	Wayne	776746	543722	583519	–39796
	Greene	472552	330786	319195	11592
	Lenoir	711951	498366	472437	25928
	Pitt	676993	473895	524966	–51071
	Jones	195863	137104	195863	–58759
	Craven	438073	306651	330268	–23617
Point	Zebulon	2087	1441	2087	–646
	Apex	7504	5197	7504	–2307
	Cary-North	53010	35679	53010	–17331
	Cary-South	50863	34386	50863	–16477
	Burlington	23274	16185	14192	1993
	Wilson	57840	39424	57840	–18416
	Wake	2310	2310	2310	0
	Raleigh	330450	220374	48269	172105
	Benson	14940	10329	7915	2414
	Johnston	28167	19267	28167	–8900
	Goldsboro	166568	112746	69451	43295
	Farmville	10215	10215	10215	0
	Kinston-Peachtree	64226	44381	64226	–19845
	Contentnea	46305	31446	13297	18150
	Kinston-North	34560	34560	29107	5453
	Dupont	8110	8110	8110	0
	New Bern	101127	69769	50648	19121
	Havelock	17568	17568	17568	0
	Basinwide	4984527	3489170	3489169	0

Note: [a] Solutions derived under county constrained module; includes cropping activities, wastewater treatment plants, and swine waste. Cropping activities are responsible for swine waste under command and control. Positive values indicate source assumes more responsibility for nitrogen loading reduction under IB compared to CAC.

Source: Schwabe (1996).

nitrogen loadings; it also imposes greater costs on the other counties identified. This is the spatial counterpart of our evaluation of including different types of production sources responsible for nitrogen in the river.

We can develop some insight into the effects of re-allocating responsibilities for meeting the 30 percent goal by comparing the average cost of a CAC versus an incentive based (IB) approach. The former is about $6.24 per pound of nitrogen removed while the IB approach is about $4.12 per pound. Table 6.3 reports the re-allocation in responsibilities for reducing nitrogen loadings in the two solutions. The first 12 rows correspond to the cropping activities by county and the 18 rows designated as point sources are the wastewater treatment plants along the river that are included in the model. Clearly the two scenarios assign responsibility for the clean-up quite differently. Moreover, this type of change probably understates what might be expected with different assignments of responsibility for nutrient regulation.[21] As Whisnant and Cherry suggest, there is no reason to expect that devolved systems will have incentives to develop the information necessary to promote assignment of responsibility based on costs, especially if those realizing the largest cost savings would be outside that system's area of jurisdiction.

Benefits and Devolution

The benefit side of environmental federalism questions is especially difficult. As we noted, environmental assets are located in space and can have implications for more than the immediate neighbors. There are not systematic means to keep track of how all these effects take place. In the case of the Neuse River, farming practices as well as the operations of the wastewater treatment plants influence water quality along North Carolina's coast around New Bern. Residents of the area suffer fish kills, algae blooms, odor, and other impacts. During recreational seasons tourists are also be affected. Measuring the benefits that might arise from different regulatory regimes requires a specification of the composition of the 'market' for all the services provided by the environmental asset(s). Often these decisions focus on the treatment of use and non-use values, where the latter is associated with people who may experience enhanced well-being from improvements in a resource but do not display any behavioral response that can be attributed to these concerns. As a result some authors have considered them speculative and argued that they should not be included in a benefit–cost analysis associated with policies intended to manage most environmental assets.[22] As a practical matter, even within the category of use values, the composition of the 'n' in equation (6.2) is rarely 'clearcut'. As in the case of those contributing to estimates of the costs of regulations, the identification of which economic agents' benefits should count is also fundamental to what can be expected from a devolved system.

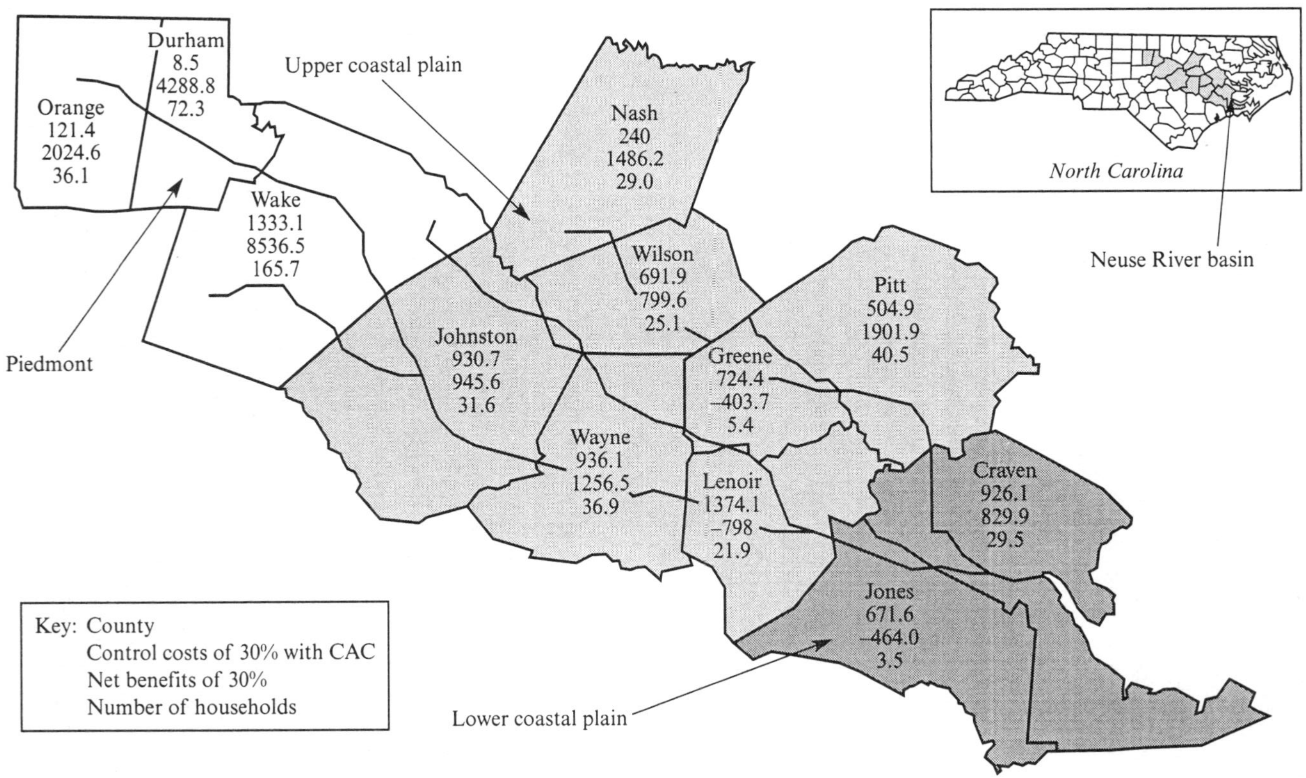

Figure 6.1 Net benefits of nutrient control by county in the Neuse River basin – CAC

Figure 6.1 illustrates how this can happen. It takes the 12 counties in the Schwabe model comprising the primary components of the Neuse watershed and computes the net benefits of the proposed 30 percent reduction in nutrient loadings for each. These estimates are derived from a fairly crude benefit transfer.[23] To illustrate the spatial differences we have placed the estimates on the map, reporting the aggregate costs (in thousands of dollars), net benefits assuming a CAC policy regime, and the number of households in each county. Table 6.4 reports the estimates by county for the CAC and IB approaches of realizing the 30 percent reduction in 1994 dollars. With the CAC policy, only three of the counties, Greene, Lenoir, and Jones, experience losses but this is enough to make our point. It is clear from the estimates in Figure 6.1 (and Table 6.4) that decisions about the composition of the region given authority for nitrogen control will influence the extent of excess demand for water quality improvements. Moreover, to make this argument in a fairly persuasive way, we do not need to extend the market area to include counties that are 'outside' the set linked through the watershed to water quality in the sound.

Table 6.4 Net benefits of a 30 percent reduction in nitrogen loadings: CAC versus IB Policies

	Net benefits$[b]	
County[a]	CAC	IB
Orange	2025	2146
Durham	4289	4297
Wake	8536	8029
Johnston	946	1440
Nash	1486	1545
Wilson	800	1278
Wayne	1256	1657
Greene	–404	–513
Lenoir	–798	–37
Pitt	1902	2397
Jones	–464	208
Craven	830	1068
Aggregate net benefit	20388	23515

Notes:

[a] Counties are ordered from most distant to most proximate location to the Pamlico Sound.

[b] Estimates are in thousands of dollars and do not adjust for the fact that benefits are in 1995 dollars and cost in 1994.

One might argue that we could devise plans (that is, assign property rights) to create incentives for those with positive net benefits to clean up and to compensate those with negative net benefits for their efforts. However, this suggestion assumes that a higher level authority sets and enforces those rights. Moreover, it does not account for the fact that regulations could easily be set for different types of sources under different levels of devolution in each source category. Thus a mix of negative and positive net benefits by level of government can be considered constraints to the processes used in devolution of environmental policies.

Our benefit estimates are derived from a telephone-mail-telephone survey. In the first stage, 1002 households in North Carolina were contacted by telephone, collecting attitudinal, demographic, and economic characteristics. In the process respondents were asked if they would be willing to participate in a second telephone interview which required them to provide their mailing address so that they could send information about issues affecting the water quality of North Carolina's rivers and coastal areas. Of the original 1002 respondents, 540 completed the second interview.[24]

To estimate the benefits of controlling nitrogen loadings that impact on the quality of coastal resources, two plans to regulate the operations of large hog farms were described in different booklets which were randomly assigned to each person who agreed to the second interview. The booklets included color photos of hog operations and described how regulations would reduce nutrients in surface and groundwater, as well as reduce the risk of future waste spills from large farms' waste handling systems into North Carolina rivers. These reductions were described in qualitative terms. The plans were also distinguished based on how much of the control costs to private operators would be shared by the state. The descriptions were closely aligned to the actual text of proposals discussed at that time in the state legislature.

The proposal we consider for our benefit estimate does not bundle private cost sharing with regulations and monitoring intended to realize nitrogen control. Neither does it guarantee the 30 percent reduction envisioned in our cost analysis. Moreover, it is described as a statewide initiative that relies on regulations imposed on large hog farms, and not one targeting the Neuse River or one affecting other sources of nitrogen – the cropping activities and wastewater treatment plants.[25]

Our benefit estimates assume the respondents' answers to discrete, take it or leave it contingent valuation (CV), questions that provide adequate measures of household willingness-to-pay (WTP) for a benefit transfer analysis. The CV questions suggest that respondents will have to pay for the regulations because state income taxes must increase from $10 to $750 each year to pay for increased monitoring associated with the proposed new rules.[26]

This transfer may well seem a considerable 'stretch' (given survey design) of the available benefit measures. It is not clear, however, that we are overstating the WTP at the household level. Indeed, the majority of the nutrient loadings on the Neuse are due to cropping and wastewater loadings, not the operations of hog farms. This focus may imply that our estimate for a household's WTP is a conservative measure of the value people might place on a plan perceived as addressing all aspects of the problem.

Equally important, we applied a conservative method to develop the aggregate estimates from our household WTP estimates. Based on the estimated median WTP (derived from fitting a Weibull survival model to the CV responses) we adjusted the estimate assigned to all the households in each county by the response rate to our final survey (66 percent).[27] This procedure assumes non-respondents had a zero value for the proposed plan to regulate hog farms. Finally, we assume only households in the 12 county areas covered by the Schwabe model of the Neuse River watershed would be willing to pay. The estimated overall benefits from the plan (with the median estimate) would be 29.6 million (in 1994 dollars). This compares with overall costs of the CAC program for a 30 percent reduction of 8.1 million dollars to yield positive net benefits.

If we used the same process and applied the median household WTP and response rate adjustment to all households in the state this estimate would be $114.2 million. Where do we stop? This is also an issue that is logically part of devolution and suggests that the 30 percent reduction could well be considered too small as the size of the aggregate net benefits increases with expansion in the set of households assumed to be concerned about the resource.[28]

IMPLICATIONS

Wally's research on federalism has emphasized the need to balance the complexity of theoretical models designed to highlight the information necessary to make jurisdictional decisions with the empirical details relevant to each application. We believe these 'details' are especially important in structuring the jurisdictional responsibilities for environmental policy. Our conclusions about the scope for devolution, in some respects, reiterate the important lessons found in the design of Kneese's environmental management efforts in the 1970s. Linkages in environmental resources create spillover effects that cannot be ignored when measuring the costs of attaining any ambient quality level and thus impact on judgments about the extent of regulation that is warranted. Our example of the Neuse River suggested that whether we identify jurisdiction by activity or location, the effects on the cost of reducing nitrogen loadings can be substantial.

This is a different perspective than most discussions of fiscal federalism, where the production component of the delivery of local public goods is considered in less detail than what is given to preference heterogeneity. In the case of environmental devolution it is clear that regulations can impact on costs in different ways that are affected by the definition of the jurisdiction assigned responsibility. A simple identification of the spillovers is not enough to assure these external effects will be taken seriously without credible oversight.

The preference component of these decisions is also, we believe, more complex than with local public goods. The spatial dimension of environmental resources implies that in a number of cases 'users' will extend beyond local residents. We expect (and for some approaches to non-market valuation we rely on the fact) that people will travel to some environmental resources to experience their services. This feature of the consumption of environmental services implies the user population is harder to define by residential location alone. Equally important, non-use values are also harder to dismiss as speculative for many environmental resources. Developing benefit estimates in these cases that identify those with very low versus zero willingness-to-pay is difficult and costly.

Both these differences are central to how one must address the extent of devolution adopted for decisions involving the direct management or the regulation of activities impacting on environmental resources. Our arguments concern differences for both the cost and the preference components of the federalism problem. They began from analyses that sought to understand the specifics of how each environmental resource is affected by and contributes to people's activities. Understanding the contribution of 'nature' expressed in these terms is an essential component of the tasks to be addressed in environmental federalism.

NOTES

* Partial support for Smith's research was provided by the UNC Sea Grant Program under project #R/MRD-32. Schwabe's research was partially supported by the North Carolina Agricultural Research Service at North Carolina State University. Thanks are due to Diane Cherry, Arvind Panagariya and Robert Schwab for comments on an earlier draft of this paper and to Kris McGee for preparing and editing it. The conclusions reported are those of the authors, not their respective employers or funding sources.

1. Musgrave's three way categorization of the functions of government (that is, allocation, distribution, and stabilization) argues that allocation issues are motivated largely through preference differences. This may be the reason why production advantages were not addressed in the same detail as preference heterogeneity in the early discussions of federalism. Oates (1991) cites Musgrave's key description of the fiscal federalism question as follows: 'The heart of fiscal federalism thus lies in the proposition that the policies of the Allocation Branch should be permitted to differ between states, depending on the preferences of their citizens.' (Musgrave (1959) pp. 181–2).
2. Schoenbrod's proposal to reform EPA is best described in his own summary: 'The Environmental Protection Agency should be stripped of its power with four exceptions. First, it

should gather and publicize information on pollution and its consequences, both on the national and the local level. Second, it should propose to Congress rules of conduct to control types of interstate pollution that are not adequately addressed by the states or that require special protection, such as the Grand Canyon. Third, it should propose to Congress rules of conduct for goods, such as new cars, when state-by-state regulation would erect significant barriers to interstate commerce. Fourth, it should draft model state environmental laws and conduct policy studies that states could use when considering whether to enact such laws. States, however, should be free to amend or reflect federal proposals in favor of different approaches to pollution control.' (p. 24).

3. Schoenbrod (1996) p. 25, bracketed term added.
4. Crandall (1985) suggested that substantial progress had been made prior to the 1970s in the case of air quality.
5. Assume the statistic used to define the ambient standard is accurately based on how that air pollution affects human health, then the physical and temporal features of the standard serve an important role in targeting specific types of improvements (that is, the severe episodes of pollution versus long term average levels).
6. There are also complications that arise with the public financing used for increments in q. A common approximation involves multiplying the *MRT* by the marginal cost of public funds (*MCF*). This adjustment arises from a recognition of the welfare losses due to the distortionary effects of most tax systems. Ballard and Fullerton (1992) provide an excellent summary of the optimal taxation literature in relation to estimates of the excess burden caused by distortionary taxes and its role in evaluating the efficiency conditions for public goods. For more recent discussions of these issues in the context of measuring the costs of environmental regulations, see Goulder et al. (1997) and Fullerton and Metcalf (1996).
7. Practical financing issues are largely outside the simplified framework of equation (6.2). It could be amended to take account of the marginal costs of public funds. Equally important, this simplified classification requires a set of separability assumptions for both individual preferences and for the process involved in producing q. If q is not separable from the activities taxed to finance increases in the public good then the simple expression (and assumption of locally constant values of the marginal cost of public funds) collapses.
8. Of course, linkages through markets can be important as well. The lessons from efforts to compute the social costs of environmental regulations suggest these are not simple adjustments (see Hazilla and Kopp, 1990 and Jorgenson and Wilcoxen, 1990).
9. To our knowledge, Haefele and Kneese (1973) provide the first integrated discussion in the economic and political economy dimensions of optimal jurisdiction. While their paper recognized the interactions between the physical or environmental limits on federalism, it seems to assume implicitly that environmental constraints define what they refer to as a 'problemshed' and limit the consideration given to other factors within this pre-defined unit of analysis.
10. One example of this role can be found in Kneese and Bower's description of how to start the analysis and design of policies to meet environmental quality management problems. They note that it is necessary to start at the regional level; for their approach, the region embodied the key unit of analysis because it incorporated environmental constraints. 'It is necessary to use a word like regional rather than terms pertaining to political jurisdictions, such as nations, states, or cities because the extent of ambient environmental quality changes resulting from the discharge of materials and energy follow the meteorological, hydrological, and biological systems rather than the boundaries of political systems.' (p. 16).
11. Botkin's (1990) arguments for a new ecology are examples of this difference in perspective. Christensen et al. (1996) have noted, based on these changing perspectives for ecosystems, that management focusing on commodity outputs alone and failing to recognize the influence of surrounding areas is not sustainable.
12. There are numerous examples of these in discussions in the double dividend literature. See Goulder et al. (1997) and Fullerton and Metcalf (1996) as examples. Deaton (1987) is often attributed with highlighting the importance and plausibility in some circumstances of the separability restrictions required for the tractable versions of optimal taxation results. We are grateful to Jim Poterba for calling this work to our attention. These have been questioned by many authors before us and a common response is that without them we have no hope of simplified policy

judgments. Of course, mistaken conclusions from simple models do not necessarily improve welfare.

13. For a discussion of these issues in the context of a computable general equilibrium model with a non-separable treatment of the effects of air pollution on people's preferences, see Smith and Espinosa (1996).
14. If we write out

$$\sum_{i} MRS^{i}_{xq} \text{ as } \sum_{i=1}^{n} MRS^{i}_{xq}$$

then it is the 'n'.

15. See Freeman (1993) for an overview of the various definitions for non-use value. The original concept of existence value is due to Krutilla (1967).
16. These authors observed, '... a state has little or no incentive to issue rules that costs its taxpayers – more importantly, its voters – for the benefit of the citizens of other states' (p. 736).
17. Anderson and Hill (1996), suggest: '... the following principle should guide environmental federalism: To minimize the costs of monitoring regulatory agencies, authority should devolve to the lowest level of government that also allows for control of pollution and other spillover effects' (p. 9).
18. As we have suggested, RFF's Quality of the Environment Program of the 1970s was organized to integrate this insight into all the models used to evaluate policy instruments. It has also been an important part of Wally's work on environmental policies with his PhD students. See Krupnick, Oates, and Van De Verg (1983), McGartland and Oates (1985) and Oates, Portney, and McGartland (1989).
19. After the research for this paper was finished, the Raleigh *News and Observer* (31 January 1997) reported that the EPA was taking steps (in response to a suit filed on 31 December 1996 by the Neuse River Foundation) to enforce a provision in the Clean Water Act that requires states to set firm thresholds on the total waste a river can absorb daily from all sources. This would make our case study directly parallel to the conceptual issues underlying regulatory federalism, not due to the geographic boundaries but rather federal mandates for consistent measures for the waste handling capacities of a river.
20. See Figure 6.1 for the definitions of these areas.
21. In these comparisons the size of the aggregate reduction in nitrogen loading was held constant.
22. Diamond and Hausman (1993) appear to equate non-use values with an expression of ethical beliefs and then conclude that monetary compensation for natural resource injury and benefit–cost evaluations should be based on individual preferences not ethical judgments. Non-use or existence values can also be argued to represent enhancements to individual preferences that parallel the effects of a pure public good (Plourde, 1975). Under this perspective one could agree to avoid ethical positions but continue to include non-use values because of their relationship to public good services.

    Diamond and Hausman (1994) would also have an objection to this position because such values would have to be measured with contingent valuation (that is, non-use values do not necessarily imply any behavioral response). They had noted that: '... contingent valuation is a deeply flawed methodology for measuring non-use values, one that does not estimate what its proponents claim to be estimating .... There is a history of anomalous results in contingent valuation surveys that seem closely tied to the embedding problem. Although this problem has been recognized in the literature for over a decade, it has not been solved. Thus, we conclude that current contingent valuation methods should not be used for damage assessment or for benefit cost analysis.' (pp. 62–3).
23. In a separate analysis Smith and Schwabe used a random utility model (RUM) developed by Liu (1995) together with a model linking nutrient loadings to sport fishing quality (Smith, Liu, and Palmquist [1993]) to evaluate the impact of a 36 percent reduction in nitrogen loadings on the Neuse. The RUM was based on a 1988 (follow-up to the 1987) National Marine Fisheries Service survey that was conducted by Nancy Bockstael and Kenneth McConnell of the University of Maryland. This follow-up involved fishing parties intercepted in North Carolina.

The per trip Hicksian consumer surplus from the quality improvement (in 1988 dollars) was estimated at $13.29. Using the estimated number of trips taken by only NC sport fishing anglers from 1991 National Survey of Fishing, Hunting, and Wildlife Associated survey, together with the number of North Carolina sport fishing anglers and the fraction of the fishing parties using locations around the Neuse River (adjusting the benefits for the higher percent of reduction), our estimates suggested between $3.25 and $5.83 million dollars of benefits. These estimates assume either 12 or 22.7 percent of the trips originate from areas affected by the Neuse River. They are limited to trips made by North Carolina anglers (estimated at 1.94 million per year).

The benefit transfer underlying the estimates in Table 6.4 and Figure 6.1 relate to all possible sources of benefits from the water quality improvement to North Carolina residents in the area. When compared with these benefits to sport fishing alone, the total benefits seem plausible.

24. Mansfield and Smith (1997) investigated the importance of selection effects with initial agreement to participate in the survey (using a model with county level aggregate data following Papke and Woolridge (1996)) and the selection effects associated with those respondents who answered the first phase survey completing the second interview. While age, education, and gender were important determinants of the likelihood of completing this survey, the results did not indicate that either selection effect was important to choice models derived for the contingent valuation question associated with the plan to regulate large hog farms.

25. The text of the question associated with the plan to regulate large hog farms was distinguished according to whether it involved some cost sharing of initial capital costs (with farmers) or not and its order in the telephone interview. Our results relate to the plan *without* cost sharing when asked first. (Respondents were reminded of the plan which involved three changes in hog farms operations.) We review the full sequence of questions as follows: The booklet described a plan with new regulations for reducing the potential contamination of coastal waters from releases of hog waste in the eastern counties of North Carolina.

9. Do you remember the plan?
   01 yes
   02 no (go to 9b)

9a. As you recall, the plan applies to large hog farms. (Go to 9c)

9b. The plan applies only to large hog farms.

9c. It would require three changes in their operations. Their waste lagoons would be required to use mechanical techniques to increase the natural decay of the waste and reduce odor. Reinforced lagoons with plastic liners and annual inspections would be required. This would reduce the chances of accident spills in the leakage of nutrients into groundwater. And finally, spraying of waste would not be allowed within 1000 feet of a wetland or a river. This plan would be in addition to other actions the state is now undertaking.

9d. Would you like me to repeat anything about the plan?
   01 yes
   02 no

10. These requirements would raise the costs of operations at hog farms. Because they would be among the most stringent in the nation, it is anticipated that some farms would close and the major firms in the industry would move some operations outside the state. This would increase unemployment in eastern North Carolina.

    Here is how the plan for increased regulations and monitoring of the large hog farms would be paid for. Large hog farms would be required to pay for the mechanical processing of hog waste, the enhanced lagoons, and the controls on spraying. The state would pay for the increased inspections to assure the plan works.

To pay for these annual inspections, there would have to be an increase in North Carolina residents' state income taxes. For your household it would be an additional (randomize and keep track: \$10, \$25, \$50, \$75, \$100, \$125, \$375, \$750) each year. This would be in addition to the amount you now pay in state income taxes. This payment would be required each year to maintain this program. Please keep in mind your current income and the things you now buy.

If this plan to regulate large hog farms were on statewide referendum with your taxes increased by (repeat amount from above) and you could vote on the plan, would you vote for or against it?

01 for the plan (go to 12a)
02 against the plan (go to 12)
03 don't know (don't offer, go to 11a)

26. By using the per household estimates for our survey (with some adjustment explained below) we are assuming these differences would not markedly impact the WTP estimates for a plan targeted at the Neuse River with the households we include in our analysis.
27. Using a Weibull survival model to estimate the responses from the first question, the estimated median WTP was \$94.90 per year. The 95 percent confidence interval was \$46.07 to \$195.50. Because the survey was conducted between November 1995 and January 1996 we used the December 1995 Consumer Price Index to adjust the benefit to 1994 dollars for the aggregate estimates. Household income was reported for the last tax year, 1994 (1995 income taxes were not filled until after the survey was completed). The adjustment implies benefit measures in 1994 dollars that were about 95 percent of the 1995 levels.

The probit choice model from the CV data suggests that the proposed tax amount was a significant determinant of stated choices. One of the models reported in Mansfield and Smith (1997) is given as follows:

State vote for plan =	–2.44	–0.0013 tax amount
	(–1.66)	(–2.70)
	+0.055 Household income	+ 0.655 College Grad.
	(1.35) (in ten thousand dollars)	(2.20) (=1)
	+0.204 Likelihood of hog waste spills	+0.125 Regulate Hog Farms
	(3.47)	(0.54) (=1)
	–0.248 Live on Farm	+0.877 IMR1
	(– 0.68) (=1)	(0.41)
	+0.475 IMR2	n = 140
	(0.38)	pseudo $R^2 = 0.159$

This model was estimated for only the respondents receiving the booklet and question relating to the plan without cost sharing. IMR1 and IMR2 correspond to the inverse Mills ratios for initial agreement to participate (based on aggregate data) and participating in second phase sample. Missing values of household income were imputed for this model. The remaining qualitative variables are defined as follows:

Likelihood of Spills is a 1 (not likely at all) to 10 (very likely) Likert scale for individual's perception of possibility of future spills of hog waste comparable to events in North Carolina in summer of 1995.
Regulate Hog Farms is an attitudinal variable that = 1 if respondent indicated regulating hog farms to reduce changes of waste spills was very important, zero otherwise.
Live on a Farm is equal to one if respondent lives on a farm and zero otherwise.

The Z statistics reported below the estimated parameters are based on robust estimates to account for potential heteroscedasticity due to selection effects.

28. Of course, expansion beyond the state of North Carolina would require redesign of the survey and not simply a benefits transfer, applying these benefit estimates to other households outside the area they were designed to represent.

REFERENCES

Anderson, Terry L. and Peter J. Hill (1996), 'Environmental Federalism: Thinking Smaller', PERC Policy Series, Number PS-8, PERC, Bozeman Montana, December.

Ballard, Charles L. and Don Fullerton (1992), 'Distortionary Taxes and the Provision of Public Goods', *Journal of Economic Perspectives*, **6** (3), 117–31.

Botkin, Daniel B. (1990), *Discordant Harmonies: A New Ecology for the Twenty-First Century*, New York: Oxford University Press.

Brennan, Geoffrey and James Buchanan (1977), 'Toward a Tax Constitution for Leviathan', *Journal of Public Economics*, **8**, December, 255–73.

Christensen, N.L., A. M. Bartuska, J.H. Brown, S. Carpenter, C. D'Antonio, R. Francis, J.F. Franklin, J.A. MacMahon, R.F. Noss, D.J. Parsons, C.H. Peterson, M.G. Turner and R.G. Woodmansee (1996), 'The Scientific Basis for Ecosystem Management', *Ecological Applications*.

Crandall, Robert W. (1985), *Controlling Industrial Pollution*, Washington, DC: Brookings Institution.

Deaton, Angus (1987), 'Econometric Issues for Tax Design in Developing Countries', in D. Newbery and N. Stern (eds), *The Theory of Taxation for Developing Countries*, New York: Oxford University Press for the World Bank.

Diamond, Peter A. and Jerry A. Hausman (1993), 'On Contingent Valuation Measurement of Nonuse Values', in J.A. Hausman (ed.), *Contingent Valuation*, Amsterdam: North Holland.

Diamond, Peter A. and Jerry A. Hausman (1994), 'Contingent Valuation: Is Some Number Better Than No Number?', *Journal of Economic Perspectives*, **8**, 45–64.

Fullerton, Don and Gilbert Metcalf (1996), 'Environmental Controls, Scarcity Rents, and Pre-Existing Distortions', unpublished paper, Department of Economics, Tufts University.

Gold, Steven D. (1996) 'Issues Raised by the New Federalism', *National Tax Journal*, **49** (2), 273–87.

Goulder, Lawrence H., Ian H.W. Parry and Dallas Burtraw (1997), 'Revenue-Raising vs. Other Approaches to Environmental Protection: The Critical Significance of Pre-Existing Tax Distortions', *Rand Journal of Economics*, **28**, 708–31.

Haefele, Edwin T. and Allen V. Kneese (1973), 'Residuals Management, Metropolitan Governance, and the Optimal Jurisdiction', reprinted as Chapter 4 in E.T. Haefele, *Representative Government and Environmental Management*, Baltimore: Johns Hopkins University.

Hazilla, Michael and Raymond J. Kopp (1990), 'Social Cost of Environmental Quality Regulations: A General Equilibrium Analysis', *Journal of Political Economy*, **98**, August, 853–73.

Henderson, J. Vernon (1996), 'Effects of Air Quality Regulations', *American Economic Review*, **86**, September, 789–813.

Jorgenson, Dale W. and Peter J. Wilcoxen (1990), 'Environmental Regulation and U.S. Economic Growth', *Rand Journal of Economics*, **21**, Summer, 314–40.

Kneese, Allen V. and Blair T. Bower (1979), *Environmental Quality and Residuals Management*, Baltimore: Johns Hopkins University.

Krupnick, Alan, Wallace E. Oates and E. Van DeVerg (1983), 'On Marketable Air Pollution Permits: The Case for a System of Pollution Offsets', *Journal of Environmental Economics and Management*, **10**, September, 233–47.

Krutilla, John V. (1967), 'Conservation Reconsidered', *American Economic Review*, **57**, September, 777–86.

Liu, Jin Long (1995), *Essays on the Valuation of Marine Recreational Fishing Along Coastal North Carolina*, unpublished, Raleigh, NC: North Carolina State University, PhD Thesis.

Mansfield, Carol and V. Kerry Smith (1997), 'Tradeoff at the Trough: Environmental Implications of the Hog Industry in North Carolina', unpublished paper under revision, Center for Environmental and Resource Economics, Duke University, August.

McGartland, Albert M. and Wallace E. Oates (1985) 'Marketable Permits for the Prevention of Environmental Deterioration', *Journal of Environmental Economics and Management*, **12**, September, 207–28.

Musgrave, Richard (1959), *The Theory of Public Finance*, New York: McGraw Hill.

Oates, Wallace E. (1972), *Fiscal Federalism*, New York: Harcourt Brace Jovanovich, Inc.

Oates, Wallace E. (1977), 'An Economists Perspective on Fiscal Federalism', in W.E. Oates (ed.) *The Political Economy of Fiscal Federalism*, Lexington, MA: Heath Lexington.

Oates, Wallace E. (1991) *Studies in Fiscal Federalism*, Brookfield, VT: Edward Elgar Publishing.

Oates, Wallace E., Paul R. Portney and Albert M. McGartland (1989), 'The Net Benefits of Incentive-Based Regulation: A Case Study of Environmental Standard Setting', *American Economic Review*, **79** (5), 1233–42.

Papke, Leslie K. and Jeffrey M. Woolridge (1996), 'Econometric Methods for Fractional Response Variables With an Application to 401 (K) Plan Participation Rates', *Journal of Applied Econometrics*, **11**, Nov/Dec, 619–33.

Plourde, Charles (1975), 'Conservation of Extinguishable Species', *Natural Resources Journal*, **15**, October, 791–7.

Schoenbrod, David (1996), 'Why States, Not EPA, Should Set Pollution Standards', *Regulation*, (4), 18–26

Schwabe, Kurt A. (1996), 'Source Heterogeneity, Resource Characteristics and the Performance of Marketable Permits', unpublished, Raleigh, NC: North Carolina State University, PhD Thesis.

Smith, V. Kerry and J. A. Espinosa (1996), 'Environmental and Trade Policies: Some Methodological Lessons', *Environment and Development Economics*, **1**, February, 19–40.

Smith, V. Kerry, Jin Long Liu and Raymond P. Palmquist (1993), 'Marine Pollution and Sport Fishing Quality: Using Poisson Models and Household Production Functions', *Economic Letters*, **42**, 111–16.

Tiebout, Charles (1956), 'A Pure Theory of Local Expenditures', *Journal of Political Economy*, **64**, October, 416–24.

Whisnant, Richard and Diane DeWitt Cherry (1996), 'Economic Analysis of Rules: Devolution, Evolution, and Realism', *Wake Forest Law Review*, **31** (3), 693–743.

PART II

Public Economics

7. Modeling urban growth controls

Jan K. Brueckner*

1 INTRODUCTION

In response to rapid population growth, communities in various regions of the US have imposed growth controls in an attempt to divert unwanted additional residents to other cities. An annual limit on building permits is the most transparent control mechanism, but a variety of other approaches are used. These include a reduction in allowable development densities, an increase in development fees paid by builders, or a timing ordinance designed to delay development (see Rosen and Katz, 1981).

The widespread use of growth controls has generated a considerable volume of research on this policy tool. Empirical researchers have studied the impact of growth controls on real estate markets, and a number of theoretical papers have attempted to explain these effects while modeling the economic forces leading to the adoption of controls. The empirical literature, which is surveyed by Fischel (1990), establishes that growth controls raise housing prices in cities where they are imposed. Recent theoretical studies provide two alternative models for explaining this empirical fact: the *amenity-creation* model and the *supply-restriction* model. In the amenity-creation model, consumers experience a negative population externality and thus become better off, other things equal, when the city's population is reduced by a growth control. Because the city is small, however, the control cannot affect the prevailing utility level in the economy, ruling out a welfare gain for local residents. As a result, the amenity created by the lower population is fully capitalized in land rents, creating a windfall for landowners.

The alternative supply-restriction view of controls asserts that the control-related increase in land prices is caused by a restriction in the supply of developable land, having no connection to amenity effects. In the supply-restriction model, the small-city assumption is abandoned because, with no amenity effect, the control will have an impact only if the city imposing it is non-negligible in size relative to the urban system. In this case, the population diverted by the control increases demand pressure throughout the system, leading to higher land rents in all cities. While these higher rents benefit landowners, consumers are hurt (amenity gains are absent). As a result, imposition of controls must be seen as the outcome of a political struggle in which landowners prevail.

The amenity-creation framework was first analysed by Brueckner (1990), who developed a dynamic model with a negative population externality where the growth control restricts the rate of spatial expansion of the city. Engle, Carson and Navarro (1992) analyse a similar static model, where the growth control restricts the city's spatial size in a stationary environment. Although actual growth is absent in such a model, the control's key effect (diversion of residents to other cities) is still present, and it can be analysed more simply than in a dynamic framework.

The supply-restriction framework is developed by Brueckner (1995), Brueckner and Lai (1996), and Helsley and Strange (1995), again using static models. While the negative population externality is absent in the first two papers, Helsley and Strange (1995) analyse a model where both the amenity-creation and supply-restriction motives for controls are present. In each model, the number of cities is small, so that one city's growth control has a non-negligible effect on the economy's supply of urban land. To show how the incentive for supply restriction depends on landownership arrangements, Brueckner and Lai (1996) relax the usual assumption that landowners are absentee, assuming instead that owners reside in the city along with a class of renters.[1]

The purpose of the present chapter is to provide a synthesis and extension of the analysis contained in the above studies. The goal is to provide a concise, self-contained treatment of the modeling approaches found in this literature, creating a useful reference for other researchers. Because of the simplicity of their framework, the analysis borrows heavily from Helsley and Strange (1995). The first key assumption of their model is that land consumption is fixed exogenously for all urban residents. The second assumption, which is necessitated by the first, is that the urban system contains one or more 'passive' cities, which do not impose growth controls. This assumption is required because, when individual land consumption is fixed, *all* cities cannot simultaneously restrict their spatial sizes without violating the requirement that everyone has a place to live. More general assumptions lead to more complex analysis, as can be seen in Brueckner (1995). In that model, land consumption is flexible and growth controls are therefore feasible in all cities. However, simple closed-form solutions like those presented below are not available.

The analysis begins by presenting the basic amenity-creation and supply-restriction models, which is done in sections 2.1 and 2.2 respectively. Section 2.3 then develops a hybrid model that illustrates the joint operation of the amenity-creation and supply-restriction forces, yielding the basic models as special cases. While the hybrid model is useful, it is unrealistic in many respects. As a result, the remainder of the chapter is devoted to showing how the model can be generalized. These generalizations demonstrate the flexibility of the basic structure, which can be modified as needed to include other features that may be deemed realistic or desirable.

The models in sections 2.1–2.3 assume that growth controls are imposed in a single city. In reality, controls are often imposed in many cities simultaneously, and this possibility is recognized in section 2.4. The model developed there allows multiple controlling cities instead of just one, a step that requires analysis of strategic interaction in the choice of growth controls, following Brueckner (1995) and Helsley and Strange (1995). In addition, since it may be unrealistic to assume that landowner interests dominate in the choice of growth controls, the analysis in section 2.5 treats the case where the utility of the mobile renter class also enters the city's objective function (this follows Brueckner, 1995). Section 2.6 eliminates another source of unrealism by modifying the assumption that landowners are absentee. Following Brueckner and Lai (1996), the model is modified to include a class of immobile resident landowners, who own all the city's land and rent out a portion to the renter class, occupying the remainder themselves. The growth control chosen by the resident landowners is compared with the one that emerges in the absentee case.

In his wide-ranging research career, Wallace Oates has never directly studied the question of growth controls. Nevertheless, the analysis in the present chapter follows a tradition that originated in his classic paper, Oates (1969). That paper focused the attention of the economics profession on the phenomenon of *capitalization*, through which public goods and other amenities in an area affect the local prices of housing and land. With the importance of capitalization made clear by Oates' original work, the effect of public-sector decisions on land rents has played a key role in most subsequent research in local public economics. By incorporating Oates-style amenity capitalization along with a supply-restriction effect, the present analysis of growth controls represents another contribution in the long line of research started by Wallace Oates.

2 ANALYSIS

Basic assumptions of the model are as follows. Each city in the economy is occupied by a class of mobile renters, who commute to work in the central business district (CBD), earning wage income y. Commuting cost from a residence x miles from the CBD is given by tx, where $t > 0$. Renters consume land, whose amount is fixed at one unit per household, and a numeraire non-land commodity, denoted c. Utility is also assumed to depend negatively on the population N of the city. Following Helsley and Strange (1995), the renters' common utility function is written $c - \beta N$, where $\beta \geq 0$ is the externality parameter. Note that since land consumption is fixed, it can be suppressed in writing the utility function. Cities in the economy are linear with a width of one unit, and the land in the region containing each city is owned by absentee landowners. In order to focus on the interests of landowners as a class, the absentee owners are assumed to share the rental income from the developed land within the city and the undeveloped land around it. Owners of undeveloped land, who are likely to oppose growth controls, are thus not recognized as a separate interest group.

The budget constraint of a renter household living at distance x from the CBD is $c + r = y - tx$, where r is rent per unit of land. Rearranging yields the bid-rent function

$$r = y - tx - c, \tag{7.1}$$

which shows the land rent paid conditional on a particular consumption level. As usual, the bid-rent function is downward sloping, indicating a rent premium for CBD accessibility, and it is linear, a consequence of fixed land consumption. The level of the function depends on consumption c, which is endogenous and determined by the urban equilibrium conditions.

2.1 The Amenity-Creation Model

Suppose that the economy is composed of a large number of cities, so that the prevailing utility level of the mobile renter class is unaffected by the growth-control choices of any one city. Then consider the growth-control decision of a particular city, denoted 0. Letting the economy's prevailing utility level be denoted u, consumption in city 0 must satisfy $c_0 - \beta N_0 = u$, where c_0 is the consumption level and N_0 is the city's population. Note that, because of the negative population externality, consumption must rise as the city's population increases in order to maintain utility at the prevailing external level. The consumption increase is made possible by a decline in land rent, as can be seen by solving for c_0 and substituting in (7.1). This yields

$$r = y - tx - u - \beta N_0, \tag{7.2}$$

so that land rent falls as N_0 increases, generating the requisite increase in consumption.

In the absence of a growth control, the city would expand until rent at the boundary equals the land rent in agriculture, assumed to be zero. Letting $\bar{x}_0$ denote the distance to the urban boundary and using (7.2), this condition is $y - t\bar{x}_0 - u - \beta N_0 = 0$. Solving for $\bar{x}_0$ requires use of the additional equality $N_0 = \bar{x}_0$, which holds because (i) a city's land area equals $\bar{x}_0$ given its linearity and unit width; (ii) the city's population and land area are equal given unitary land consumption.[2]

Substituting $N_0 = \bar{x}_0$ into the above equation, the condition determining $\bar{x}_0$ is then $y - t\bar{x}_0 - u - \beta\bar{x}_0 = 0$. Solving yields the market-equilibrium value of $\bar{x}_0$,

$$\bar{x}_0^e = \frac{y-u}{\beta+t}, \tag{7.3}$$

where the *e* superscript denotes equilibrium.

Now consider the case where the city adopts a growth control, which restricts $\bar{x}_0$ below its equilibrium value. This restriction diverts some of the city's residents to other cities in the economy, with no effect on their welfare. The growth control is chosen in the interests of the city's landowners, which calls for maximizing total land rent in the region containing the city. Recalling that agricultural rent is zero, this requires maximizing total urban rent.

To see that this goal requires restricting the spatial size of the city, consider the effect of a marginal reduction in $\bar{x}_0$ below $\bar{x}_0^e$. On the one hand, the reduction returns land at the boundary to agricultural use. This switch has no effect on rental income, however, because boundary land earns zero rent in urban use. The marginal reduction in $\bar{x}_0$ also shrinks the urban population slightly, which from equation (7.2) increases the level of the land-rent function throughout the city. Land rents rise because, given the population externality, renters are willing to offer more to live in a smaller urban area. Since rental income is unaffected by the loss of boundary land, total rent in the city therefore increases as $\bar{x}_0$ is marginally reduced below $\bar{x}_0^e$.

Once $\bar{x}_0$ is driven below $\bar{x}_0^e$, boundary rent is positive, and further reductions lead to a sacrifice of rental income at the edge of the city. This loss is accompanied by a gain in interior rents owing to an increase in the level of the land-rent function, as shown in Figure 7.1. Total land rent is maximized when these two effects exactly offset one another. To see this, consider the expression for total land rent, which equals

$$V_0 \equiv \int_0^{\bar{x}_0} (y - tx - u - \beta N_0)dx = \int_0^{\bar{x}_0} (y - tx - u - \beta\bar{x}_0)dx. \tag{7.4}$$

Differentiating (7.4) with respect to $\bar{x}_0$ yields

$$\begin{aligned}\frac{\partial V_0}{\partial \bar{x}_0} &= y - t\bar{x}_0 - u - \beta\bar{x}_0 - \int_0^{\bar{x}_0} \beta dx \\ &= y - t\bar{x}_0 - u - 2\beta\bar{x}_0.\end{aligned} \tag{7.5}$$

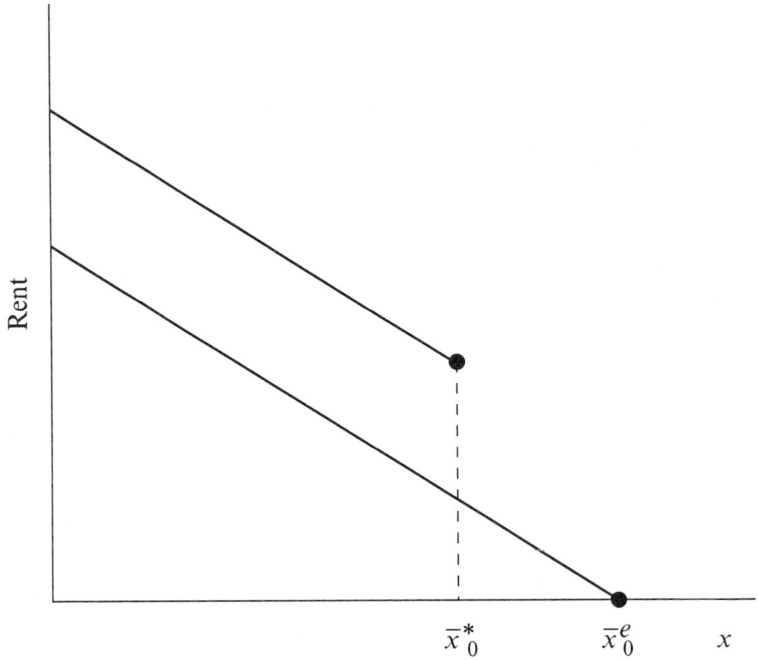

Figure 7.1 *Land-rent functions*

In the first line of (7.5), the integral is the gain in interior land rent associated with a decrease in $\bar{x}_0$, which comes from the increase in the level of the land rent function. The remaining terms represent the accompanying loss in rent at the boundary. Since the second derivative $\partial^2 V_0/\partial \bar{x}_0^2$ is negative, V_0 is maximized when these two expressions are equal. Setting the last line of (7.5) equal to zero, the optimal value of $\bar{x}_0$ under the growth-control ordinance is then

$$\bar{x}_0^* = \frac{y-u}{2\beta + t}. \tag{7.6}$$

Comparing (7.6) and (7.3), it follows that $\bar{x}_0^* < \bar{x}_0^e$, so that the control does indeed restrict the size of the city. Note also that since $\partial \bar{x}_0^* / \partial \beta < 0$, a higher value of β leads to a more stringent control. The reason is that when the population externality is stronger, land-rent escalation is more pronounced as $\bar{x}_0$ falls. A greater reduction in $\bar{x}_0$ is then needed before the loss of boundary rent balances the gain from higher interior rents.

A related point is that when the population externality is absent, with $\beta = 0$, $\bar{x}_0^*$ from equation (7.6) equals the market-equilibrium value, given by $(y - u)/t$. The explanation is that, in the absence of the externality, a reduction in $\bar{x}_0$ does not lead to escalation of land rents. The control's only effect is lost boundary rent, which is avoided by following the market equilibrium.

2.2 The Supply-Restriction Model

To develop the supply-restriction model, the population externality is suppressed by assuming $\beta = 0$. In addition, the economy is assumed to contain just two cities, denoted 0 and 1, with city 1 being passive. The economy's renter population, which is again mobile between the cities, has total size $2P$. Because the externality is absent, utility equalization among cities now implies equalization of consumption. Therefore, the consumption variable c no longer has a city subscript, and this implies that the land-rent function is the same in both cities, being given by equation (7.1).

Instead of being exogenous, the renter utility level is now determined endogenously. One requirement is a market-clearing condition, which says that the renter population fits in the two cities. Recalling that a city's population is equal to its $\bar{x}$ value, this condition is written

$$\bar{x}_0 + \bar{x}_1 = 2P. \tag{7.7}$$

An additional condition comes from the assumption that city 1 is passive, foregoing a growth control. Passive behavior means that the city expands until its boundary rent equals zero, implying

$$y - t\bar{x}_1 - c = 0. \tag{7.8}$$

Equations (7.7) and (7.8) can be solved for the consumption level c, yielding

$$c = y + t(\bar{x}_0 - 2P). \tag{7.9}$$

A key implication of (9) is that consumption is increasing in $\bar{x}_0$. This implies that renters throughout the economy are hurt when city 0 restricts $\bar{x}_0$ via a growth control. From equation (7.1), the consumption loss is associated with an increase in rent, which rises at all locations in both cities as the growth control tightens the supply of urban land.

Assume as before that the growth control is chosen in the interests of city 0's landowners. Then, the same considerations as before affect the choice of the control, and Figure 7.1 remains relevant. Restriction of $\bar{x}_0$ leads to a loss of boundary rent together with an escalation of interior rents, which is now due to supply restriction rather than amenity creation. The control is set optimally when these two effects offset one another. The goal is again to maximize total land rent, which is written

$$V_0 \equiv \int_0^{\bar{x}_0} (y - tx - c)dx. \tag{7.10}$$

Substituting the c solution from (7.9) into (7.10), total rent is then only a function of $\bar{x}_0$. Differentiating this expression with respect to $\bar{x}_0$, setting the result equal to zero, and solving for $\bar{x}_0$ yields

$$\bar{x}_0^* \equiv \frac{2P}{3}. \tag{7.11}$$

To understand (7.11), observe that the market equilibrium value of $\bar{x}_0$ equals P, which reflects an equal division of the renter population between the cities. Therefore, it follows from (7.11) that city 0's population shrinks by one-third as a result of the growth control, with city 1's population growing by one-third. From equation (7.9), the reduction in $\bar{x}_0$ hurts renters, whose consumption falls because of escalating land rents.

2.3 A Hybrid Model

The models considered above are special cases of a more general model that includes a population externality along with an endogenously-determined renter utility level. To construct such a hybrid model, let there be $n - 1$ passive cities and one controlling city. The relevant equilibrium conditions are

$$\bar{x}_0 + (n - 1)\bar{x}_1 = nP \tag{7.12}$$

$$c_0 - \beta\bar{x}_0 = c_1 - \beta\bar{x}_1 \tag{7.13}$$

$$y - t\bar{x}_1 - c_1 = 0. \tag{7.14}$$

Equation (7.12) says that the total renter population of nP fits in the economy's n cities. Note that each passive city has the same value of $\bar{x}$, denoted by $\bar{x}_1$. Equation (7.13) requires utility equalization between the controlling city and each passive city, and (7.14) says that boundary rent is zero in the passive cities. The system (7.12)–(7.14) can be solved for c_0 and c_1, which yields

$$c_0 = y + \frac{(t+\beta n)\bar{x}_0 - (t+\beta)nP}{n-1} \tag{7.15}$$

$$c_1 = y + \frac{t(\bar{x}_0 - nP)}{(n-1)}. \tag{7.16}$$

The renter utility level, which equals $c_0 - \beta\bar{x}_0$, is then equal to

$$u = y + \frac{(t+\beta)(\bar{x}_0 - nP)}{n-1}. \tag{7.17}$$

Equations (7.15) and (7.16) show that consumption falls in both the controlling and passive cities as $\bar{x}_0$ is reduced, a consequence of higher land rents in both cities. Utilities are also affected by changing city populations, but (7.17) shows that the net result is a reduction in renter utility as $\bar{x}_0$ decreases. Thus, as before, the renter class is harmed when city 0 restricts its spatial size via a growth control.

Total land rent in city 0 is now written

$$V_0 \equiv \int_0^{\bar{x}_0} (y - tx - c_0)dx, \tag{7.18}$$

and substituting equation (7.15) in place of c_0 gives V_0 as a function of $\bar{x}_0$ alone. The optimal growth control is found by setting the derivative equal to zero and solving, which yields

$$\bar{x}_0^* = \frac{(\beta+t)nP}{(2\beta+t)n+t}. \tag{7.19}$$

It is easily seen that, when n is finite, (7.19) is less than the market-equilibrium value of P, indicating the presence of a control.

To explore special cases, suppose $\beta = 0$, so that the population externality is absent. If $n = 2$ in this case, then equation (7.19) yields the $\bar{x}_0^*$ solution for the simple supply-restriction model, given by equation (7.11). Writing (7.19) as

$P/(1 + 1/n)$, it also follows that $\bar{x}_0^*$ increases as n rises, converging to the market-equilibrium value of P as n approaches infinity. The explanation is that city 0's market power, namely its ability to raise its own rents as well as those in other cities through a growth control, diminishes as the economy becomes larger. With control-induced rent escalation weakening as n rises, the sacrifice of boundary rent is less worthwhile, and the control becomes less stringent. In the limit, rent escalation disappears and there is no benefit from restricting $\bar{x}_0$.

Now reintroduce the population externality, so that $\beta > 0$. As above, it remains true that $\bar{x}_0^*$ is increasing in n, a consequence of city 0's waning market power. However, instead of converging to P, the limit of (7.19) as n approaches infinity equals $(\beta + t)P/(2\beta + t)$. Two aspects of this result deserve note. First, the limiting value is consistent with the solution (7.6) from the basic amenity-creation model. This follows because the denominators are the same and because the numerator $(\beta + t)P$ equals the limiting value of $y - u$ as n approaches infinity, as can be seen from equation (7.17). This verifies that the basic amenity-creation model applies to an infinitely-large economy.

The second observation is that, in contrast to the $\beta = 0$ case, the limiting value $(\beta + t)P/(2\beta + t)$ is less than P, indicating that the control persists as the economy becomes large. To understand this result, it is useful to contrast the operation of the hybrid model with that of the supply-restriction model. In the latter model, rents rise in parallel fashion in all cities as the control restricts the supply of urban land. When the amenity effect is present, however, these changes create a utility differential between cities, with renters better off in city 0 because of its smaller population. To equate utilities, rents must rise an additional amount in city 0, further depressing the consumption of its residents. As the number of cities increases, reducing city 0's market power, the parallel rent increases from supply restriction become smaller, disappearing eventually in the limit. However, the amenity-driven rent increase in city 0 persists as n becomes large. The persistence of this rent gain maintains city 0's incentive to impose a growth control. Note that because the rent gain is greater the larger is β, the control becomes tighter for given n as β increases ($\partial\bar{x}_0/\partial\beta < 0$ holds in (7.19)).

A final question concerns the efficiency of growth controls. A social welfare function is needed to address this issue, and since utility is measured in units of consumption, total utility plus total land rent in the economy is the proper function. Social welfare is then given by

$$nPu + \int_0^{\bar{x}_0} (y - tx - c_0)dx + (n-1)\int_0^{\bar{x}_1} (y - tx - c_1)dx. \qquad (7.20)$$

To express (7.20) as a function of $\bar{x}_0$, the c_0, c_1, and u solutions from (7.15) – (7.17) are substituted along with the corresponding $\bar{x}_1$ solution, which equals $(nP - \bar{x}_0)/(n - 1)$. It can be shown that the resulting function reaches a maximum at $\bar{x}_0 = P$, indicating that the market equilibrium maximizes welfare and that growth controls are inefficient. The explanation is that even though the population externality favors smaller cities, a unilateral attempt by one city to shrink its size is welfare-reducing.[3]

2.4 Multiple Controlling Cities

In contrast to the hybrid model, which assumes a single controlling city, use of growth controls is widespread in fast-growing regions of the US. As a result, a more-realistic model should allow for multiple controlling cities. Once this modification is introduced, however, the possibility of strategic interaction among controlling cities enters the analysis. The controls that are ultimately imposed then represent the Nash equilibrium of a growth-control game played among cities in the region.

To see how such an equilibrium emerges, suppose that in addition to city 0, there are k other controlling cities. Letting the subscript 2 denote these cities, and keeping the other assumptions from the hybrid model, the equilibrium system (7.12)–(7.14) is replaced by

$$\bar{x}_0 + (n - 1)\bar{x}_1 + k\bar{x}_2 = (n + k)P \tag{7.21}$$

$$c_0 - \beta\bar{x}_0 = c_1 - \beta\bar{x}_1 \tag{7.22}$$

$$c_0 - \beta\bar{x}_0 = c_2 - \beta\bar{x}_2 \tag{7.23}$$

$$y - t\bar{x}_1 - c_1 = 0. \tag{7.24}$$

Equation (7.21) is the modified market-clearing condition, while (7.22) and (7.23) express the requirement that utility is equal among all cities. Note that the growth-control choices and consumption levels in all controlling cities are ultimately identical. The distinction between these variables in (7.21)–(7.24) is needed to characterize the Nash equilibrium.

Solving (7.21)–(7.24) for c_0 as a function of $\bar{x}_0$ and $\bar{x}_2$ yields

$$c_0 = y + \frac{(t + \beta n)\bar{x}_0 + (t + \beta)\left[k\bar{x}_2 - (n + k)P\right]}{n - 1}. \tag{7.25}$$

To find the optimal value of $\bar{x}_0$ conditional on $\bar{x}_2$, (7.25) is substituted into (7.18), the expression for total land rent, and the derivative is set equal to zero. The solution for $\bar{x}_0$ yields city 0's reaction function, which gives its best response to a common value of $\bar{x}_2$ for the other controlling cities. Since the controlling cities are identical, however, their equilibrium choices must be the same. Setting $\bar{x}_0 = \bar{x}_2$ and solving for $\bar{x}_0$ then yields the symmetric Nash-equilibrium value, which equals

$$\bar{x}_0^* = \frac{(\beta + t)(n+k)P}{(\beta + t)(n+k) + \beta n + t}. \tag{7.26}$$

It remains true that (7.26) is less than the market-equilibrium value P for finite n and k. Also, the limit of $\bar{x}_0^*$ as n approaches infinity is $(\beta + t)P/(2\beta + t) < P$, as before. However, the limit of $\bar{x}_0^*$ as k approaches infinity equals P. Therefore, while growth controls persist as the number of passive cities grows without bound, controls vanish as the number of controlling cities approaches infinity. This shows that other controlling cities are more effective than passive cities in limiting any given city's growth-control behavior, a consequence of the competition they provide. Another way of seeing this fact is to alter the mix of controlling and passive cities, holding the total number of cities fixed, and investigate the impact on $\bar{x}_0^*$. Inspection of equation (7.26) shows that, when $n + k$ is fixed, $\bar{x}_0^*$ increases as n falls. This shows that controls become looser as the city mix shifts away from passive and towards controlling cities.

The changed role of passive cities is also evident in the fact that an increase in their number may no longer lead to a loosening of controls. While $\bar{x}_0^*$ is increasing in k, calculation shows that $\partial\bar{x}_0^*/\partial n$ has the sign of $t - \beta k$, which can be either positive or negative. If $\beta = 0$ or $k = 0$, then $\bar{x}_0^*$ increases with n, as in the hybrid model of section 2.3. However, if $\beta > 0$ and k is sufficiently large, then growth controls become tighter as n increases. Evidently, when many controlling cities exist, passive cities no longer play the same role as before in limiting their market power.

2.5 Introducing Renter Political Power

The maintained assumption that landowners dominate the political process, with growth controls chosen in their interest, may be unrealistic. Instead, the choices made by city governments may be partly influenced by the renter population, which can express its wishes through voting. To formalize this notion, Brueckner (1995) assumes that the city government maximizes an objective function that takes both renter and landowner interests into account. The function is a weighted average of renter utility and total land rent, given by

$$\lambda u + (1-\lambda)\int_0^{\bar{x}_0}(y - tx - c_0), \tag{7.27}$$

where $0 \leq \lambda \leq 1$. If renter interests carry no weight ($\lambda = 0$), then the $\bar{x}_0$ solution is (7.19). If landowner interests carry no weight ($\lambda = 1$), then the solution is the market equilibrium value P. This follows because utility is increasing in $\bar{x}_0$ (see equation (7.17)), which implies that the largest possible value is optimal (values above P are not feasible). To find the optimal $\bar{x}_0$ in intermediate cases, equations (7.15) and (7.17) are used to eliminate c_0 and u in (7.27), and the derivative is set equal to zero. If the resulting solution for $\bar{x}_0$, which equals

$$\frac{(\beta + t)[nP + \lambda/(1-\lambda)]}{(2\beta + t) + t}, \tag{7.28}$$

is less than P, it represents the optimal value. Otherwise, P itself is the optimum, indicating the absence of a control. Naturally, (7.28) is increasing in λ, indicating that any growth control becomes looser as renter power rises.

2.6 A Model with Resident Landowners

A major drawback of the models considered so far is that the group that benefits from growth controls, namely landowners, lives outside the city. In reality, the political impetus behind controls appears to come from the class of *resident landowners*, which constitutes the majority group in most cities. To make the model more realistic, it can be modified to include such a class. The resulting model is considerably more complex than those considered above, but it captures a crucial element of the urban environment in which growth controls are actually imposed.

Following Brueckner and Lai (1996), suppose that all the land in the city is owned by a group of resident landowners. These individuals, who are immobile, occupy a portion of the urban land while renting out the remainder to a group of mobile renters. The landowners again divide the city's rental income, but a portion of this income now comes from rent they pay to themselves for the urban land they occupy. Letting R_0 denote rental income per landowner in city 0, the landowner budget constraint is $c_0^h + r = y^h - tx + R_0$ (the h superscript stands for 'homeowner,' the class that the landowners represent). The landowner bid-rent function is then $r = y^h + R_0 - tx - c_0^h$.

Realistically, it is assumed that renters consume less land than landowners, with consumption equal to $\alpha < 1$. The renter budget constraint is then $c_0^r + \alpha r = y^r - tx$ and their bid-rent function is $r = (y^r - tx - c_0^r)/\alpha$. Given lower land consumption, renters have a steeper bid-rent function than landowners (the slopes are $-t/\alpha$ and $-t$ respectively). As a result, renters live in the central part of the city, between $x = 0$ and $x = \hat{x}_0$, while landowners live between $\hat{x}_0$ and $\bar{x}_0$. The city's population can then be written $N_0 = (\bar{x}_0 - \hat{x}_0) + \hat{x}_0/\alpha$. Parallel statements apply to the economy's passive cities, of which there is assumed to be just one.

Each city contains P^h immobile landowners, and the economy contains $2P^r$ mobile renters. The market-clearing conditions are then

$$\bar{x}_i - \hat{x}_i = P^h,\ i = 0,1 \tag{7.29}$$

$$\frac{\hat{x}_0 + \hat{x}_1}{\alpha} = 2P^r. \tag{7.30}$$

Equation (7.29) says that city i's landowner population fits between $\hat{x}_i$ and $\bar{x}_i$, $i = 0,1$, while (7.30) says that the renter areas in both cities are sufficient to house the total renter population. The equal-utility condition for the mobile renter class is

$$c_0^r - \beta[\bar{x}_0 - \hat{x}_0) + \hat{x}_0/\alpha] = c_1^r - \beta[(\bar{x}_1 - \hat{x}_1) + \hat{x}_1/\alpha], \tag{7.31}$$

where the above expression for city population is used. Boundary rent is again zero in the passive city, so that

$$y^h + R_1 - t\bar{x}_1 - c_1^h = 0. \tag{7.32}$$

In addition, the bid-rent curves of renters and landowners must intersect in city i at $\hat{x}_i$, $i = 0,1$, which requires

$$\frac{y^r - t\hat{x}_i - c_i^r}{\alpha} = y^h + R_i - t\hat{x}_i - c_i^h, \quad i = 0,1. \tag{7.33}$$

The final condition is the definition of rental income per landlord, which is written

$$\int_0^{\hat{x}_i} \frac{y^r - tx - c_i^r}{\alpha} dx + \int_{\hat{x}_i}^{\bar{x}_i} \left(y^h + R_i - tx - c_i^h\right) dx = P^h R_i, \quad i = 0,1. \quad (7.34)$$

P^hR^i in (7.34) is total rental income, which must equal the area under the city's bid-rent curves, given by the expression on the left-hand side. Integrating the R_i term on the left and using equation (7.29), it cancels the term on the right. Integrating c_i^h on the left and rearranging, (7.34) then reduces to

$$c_0^h = \frac{1}{P^h}\left(\int_0^{\hat{x}_0} \frac{y^r - tx - c_0^r}{\alpha} dx + \int_{\hat{x}_0}^{\bar{x}_0} \left(y^h - tx\right) dx\right) \quad (7.35)$$

for city 0, with a parallel expression pertaining to city 1.

Assuming that city 0's growth control is chosen by its landowners, their goal is to maximize utility, which equals $c_0^h - \beta N_0$. This contrasts with the hybrid model, where the absentee landowners' goal was to maximize rental income. Greater rental income boosts consumption, as before, but landowners now experience an amenity gain from a smaller urban population, which was not felt when they were absentee.

To maximize utility, the derivative of $c_0^h - \beta N_0$ is set equal to zero, which requires $\partial c_0^h/\partial\bar{x}_0 = \beta\partial N_0/\partial\bar{x}_0$. Since $\partial N_0/\partial\bar{x}_0$ is equal to $1/\alpha$ using $N_0 = (\bar{x}_0 - \hat{x}_0) + \hat{x}_0/\alpha$ and equation (7.29), the first-order condition then reduces to $\partial c_0^h/\partial\bar{x}_0 = \beta/\alpha$. The derivative $\partial c_0^h/\partial\bar{x}_0$ is computed by solving (7.29)–(7.34) for c_0^r, substituting in (7.35), and differentiating with respect to $\bar{x}_0$.[4] When this is done and the result is substituted into the first-order condition above, the $\bar{x}_0$ solution is

$$\bar{x}_0^* = \frac{\left[3t\alpha + (4-\alpha)\beta\right]P^h + 2\alpha(\alpha t + \beta)P^r}{3t\alpha + 4\beta} \quad (7.36)$$

It is easily seen that $\bar{x}_0^*$ is less than $P^h + P^r$, the market-equilibrium value, which indicates the presence of a growth control. As before, it can be shown that $\partial\bar{x}_0/\partial\beta < 0$, indicating that the control becomes tighter as the population externality strengthens.

It is interesting to ask how (7.36) compares to the $\bar{x}_0$ value that would be chosen by absentee landowners. To make this comparison, let the resident landowner group be transformed into a group of immobile renters. This requires setting the

R_i terms in (7.29)–(7.33) equal to zero and deleting (7.34). Then let $\bar{x}_0$ be chosen to maximize city 0's total land rent,

$$V_0 \equiv \int_0^{\hat{x}_0} \frac{y^r - tx - c_0^r}{\alpha} dx + \int_{\hat{x}_0}^{\bar{x}_0} \left(y^h - tx - c_0^h\right) dx. \tag{7.37}$$

The c_0^r solution, which is the same as before, is substituted into (7.37) along with a new solution for c_0^h.[5] Differentiating with respect to $\bar{x}_0$, the optimal value is

$$\bar{x}_0^* = \frac{[\alpha t(1+\alpha)+2\beta]P^h + \alpha(\alpha t+\beta)P^r}{3t\alpha + 4\beta}. \tag{7.38}$$

The only difference between (7.38) and (7.36) is in the P^h coefficients, and it is easily seen that term in (7.36) is larger. Therefore, resident landowners choose a looser growth control than absentee owners. This is the result found by Brueckner and Lai (1996), who assume $\beta = 0$, and they explain it by noting that a portion of urban rent is paid by the resident landowners to themselves. As a consequence, the increase in land rents caused by a reduction in $\bar{x}_0$ is worth less than it is to absentee owners, and this leads resident owners to choose a looser control. While the same force is at work in the present model, where $\beta > 0$, a countervailing effect comes from the amenity gains experienced by resident landowners, which cause them to favor a *tighter* control than absentee owners. Interestingly, the analysis shows that this amenity force is dominated by the effect identified by Brueckner and Lai, leading resident owners to impose a looser control.

By including both resident landowners and amenity-creation effects, the above model provides a nearly-complete depiction of the forces leading to the adoption of growth controls in existing cities. On the one hand, resident landowners benefit from higher rental income when a growth control is imposed, an effect similar to the housing capital gains enjoyed by homeowners in controlling cities. This rent escalation comes partly from the supply-restriction effect, but it also reflects the amenity gain from an improved quality-of-life. While the benefits of this amenity gain are nullified for the renter population through higher rents, no force works to offset the amenity for resident landowners. Therefore, the landowner class enjoys a dual gain when controls are imposed: increased wealth and better quality-of-life. Commentators on the growth-control process sometimes point to this dual gain as providing the political impetus for controls, and the model provides a formalization. Finally, it should be noted that a missing element in the above model is strategic interaction in the choice of controls. However, this element can be added easily, following the approach in section 2.4.

3 CONCLUSION

Growth controls are now commonplace in fast-growing regions of the country, and a challenge for urban and public economics is to provide a coherent theoretical picture of the forces leading to the adoption of controls. The models sketched in this chapter offer such a picture, building on the notion that growth controls are imposed to serve the interests of landowners. Landowner gains arise in part from the amenity-creation effect, where the benefits of a smaller urban population are capitalized in land rents. By relying on the capitalization phenomenon, the analysis in this chapter ultimately draws on the classic contribution of Oates (1969), which taught the economics profession the central importance of capitalization.

Although there is a large empirical literature on the effects of growth controls, the above analysis suggests that the *adoption* of controls deserves more empirical study. Glickfeld and Levine (1992) conduct such an investigation, using data from their elaborate survey of growth-control practices in California cities and counties. Brueckner (1998) conducts a related study using the same data, with the goal of testing for the existence of strategic interaction among cities in the choice of controls. His results suggest that, as in the model of section 2.4, California cities are indeed playing a growth-control game.

NOTES

* I wish to thank Richard Martin, Arvind Panagariya, and Robert Schwab for comments. Any shortcomings in the chapter, however, are my responsibility.

1. For growth-control models that do not easily fit into the amenity-creation or supply-restriction categories, see Cooley and LaCivita (1982), Epple, Romer and Filimon (1988), Frankena and Scheffman (1981), and Sakashita (1995). For related work on the economics of urban density restrictions, see Arnott and MacKinnon (1977), Pasha (1992), Sheppard (1988), and Turnbull (1991).
2. Note that since the city extends in both directions away from the CBD, N_0 actually represents half of the urban population. This convention is maintained in what follows.
3. Note that while the externality could be addressed by reducing average city size (increasing n for a given total population), the model rules this out by assuming that the total population and n are proportional.
4. The c_0^r solution is $y^r + (t + 2\beta/\alpha)[\bar{x}_0 - (1 + \alpha)P^h - \alpha P^r] + 2\beta P^h + \beta P^r$.
5. The c_0^h solution is $y^h - y^r/\alpha + (1 - \alpha)(t\bar{x}_0 - P^h)/\alpha + c_0^r/\alpha$.

REFERENCES

Arnott, R.J. and J.G. MacKinnon (1977), 'Measuring the costs of height restrictions in a general equilibrium model', *Regional Science and Urban Economics*, **7**, 359–75.

Brueckner, J.K. (1990), 'Growth controls and land values in an open city', *Land Economics*, **66**, 237–48.

Brueckner, J.K. (1995), 'Strategic control of growth in a system of cities', *Journal of Public Economics*, **57**, 393–416.

Brueckner, J.K. (1998), 'Testing for strategic interaction among local governments: The case of growth controls', *Journal of Urban Economics*, **44**, 438–67.

Brueckner, J.K. and F.-C. Lai (1996), 'Urban growth controls with resident landowners', *Regional Science and Urban Economics*, **26**, 125–44.

Cooley, T.F. and C.J. LaCivita (1982), 'A theory of growth controls', *Journal of Urban Economics*, **12**, 129–45.

Engle, R., R. Carson and P. Navarro (1992), 'On the theory of growth controls', *Journal of Urban Economics*, **32**, 269–83.

Epple, D., T. Romer and R. Filimon (1988), 'Community development with endogenous land use controls', *Journal of Public Economics*, **35**, 133–62.

Fischel, W.A. (1990), *Do growth controls matter: A review of empirical evidence on the effectiveness and efficiency of local government land use regulation*, Cambridge, MA: Lincoln Institute of Land Policy.

Frankena, M.W. and D.T. Scheffman (1981), 'A theory of development controls in a "small" city', *Journal of Public Economics*, **15**, 203–34.

Glickfeld, M. and N. Levine (1992), *Regional Growth ... Local Reaction*, Cambridge, MA: Lincoln Institute of Land Policy.

Helsley, R.W. and W.C. Strange (1995), 'Strategic growth controls', *Regional Science and Urban Economics*, **25**, 435–60.

Oates, W.E. (1969), 'The effects of property taxes and local public spending on property values: An empirical study of tax capitalization and the Tiebout hypothesis', *Journal of Political Economy*, **77**, 957–71.

Pasha, H.A. (1992), 'Comparative statics analysis of density controls', *Journal of Urban Economics*, **32**, 284–98.

Rosen, K.T. and L. Katz (1981), 'Growth management and land use controls: The San Francisco Bay area experience', *Journal of the American Real Estate and Urban Economics Association*, **9**, 321–44.

Sakashita, N. (1995), 'An economic theory of urban growth control', *Regional Science and Urban Economics*, **25**, 427–34.

Sheppard, S. (1988), 'The qualitative economics of development control', *Journal of Urban Economics*, **24**, 310–30.

Turnbull, G.K. (1991), 'A comparative dynamic analysis of zoning in a growing city', *Journal of Urban Economics*, **29**, 235–48.

8. Congestion and taxation in lumpy countries

David L. Hummels, Paul N. Courant, and Alan V. Deardoff

I INTRODUCTION

In recent years, some first steps have been taken to marry the fields of trade theory and location theory. As Paul Krugman (1993) argues, the two fields are concerned with very similar issues – the questions of who produces what and where – but their methodological approaches are sufficiently different to render them separate and to make cross-field communication difficult. Trade theory typically fails to include space in its models, ignoring the economic consequences of distance in general, transportation costs in particular, and regional heterogeneity within nations, while often also ignoring distance costs between nations. Location theory and much of the regional economics literature fails to include general equilibrium concepts, treating each location as small and locational allocation as unable to affect prices. A fruitful union of the two fields would borrow general equilibrium insights from trade theory, and the treatment of economic forces in space from location and regional theory.

Two previous papers on lumpy countries (Courant and Deardorff, 1992, 1993) address what trade theory can learn from location theory. In these, two of the present authors consider nations not as dimensionless points but a heterogeneous, hence 'lumpy,' places.[2] In the first paper, we find that regional heterogeneity can affect international and intranational production and trade. In the second paper we consider in some detail the effect of regional variation in amenities, showing that such variation will generally lead to violations of factor price equalization and hence that it will generally have implications for the pattern of international trade. Such a result is not a theoretical curiosum: there is a large literature in urban economics that establishes firmly, both theoretically and empirically, that amenity-induced wage differentials between regions are the rule rather than the exception.[3]

In this chapter, we ask what theories of location, regional economics, and local public economics can learn from trade theory.[4] Specifically, we turn to the welfare economics of amenities and congestion to see if general equilibrium concepts provide additional insight into optimal congestion taxation. We analyse taxes on congestible amenities[5] in a lumpy country model with one mobile factor (labor) and one immobile factor (land). We investigate optimal congestion taxes first with one, and then with two traded goods, and we examine how optimality rules differ from the perspectives of a federal planner and of a local government.

The local government, in the spirit of Oates (1969), is well aware of the fact that government behavior is capitalized into land values, and cares both about tax revenue *per se* and about the effects of its fiscal policies on the value of land. Given Oates's lifelong interests in both local government and environmental issues, it is especially fitting that it is an environmental amenity that provides government with the opportunity to improve (or to diminish) welfare. It is also a mark of Wally Oates's infectious enthusiasm for these subjects that one of us (Courant) has continued to work on them off and on for over twenty-five years, entirely due to having taken a public finance course from Wally in 1971.

In section II, we examine a congestible amenity in an economy with one good – either a closed one-sector economy or an open economy that has specialized in the production of a single traded good that it exchanges on world markets for other goods that it does not produce. We find that, in the absence of congestion tolls, labor will move into an amenity-endowed region, over-congesting the amenity, and, generally, causing a decline in national output. That a congestible public good will be over-congested in the absence of a toll is a standard result in the literature. However, the standard treatment does not take into account that, when a congestible amenity differs by region, the same reallocations of population and labor that lead to congestion also will affect factor prices and output in all regions of an economy.[6]

Optimal federal policy picks a regional labor allocation that trades off amenity losses against national output gains. This implies an optimal degree of congestion that will in general be different than if there were no effect on national output. We also find (in section IV) that a local government will always prefer a smaller amount of labor in the amenity-endowed region than does the federal planner.

In section III we add a second traded good, with the relative price of the traded goods fixed on world markets, leading to two interesting changes in results. First, under some circumstances, the optimal congestion toll chosen by the national planner (a Pigouvian toll equal to the difference between the private average benefit and the net social marginal benefit from migration) can restore factor price equalization across regions, a condition that cannot hold in the one-good model. Moreover, as we establish in section IV, when the optimal national toll would restore factor price equalization, the optimal regional toll does so, as well. Thus, there are conditions (again, only with more than one traded good) under which local governments will choose policies that lead to nationally optimal congestion.

II THE ONE-SECTOR MODEL

In this section we introduce the basic model structure used throughout the paper, including a description of the amenity, and the nature of the labor allocation equilibrium. The one-sector model offers an expositionally simple baseline against which to compare subsequent complications posed by an additional sector or strategic local government behavior.

Consider, then, a country consisting of two regions, but only one sector. Each region uses the same constant returns to scale production function to produce a single good X using labor L and land T, $X = F(L, T)$. Land is specific to each region. Labor is mobile between regions, and the wage in each region is given by

$$W_1 = \frac{\partial F(L_1, T_1)}{\partial L_1} = f_{L,1} \tag{8.1}$$

and

$$W_2 = \frac{\partial F(L_2, T_2)}{\partial L_2} = f_{L,2} \tag{8.2}$$

Figure 8.1 shows the value of output and the wage differential between regions for alternative allocations of labor in the special case of a land endowment that is equally divided between the regions. Labor in region 1 is measured to the right from O_1, labor in region 2 to the left from O_2, the distance O_1O_2 being the labor endowment of the country, $\bar{L}$. Output is maximized at L_1^* where the labor endowment is also shared in proportion to land – in this case equally. This is because $f_{L,2} = f_{L,1}$; the marginal productivity of labor is equalized across the regions when the land to labor ratio is the same in both places. For labor allocations to the left of L_1^*, $f_{L,2} < f_{L,1}$, so that $W_2 < W_1$. Similarly, for labor allocations to the right of L_1^*, $W_2 > W_1$. This gives us the bottom panel of Figure 8.1, the $W_2 - W_1$ curve.[7]

Now suppose that laborers in region 1 enjoy a congestible consumption amenity.[8] Figure 8.2 shows three curves that plot total, average and marginal valuations of the amenity against regional allocations of labor. The total value of the amenity (the sum of individual valuations) is given by the $TA(L_1)$ curve. We assume that all residents of the region share equally in the amenity, each receiving the average value of the amenity in region 1, $TA(L_1)/L_1$, as given by the $AA(L_1)$ curve. The marginal effect of adding additional population and hence workers to region 1, or $dTA(L_1)/dL_1$ is given by the marginal amenity curve, $MA(L_1)$. Congestion is indicated by the downward slope of AA. In the case drawn, congestion is such that the total amenity also declines with L_1 after a point and indeed tends toward zero.[9]

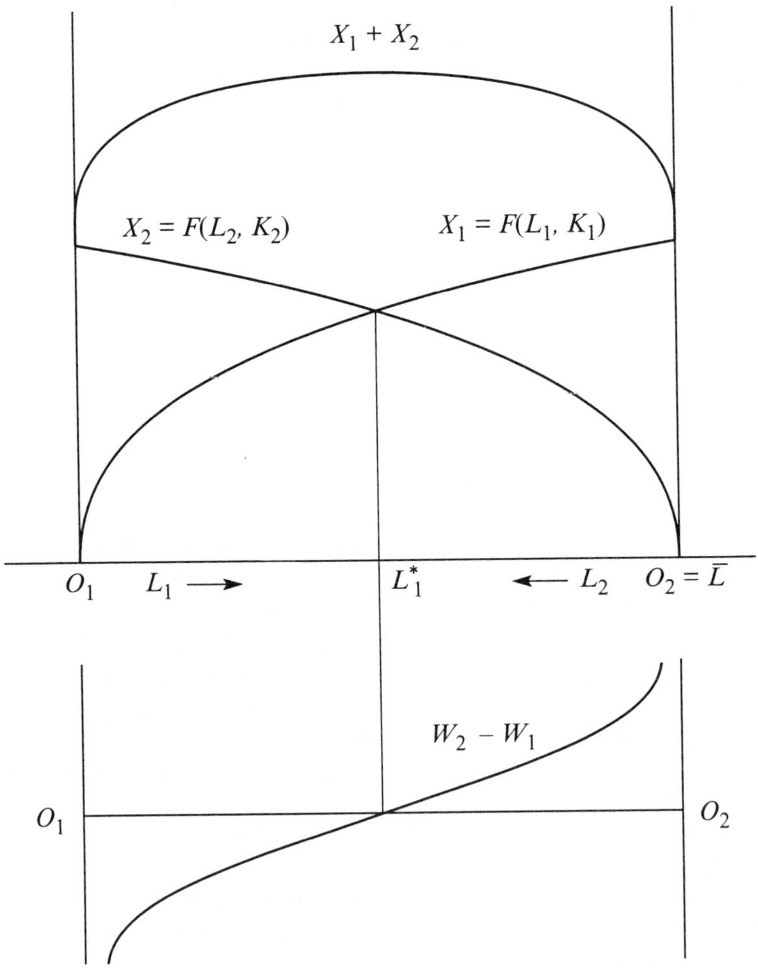

Figure 8.1 Value of output and wage differential between regions

In the absence of the amenity, labor moves between regions seeking the highest available wage. In equilibrium, mobile factor prices are equalized, $W_1 = W_2$. This occurs at L_1^* of Figure 8.1, the output maximizing point. However, with the amenity, labor moves between regions seeking to maximize factor utility, given by the wage plus the average amenity (if any) in each region. In equilibrium, we have factor utility equalization for labor. Following the assumption that we have an amenity only in region 1, labor market equilibrium requires

$$W_1(L_1) + AA(L_1) = W_2(L_1)$$

or

$$W_2(L_1) - W_1(L_1) = AA(L_1) \tag{8.3}$$

Figure 8.3 shows this equilibrium at L_b. To characterize this equilibrium, we note that L_b is to the right of L_1^*, the output maximizing point. Recalling Figure 8.1, the value of total output is therefore decreasing in L_1 at L_b. Because the amenity draws labor into region 1, the marginal product of labor is unequal in

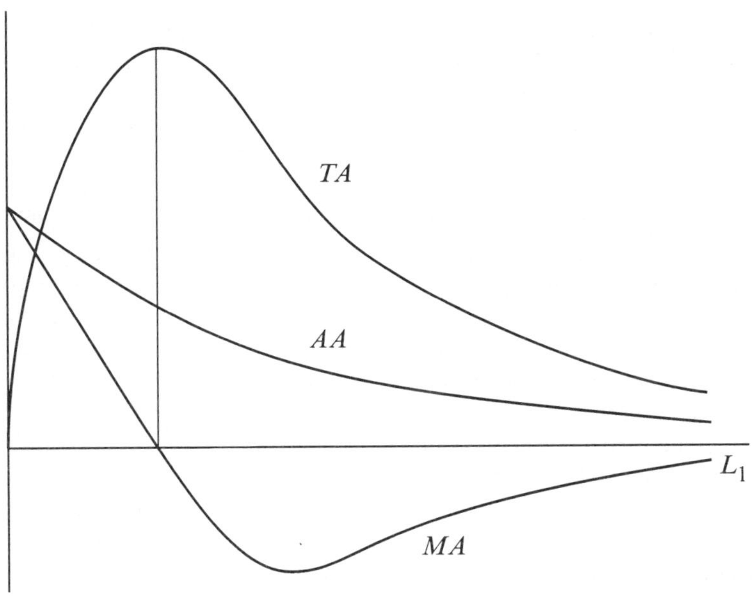

Figure 8.2 Total, average and marginal amenity valuations against regional labor allocations

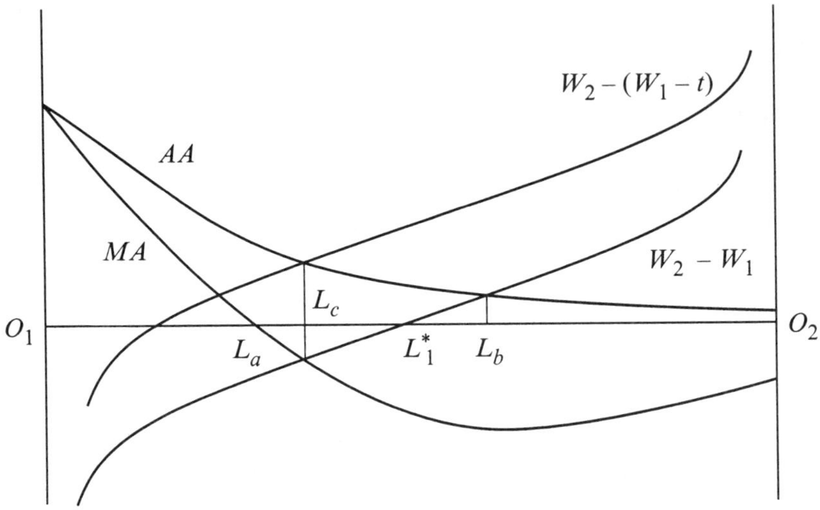

Figure 8.3 Qualitative analysis of labor market equilibrium

the two regions, and the economy is no longer maximizing output. Further, note that the total value of the amenity would be maximized at L_a, where $MA(L_1)$ equals zero, and that L_b lies to the right of L_a.[10]

Addition of a non-traded good (for example, housing) to the model changes the location of the equilibrium but not the basic story. The presence of such a non-traded good will make the $W_2 - W_1$ function of Figure 8.3 steeper but, assuming no regional asymmetry in the endowment of the non-traded good, will not affect the location of L_1^*. The reason that the curve becomes steeper is that, as L_1 increases, the marginal product of labor (hence, the wage in terms of tradables) falls and the price of the non-tradables rises. This implies that the derivative of the real wage with respect to the labor allocation is everywhere larger in absolute value. This would shift L_b closer to the optimum but, because the amenity is still unpriced, would not remove the inefficiency, and so does not change the qualitative analysis of Figure 8.3.

This economy here is in a wretched state. The labor movement induced by the amenity reduces both the output of the economy and the total value of the amenity. We now introduce a federal social planner whose objective is to maximize the sum of total output and total amenity value. This planner may impose a congestion tax t that can be levied equally on all laborers in one region and redistributed lump sum to all laborers in both regions.

The federal planner's problem is to

$$\underset{L_1}{\text{maximize}}\ GDP(L_1) + TA(L_1)$$

the first order condition for which is

$$GDP'(L_1) = -\,TA'(L_1) \tag{8.4}$$

That is, the social planner picks L_1 so that the marginal gain in output from adding more labor to region 1 is offset by the marginal loss in amenity caused by that labor movement.[11]

Perhaps a more intuitive interpretation of this result is given in Figure 8.3. With the tax, laborers move between regions until,

$$W_2(L_1) - [W_1(L_1) - t] = AA(L_1) \tag{8.5}$$

The tax causes a parallel upward shift of the $W_2 - W_1$ curve. At point L_b, workers have moved into region 1 until the wage differential has become equal to the average value of the amenity. However, in the presence of congestion, optimality requires that workers respond to marginal, not average, amenity returns. This occurs at point L_c in Figure 8.3, at the intersection of the $W_2 - W_1$ and $MA(L_1)$ curves. To reach L_c, the social planner sets a tax equal to the difference between the average and marginal amenity values at that point.

The preceding differs somewhat from standard results on congestion tolls because it explicitly recognizes the amenity-induced wage differential between regions. Were no wage differential to exist (that is, if the $W_2 - W_1$ curve were constant and equal to zero for all labor allocations), the optimum in Figure 8.3 would occur at L_a, where total amenity value is maximized.[12] This would mean that the total output curve would be exactly flat in the neighborhood of L_a. The solution to the federal social planner's problem, equation (8.4), would be satisfied only at the amenity peak, L_a.

The point here is that the population of a region matters for more than just its effect in congesting the amenity. Population also has an effect on output and upon market wage levels. This is true, incidentally, even if the region is small. In our figures we have assumed for simplicity that the two regions have equal endowments of land. However, one could equally well examine a small region, the population of which would not matter for the marginal product of labor, and therefore the wage, in the rest of the country. The size of the region's labor force would matter for its own wage, however, and we would still have an upward-sloping relationship between $W_2 - W_1$ and L_1. This together with the configuration of amenities in the region is enough to generate all of our results.

Before proceeding to the next section, a final note on the nature of the amenity in question is warranted. Courant and Deardorff (1993) consider pure consumption and production amenities as well as the presence of non-traded goods produced using a factor not used in the production of the traded good. They note there that analysis of equilibrium is the same for amenities and non-traded goods, but we show here that the welfare implications are very different. Equilibrium obtains when labor has the same utility in both the amenable (non-traded-abundant) region and the less well endowed region. However, in the case where one region is able to produce a non-traded good more cheaply, the equilibrium is also an optimum, because the price of the non-traded will be equal to its marginal cost. In the case of the congestible amenity, the optimum diverges from the market equilibrium because of the congestion externality, which causes the average amenity attained by the marginal worker to exceed the marginal amenity attained by all workers due to immigration of the marginal worker.

III THE TWO-SECTOR MODEL

In this section, we add a second traded good to the model set forth in section II. The relative price of the two traded goods is assumed to be fixed on the world market. The top panel of Figure 8.4 shows an Edgeworth-like box diagram for a country with two regions, two factors of production and two produced goods.[13] Given the world prices of goods X and Y, and assuming the absence of factor intensity reversals, there will exist a single set of factor prices consistent with incomplete specialization.[14] Corresponding to those factor prices will be a pair of least cost techniques of production for producing goods X and Y. Call the ratios of land to labor employed by these techniques t_X and t_Y, respectively, and draw rays t_X^1 and t_Y^1 from O^1, and t_X^2 and t_Y^2 from O^2. For each region, only those factor allocations that lie between these rays are consistent with their producing both goods while maintaining full employment of both factors. Therefore, in the parallelogram O^1RO^2S lie all of those factor allocations for which both regions can be incompletely specialized. Since factor prices are equalized (and constant) within this area, we refer to it as the FPE (factor-price-equalization) parallelogram.[15]

As before, we assume that labor is mobile and that land is immobile between regions. By drawing a horizontal line through the box diagram, T^0, we partition the land endowment of the economy into the two regions. Movements left and right along this line represent movements of labor between regions. We now consider the effects these movements have on factor prices and output in the economy, summarizing the results in the middle and bottom panels of Figure 8.4.

In the top panel, consider a point on T^0 immediately to the right of A. Both regions are diversified (although region 1 is producing mostly X), and factor prices are equalized. Now reallocate labor from region 2 to region 1. This

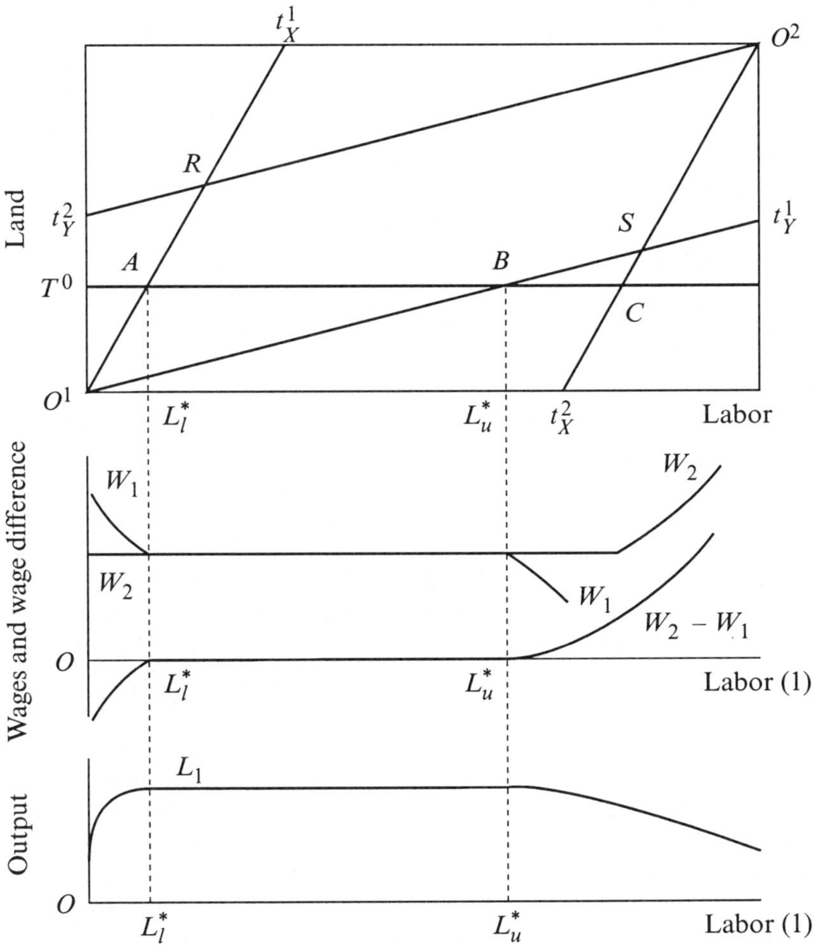

Figure 8.4 *A country with two regions, two factors of production, and two produced goods*

rightward movement along T^0 causes a reallocation of production. The ratio of labor to land in each sector of each region is unchanged, but region 1 absorbs its increase in the ratio of labor to land by producing more Y (the labor-intensive good) and less X (the land intensive good.) The value of region 1 total production has increased slightly and the value of region 2 production has decreased slightly.[16] Since neither total factor endowments nor factor prices have changed, the value of total output of the whole economy is unchanged. Therefore, for all labor allocations which preserve factor price equalization, total output is maximized and constant.[17]

Moving left and right outside of the FPE set, the value of output decreases. Moving left along T^0 from point A, we remain in region 2's diversification cone, but we are outside region l's cone. Region 1 now has a higher land to labor ratio than is used by the least cost method of producing the most land intensive good. The region 1 wage must therefore rise, and total output falls as we move to the left. Similarly, moving to the right along T^0 from point B, we remain in region 2's diversification cone, but we are again outside region l's cone. Here, region 1 has a lower land to labor ratio than is used by the least cost method of producing the most labor intensive good. The wage in region 1 must fall, and value of total output falls as we move to the right. Continuing to the right on T^0 past point C, we are finally also outside of region 2's diversification cone. Region 2 now has a higher land to labor ratio than is used by the least cost method of producing the most land intensive good, and the wage in region 2 must rise. Finally, note that the set of labor allocations which preserve factor price equalization depends on the land endowment. A slight, parallel upward shift of T^0 moves the FPE set rightward in the labor allocation and enlarges it slightly. Consequently, the sets of points for which the output and wage differential curves are constant, increasing, or decreasing depend on the land endowment.

To complete our description of this economy, we now give region 1 an amenity. This would be shown by a diagram similar to Figure 8.2 for the one-sector economy. The description of the labor allocation equilibrium and the federal planner's problem is similar to that shown in section II. In the absence of the amenity, labor moves between regions seeking the highest available wage. Denote the upper and lower bounds of the labor allocations that preserve FPE as L_u^* and L_l^*. Because there now is an entire range of labor allocations where factor prices are equalized (and where output is maximized), we cannot say precisely where equilibrium will occur, only that it will lie in the FPE set (between L_u^* and L_l^*). With the amenity, however, labor moves between regions seeking to maximize worker utility, given by the wage plus the average amenity (if any) in each region. In equilibrium, we have factor utility equalization for labor, and equation (8.3) is satisfied. Several possibilities emerge depending on the shape of the amenity schedule relative to the FPE set.

If there is no congestion tax, the presence of the amenity in region 1 will in all cases attract labor until a wage differential opens up favoring region 2. This means that the untaxed equilibrium, L_b, always lies to the right of the FPE set, and therefore that region 1 specializes completely in the labor-intensive good.[18] If we allow a congestion tax, different cases arise depending on whether the allocation that maximizes the total amenity, L_a, lies inside the FPE set, or to its right or left.

Most similar to the case we showed for the one-sector economy is the situation in Figure 8.5. Here the amenity itself would be maximized, at L_a, to the left of the FPE set, where region 1 specializes in the land-intensive good. The social optimum is again found at L_c, where the marginal amenity equals the wage differential, $MA = W_2 - W_1$. This point must also lie to the left of the FPE set. Whereas, absent a tax, the amenity draws so much labor to the region that it specializes in the labor intensive good, an optimal congestion tax may lead it to the opposite extreme of specialization. This is an extreme case, of course, but there is no basis to rule it out, as it will occur whenever the amenity maximum corresponds to a labor allocation less than L_l^*.

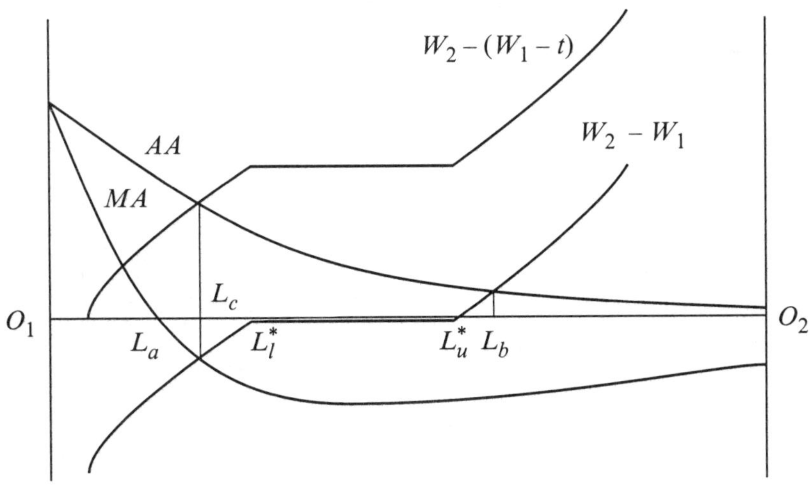

Figure 8.5 Amenity maximum – labor allocation equilibrium

Figure 8.6 shows a case where L_a lies between L_l^* and L_u^*. In this case, the social optimum occurs where the amenity is maximized since, within the FPE set, variations in L_1 do not change the value of the country's output. Thus $L_c = L_a$.

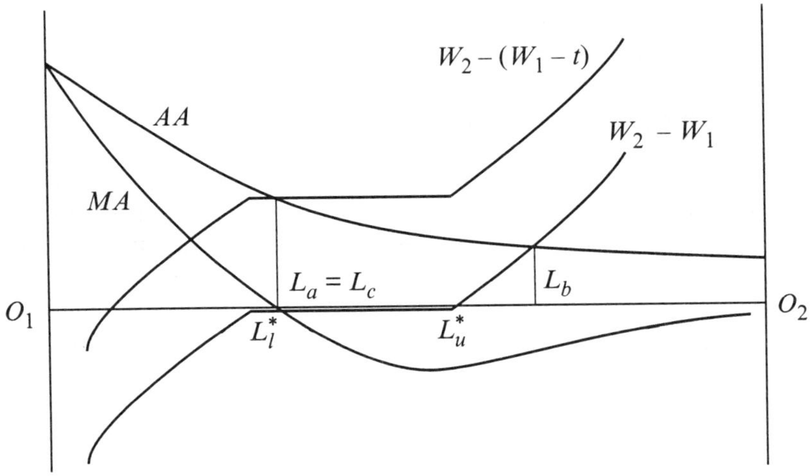

Figure 8.6 Tax-removed wage differential

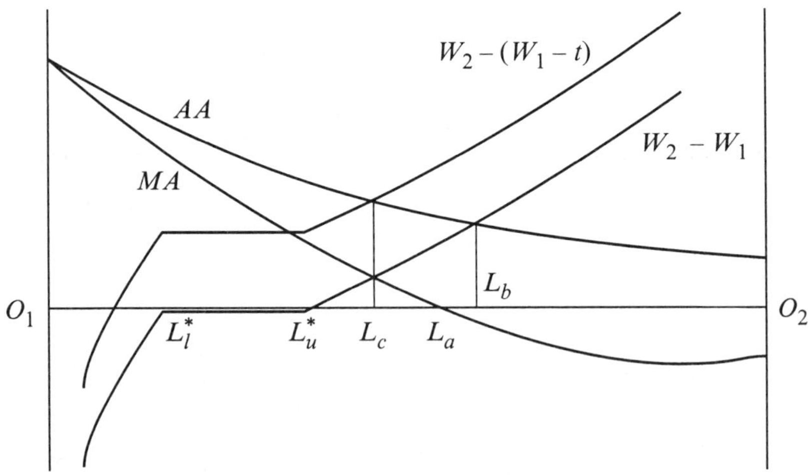

Figure 8.7 Amenity maximum – social optimum equilibrium

Here the addition of the second traded good markedly changes the analysis: optimal congestion tolls restore the economy to the FPE set. With only one traded good, the imposition of an optimal tax always, except on a set of measure zero, leaves some amenity-induced wage differential in place. Here, in contrast, the tax removes this differential completely.

Finally, in Figure 8.7, the amenity maximum occurs to the right of the FPE set, and the social optimum, at L_c, occurs there as well. In this case, the complications of the two-sector economy play no role, since region 1 is specialized completely in the same sector for all of the equilibria that we consider.

Note that each case implies different patterns of specialization for the socially optimal allocation. However, in all cases, the optimal congestion tax, following the standard public finance result, is equal to the difference between the average amenity and the marginal amenity.[19]

IV THE LOCAL GOVERNMENT

In this section, we extend the model of the previous sections to examine the role of a local government. Specifically, we want to see how the optimal labour allocation chosen by the local government differs, both from the federal planner's optimum and from the allocation in the no-tax equilibrium.

We now change the model slightly so that region 1 has a local government that has been captured by landowners who use tax policy to maximize local welfare. Alternately, and in the spirit of much urban development literature, we could assume that all the land in region 1 is owned by a single developer. Further, we also assume that, in either case, the other region of the country either fails to act strategically, or it is incapable of doing so. If, for example, region 2 is simply an aggregation of many small and separate regions, there would be no strategic response to tax policies in region 1. Allowing strategic interactions between local governments is a difficult and interesting complication that lies beyond the scope of this paper.

The local government attracts or 'hires' labour into the region by offering a combination of wage, amenity, and tax that leaves labor at least as well off as its next best alternative. The local government wants to hire an amount of labor that maximizes the return to land plus tax revenue. The local government benefits from a large amount of labor because land rent is non-decreasing in labor. However, too much labor drives down the wage and congests the amenity, reducing the size of tax that the local government can assess. Note that our setting up the problem in this way follows directly from Oates's seminal paper on capitalization (1969). In particular, the local government is fully aware of the fact that its fiscal behavior will be capitalized into land values, and it sets up its optimization problem accordingly.

Land rent is given by region 1 output, less the wage bill.[20]

$$R_1 = X_1 - W_1L_1 \tag{8.6}$$

Labor market equilibrium occurs when the after-tax regional wage differential equals the average amenity value: $W_2 - (W_1 - t) = TA/L_1$. Rearranging this gives a head tax of $t = W_1 - W_2 + TA/L_1$ Total revenue is just the head tax multiplied by the region 1 labor force. $TR = tL_1 = L_1(W_1 - W_2) + TA$.

The local government's problem is then to

$$\begin{aligned} &\underset{L_1}{\text{maximize}}\ R_1 + TR \\ &= X_1 - W_1L_1 + W_1L_1 - W_2L_1 + TA \\ &= X_1 - W_2L_1 + TA \end{aligned} \tag{8.7}$$

Differentiating we get the local government's first order condition,

$$\frac{dX_1}{dL_1} + \frac{dTA}{dL_1} - W_2 - L_1\frac{dW_2}{dL_1} = 0$$

The first term is simply the region 1 wage. The second term is the marginal value of the amenity. Rearranging, we get,

$$W_2 - W_1 = MA - L_1\frac{dW_2}{dL_1} \tag{8.8}$$

The local government's optimum, therefore, equates the wage differential to the marginal value of the amenity, less an additional term. The solution to the federal planner's problem is to equate the wage differential to the marginal value of the amenity only, or $W_2 - W_1 = MA$. The difference in the two solutions is the last term in equation (8.8). This term describes the marginal effect on region 2 wages of adding more labor to region 1, multiplied by the number of region 1 laborers. As the local government adds labor to region 1, it raises the wage in region 2. Since this is the next best alternative for region 1 labor, the local government must compensate each worker by the amount of the region 2 wage increase. The region 2 wage is non-decreasing in L_1, so this term is always non-negative.

The solution to the local government's problem is shown in Figure 8.8 for a one-sector economy. As before, L_1^* is the output maximum, L_a is the amenity maximum, L_b is the no-tax equilibrium, and L_c is the solution to the federal

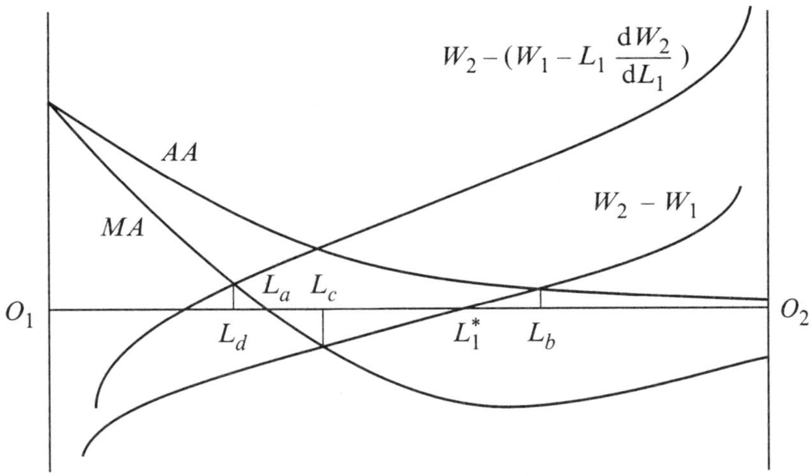

Figure 8.8 Local government's optimum solution in a one-sector economy

planner's problem. To find the local government's optimum, we shift the wage differential curve up by an amount $L_1[dW_2/dL_1]$.[21] The solution to equation (8.8) is found at point L_d, the intersection of this new curve and the marginal amenity curve.

If the term $L_1[dW_2/dL_1]$. non-zero in the vicinity of L_c, the point L_d must lie to the left of the federal optimum, and it may lie to the left or right of L_a, the amenity maximum point. Only if $L_1[dW_2/dL_1]$ were zero would the local government and the federal planner choose the same allocation. In a one-sector economy, this can happen only in the limit as the size of the region becomes very small, so that it takes the wage in region 2 as given.[22] In a two-sector economy, however, this will happen anywhere in the FPE set. Once again, the addition of the second traded good affects the results of the model. Here, the regional and national optima will coincide with positive probability, rather than on a parameter set of measure zero.

The local government's problem is the same in the two-sector and one-sector models, with only the shapes of the relevant curves being affected by the presence of the FPE set. Figure 8.9 shows three curves. The R_1 curve shows region 1 land rents. It is constant inside the FPE set and increasing in L_1 otherwise. The total amenity curve, *TA*, is given by the smooth curve, including the two thin segments at either end. The total revenue curve for the local government is shown by the thick curve, with kinks at L_l^* and L_u^*. Recall that total revenue is given by

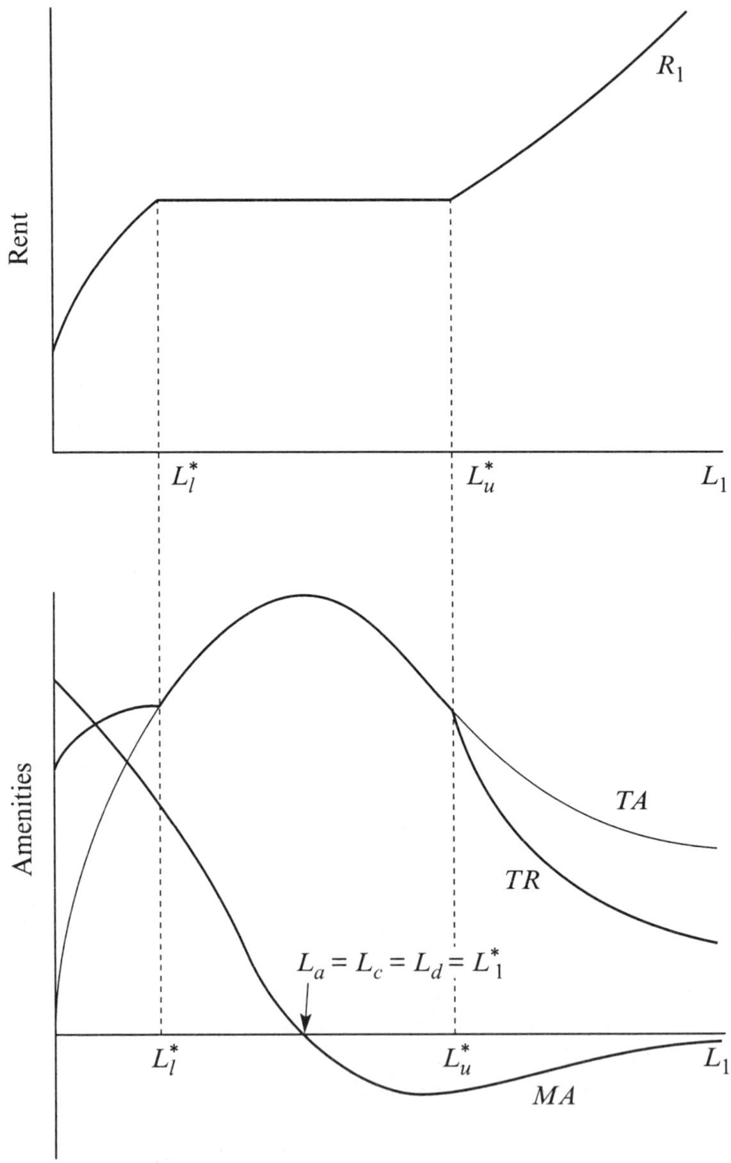

Figure 8.9 Local government's optimum solution in a two-sector economy

$TR = TA + L_1(W_1 - W_2)$. Inside the FPE set, $W_1 = W_2$, so that the total revenue attainable is just the total value of the amenity. Since wages are equal and unchanging in L_1 inside FPE, the local government sets a tax that extracts all of the amenity value from labor. To the left of FPE, the *TR* curve lies above *TA* because $W_1 > W_2$. Here, the local government can take advantage of the wage differential to set a tax higher than the value of the amenity. To the right of FPE, the *TR* curve lies below *TA* because $W_1 < W_2$, and the local government must use some of the amenity's value to offset the wage differential.

The federal planner equates the wage differential to the marginal amenity curve. This occurs at point L_c, equal in this drawing to L_a, the amenity peak. The local government, on the other hand, equates the wage differential to the marginal amenity, less an additional term, $L_1[dW_2/dL_1]$. However, the region 2 wage is constant for changes in the labour allocation inside the FPE set, so this last term drops out.[23] The local government's optimum is at L_d, equal to the federal optimum L_c.[24]

V CONCLUSIONS AND IMPLICATIONS

In this paper we have taken some first steps in asking what location and regional economics theory can learn from trade theory. Specifically, we have examined the welfare economics of amenities and congestion to see if general equilibrium concepts provide additional insight into optimal congestion taxation. General equilibrium matters, and so does having two traded goods rather than one. By looking at congestion tolls in general equilibrium, we see that the optimal toll (even in a small, open region) generally involves a trade-off between the amenity and the total (national) production of marketed output.

Adding a second traded good to the model raises the possibility that the trade-off disappears. With two traded goods, it is possible that the optimal toll would lead to an allocation of labour that is consistent with factor price equalization for the economy. When there is one traded good and a non-congestible amenity, Roback (1982) has shown that equilibrium generally involves a regional wage differential. No one, to our knowledge, has yet worked out what happens with two traded goods and a non-congestible amenity.

Given the two preceding results, it is unsurprising to find that in the second case, where partial equilibrium results hold exactly in general equilibrium, local governments will price local amenities optimally. Where the partial equilibrium welfare analysis goes astray, because amenity pricing affects productive efficiency in marketed goods, pricing by a local government will be non-optimal.

One could extend the analysis to consider mobile capital and capital taxation. An important distinction between capital and labor, of course, is that capital movements will always equalize factor prices, rather than the utilities of factor owners, as is the case with labor.

NOTES

1. The authors have benefited from the comments of Carsten Kowalczyk, from the comments of anonymous referees, and from comments from the editors of this volume.
2. A lumpy country is one in which any variety of differences may exist across regions within it, including differences in relative factor endowments, technologies, and in amenities that matter for the quality of life of the population.
3. All that is required for this conclusion is that workers with similar tastes and endowments inhabit locations of different amenity value. Equilibrium requires that utilities, rather than wages, be equalized across locations. See, for example, Tolley (1974), Roback (1982, 1988), Diamond and Tolley (1982), Knapp and Graves (1989), and Beeson (1991).
4. We note that Wally Oates's first published work was in international economics, implying that international economics and local public economics have had some connection for at least 30 years.
5. Strictly speaking, our tax is not on the amenities directly, but on the location of population, which we equate with the number of workers and hence the labor supply in a region. Thus our taxes on amenities are therefore modelled formally as taxes on labor.
6. See Oakland (1987) for a treatment of congestible public goods that does not consider output effects. Tolley (1974) considers the output effects of congestion, but does so in the context of a pure congestion externality, rather than a congestible amenity.
7. Under the Inada conditions the $W_2 - W_1$ curve goes to negative infinity as L_1 goes to zero, and to positive infinity as L_2 goes to zero. For all allocations of labor, the $W_2 - W_1$ curve will normally have strictly a positive slope.
8. While we will describe the amenity here as only being present in region 1, it works equally well to have amenities in both regions, where the total value of the region 1 amenity is larger than the region 2 amenity for all allocations of labor.
9. We could also consider the case of an amenity whose benefits are entirely exhausted at some finite level of population, as in Courant and Deardorff (1993). We have taken to calling this the 'Yogi Berra' case, after the Yankee catcher who once said of a famous New York restaurant, 'That place is so crowded no one goes there anymore.' Here, we consider Yogi's insight in footnotes. The Yogi Berra case can only be relevant if the amenity is exhausted at a population size in region 1 small enough so that $W_1 > W_2$.
10. Tolley (1974) derives a similar result in a model that has congestion but no explicit amenities. See his figures 2 (p. 332) and 3 (p. 335) and the associated discussion.
11. It is possible to draw these curves so that the amenity peak, L_a, lies to the right of the output peak L^*. In this case, equation (8.4) can be interpreted to say that the planner picks L_1 so that the marginal output *losses* from adding more labor to region 1 are offset by marginal amenity gains.
12. At point L_a, the $W_2 - W_1$ curve and the marginal amenity value curve would intersect at zero. This is just the sort of problem analysed in Oakland (1987).
13. This diagram was first used to illustrate allocations of factors between two countries by Dixit and Norman (1980). In their analysis, the dimensions of the box are the factor endowments of the world economy, and the diagram is used to illustrate the allocations of factors across two separate countries that would permit free trade between them to duplicate the equilibrium of the 'integrated world economy,' that is, the equilibrium in the absence of barriers to movement of both goods and factors.

    Used for a lumpy country in Courant and Deardorff (1992), the dimensions of the box are the country's factor endowments and points within the box indicate allocations across two regions within the country.
14. This is the Factor Price Equalization Theorem of Samuelson (1949).

15. Note that allocation movements that are outside of the FPE parallelogram, but still inside one region's diversification cone, will not change factor prices in that region.
16. The composition of production in each region has also changed somewhat. Region 1 is producing a little less X and a little more Y, as in the Rybczynski Theorem, and vice versa for region 2.
17. And, of course, for all labor allocations within the FPE set, the wage differential curve is constant at zero.
18. In the Yogi Berra case where the amenity is completely congested by finite labor, L_b could be inside the FPE set.
19. The relationship between congestible amenities and non-tradables discussed in the last paragraph of section II holds in the models discussed in this section.
20. All the variables in the following equations are functions of L_1.
21. Note that this is not a parallel shift of the wage differential curve. The $L_1(dW_2/dL)$. term is increasing (and for most technologies, probably at an increasing rate) in L_1.
22. This is the case considered in Oates and Schwab's (1988) analysis of local capital taxation.
23. If L_a lies outside FPE, then the region 2 wage is changing in L_1, and the federal and regional optima are not equal.
24. Another way to see the local government's optimum point is to note that it wants to maximize land rent plus tax revenue. Since land rent is constant in FPE, and the FPE set contains the amenity peak, its objective function must be maximized at the amenity peak.

REFERENCES

Beeson, P.E. (1991), 'Amenities and regional differences in returns to worker characteristics', *Journal of Urban Economics*, **30**, 224–41.

Courant, Paul N. and Alan V. Deardorff (1992), 'International Trade with Lumpy Countries', *Journal of Political Economy*, **100**, February, 198–210.

Courant, Paul N. and Alan V. Deardorff (1993), 'Amenities, Nontraded Goods, and the Trade of Lumpy Countries', *Journal of Urban Economics*, **34**, July, 299–317.

Diamond, D.B., Jr and George S. Tolley (1982), 'The Economic Roles of Urban Amenities', Ch. 1 of Diamond and Tolley (eds), *The Economics of Urban Amenities*, New York: Academic Press, pp. 3–54.

Dixit, Avinash K. and Victor Norman (1980), *Theory of International Trade*, London: Cambridge University Press.

Knapp, Thomas A. and Philip E. Graves (1989), 'On The Role of Amenities in Models of Migration and Regional Development', *Journal of Regional Science*, **29** (1), 71–87.

Krugman, Paul (1993), 'On the Relationship between Trade Theory and Location Theory', *Review of International Economics*, **1**, June, 110–22.

Oakland, William (1987), 'Public Goods', in Auerbach and Feldstein (eds), *Handbook of Public Economics*, Amsterdam: North-Holland, Ch. 9, pp. 485–535.

Oates, W.E. (1969), 'The Effects of Property Taxes and Local Public Spending on Property Values: An Empirical Study of Tax Capitalization and the Tiebout Hypotheses', *Journal of Political Economy*, **77** (6), 957–71.

Oates, W.E. and R.M. Schwab (1988), 'Economic Competition Among Jurisdictions: Efficiency Enhancing or Distortion Inducing?' *Journal of Public Economics*, **35**, 333–54.

Roback, J. (1982), 'Wages, Rents and the Quality of Life', *Journal of Political Economy*, **90**, 1257–78.

Roback, J. (1988), 'Wages, Rents, and Amenities: Differences among Workers and Regions', *Economic Inquiry*, pp. 23–41.
Samuelson, Paul A. (1949), 'International Factor-Price Equalisation Once Again', *Economic Journal*, **59** (June), 181–97.
Tolley, G.S. (1974), 'The Welfare Economics of City Bigness', *Journal of Urban Economics*, **1**, 324–45.

9. The effects of educational vouchers when schools track students by ability*

Dennis Epple, Elizabeth Newlon, and Richard E. Romano

1 INTRODUCTION

Wallace Oates laid out a major challenge for research on local public economies by highlighting that the production function for locally provided public services depends not only on conventional inputs such as labor and capital but also on the characteristics of individuals who comprise a community (Oates, 1981). In the context of education, he stressed that individual characteristics play a particularly significant role via peer group effects. He argued that, as a result, one cannot come to terms with major school policy issues by focusing only on variations in expenditure per pupil. Our paper seeks to contribute to the research inspired by Oates's challenge.

A practice common in public schools is the tracking of students by ability as measured by performance on standardized examinations. Tracking can be within schools (accelerated course programs), or it can be across schools, with certain schools restricted to only the most able students. The implicit presumption in the literature on ability tracking has been that school policy regarding tracking is driven by normative considerations about what arrangement best achieves a school's educational goals. In Epple, Newlon, and Romano (1997) we study the use of tracking as a device by which schools compete for students. We find that tracking has significant effects on the allocation of students across public and private schools. We also find that tracking has large effects on the distribution of achievement across students and on the distribution of welfare across students' households. In light of this, it is natural to expect that the effects of educational vouchers may be quite different when schools use tracking than when they do not.

In this chapter, we study an environment in which students differ by ability and household income. Student achievement depends on peer student abilities as well as on own ability. We consider a public school system that practices ability tracking and competes with a private sector for students. We examine how the introduction of educational vouchers in the presence of tracking affects the allocation of students of differing incomes and abilities among public and private schools. We investigate how achievement and welfare of students of different income and ability are affected by vouchers when public schools use tracking.

We find that vouchers which cover part of average educational cost induce students to exit each of two public school tracks and enter private schools. Because relatively higher-ability students in each track are the first to exit when given a voucher, the peer group and educational quality in each track decline. Consequently, those that stay behind in public school experience achievement and welfare losses. However, relative to when there is no tracking, the exodus to the private sector caused by increasing vouchers is decelerated and achievement of students remaining in public school declines less rapidly. This is because tracking provides a means for public schools to better retain higher-ability students who qualify for the high track, and their retention provides positive peer benefits to all public school students.[1]

The increased demand for private education caused by vouchers increases the marketability of student ability which private schools value for its peer effects. This is manifest in rising tuition discounts to ability in private schools as vouchers increase. The largest beneficiaries of vouchers are then low-income, high-ability students. Most students who depart public schools as vouchers rise gain in welfare, but there are conflicting effects. A few such students lose on net because they are driven to the private sector by the deterioration of their public school track. Many wealthy students in private schools without a voucher experience achievement losses when a voucher is introduced because fierce competition for high-ability students from new private schools which enter the market lowers the quality of the top private schools. Nevertheless, welfare of these (wealthy) students rises due to the vouchers' subsidy to their tuition and lower tax rates. Lower tax rates result for moderate level vouchers because cost reductions from educating fewer students in the public sector outweigh the public costs of funding partial vouchers.

We analyse vouchers computationally employing a theoretical model of the educational environment developed in earlier research (Epple and Romano, 1997, and Epple, Newlon, and Romano, 1997). To understand the effects of vouchers, one must become familiar with this model. Section 2 reviews the theoretical model, and section 3 develops its equilibrium properties. Vouchers are introduced in section 4 and their effects examined. Section 5 concludes.

2 THE MODEL

A Household and Educational Technology

In Epple, Newlon, and Romano (1997), we extend the model in Epple and Romano (1997) to the consideration of student tracking in schools. We apply the former model in order to consider the effects of vouchers in this paper. As a backdrop for this analysis, we outline our model and present a summary of results from these earlier papers. Ignore vouchers for the time being. In our model, household income is denoted y, and each household has a student of ability b. The joint marginal distribution of ability and income in the population is denoted $f(b,y)$, and is assumed to be continuous and positive on its support, $S \equiv (0,b_{max}] \times (0,y_{max}]$. All students attend a school since we assume free public schooling is preferred to no schooling. The household decision maker's utility function, $U(\cdot)$, is increasing in numeraire consumption and the educational achievement of the household's student, and is continuous and twice differentiable in both arguments. Achievement, $a = a(\theta,b)$, is a continuous and increasing function of the student's ability and the educational quality of the student's track in the school attended, θ. Let y_t denote after-tax income and p tuition expenditure, the latter equal to zero if a public school is attended. Thus, $U = U(y_t - p, a(\theta,b))$, with U_1, U_2, a_1, and a_2 all positive.

Peer student abilities exclusively determine track qualities in our model.[2] We permit at most two tracks in a school for simplicity. With tracking, students are assigned to a high or low track by the process discussed below. Track quality equals the mean ability of peer students per unit of time in classes. A 'mixing' value, $m \in [0,1]$. equals the proportion of class time (proportion of subjects studied) over which students attend non-track-segregated classes, with the remaining time (subjects studied) in classes with students assigned exclusively to their track. Let $\bar{b}_h > \bar{b}_l$ denote the mean ability of students assigned to the high and low tracks respectively, and $\bar{b}$ the mean student ability in the school. Quality of track $i \in \{\ell,h\}$ is then given by[3]

$$\theta_i = (1 - m)\bar{b}_i + m\bar{b}. \tag{9.1}$$

Pure tracking has $m = 0$ and no tracking $m = 1$.

U is also assumed to satisfy everywhere the 'single-crossing' condition:

$$\partial\left[\frac{\partial U / \partial\theta}{\partial U / \partial y_t}\right] \Big/ \partial y_t > 0. \qquad \textbf{(SCI)}$$

Hence, for students of the same ability, any indifference curve in the (θ,p)-plane of a higher-income household cuts any indifference curve of a lower-income household from below. This condition corresponds to an income elasticity of demand for educational quality that is positive at all qualities for all types.

Preferences for school quality might also depend on ability. We say preferences satisfy *weak single crossing in ability* if $\partial(\partial U/\partial\theta)/(\partial U/\partial y_t)/\partial b \geq 0$, which implies a weakly positive ability elasticity of demand for quality. However, because the pertinent empirical evidence is mixed and scarce, we avoid use of this assumption for almost all of our theoretical results. We will indicate explicitly any points where this assumption is used. In our computational model we adopt a Cobb–Douglas specification of the utility function:

$$U = (y_t - p)a(\theta,b); \quad a(\theta,b) = \theta^{\gamma}b^{\beta}; \quad \beta > 0, \gamma > 0. \tag{9.2}$$

While (9.2) satisfies **SCI**, it embodies the 'neutral' assumption of zero ability elasticity of demand: $\partial(\partial U/\partial\theta)/(\partial U/\partial y_t)/\partial b \geq 0$.

Since peer effects are prominent in our model, it is appropriate to comment briefly on the role of peer effects in this analysis and on the empirical evidence for peer effects. Two consequences of peer effects arise in our model. First, the preference for high-ability peers coupled with differences in student ability and household income lead to equilibria in which average student ability differs across schools and to sorting of students by income and ability across those schools. Second, peer quality affects individual student performance.

Predictions that our model provides about differentiation across schools and sorting of students across schools arise from the preference effect even if the performance effect is absent. There is little doubt that the preference effect is pervasive; individuals clearly care about the characteristics of their peer group. In large urban school districts, differences in average student ability across schools and sorting across schools are commonplace even when there are no differences across schools in expenditure per student.[4] Of course, this sorting is likely to reflect preferences for many different peer characteristics, but concern for school peers is surely one of them.

The performance effect of peer groups is more difficult to measure and more controversial. If individuals group together for the preference effect and there are unobserved characteristics of individuals which affect performance, then performance may appear to be affected by peer quality when, in fact, the performance differences are simply a manifestation of differences in unobserved characteristics. In studying teenage pregnancy, Evans, et al. (1992) find that, once one controls for the common unobserved characteristics of individuals who group together, there is little evidence of a direct effect of peers on teen pregnancy. They are careful to emphasize that their work does not rule out peer effects. Rather they demonstrate that much evidence cited in support of peer effects is suspect. While work on peer effects in education has, to varying degrees, reflected concern for the selection effects highlighted by Evans, et al., little of that work reflects the sophistication that those authors bring to dealing with this issue. Our reading of the evidence (see Epple and Romano, 1997) is that peer quality does affect individuals' performance in education, but more definitive empirical work is clearly needed.

A school's costs depend only on the number of students in each track since we hold fixed the quality of educational inputs (other than peer student ability; see note 2). Let k_i, $i \in \{\ell, h\}$, equal the number of students in track i, and $k \equiv k_\ell + k_h$ the number of students in the school. $C(k_\ell,k_h)$ denotes total cost. We require that $C(k_\ell,k_h) = C(k_\ell, + k_h,0) = C(0,k_\ell + k_h)$ if $m = 1$, that is, if there is no real tracking. We say that diseconomies (economies) of scope in tracking are present if:

$$C(k_l,k_h) \geq (\leq)\ C(k_\ell,0) + C(0,k_h)\ \forall\ k_i > 0,\ i \in \{l,h\}. \tag{9.3}$$

In our computational analysis we investigate the neutral case of 'constant scope economies,' that is where (9.3) holds with equality. There we assume track costs are given by

$$V(k_i) + F; \quad V' > 0,\ V'' > 0 \tag{9.4}$$

which also equals the cost of a school that does not track having $k = k_i$. For this specification, let k_i^* denote the 'efficient scale' of a track (or school in the no-tracking case):

$$k_i^* \equiv \text{ARGMIN}\ [C(k_i)/k_i]. \tag{9.5}$$

This presumes the presence of scale economies in schooling is realistic (Kenny, 1982) and precludes an unrealistic continuum of private schools that would otherwise result (Epple and Romano, 1997).

B Public Sector Schools

Public sector schools all follow the same policies. They offer free admission to all students. They track by ability using the same threshold ability, B, and adopt the same mixing value, m. Students are assigned to the upper (lower) track as their own ability $b \geq (<) B$.[5] We take B and m to be exogenous rather than specify a public sector objective function.[6] Public sector schools are homogeneous, as would be the case if frictionless choice among public schools induced equalization of the θ_is. Epple and Romano (1995) study the alternative of neighborhood school systems that impose residence requirements in a model without tracking. Given homogeneity of public schools, one can think of the public sector as one (possibly large) public school.

Public sector schooling is financed by a proportional income tax, t, paid by all households, whether or not the household's child attends public school. The public sector chooses the integer number of schools to minimize the total cost of providing schooling. Households are atomistic, so there is no tax consequence of any single household choice. The tax rate adjusts with household choices to balance the public-sector budget.

C Private Sector Schools

Private sector schools maximize profits and there is free entry and exit.[7] They can practice tracking and optimally choose the mixing value m, but again we allow no more than two tracks for simplicity. Student type is observable, implying tuition and track assignment can be conditioned on ability and income as competition permits.[8] Note that track assignment need not depend only on ability. Following the literature on competitive club economies, we model schools as utility takers (see Scotchmer, 1994). Private schools believe they can attract any student-type by offering admission and track assignment at a tuition yielding at least the maximum utility the student could obtain elsewhere.

We now summarize a private school's optimization problem (see Epple, Newlon, and Romano (1997) for a detailed development). It is convenient (and without loss of generality) to describe schools as choosing an admission and tuition policy. Let an i subscript, $i = 1,2,..,n$, indicate a value for the ith private school. A zero subscript does the same for 'the' public school. Let $\alpha_i(b,y) \in [0,1]$ denote the proportion of type (b,y) in the population that school i admits, with any $\alpha_0(b,y)$ 'optimal' for the public sector. (The equilibrium $\alpha_0(b,y)$ is determined by the residual demand for public education.) Let $\varphi_i(b,y) \in [0,1]$ denote the proportion of school i's admitted students of type (b,y) assigned to the high track, hence, $1 - \varphi_i$ the proportion assigned to the low track. Public school policy dictates that $\varphi_0 = 1$ (0) for $b \geq (<)$ B. Finally, let $p_{ih}(b,y)$ and $p_{i\ell}(b,y)$ denote school i's tuition functions for the high and low tracks respectively. Public school policy dictates that $p_{0h} = p_{0\ell} = 0$ for all (b,y), but the price of zero for the high track is contingent on admission to that track.

Private school i chooses its admission and tuition policies, track assignments, and between track mixing parameter to maximize profits:

$$\pi_i \equiv \iint_S \{p_{i\ell}(b,y)[1 - \varphi_i(b,y)] + p_{ih}(b,y)\varphi_i(b,y)\}\, \alpha_i(b,y) f(b,y)\, db\, dy - C(k_{i\ell},k_{ih}). \tag{9.6}$$

This objective is maximized subject to several constraints. A school admits no more of a type than exists in the population, all admitted students are assigned to one of the two tracks, and the mixing parameter must fall in the interval [0,1]. Definitional constraints specify attendance in each track, average ability in each track, and average ability in the school as the appropriate integrals over the set of students admitted. Track peer qualities are then determined by (9.1). Finally, the utility-taking assumption requires that a school expects (correctly in equilibrium) to attract a student if it offers the student tuition and track quality yielding the same utility obtainable elsewhere.

D Equilibrium

The private/public equilibrium can be described by the following conditions.[9] Households choose a school/track that maximizes utility while taking as given school/track qualities, admission/track-assignment/tuition policies, and the tax rate. Private schools maximize profits as discussed above. Zero profits for private schools is necessary and sufficient for no entry or exit. Public schools charge zero tuition and admit all students to a track who wish to attend and who meet the ability constraint for that track. The income tax rate is set to satisfy the public school budget constraint. Finally, there is market clearance; all students attend a school.

3 THEORETICAL RESULTS WITHOUT VOUCHERS

A Equilibrium Without Tracking

As a benchmark, we first review equilibrium properties with tracking precluded in both private and public schools. These results are developed in Epple and Romano (1997) where more detail and proofs are provided. By requiring that m equals 1 in all schools this simplified model is obtained. School quality, θ, then equals mean student ability in each school (see (9.1)). The issue of track assignment disappears, and the private school's problem is considerably simplified. We can drop the subscript $j \in \{\ell, h\}$ from values describing school variables. Note that the ith private school has a single tuition function $p_i(b,y)$ rather than one for each track. Last, this analysis employs the simple school cost function in (9.4) for all schools.

The solution to the ith private school's profit maximization problem is summarized as follows:

$$p_i(b,y) = p^*(b,y,\theta_i) \quad \forall \; (b,y) \in S; \tag{9.7a}$$

$$\eta_i = \frac{1}{k_i} \iint_S \frac{\partial p^*(b,y,\theta_i)}{\partial \theta} \alpha_i(b,y) f(b,y)\,db\,dy; \tag{9.7b}$$

and

$$\alpha_i(b,y) \begin{pmatrix} =1 \\ \in [0,1] \\ =0 \end{pmatrix} \text{ if } p^*(b,y,\theta_i) \begin{pmatrix} > \\ = \\ < \end{pmatrix} EMC_i(b) \quad \forall \; (b,y) \in S \tag{9.7c}$$

where

$$EMC_i(b) \equiv V'(k_i) + \eta_i(\theta_i - b). \tag{9.7d}$$

Condition (9.7a) indicates that all students face a tuition to school i equal to their type's *reservation price*, denoted $p^*(\cdot)$, for attending a school of quality θ_i. Condition (9.7b) defines a Lagrangian multiplier that equals the marginal willingness-to-pay for quality increases per household in school i's student body. We define the 'effective marginal cost' (EMC) of admitting a student of ability b as equal to the resource cost of educating the student plus the revenue change deriving from that student's effect on school quality. Expression (9.7d) indicates the latter peer effect equals the change in θ_i from admitting student of type b (equal to $(b - \theta_i)/k_i$) multiplied by the optimal tuition adjustments (equal to $k_i\eta_i$). Note that the peer-effect 'cost' of admission is negative for students of ability higher than the mean ability in the school. Condition (9.7c) indicates all (no) students of type (b,y) who are willing to pay more (less) than their EMC are admitted, and indifference to admission obtains for types with $p^* = EMC$.

The peer effect on quality is central to the nature of equilibrium. Private schools fully internalize this externality in admission decisions. The relative values of the ηs across schools of differing quality play a role in the analysis, and we argue below that higher quality schools are likely to be characterized by higher η values.

Turning to market properties, the analysis is complicated by an existence problem. Formally, the market equilibrium conditions cannot be satisfied except in special cases of $f(b,y)$. The existence problem is generic to club economics (see Scotchmer, 1994), derives from the discreteness of schools (that is, their fixed costs), and is manifest in an inability to have all (profit-maximizing) private schools' profits equal exactly zero. Our resolution is to examine an 'epsilon competitive equilibrium,' that replaces the profit-maximization and zero-profit conditions with requirements that private schools are at local profit maxima (implying satisfaction of first-order conditions) but allowing profit levels to differ from zero by a positive value $\in$. Hence, entry will not occur unless $\pi_i > \in$ for some private school, nor would an incumbent school pursue non-local changes in admission/tuition policies unless it could gain more than $\in$. Of course, the smaller is the value of $\in$ consistent with the equilibrium, the less troubling is the approximation. In our computational analysis, we have found equilibrium with values of $\in$, on the order of eleven percent of cost. The 'equilibrium' results reported below apply to our approximate equilibrium as well as exact equilibrium ($\in = 0$) when it exists.

To interpret the equilibrium properties discussed below, refer for an example to Figure 9.1 from our computational analysis. This case has no tracking in public schools (that is, $m = 1$) or private schools. The triangle in the (b,y)-plane with vertex at the origin comprises the student body or *admission space* of the public sector (with the vertical track boundary irrelevant since $m = 1$), and the remaining diagonal slices of the plane each correspond to the admission space of a private school. We refer to the loci that divide schools' admission spaces as *boundary loci*. Epple and Romano (1997) establish Results 1 through 4 below.

Result 1 A strict hierarchy of schools results with the public sector having the lowest ability peer group $\theta_n > \theta_{n-1} > \ldots > \theta_1 > \theta_0$.

Result 2a Along a boundary locus between schools i and j, $p_i = EMC_i(b)$ and $p_j = EMC_j(b)$ for any i and/or $j \neq 0$ (that is, for private schools). Private school pricing on boundary loci is strictly according to ability.

b $p_i(b,y) > EMC_i(b)$ for $i \neq 0$ in the interior of private school i's admission space; private school pricing off boundary loci depends on income.

c The attendance pattern is the same if all private schools instead set p_i equal to the equilibrium EMC_i for all students.

Result 3a Student choice of school is characterized by *stratification by income* (SBI) meaning, for a given ability, attendance at a higher quality school implies weakly higher household income.

b If preferences satisfy weak single crossing in ability and the ηs weakly ascend in private schools (that is, $\eta_n \geq \eta_{n-1} \geq \ldots \geq \eta_1$), then *stratification by ability* (SBA), analogously defined, also characterizes school choice.

The minimum quality of public sector schools in *Result 1* is simply because public schools are free and open to all, while at least some students must pay positive tuition to any private school. The strict hierarchy among private schools of *Result 1* derives from **SCI** and an associated incentive of higher income types to compensate higher ability types for attending 'their' schools.

Along boundary loci students are indifferent to which of the adjacent schools they attend, implying perfect competition for these students and tuition equal to effective marginal cost (*Result 2a*). Hence, tuition to private school i is discounted to ability at rate η_i along school i's boundary loci. Students of type in the interior of a private school's admission space would have a strict preference for that school if it charged tuition equal to *EMC*. This is because preference for quality rises with income **(SCI)** while *EMC* is independent of income. The school increases tuition to such students, squeezing away all consumer surplus (*Result 2b*). Because it is perfect (first-degree) discrimination, the allocation is as though schools compete perfectly (*Result 2c*), with normative implications discussed below. In spite of the discrimination, competition from rival schools for students of higher ability is enough to guarantee discounting to ability (for given income) in the admitting school for some utility functions (for example, Cobb–Douglas). Further, if the efficient scale of schools is small relative to the population, then private schools will be numerous and not very differentiated, and discrimination is of little consequence and can be safely ignored in any case.

Result 3a's assertion of SBI follows easily from the normality of demand for educational quality (**SCI** again). Because of the discounting to ability, one expects also to find SBA. However, there is a potential for this effect to be offset if preference for quality declines with ability. Hence, we must assume weak single crossing in ability to guarantee SBA. In addition, if lower quality schools were to give higher discounts to ability (that is, if η's fail to weakly ascend), then weaker schools might attract higher ability students over some ranges. Because η_i is the willingness-to-pay for quality increases per student in school i, we expect it to rise with school quality due to **SCI** and that equilibrium is characterized by income stratification. We have consistently found strictly ascending ηs in varied computational analysis. Although a reversal of ascending ηs seems pathological, we have not been able to reject it theoretically.[10] The combination of SBI and SBA conforms to the diagonal admission spaces of private schools.[11]

We now turn to normative results. Pareto efficiency requires: (A) a student allocation that internalizes the peer-group externality given the number of schools; and (B) entry whenever aggregate household net willingness to pay for an allocation with one more school exceeds the change in all schools' costs. An equilibrium with only private schools satisfies efficiency condition (A) by *Result 2c*. However, entry to the point of zero profits entails externalities so that condition (B) fails to hold in a purely private equilibrium.

Introduction of the free public sector implies deviations from both efficiency conditions. In general, the public sector displaces multiple differentiated private schools, substituting the equivalent of one 'large' homogeneous school. This effective reduction in the number of schools is without attention to costs and benefits, implying a deviation from efficiency condition (B). Free tuition to public schools violates condition (A).

Collecting these results, we have:

Result 4a The allocation in a fully private equilibrium is (Pareto) efficient given the number of schools. The equilibrium number of schools is not, however, generally efficient.

b The public–private sector equilibrium has neither an efficient number of schools, nor an efficient student allocation given the number of schools.

The normative results above treat educational achievement as a consumption good. An alternative interpretation of the model views achievement as an investment good, with offspring income a linear function of achievement. Household utility is a linear combination of utility of parental consumption and utility of offspring's consumption. Efficiency requires an allocation of types across schools that maximizes aggregate achievement (net of the relative cost of education). For Cobb–Douglas achievement specification, the efficient allocation entails ability stratification but no income stratification. Our positive results carry over if households face imperfect loan markets for financing education that are binding. In particular, the relevant indirect household utility function then satisfies **SCI.**[12] The stratification by income that characterizes equilibrium with private schools implies inefficiency.

To accommodate both normative interpretations, we examine two welfare measures in the computational analysis. Relevant to achievement as a consumption good, we calculate changes in compensating variation. Relevant to achievement as an investment good, we calculate changes in a normed measure of achievement discussed below.

B Equilibrium with Tracking

We now summarize results for the model with tracking. Further detail and proofs are provided in Epple, Newlon, and Romano (1997). We allow private school i to track and consider its profit-maximization problem (recall (9.6)). We suppress the i subscript for the time being. In addition to the constraints themselves, the first-order conditions are:

$$p_t(b,y) = p^*(b,y,\theta_t),\ t \in \{\ell,h\}\ \forall\ (b,y) \in S; \tag{9.8a}$$

$$\eta_\ell = \frac{1}{k_\ell}\iint_S \frac{\partial p^*(b,y,\theta_\ell)}{\partial\theta}(1-\phi(b,y))\alpha(b,y)dbdy; \tag{9.8b}$$

$$\eta_h = \frac{1}{k_h}\iint_S \frac{\partial p^*(b,y,\theta_h)}{\partial\theta}\phi(b,y)\alpha(b,y)dbdy; \tag{9.8c}$$

$$\alpha(b,y)\begin{pmatrix} =1 \\ \in[0,1] \\ =0 \end{pmatrix} \text{ if } \phi(b,y)\left[p^*(b,y,\theta_h) - EMC_h(b)\right]$$

$$+\ (1-\phi(b,y))\left[p^*(b,y,\theta_\ell) - EMC_\ell(b)\right]\begin{pmatrix} > \\ = \\ < \end{pmatrix} 0\ \forall\ (b,y) \in S; \tag{9.8d}$$

$$\phi(b,y)\begin{pmatrix}=1\\ \in[0,1]\\ =0\end{pmatrix} \text{if } p^*(b,y,\theta_h)-EMC_h(b)\begin{pmatrix}>\\ =\\ <\end{pmatrix} p^*(b,y,\theta_\ell)-EMC_\ell(b)\ \ \forall\ (b,y)\ \in\ S; \tag{9.8e}$$

and

$$m\begin{pmatrix}=1\\ \in[0,1]\\ =0\end{pmatrix} \text{if } \left(\bar{b}_h-\bar{b}_\ell\right)\left(\eta_h-\eta_\ell\right)\begin{pmatrix}<\\ =\\ >\end{pmatrix}0; \tag{9.8f}$$

where

$$EMC_h(b)\equiv\frac{\partial C}{\partial k_h}+(1-m)\left(\bar{b}_h-b\right)\eta_h+m\left(\bar{b}-b\right)\left[\frac{k_h}{k}\eta_h+\frac{k_\ell}{k}\eta_\ell\right]; \tag{9.8g}$$

and

$$EMC_\ell(b)\equiv\frac{\partial C}{\partial k_\ell}+(1-m)\left(\bar{b}_\ell-b\right)\eta_\ell+m\left(\bar{b}-b\right)\left[\frac{k_h}{k}\eta_h+\frac{k_\ell}{k}\eta_\ell\right]. \tag{9.8h}$$

Most of the conditions have very similar interpretations to those when tracking is precluded. Students face their reservation prices by (9.8a), but now a different one for each track. Conditions (9.8b) and (9.8c) describe the marginal value of changes in quality per student of those in the low and high tracks respectively. By (9.8e), all students are assigned to the track that maximizes the difference between their reservation price for the track and effective marginal cost of admission to the track. There is a strict preference for assigning the total proportion of students of type (b,y) to one track, that is, ϕ will equal 0 or 1 except along a one-dimensional track boundary in the (b,y)-plane. The admission criterion (9.8d) is then seen to be analogous to that in the case of no tracking (recall (9.7c)). Condition (9.8f) describes the mixing choice discussed further below. Expressions (9.8g) and (9.8h) define respectively the effective marginal cost of assignment of student with ability b to the high and low tracks. As in the no tracking case, effective marginal cost is the sum of the resource cost and the ‘cost’ of the peer externality. Now the latter is a weighted sum of the revenue changes from other students who attend the assigned student's track and from the entire student body, the weights dependent on the degree of mixing.

Recall that $m = 1$ corresponds to no tracking.[13] Henceforth, when we refer to the practice of tracking, we mean the non-degenerate case with $m < 1$. For $m < 1, \bar{b}_h > \bar{b}_\ell$ by definition of the tracks. From (9.8f), then $\eta_h \geq \eta_\ell$ if $m \in [0,1)$. When a private school tracks, the partition satisfies:

Result 5 There is stratification by income across a private school's tracks. For Cobb–Douglas preference/achievement, stratification by ability across tracks also results.

The two types of within-school stratification across tracks arise for analogous reasons to the across-school stratification induced by private schools that cannot track (*Result 3* above). Cobb–Douglas utility is not necessary to get both forms of stratification. **SCI** is enough for stratification by income, and **SCI** and weak single crossing in ability are 'likely' to be enough for stratification by ability.

Given **SCI** and the partition across tracks, it is likely that $\eta_h > \eta_\ell$ (as it is likely that η's will strictly ascend in the model without tracking). Then:

Result 6 Private school tracking has $m = 0$ if $\eta_h > \eta_\ell$.

This follows immediately from (9.8f). Hence, in most cases, tracking in private schools will have no mixing across tracks. Combining *Results 5* and *6* we see that private-school tracking produces a similar partition of students as results from competition of private schools that cannot track.

The apparent substitutability of individual private-school tracking for competitive provision of private schooling raises the question as to the extent to which tracking persists with free entry. *Result 7* confirms one's intuition:

Result 7 If tracking by schools were characterized by $\eta_{ih} > \eta_{i\ell}$ in all private schools in that track, then, absent *strict* scope economies in tracking, no private school will track in free-entry equilibrium.

The proof shows that if an incumbent school were to track students in any case without strict scope economies in tracking, then a non-tracking entrant could attract a subset of students from the incumbent school and earn positive profits. Thus, private-school tracking cannot occur in equilibrium.

Henceforth, we assume costs are track specific and given by (9.4), implying constant scope economies. This is for simplicity and is a 'neutral assumption,' given the lack of evidence on tracking costs. Although we have not proved private-school tracking could never result under such circumstances (because

Result 7 requires track-ascending η's), we ignore it as a possibility in the market equilibrium analysis that follows.

The last results to review concern properties of market equilibrium with tracking. Recall that we assume the public sector runs two tracks with track boundary at exogenously determined ability B and with exogenous mixing parameter $m \in [0, 1)$. The gains from partitioning students by cross subsidization imply again a strict hierarchy among private schools. The high track in the public sector can, however, be of higher quality than some private schools, implying *Result 1* must be modified.

Result 8 Equilibrium with public sector tracking has a strict hierarchy of private schools, each of strictly higher quality than the lower track in the public sector. The quality of the higher track in the public sector can exceed that of any private school.

Panels (c) and (d) of Figure 9.2, discussed further below, depict examples from our computational analysis of vouchers for which a subset of private schools are inferior to the high public track as in *Result 8*.

The pricing properties collected in *Result 2* carry over, and private schools continue to discount to ability. The income-stratification property of *Result 3* also holds. Public-school tracking can, however, disrupt the simple ability stratification that is typical without tracking.

Result 9 For equilibrium with weakly ascending η's across private schools (that is, $\eta_1 \leq \eta_2 \leq ... \leq \eta_n$), stratification by ability holds among students that attend private schools, but not generally when upper-track, public-school students are included.

The reversal of SBA can occur when the upper track is of higher quality than a private school as illustrated again by panels (c) and (d) of Figure 9.2.

Any of the examples in Figure 9.2 depict a general and more fundamental property of the equilibrium partition with tracking.

Result 10 The boundary locus between the public and private sector is discontinuous at the track boundary B, where there is a discrete increase in household income.

The discrete jump in public school quality as ability rises above the track boundary implies that discretely higher income is necessary for a household to be indifferent between public-sector and private-sector schooling. The graphic counterpart of *Result 10* is the 'notch' in the public-private sector boundary locus in the cases of Figure 9.2. The introduction of tracking renders the public sector more effective in competing for higher ability students who qualify for the upper track but less effective in attracting lower ability students.

Last, consider briefly the normative implications of tracking. First, treat school quality as a consumption good. *Result 4a* continues to apply since it regards a fully private equilibrium. The public sector with tracking will not produce an efficient allocation as in *Result 4b*. The effective track tuitions, zero to track qualifiers and infinity to non-qualifiers, fail to reflect the social cost of admission.

4 VOUCHERS AND COMPUTATIONAL RESULTS

We examine computationally the effects on equilibrium of tax-financed vouchers redeemable by private schools.[14] Each student who attends a private school receives a voucher of exogenously determined magnitude v. Reformulate the model by everywhere adding v to y_t for households that choose a private school, and modify the public-sector budget constraint by adding to the expenditure side the cost of the voucher for all students who attend private school: $v\sum_{i=1}^{n} k_i$. Vouchers lower the private cost of education leading to lower real tuitions and increased demand for private schooling.

A computational model allows us to explore how the introduction of vouchers affects attendance and quality in the public school tracks and the number and quality of private schools. We view the results as more than illustrative examples. We have calibrated the computational model to existing empirical evidence. In interpreting our results, however, it is important to keep in mind that empirical evidence is limited on some important parameters of the model.

A Specification and Calibration

We adopt the computational model in Epple and Romano (1997) extended to include public school tracking in Epple, Newlon, and Romano (1997). We briefly summarize the calibration here. The computational model entails a choice of joint density function for income and ability, utility and achievement functions, and the cost function for education.

Income and ability follow a joint lognormal distribution: $\begin{bmatrix}\text{Ln(b)}\\ \text{Ln(y)}\end{bmatrix}$ is distributed bi-variate normal with mean $\begin{bmatrix}\mu_b\\ \mu_y\end{bmatrix}$ and covariance matrix

$$\begin{bmatrix}\sigma_b^2 & \rho\sigma_b\sigma_y\\ \rho\sigma_b\sigma_y & \sigma_y^2\end{bmatrix}.$$

Calibrating the marginal distribution of income to mean (\$36 250) and median (\$28 906) income in 1989 yields $\mu_y = 3.36$ and $\sigma_y = 0.68$.

The distribution of ability is calibrated as follows. We assume the ability distribution to be a primitive, that is, independent of policy changes. We further assume that future earnings are linear in normed achievement, a_N. The latter is obtained by raising the assumed achievement function, $a = \theta^{\gamma}b^{\beta}$, to the power $1/\beta$ and multiplying by a constant: $a_N \equiv \Lambda_0\theta^{\gamma/\beta}b$. Hence, normed achievement is measured in the same units as ability, and both are measured in dollars. Results from Henderson et al. (1978) imply an elasticity of achievement with respect to peer ability at least 20 percent as large as the elasticity with respect to own ability: $\gamma/\beta = 0.2$. Parameters for the ability distribution are then chosen to give rise to an approximate steady-state equilibrium when there is no tracking.[15] That is, the distribution of normed achievement in each generation (approximately) replicates the distribution of income of the parent generation. A final step adjusts for the difference between ratios of employed workers per household and students per household. The outcome of this calibration process is $\mu_b = 2.42$ and $\sigma_b = 0.61$.

Recent evidence (Solon, 1992; Zimmerman, 1992) indicates that the correlation between father's income and son's income is approximately 0.4. This correlation is an upper bound on the correlation between father's income and son's ability because the intergenerational correlation of income arises both from intergenerational correlation of ability and from the choice of higher quality private schools by some higher income households. For our benchmark case, we set $\rho = 0$. Sensitivity analysis demonstrates only minor effects of increasing ρ to 0.4. This completes the calibration of $f(b,y)$.

The combined utility-achievement function is assumed Cobb–Douglas (recall (9.2)), and implies unitary price and income elasticities of demand for school quality, θ. It also implies zero ability elasticity of demand for school quality. The assumption that the effect of peer group is not biased toward either high- or low-ability types seems an appropriate choice for a baseline model given the mixed empirical evidence about whether an improvement in peer group is more beneficial to high- or low-ability students.

The share of disposable personal income spent on education in the US is approximately 0.056. Parameter γ is chosen to yield the observed expenditure share if school quality could be purchased at a constant price per unit of quality, implying $\gamma = 0.06$. This and $\gamma/\beta = 0.2$ from above yield the calibrated utility function $U = (y_t - p)\theta^{0.06}b^{0.012}$.

We measure a school's or track's size, $k \in [0,1]$, as the proportion of the population's households (or students) using the school. The cost function for private schools and for each track in a public school is quadratic in k, $F + V(k) = C_0 + C_1 \cdot k + C_2 \cdot k^2$. Expenditure per student in public schools in 1988 was \$4222 (Statistical Abstract, 1991, p. 434), and there was approximately 1/2 student per household (Statistical Abstract, 1992, p. 46 and p. 136). Thus, educational expenditure per household was approximately \$2 100, and the cost function parameters were chosen such that average cost reaches a minimum at this value (and to satisfy second-order conditions). For our simulations, we use the following cost function: $F + V(k) = 12 + 1300 \cdot k + 13333 \cdot k^2$. This function yields a minimum average cost per household of \$2 100 when k^* (efficient scale) = 3 percent of the student population.[16] The cost function and other parameters presented thus far are those used in Epple and Romano (1997).

In addition to presuming constant scope economies in tracking, two parameters characterize tracking in our model and are taken from Epple, Newlon, and Romano (1997). These are the public school track boundary, B, and the mixing parameter, m. Data presented in Gamoran (1992) suggest that there is typically some mixing between tracks, which we reflect by a mixing parameter of 0.25. The track boundary B is set so that the percentage of public school students in the high track in equilibrium without vouchers equals the average value of 30 percent reported by Gamoran (1992). The resulting value of B equals 14.4 and is roughly at the 65th percentile of our ability distribution.

B Computing Equilibrium

Several factors that complicate the computation of equilibrium are discussed here. Recall that the existence problem leads us to examine an epsilon-competitive equilibrium, so a value of epsilon must be specified. We chose, of course, the minimum value consistent with the comparative statics we perform. Our epsilon value is 7, and is approximately 11 percent of total school cost at the efficient scale.

Consider the determination of boundary loci. Let an *indifference locus* between two private schools consist of the set of types (b,y) indifferent between them when tuition at each school equals effective marginal cost. Let an indifference locus between a private school and a public school track consist of indifferent students who qualify for the track while facing zero tuition at public school and again tuition equal to effective marginal cost at the private school.[17] When there are no intersections of the indifference loci in the support of $f(b,y)$, boundary loci are simply determined, equal to the subset of indifference loci between schools/tracks of adjacent quality. This occurs, for example, in our equilibrium with no tracking (Figure 9.1). However, the cases of tracking typically result in crossing of indifference loci which is seen to be manifest in kinks in the boundary loci (for example, Figure 9.2). This complicates the characterization of admission spaces. In the appendix to Epple, Newlon, and Romano (1997), we demonstrate how admission spaces and boundary loci are then determined.

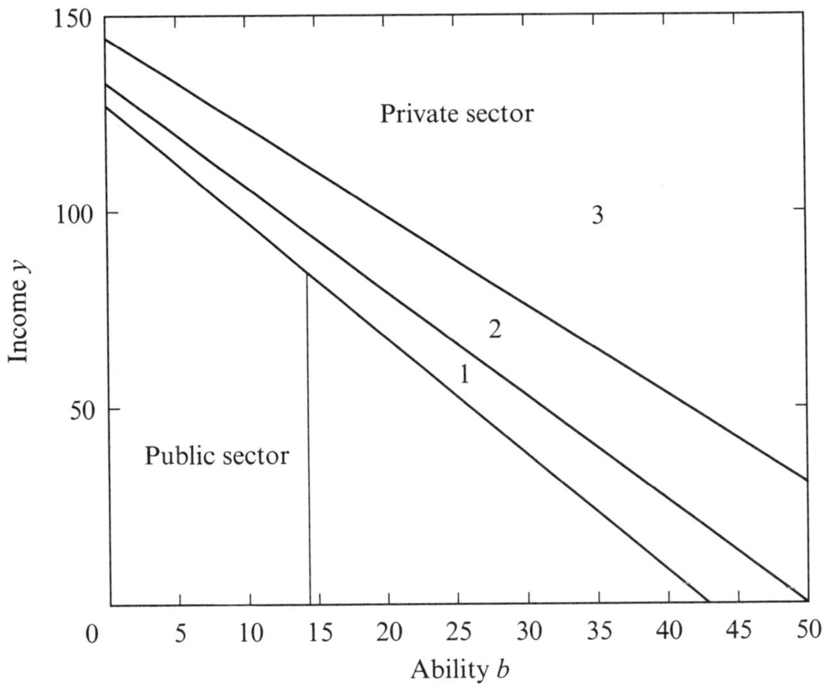

Figure 9.1 School admission spaces with no tracking and no voucher

To compute the profit of a private school, it is necessary to determine the utility each student in that school could obtain in the student's next best alternative school. While an analytic characterization is easily obtained, this proves to be an exceedingly difficult computational problem when indifference loci of schools cross. Hence, we approximate by characterizing the equilibrium obtained when schools set price equal to effective marginal cost, that is, they do not price discriminate by income. We know that this is the limiting outcome as private school size approaches zero. In our computational model, schools are small, and this approximation is likely to be a good one.

C Results

As a benchmark, the equilibrium partition of students with no tracking and no voucher is illustrated in Figure 9.1. The inoperative track boundary is included for comparisons to follow. The public school sector attracts 90 percent of the student population. There are three private schools, each serving approximately 3 percent of the student population. The effects of tracking with no voucher are illustrated in panel (a) of Figure 9.2. The public school sector attracts 93 percent of the student population. The introduction of tracking lowers private school profits when three private schools are present, inducing one private school to exit. In the equilibrium with tracking, the high track of the public school sector serves 31 percent of the aggregate student population and the low track serves 62 percent. In the absence of tracking, the corresponding figures are 27 percent and 63 percent. Thus tracking causes an increase in attendance in public schools among students who qualify for the high track by more than it reduces attendance among students who do not qualify for the high track. Further results regarding the effects of tracking without vouchers may be found in Epple, Newlon, and Romano (1997).

The effects of $2000, $3000, and $3600 per student vouchers in the presence of tracking are illustrated in panels (b), (c), and (d) of Figure 9.2. Keep in mind the average cost of schooling is about $4200. The voucher induces entry by private schools and results in a concurrent shrinkage in the size of both the low and high public school tracks. The number of private schools grows from 2 in panel (a) of Figure 9.2 to 22 in panel (d).

For the public sector and selected private schools, school/track qualities, sizes, and shadow prices of ability (the ηs), and the income tax rates are presented in Table 9.1 without a voucher and with vouchers of $1000, $2000, $3000, and $3600. The ℓ (h) subscript indicates a value for the low (high) track in the public sector. The table shows that both public tracks shrink in size as the voucher is increased. For example, with a $3000 voucher, attendance in the high public school track shrinks to 15 percent of the student population and attendance in the low track falls to 47 percent of the student population. The drop is proportionately greater in the high track because private schools give tuition discounts to attract high-ability students, including scholarships to very able students. Together with the decline in public school attendance, there is a concurrent drop in peer quality in both tracks, as the table shows.

In addition to results for both public school tracks, the table also provides results for the worst, median, and best quality private schools (subscripted w, m, and b respectively). It also reveals several aspects of the way in which the voucher affects the equilibrium characteristics of private schools. In the presence of the voucher, there is a much greater range of private school qualities. With a sufficiently high voucher (for example, $3000) the lowest quality private school has lower peer quality than the high public track.

The deterioration of the low public school track when this voucher is introduced leads students of higher income and ability from the lower track to switch to private school. In panel (c) of Figure 9.2, this group switching to the lowest quality private school is a triangle just to the left of the track boundary

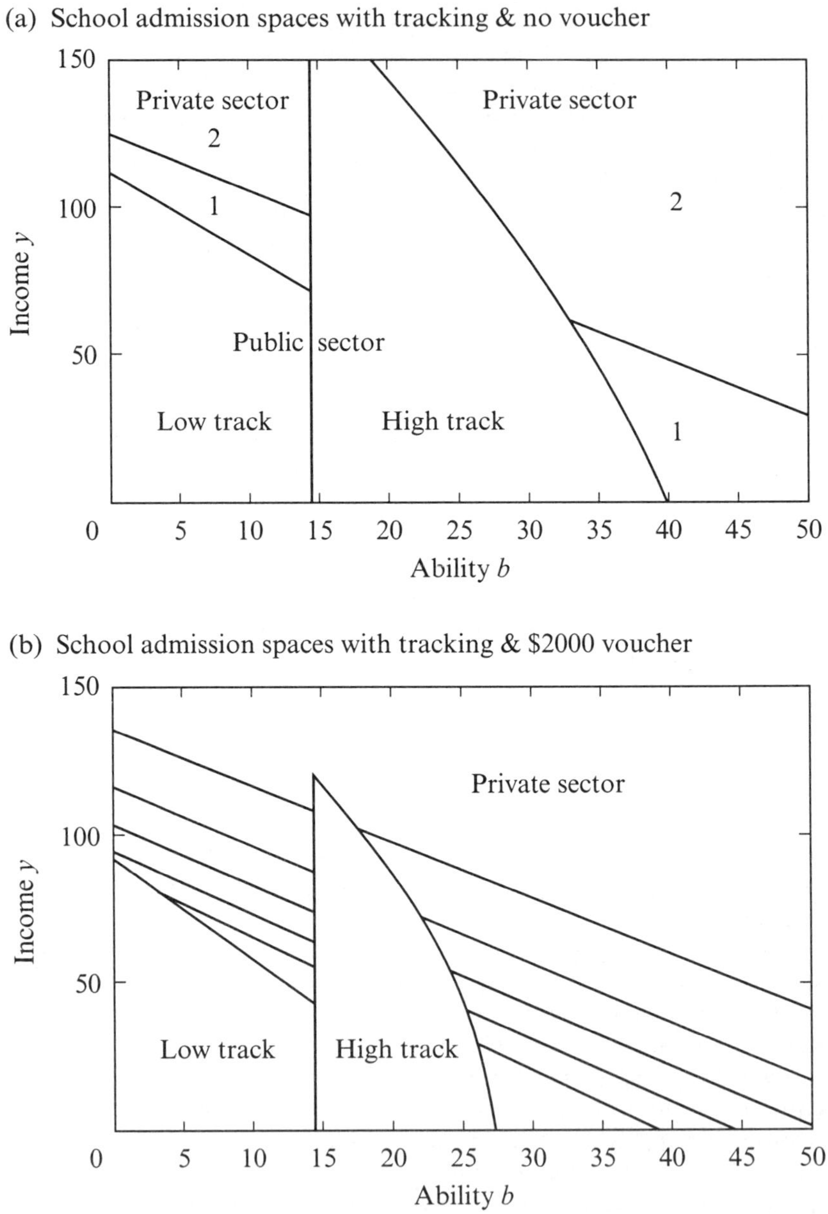

Figure 9.2 School admission spaces with tracking and various vouchers

(c) School admission spaces with tracking & $3000 voucher

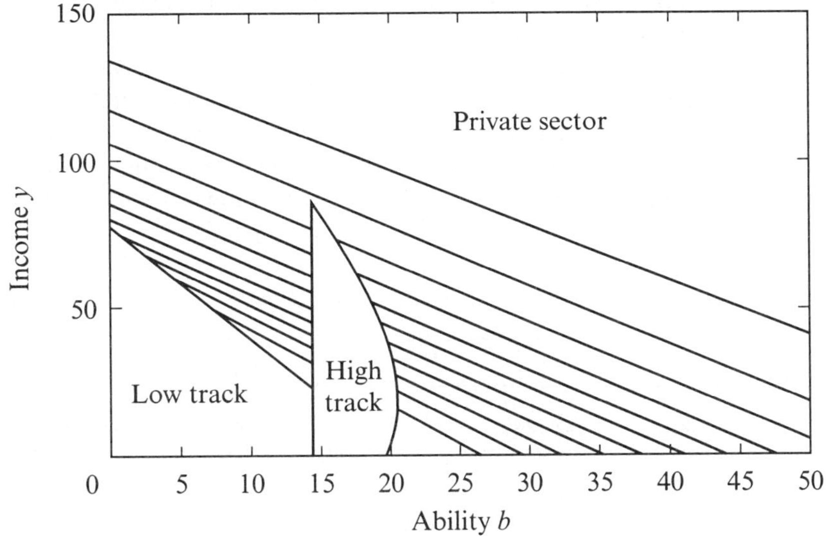

(d) School admission spaces with tracking & $3600 voucher

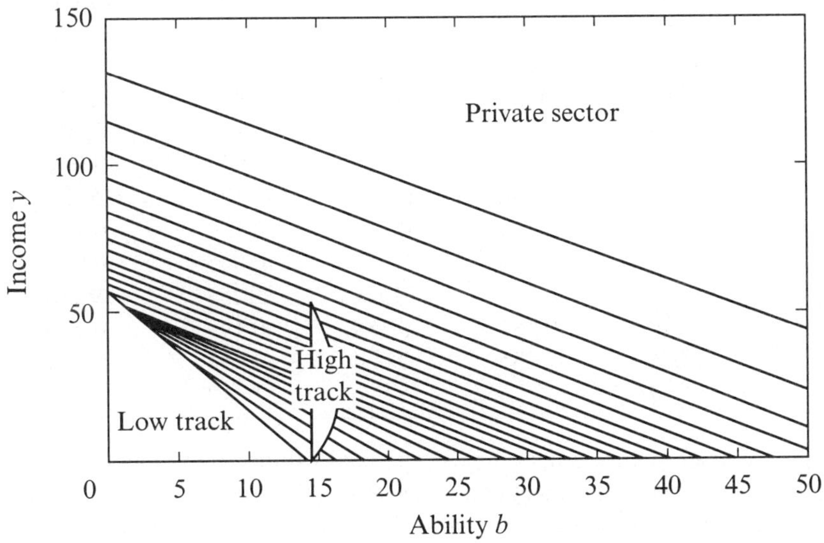

Figure 9.2 continued

and immediately above the public–private boundary. While the peer quality they attain is lower than that in the high public track (for which they do not qualify) these students attain a higher peer quality than in the low public school track by attending a private school that attracts high-ability poor students (who do qualify for the high public track). In panel (c) of Figure 9.2, these high-ability, poor students in the lowest quality private school are in the triangle adjoining the horizontal axis and lying to the right of the boundary of the high public track. In this case, these students attend a private school of lower quality than the public track for which they qualify. They are compensated by scholarships financed by tuitions exceeding average cost paid by students drawn from the lower track.[18]

Table 9.1 Results of tracking and vouchers in both public and private sectors

	Voucher				
	\$0	\$1 000	\$2 000	\$3 000	\$3 600
k_ℓ	0.619	0.597	0.567	0.473	0.253
θ_ℓ	9613	9446	9446	8590	6986
η_ℓ	0.187	0.182	0.174	0.162	0.158
k_h	0.311	0.284	0.245	0.150	0.049
θ_h	18794	17895	16943	15092	13436
η_h	0.102	0.104	0.106	0.109	0.106
k_w	0.033	0.030	0.032	0.032	0.033
θ_w	24662	20853	18406	14415	10672
η_w	0.147	0.137	0.133	0.117	0.100
k_m		0.029	.031	0.031	0.032
θ_m		23156	21227	19126	15021
η_m		0.149	0.149	0.153	0.145
k_b	0.029	0.24	0.026	0.025	0.025
θ_b	31079	31677	30934	30053	29236
η_b	0.170	0.181	0.189	0.199	0.210
t	0.056	0.055	0.054	0.053	0.054
n	2	4	6	12	22

The voucher increases households' marginal willingness-to-pay for school quality. This intensifies competition for the most able students, resulting in more generous tuition discounts for the most able students. For example, as shown in Table 9.1, in the best private school, η_b rises from 0.170 when there is no voucher to 0.189 when there is a \$2000 voucher. These correspond to tuition discounts for a one standard deviation increase in student ability of $3060 and $3402 respectively.[19]

The introduction of the voucher also results in a reduction in the tax rate, up to a voucher of $3000, as shown in Table 9.1. While the voucher is tax financed, a voucher of $3000 covers only a portion of the cost of attending school. By inducing students to switch from public to private school, the voucher results in a reduction in expenditures for public schools. The associated tax savings more than offsets the tax revenues needed to fund the voucher. Of course, for a sufficiently high voucher, this effect must be reversed, since a voucher high enough to cover the full cost of education would necessitate a tax rate higher than the zero-voucher tax rate. As the voucher rises above $3000, the tax rate increases.

The top panel of Figure 9.3 shows the public-private sector boundaries with and without the voucher, and welfare contours due to implementation of a $3000 voucher. The two sets of public–private sector boundaries delineate the six areas labeled *A*, *B*, and so on. The welfare measure is the compensating variation associated with introduction of the voucher as a percentage of the student's household income. Consider first students eligible only for the low public track. The welfare impact on those who remain in the public school (Area A) is relatively small (a decline of 0.4 percent). This is despite the decrease in the low track average peer quality from 9613 to 8590. The drop in peer quality for these students is partially offset by a decrease in the tax rate from 0.056 to 0.053. Most low-ability students who switch to the private sector experience modest proportionate welfare gains (up to 2.2 percent), that is, those in Area B above the 0 percent-contour. Those below the latter contour in Area B experience small welfare losses. Though their switch to the private sector yields achievement gains relative to before the voucher and is heavily subsidized, they prefer the foregone option of the free, somewhat higher-quality low track available before the voucher. Those already in the private sector (Area C) also experience modest welfare gains from the voucher.

For those eligible for the high track, almost all students induced to move from the public to the private sector (Area E) are made better off by the voucher as are all students who initially attend private school (Area F). Those who remain in the high track in the presence of the voucher (Area D) are worse off because of the reduction in the quality of their peer group as are a few students who exit public school due to this deterioration. The greatest proportionate welfare gains accrue to low-income, high-ability students, those in the lower-right part of Figure 9.3(a).[20] This is because the introduction of the voucher further increases the premium on peer quality in private schools.

The lower panel of Figure 9.3 provides additional information about the welfare effects of the voucher, detailing the welfare effects on households of three different income levels as ability varies. Consider first households whose

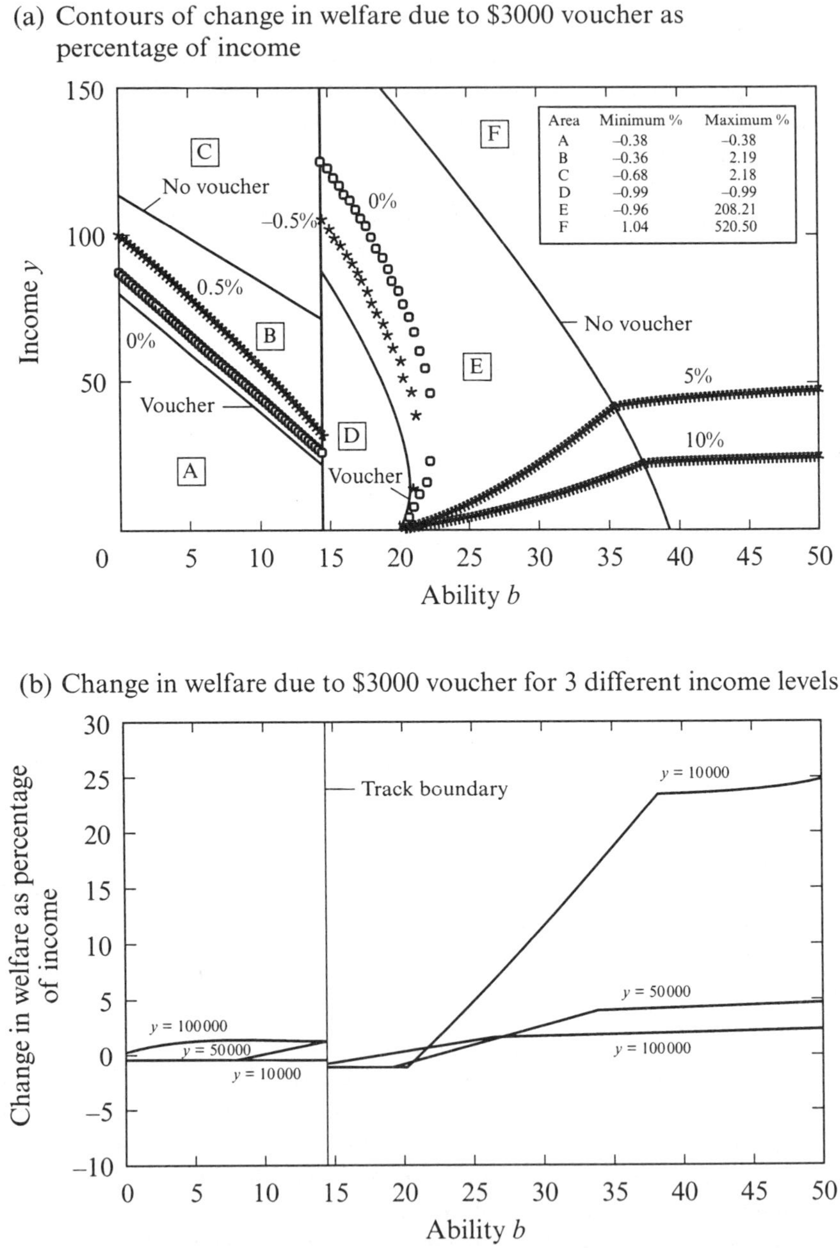

Figure 9.3 Effects of change in welfare due to voucher as percentage of income

students do not qualify for the high track. Welfare effects are small relative to income at all income levels. Students with household incomes of \$10000 are in the low public sector track both in the presence and the absence of the voucher. As we noted above, these households experience a small welfare loss. For students from households with a \$50000 income, lower ability students are in the low public track with or without the voucher. Higher-ability students with this household income move from the lower public tract to the private sector when the voucher is introduced. Most students who do not qualify for the high track and have a household income of \$100000 are in the private sector even absent the voucher. Students of this income level experience small proportional welfare gains.

Next consider students who qualify for the high track. As the bottom panel of Figure 9.3 shows, the welfare effects on households with income of \$10000 vary substantially with student ability. Households whose students remain in the high public track when the voucher is introduced experience a 1 percent welfare loss. Higher ability students from households of this income level move from the high public track to private school and then experience relatively large proportionate welfare gains (up to 25 percent). For households with income of \$50000 the pattern of welfare effects is similar, but the magnitudes of the effects, as a percentage of income, are smaller. For households with incomes of \$100000 the proportionate welfare effects are positive but comparatively small.

Figure 9.4 shows the effects of the voucher on achievement measured in percent changes. The upper panel shows the same six groups but leaves off iso-achievement contours which are poorly behaved (hence confusing). All students who are in the low track both with and without the voucher (Area A) experience an achievement loss of 2.2 percent relative to the no-voucher equilibrium. Those who switch from the low public track to private school (Area B) experience large achievement gains, ranging from 8.4 percent to 19 percent. The effects on those in private school both in the presence or absence of the voucher (Area C) vary with ability. As competition among schools for high-ability students increases, the very top schools deteriorate some (for example, see the θ_b row of Table 9.1). The poorest and most able of the students in Area C are attracted to better private schools in the presence of the voucher but most students in Area C attend private schools of lower quality. Thus, some students in Area C have gains as large as 0.5 percent while others have losses as large as 4 percent.

Turning to the effects on achievement among those who qualify for the high track, we see that all who remain in the high public track (Area D) experience achievement losses of 4.2 percent. Achievement impacts on those who switch from public to private school (Area E) range from a loss of 5.2 percent to a gain of 9.8 percent. The more able who switch from the high public track due to the voucher move to a private school of higher quality than the high public track

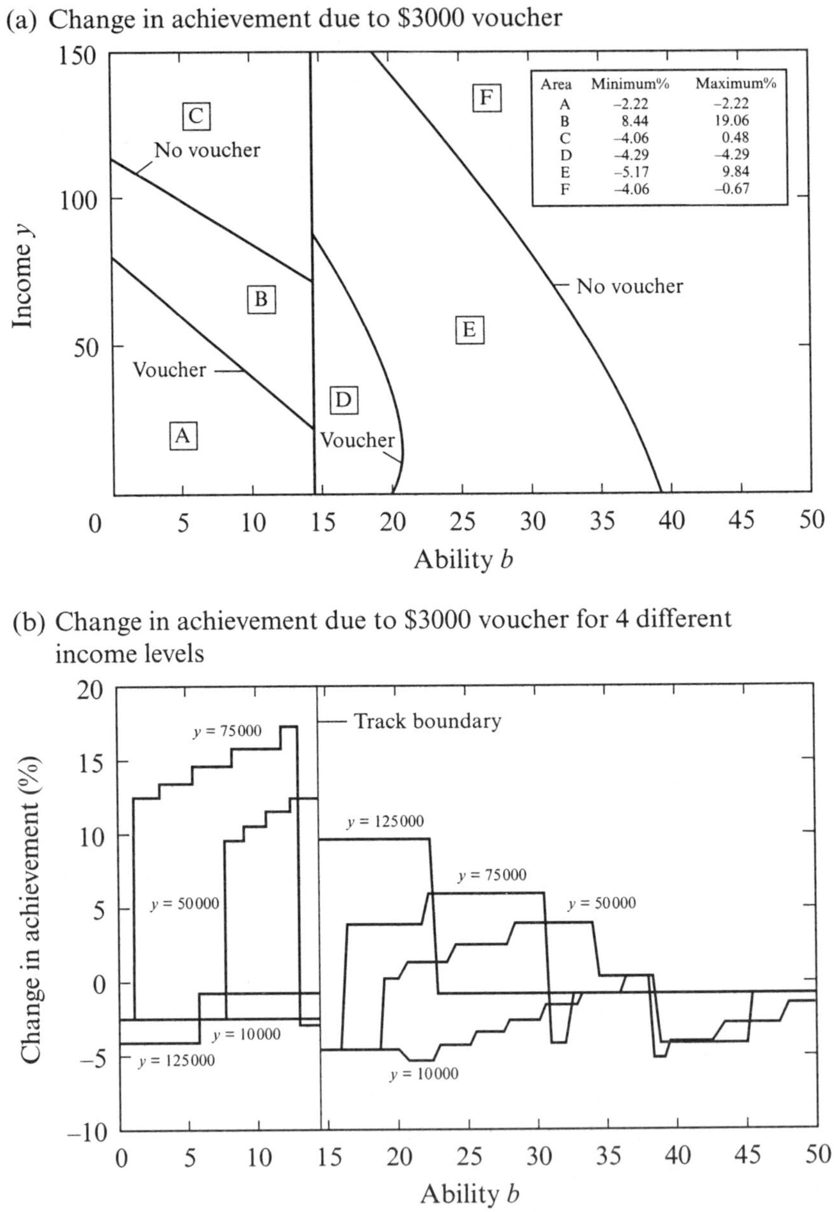

Figure 9.4 Effects of the voucher on achievement in percentage change

they attended when there was no voucher; the less able switch to a private school of lower quality. Those in private school both in the presence and absence of the voucher (Area F) experience achievement losses. In the presence of the voucher, private schools find it profitable to admit students previously in the high public track even though this lowers peer quality relative to the no-voucher equilibrium. Losses in achievement of those in Area F range from 0.7 percent to 4 percent.

The bottom panel of Figure 9.4 details the effects of the $3000 voucher on achievement of students in households of several different income levels as ability varies. Consider first students from households with income of $10 000. All such students who were in the low public track in the absence of the voucher remain there when the voucher is introduced. They experience an achievement loss of 2.2 percent. Continuing to the right, we see that some students with income of $10 000 remain in the high public track when the voucher is introduced. They experience an achievement loss of 4.3 percent. As we look at increasingly higher ability students at this income level, we see students induced to move from the high public track to private schools. For most of these students the private schools to which they move are of lower quality than the high track when there is no voucher. The very highest ability students at this $10000 income level were in private school before introduction of the voucher, and they attend private schools of somewhat lower quality when the voucher is introduced. The magnitude of the achievement effect for the students who switch to private schools or to a changed private school is seen to vary considerably.

As a second example from the lower panel of Figure 9.4, consider students from households with income of $50000. The lowest-ability students at this income level remain in the low track when the voucher is introduced and also have an achievement loss of 2.2 percent. At somewhat higher ability levels, students from households of this income move to private school from the low public track and experience substantial achievement gains. Looking to the right of the track boundary, we see that some students in households with income of $50 000 remain in the high public track when the voucher is introduced. They have an achievement loss of 4.3 percent. At higher ability levels, students with this household income move from the high public track to higher quality private schools and have modest achievement gains. Once ability is high enough that students with this income attend private school with no voucher, achievement changes from the voucher fluctuate with variation in the private school attended.

The effects of tracking and vouchers on the distribution of students by ability in the public school sector is shown in Figure 9.5.[21] Note that tracking leads to a jump in the distribution at the track boundary whether or not there is a voucher. More than 90 percent of students attend public school in the equilibrium without the voucher. As Figure 9.5 illustrates, vouchers draw students out of both tracks. Also, the figure shows, the relatively higher ability students in each track are disproportionately drawn to the private sector. This is a consequence of the tuition discounts (and scholarships for some) which private schools grant high-ability students.

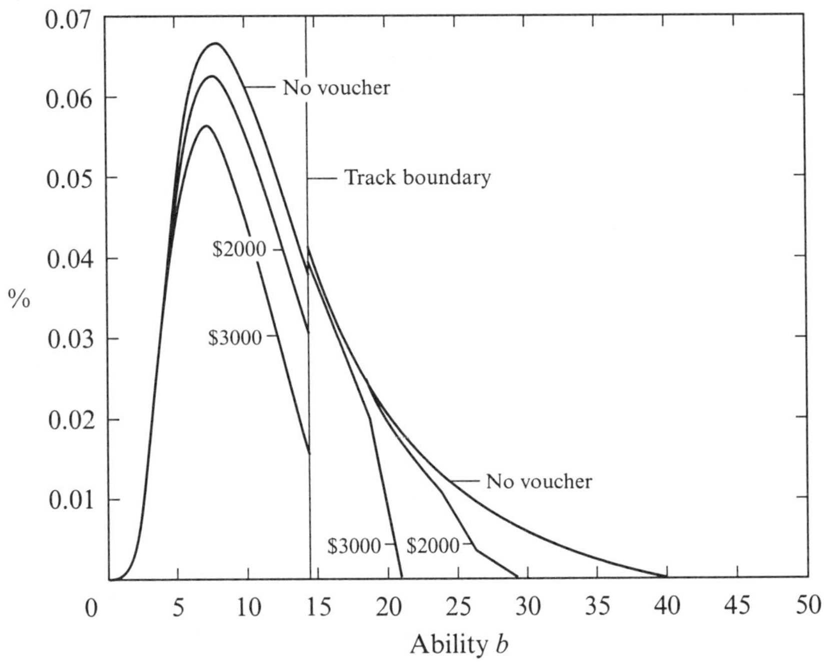

Figure 9.5 Effects of $2000 and $3000 vouchers on the distribution of abilities of students attending public schools

Figure 9.6 portrays attendance in each public school track as a function of the voucher both for the case in which public schools track and the case in which they do not. While the voucher draws students out of the public schools in either case, we see that tracking enables public schools to retain more high-ability students than are retained in the absence of tracking. This difference becomes quite striking at higher voucher values. Indeed, at high voucher levels ($3000 and above), the public sector with tracking retains more students in each track than it would retain of those groups in the absence of tracking. We now explain this somewhat surprising result.

We have seen that the quality of the public school sector declines with the voucher (see for example, Table 9.1). It is also of interest to compare the

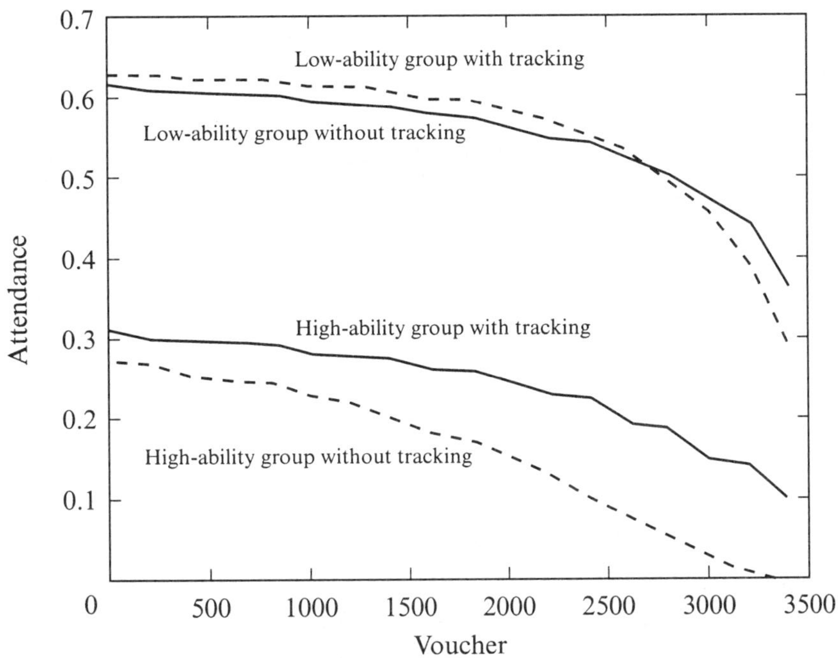

Figure 9.6 *Effects of tracking on public school attendance in each ability group as a function of the voucher*

relative quality of the public school sector with and without tracking as the voucher is increased. This comparison is presented in Figure 9.7. The upper curve shows the ratio of normed achievement in the high public track when there is tracking to normed achievement of the high public 'track' when there is no tracking. Similarly, the lower curve shows ratios of normed achievement in the low track. Not surprisingly, the high public track is better in the presence of tracking at each voucher value. Also, as expected, the low public track is of lower quality with tracking than without for most voucher values. However, for high voucher values, peer quality is higher in the low track in the presence of tracking. This reflects the benefits of mixing with students from the high track. For example, with a voucher of $3000, virtually no students of ability greater than B remain in the public sector when there is no tracking. When there is tracking, some students with ability greater than B remain in the public school. Students in the low track benefit, via mixing, from the presence of these high-ability students.

We have not postulated an objective function for public school administrators. However, it seems likely that public school attendance and average ability

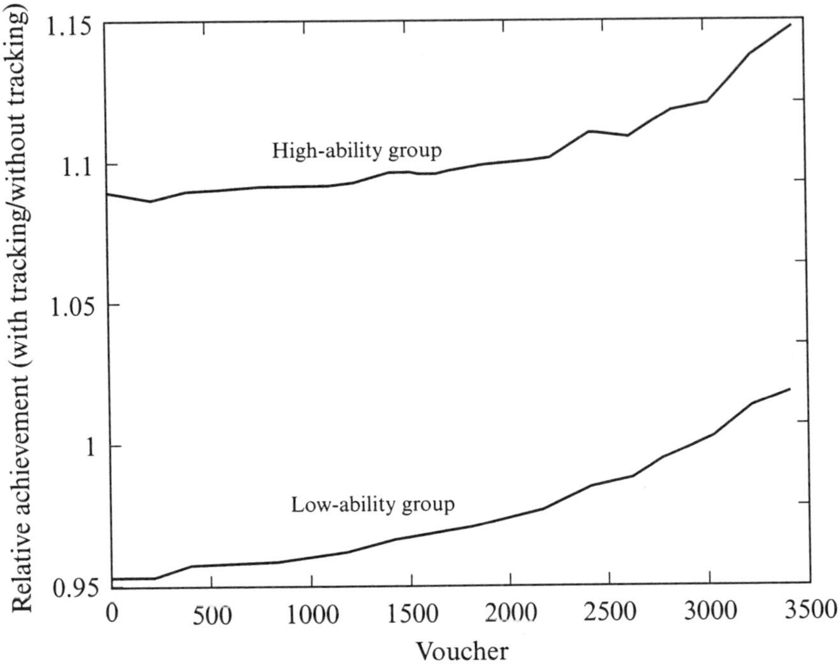

Figure 9.7 Effects of tracking on achievement in each ability group as a function of the voucher

would be important arguments in such an objective function. The results in Figures 9.6 and 9.7 suggest that a voucher program would increase the impetus for public schools to adopt or retain tracking.

5 CONCLUDING REMARKS

Our goal in this paper has been to investigate how vouchers affect the composition of public and private schools when there is tracking and to study the implications for student achievement and household welfare.

Our previous theoretical results (Epple, Newlon, and Romano, 1997) reveal that private schools have limited incentive to engage in tracking. Private schools can select students and set tuition levels that reflect differences in student abilities. Given these mechanisms for determining the composition of the school student body, competition among private schools leaves them with little, if any, incentive to separate students into subgroups within schools.

Therefore, in investigating the effects of vouchers we consider outcomes when public schools engage in tracking but private schools do not. Our analysis of the welfare effects of vouchers reveals that vouchers tend to be of particular benefit to low-income households with high-ability students. In addition, vouchers benefit most of the households with students who move from the public to the private sector as a result of the voucher. The latter group includes students from both the low and high tracks. The most substantial adverse welfare effects of the voucher fall on households with students who remain in the high track in the presence of the voucher. They attend a public school with lower peer quality as a result of the voucher experiencing achievement losses of 4.3 percent and welfare losses of 1 percent. In the low track, public school quality is also reduced. Students remaining in the low track when the voucher is introduced experience achievement losses of 2.2 percent and welfare losses of 0.4 percent For both groups, the lower peer quality of the school reduces welfare, but the reduced tax rate that results with the voucher partially offsets the welfare loss.

Public schools have few direct mechanisms to control student body composition. Our computational results reveal that tracking can significantly affect public school composition. By grouping students by ability, a public school can offer a relatively high-quality peer group to more able students, attracting more such students to the school. Tracking also helps the public school sector retain students when the voucher is introduced. The public sector loses high ability students much more rapidly when there is no tracking than when there is tracking as the voucher increases. At high voucher levels, attendance and peer quality are higher in both tracks when students are grouped by ability than when they are not.

NOTES

* The authors thank Thomas Downes and Robert Schwab for helpful comments and also seminar participants at the 1996 ASSA Meetings, the 1996 Public Choice Meetings, the May 1997 MacArthur Research Network Conference on Inequality and Economic Performance (Cambridge, MA), the University of Houston, and the University of Southern California. Epple and Romano appreciate financial support for this research provided by the National Science Foundation.

1. Students in the lower public school track interact in a subset of classes with higher ability students assigned in the high track so that the former gain some from being in school with the latter.
2. In work in progress, Epple and Romano are extending the model to include variation in per student expenditure.
3. Consistency of the time-in-class and subjects-studied interpretations of mixing require that the same class time is devoted to each subject and students in both tracks take the same number of subjects.
4. Epple and Romano (1995) show how housing price differences can sustain such sorting in equilibrium.
5. We assume that ability is observable, for example, through testing. Note that there is no incentive to underperform on placement tests.

6. In Epple, Newlon, and Romano (1997), we examine how varying B and m would affect various possible public sector objectives.
7. See Epple and Romano (1997) for justification of this assumption.
8. As observed in note 5, abilities can be determined through testing, and we assume further that required financial disclosures permit determination of household income.
9. Again, see Epple, Newlon, and Romano (1997) for more detailed, including mathematical, development.
10. For Cobb–Douglas specification of utility/achievement in (9.2), Epple and Romano (1997) prove SBA without ascending ηs, substituting the requirement that b and y are stochastically independent in the population.
11. The linear boundary loci derive from the Cobb–Douglas preference specification in the computational analysis.
12. Details on this are available from us on request.
13. When $m = 1$, there is a degree of freedom in the choices of k_ℓ and k_h since all that is relevant is their sum.
14. Our model has no role for vouchers in the public sector since public schools are homogeneous.
15. Because some students attend private sector schools, normed achievement is not exactly lognormally distributed. Our approximate steady state equates the mean and variance of the income and normed achievement distributions.
16. In Epple, Newlon, and Romano (1997), we use a cost function that reaches a minimum at 0.9 percent of the student population. Vouchers induce entry by private schools, and the increased number of schools increases the computational complexity of the model. The computational burden associated with analysing vouchers is reduced by letting efficient scale be larger so that there are fewer, larger private schools in equilibrium. By sensitivity analysis we have found that, as long as the minimum of the average cost function is unchanged, equilibrium allocations are relatively insensitive to variations in efficient scale (for example, the proportions of students in the private sector and each public school track), at least for values of k^* up to 4 percent of the student population.
17. Hence, the domain of the (b,y) plane over which these are defined is restricted to $b < (\geq)\ B$ for the low (high) track.
18. The areas of the triangles of students that make up the school are misleading indicators of the relative numbers since the distribution of types is not uniform. A substantial majority of the student body in this school is made up of those who fail to qualify for the high track.
19. The shadow prices of ability in the public sector (η_ℓ and η_h) are not relevant to tuitions since public schooling is free. But these values do indicate per student willingness to pay for increases in θ within the track. A track's η is increasing in average income (due to **SCI**) and decreasing in quality (due to diminishing returns to quality in the achievement function). That $\eta_\ell > \eta_h$ at all vouchers reflects the lower quality of the low track (in spite of higher average income in the high track). As the voucher rises, the conflicting effects in the high track of lower track quality and lower average income result in the inversion of η_h.
20. The percentage welfare changes actually tend toward infinity as income approaches zero for some students, while the maximum we indicate in Figure 9.3 conforms to a dense grid. The huge proportionate welfare gains should be appropriately interpreted, and we do not take the extremes seriously.
21. The heights of the curves drawn equal the density of students that attend public school in the entire population of students. Hence, the heights reflect the numbers of students in public school, and the area under the curve declines as students are drawn into the private sector by vouchers.

REFERENCES

Epple, Dennis and Richard Romano (1995), ‘Public School Choice and Finance Policies, Neighborhood Formation, and the Distribution of Educational Benefits’, University of Florida working paper, July.

Epple, Dennis and Richard Romano (1997), 'Competition Between Private and Public Schools, Vouchers, and Peer Group Effects', *American Economic Review*, **88**, March, 33–62.

Epple, Dennis, Elizabeth Newlon and Richard Romano (1997), 'Ability Tracking, School Competition, and the Distributional Educational Benefits', Carnegie Mellon University, June.

Evans, William N., Wallace E. Oates and Robert M. Schwab (1992), 'Measuring Peer Group Effects: A Study of Teenage Behavior', *Journal of Political Economy*, **100**, October, 966–91.

Gamoran, Adam (1992), 'The Variable Effects of High School Tracking', *American Sociological Review*, **57**, December, 812–28.

Henderson, V., P. Mieszkowski and Y. Sauvageau (1978), 'Peer Group Effects in Educational Production Function', *Journal of Public Economics*, **10**, August, 97–106.

Kenny, Lawrence (1982), 'Economies of Scale in Schooling' *Economics of Education Review*, **2** (1),Winter, 1–24.

Oates, Wallace E. (1981), 'On Local Finance and the Tiebout Model', *American Economic Review Papers and Proceedings*, **71**, May, 93–8.

Scotchmer, Suzanne (1994), 'Public Goods and the Invisible Hand', in J. Quigley and E. Smolensky (eds), *Modern Public Finance*, Cambridge, MA: Harvard University Press.

Solon, Gary (1992), 'Intergenerational Income Mobility in the U.S.', *American Economic Review*, **82**, June, 393–409.

U.S. Bureau of the Census (1991), *Statistical Abstract of the United States: 1991*, 111th edition, Washington, DC.

U.S. Bureau of the Census (1992), *Statistical Abstract of the United States: 1992*, 112th edition, Washington, DC.

Zimmerman, David J. (1992), 'Regression Toward Mediocrity in Economic Stature' *American Economic Review*, **82**, June, 409–29.

10. On designing intergovernmental transfers with an application in the new South Africa

Robert P. Inman[1]

I INTRODUCTION

The decline of the centralized, autocratic political orders in Eastern Europe, South America, and most recently in South Africa has raised new hopes for more open and democratically decided economic policies. A prominent institutional feature of the new democratic orders has typically been a move away from central government domination of economic policy-making towards increased reliance upon often newly created provincial (or state) and local governments for the financing and provision of local services. There are good reasons to think such a re-allocation of fiscal responsibilities makes sense. Wallace Oates (1972) in his now classic *Fiscal Federalism* emphasized the virtues of policy decentralization for efficient resource allocations. Samuel Beer (1993) in his overview of the intellectual foundations of American federalism championed policy decentralization for its contribution to political participation and democratic institution-building. Most recently, Barry Weingast (1995) has made the case for policy decentralization as a means to protect and thereby encourage capital accumulation, entrepreneurship, and ultimately country economic development and growth.[2]

The construction of an institutionally viable and economically efficient federalist public sector requires the assignment of tax and spending responsibilities to the central, provincial, and local levels of government. This chapter studies one important complementary policy to tax and spending assignments: the design of intergovernmental transfers between the tiers of government. For each possible tax and spending assignment there is a corresponding set of intergovernmental transfers which can facilitate the efficient and fair economic performance of the resulting federalist public economy. This essay reviews the current theory of intergovernmental transfers – offering an updating of *Fiscal Federalism*'s Chapter 3 – and applies this theory to evaluate the recently proposed system of intergovernmental transfers for the new provinces of South Africa.

II THE DESIGN OF INTERGOVERNMENTAL TRANSFERS FOR EFFICIENCY AND EQUITY

A Intergovernmental Transfers for Economic Efficiency

While decentralized provincial and local governments have much to recommend them for the provision of public goods (see Wildasin, 1986), there are three instances when such governments might lead to a less than efficient allocation of public and private goods. First, fiscal competition between governments may create incentives for the inefficient location of private factors of production. Second, when setting provincial and local service levels and taxes, elected political leaders may fail to take into account spillover benefits or costs to neighboring communities or to community residents not in their winning coalition. Third, and of particular importance in emerging democratic societies, new provincial and local governments may lack the administrative structure needed to collect government revenues. In each case, a central government grant to a provincial or local government can be designed to correct these market and administrative failures.

1 Grants for efficient private goods production

To ensure private sector economic efficiency, the tax and spending decisions of provincial and local governments should leave untouched the private incentives of factors of production to seek their most efficient location. For efficient capital location, the value of capital's private marginal product must be equalized across all locations. Generally, this can be achieved through tax assignment by allowing only the central government to tax capital; see Boadway and Flatters (1982, p. 682) or Wilson (1986) generally. Unfortunately, the efficient allocation of labor in a decentralized fiscal economy is not so easily achieved; here efficiency may require a combination of local taxation and central government grants-in-aids.

Following Boadway and Flatters (1982), production of provincial private output in province p (X_p) depends on a variable factor, the number of worker-residents (L_p) in the province, and a fixed factor of production (N_p): $X_p = F(L_p;N_p) = f_p(L_p)$, where $f_p'(L_p) > 0$ and $f_p''(L_p) < 0$. Production of provincial public services (g) also depends on the number of worker-residents according to the 'congestion' technology: $g_p = G_p/L_p^{\alpha}$, where G_p is the public facility costing G_p dollars to build, L_p are the number of resident-users of this facility, and α is the congestion elasticity ranging from 0 in the case of pure public goods to 1 in the case of pure private goods. Each province is assumed to levy an equal per resident tax ($= G_p/L_p$) to buy the public facility at cost G_p and to fully tax the rents earned by the fixed factor of production. Revenues from this provincial (that is, source-based) taxation of rents are redistributed back to resident-workers as a per worker grant.

The use of source-based taxation of rents coupled with the per capita redistribution of the proceeds allows worker-residents to receive the average private product ($=f_p(L_p)/L_p$) from provincial production.[3] A typical resident's welfare derives from her consumption of the private good equal to average income minus taxes – $x_p = [f(L_p) - G_p]/L_p$ – and her consumption of the public good allowing for congestion – $g_p = G_p/L_p^{\alpha}$: $v = v(x_p, g_p) = \mathrm{v}(L_p, G_p)$. Provincial governments maximize resident welfare by selecting G_p, conditional upon the number of residents in their provinces. The optimal level of public facilities is adjusted as a province's population changes; evaluated at this optimal level of public facilities, household welfare becomes $V(L_p)$. Worker-residents are assumed to move among provinces until $V(L_p)$ is equalized across all locations.

While it is reasonable to assume a location equilibrium will exist in this decentralized public goods economy (see Boadway and Flatters, 1982, Figure 1), there is no guarantee that this equilibrium will efficiently allocate individuals across all provinces. National location efficiency requires that there be no gain to the country as a whole of moving one resident from one province to another. This will be true when the sum of the marginal benefits to current residents of a province from adding (or subtracting) one more resident are equal across provinces. The net welfare gain to the existing L_p residents of an additional worker-resident to any province p (MB_p) will equal:

$$MB_p = L_p V'(L_p) = v_x[(1 - \alpha_p)(G_p/L_p) - R_p/L_p]. \qquad (10.1)$$

This specification of MB_p has an intuitive interpretation. First, within brackets, the net income gain from one more resident equals their tax contribution of G_p/L_p to cover current public good costs less the extra spending of $\alpha_p \cdot (G_p/L_p)$ required to offset public service congestion they impose when using existing facilities[4] less their share of rents – R_p/L_p – captured through source-based taxation. This income gain is then multiplied by the marginal utility of income (v_x) of a typical current resident. MB_p should be equalized across provinces to ensure location efficiency.

Two special cases often discussed in the local public finance literature ensure that MB_p will be equal across provinces. The first is the Tiebout economy. Here all local public goods are fully congestible at the margin ($\alpha_p = 1$) and production takes place in a 'spaceless' economy without rents ($R_p = 0$); see Bewley (1981). The second is the Henry George economy. Here all provincial public services are fully public ($\alpha_p = 0$) and land rents per capita (R_p/L_p) just equal the costs per capita (G_p/L_p) of producing the provincial public good; see Arnott and Stiglitz (1979). In both these special cases, $MB_p = 0$ across all provinces at the location equilibrium. Welfare maximizing provinces and utility maximizing residents will ensure the efficient location of mobile resident-workers in these two cases.

Often, however, production rents are earned and taxed by residents, and local public goods are congestible. If so, location efficiency for labor is not guaranteed with decentralized financing of local public goods. What can be done to ensure the MB_ps are equalized across provinces? Boadway and Flatters suggest a central government intergovernmental efficiency transfer per resident (E_p) to the provincial governments of the general form:

$$E_p = (MB_p/v_x) - \beta = [(1 - \alpha_p)(G_p/L_p) - R_p/L_p] - \beta, \qquad (10.2)$$

where β is the national uniform social benefit of one additional resident to any province beyond the unique provincial effects of that location. Larger values of β imply lower overall levels of provincial aid across all provinces. Transfers per resident E_p are transfers net of per resident taxes paid to the central government to support the aid program. Thus E_p will be positive for some provinces and negative for others.[5] Provinces which are less congested (lower α_p) in the provision of provincial public goods receive larger transfers. More efficient provincial governments are therefore rewarded with larger transfers. In the extreme when $\alpha_p = 0$ and the provincial good is a pure public good, the central government provides aid sufficient to fund the full provision of that service – that is, pure public goods are centrally financed as they should be. Further, provinces rich in rental incomes from agglomeration advantages, unique locations, or natural resource advantages receive lower transfers per resident *dollar for dollar*. In effect the revenues from provincial source-based taxes are 'taxed away' by the central government. This too makes good economic sense. Provincial source-base taxation paid to residents is a cause of location inefficiencies when households are mobile. Such rents should only be taxed and then spent by that level of government where household mobility is unaffected. This is the central level of government and the E_p grants formula is just such a tax.

2 Grants for efficient public goods production

The analysis above designing grants for private market efficiency assumes that public goods are efficiently provided within each province. This may not be true, for either of two reasons. Residents in a province p's ruling coalition may ignore spillover benefits or costs from the provision of their public services to residents (inside or outside the province) not in the ruling coalition, or residents in the ruling coalition receive, or pay, a subsidy from those outside the coalition when buying the public service. Either is a cause of public goods inefficiency within the province and a potential reason for central government intergovernmental transfers.

The efficient allocation of provincial public services requires that the social marginal benefit in province p of another unit of the public service equal the social marginal costs of providing that unit: $SMB_p = SMC_p$. Actual allocations within a province will be determined, however, by the balancing of political marginal benefits (PMB_p) and costs (PMC_p) to the province's ruling coalition (for example, the median voter): $PMB_p = PMC_p$. Social efficiency will be achieved when the ruling coalition by setting $PMB_p = PMC_p$ also ensures that $SMB_p = SMC_p$.

Public sector efficiency is not guaranteed. When provincial allocations generate positive (negative) spillovers to non-residents, or to residents within the province but outside the provincial ruling coalition, then $\phi_p \cdot PMB_p = SMB_p$, where $\phi_p > 1$ (< 1) for positive (negative) spillovers. When the ruling political coalition in a province receives (pays) a tax subsidy from (to) non-residents or residents when purchasing public services through taxation, then $PMC_p = \rho_p \cdot SMC_p$, where $\rho_p < 1$ (> 1) when a subsidy is received (paid).

In the simplest case of proportional taxation, $\rho_p = (y_p/Y_p)$, where y_p is the tax base of a member of the ruling coalition and Y_p is the average tax base per resident in the province. Typically, $y_p < Y_p$, and thus $\rho_p < 1$. Two offsetting pressures may push ρ_p greater than 1, however. First, when provincial tax base is mobile with respect to changes in tax rates – business capital is the most likely example – then as one province raises its tax rates above those found in neighboring provinces, tax base exits. This loss of tax base because of exit is a burden on the province raising taxes and included in its PMC of funding public services. But other provinces gain this exiting tax base. From society's point of view, the gain in tax base and revenues in other provinces offsets the initial costs in the province raising taxes; see Wildasin (1989). Thus the *SMC* of a provincial tax on mobile tax bases will be less than the *PMC* felt by the province itself: $PMC_p = \rho_p \cdot SMC_p$, and $\rho_p > 1$ and too little provincial public goods will be purchased in this case; see Zodrow and Mieszkowski (1986). Second, if the ruling coalition in a province wishes to provide low income assistance greater than that available in neighboring provinces, poor residents from other provinces may move in and its own taxpayers may exit. Because poorer families enter and richer taxpayers leave, the cost to the ruling coalition of transfers to its poor may be greater than the true social costs of those transfers ($\rho_p > 1$); see Inman and Rubinfeld (1997b). The consequences of these added costs may be a 'race to the bottom' together with too little income support provided by each province; see Gramlich and Laren (1984) and Brown and Oates (1987).

In the special case where there are no spillovers ($\phi_p = 1$) and the ruling coalition bears the full social costs of its spending choices ($\rho_p = 1$), then $PMB_p = PMC_p$ ensures that $SMB_p = SMC_p$. Efficiency also occurs in the happy circumstance where $\phi_p\rho_p = 1$, for then $PMB_p = PMC_p$ implies that $SMB_p/\phi_p = \rho_p SMC_p$ or $SMB_p = \phi_p\rho_p SMC_p = SMC_p$.

More generally, however, $\phi_p\rho_p \neq 1$. Efficiency can still be achieved in this general case, however, if ϕ_p and ρ_p are known to the central government. A matching intergovernmental grant from the central government for provincial spending at the rate s_p specified as:

$$s_p = 1 - (1/\phi_p\rho_p), \tag{10.3}$$

will induce the ruling provincial coalition setting $PMB_p = PMC_p$ to provide the socially efficient ($SMB_p = SMC_p$) level of provincial public services.[6] Provinces whose ruling coalitions provide services with large positive spillovers ($\phi_p > 1$) or who cross-subsidize the financing of those services for other taxpayers ($\rho_p > 1$) will receive larger matching grants as a reward for their contribution to social welfare. Conversely, provinces which produce negative externalities ($\phi_p < 1$) and/or whose taxes are subsidized ($\rho_p < 1$) may be required to pay revenues to the central government ($s_p < 0$) for public sector efficiency.

3 Grants for efficient provincial fiscal administration

To achieve their potential as efficient providers of public services, provincial governments must have the administrative capacity to collect and spend public revenues. This capacity may be lacking in the provinces of newly emerging democracies, particularly so for the administration of local taxation. Economically preferred taxes for provincial and local governments include residential income and property taxation, both of which require the ability to assess the incomes and property values of residents. Tracking incomes of residents who work outside the province will require the cooperation of all provinces. Measuring property values – or even assigning ownership – may be difficult in developing economies with newly emerging private property markets. Alternative taxes include a provincial business profits tax or a tax on sales within the province. The collection of these provincial taxes, however, is likely to be even more difficult. Further, even if such taxes could be administered at the provincial level, they are likely to induce the inefficient location of investment and retailing; see Inman and Rubinfeld (1996a). In emerging democratic economies, the provincial and local capacity to raise revenues may be limited for a time.

Until revenue raising capacity is in place, the central government stands as the most plausible substitute for provincial tax collection; see Oates (1972, pp. 148–9). Centrally collected revenues can be returned to the provinces via intergovernmental grants, often called 'revenue sharing' grants using the general specification:

$$A_p = \lambda_0 + \lambda_1[\tau_p \cdot Y_p], \tag{10.4}$$

where Y_p is the tax base per resident in the province, and τ_p is the provincially decided tax rate to be applied to that base. Here, the central government's only role is to serve as a tax collection agent; λ_0 (< 0) is the province's contribution to the fixed cost of administering the tax system and λ ($0 < \lambda_1 \leq 1$) returns provincial revenues net of any marginal costs to revenue collection.

In developing economies, the fixed costs of tax collection will have already been made by the central government for most taxes. The marginal costs of enforcement and collection are likely to be lower at the central level as well. If so, provinces can simply 'piggy-back' their tax decisions on to central government tax collections – that is, add a provincial rate τ_p, *decided through provincial politics*, to the central government rate for taxes collected within the province. Only resident-based taxes, not source-based taxes, should be piggy-backed. Source-based taxation of business profits, worker earnings, location rents, and sales will encourage inefficient location of the taxed activity; see Inman and Rubinfeld (1996a).

The central government's role may extend beyond simple tax administration, however. When tax bases are shared between the central government and provinces, the central government may need to play a role as a tax coordinator as well. Again, intergovernmental transfers are an appropriate policy tool. For example, Boadway and Keen (1996) use a variant of the shared revenue formula above to facilitate efficient second-best taxation of the shared tax base. With shared tax bases, an economic inefficiency may arise when government(s) at one level, most likely the individual provinces, ignore the consequences of their taxing decisions on the choices available to the other level, most likely the central government. Boadway and Keen show that when provinces set their tax rates without considering the likely adverse effects on the central government tax base – for example, high provincial rates on workers discourage work effort raising the marginal cost of taxation to the center – then the provinces 'over-tax' relative to a more economically efficient, coordinated allocation. The central government can use grants-in-aid to achieve the coordinated solution. One 'grant' is paid directly to those being taxed to correct for excessive provincial taxation. The other grant is a lump-sum transfer *from* the provinces *to* the central government to help pay for the corrective tax subsidy. This second grant is specified as $\lambda_0 < 0$ in the shared revenue formula above. Important to this solution is the fact that provinces or the central government have a second tax instrument to raise revenues and pay the subsidy; in Boadway and Keen this second tax is a tax on rents.

B Intergovernmental Transfers for Fiscal Equity

Economic equity has three dimensions. *Vertical equity* balances the economic opportunities of households with different economic abilities. It is a society's commitment to vertical equity or economic fairness that determines the overall distribution of income in the economy. *Horizontal equity* requires that citizens with identical economic abilities have equal opportunities to earn identical private incomes and to pay identical prices for the private and public goods they buy. *Public goods equity* seeks to guarantee all households equal access to certain socially meritorious goods and services; education, health care, and personal safety are often argued to be such goods.

The motivation for these equity standards is crucial to specifying how each is best achieved in a federalist public economy. If these equity standards arise only from the preferences of current residents as expressed through democratically elected governments, differences in provincial tax structures and public goods should be allowed; see Pauly (1973). Only to the extent the fiscal interplay of provincial governments prevents the citizens of those governments from achieving all Pareto-improving transfers – for example, because of free-riding and/or mobile tax bases – should the central government become involved. The appropriate central government policy in this case would be matching grants to each province as specified in equation (10.3) above. This is perhaps the most plausible motivation for how equity policies are set in the United States.

Alternatively, equity standards may be constitutionally-based, set through 'behind-the-veil' deliberations at the time the constitution is first written or amended. When society finds its equity principles not in daily politics but in its constitution, then those standards play a role as equity constraints on current fiscal policy-making. In such economies, the central government is the appropriate institution for enforcing the constraints. Constitutionally based standards for vertical equity are best achieved through central government tax and transfer policies targeted to individuals. Provincial governments have no role to play in meeting these standards; the sole task of provincial governments is to provide public services efficiently. To that end, provincial revenues should be raised through head taxes or user fees to approximate efficient benefit taxation; to the extent those taxes are administratively infeasible, proportional provincial taxes should be allowed. Redistributive taxation is solely a central function, however.

Meeting constitutionally-based national standards for horizontal equity and public goods equity is also the responsibility of the central government, though here provincial finances, and thus intergovernmental transfers, may play a more active role. To the extent that provinces are allowed access to proportional taxes and residents reside in income-heterogeneous communities, a horizontal equity constitutional constraint to treat economic equals equally may be violated.[7] If for reasons of allocative efficiency, provinces are the primary providers of meritorious public services, a constitutional constraint for equal public goods provisions may be violated.[8] In both cases, appropriately designed intergovernmental transfers from the center to the provinces can be used to meet the constitution's equity constraints.

1 Grants for horizontal equity

Horizontal equity in a federalist public economy will typically require that economically equally endowed households have equal opportunities to purchase public and private goods. If all households are fully mobile across provinces this requirement is satisfied trivially; see Boadway and Flatters (1982). Horizontal inequities arise when one province offers their citizens economic opportunities significantly different from those available to identically endowed households located in another province, but the disadvantaged households cannot move. In effect, identically endowed households face different prices for the purchase of public and private goods because they live in different provinces; see Oates (1972, p. 83). One important source of such inequities is differences in the cost of buying public services through a tax system, arising because of disparities in the cost of providing public services or because of differences in tax bases across provinces.[9]

Intergovernmental transfers from the central government to the provinces can correct violations of horizontal equity because of variations in public goods prices. The following grants policy will equalize the cost of buying public services across provinces where those services are financed through provincial taxes:

$$T_p = \{(Y^*/SMC^*)/(Y_p/SMC_p) - 1\}[\tau_p \cdot Y_p], \tag{10.5}$$

where Y^* is a national target level of tax base per resident, SMC^* is a target cost of providing provincial services, Y_p is the province's own tax base per resident, and SMC_p is the province's own production cost per resident of providing services.[10] As specified here, T_p will be paid in nominal dollars per resident to each province. T_p can also be specified as:

$$T_p = \tau_p \cdot Y^* \cdot (SMC_p/SMC^*) - Y_p \cdot \tau_p, \tag{10.5'}$$

showing that assistance for horizontal equity in public goods prices gives more aid to those provinces with higher production costs (SMC_p) and less aid to provinces with high per resident tax bases (Y_p). Horizontal equity aid can be negative for the very rich provinces ($Y_p > Y^*$) or provinces with very low public good production costs ($SMC_p < SMC^*$). Care must be given to ensure that the cost index used to measure SMC_p depends only upon cost factors exogenous to the province.

Finally, horizontal equity is achieved. Total real revenues per resident (R_p) from a common tax rate is fully equalized by this aid formula as:

$$R_p = T_p/SMC_p + (Y_p \cdot \tau_p)/SMC_p,$$

or, using the definition of T_p:

$$R_p = \tau_p \cdot Y^*/SMC^*.$$

Differences in production costs and tax bases are now irrelevant to what a province can provide its citizens.

2 Grants for public goods equity

Certain goods provided by provincial or local governments may be viewed as 'merit' goods demanding equal provision to all residents, at least to some minimum standard. Provision beyond the minimum would then be voluntary and allowed to reflect citizen preferences and incomes. If these goods are provided by provincial governments then matching grants are the cost-effective grants policy, achieving the target level of provincial provision at a lowest expenditure of central government resources; see Oates (1972, pp. 92–3). The matching rate, which may vary by province, is set to ensure all citizens receive at least the targeted minimum of services.

The level of the 'merit good' public service provided in each province will be decided by that province's ruling political coalition. That coalition's demand for services will depend negatively upon the price of the public service (PMC_p) and positively upon other demand determinants (D_p) (for example, income): $g_p = \delta \cdot D_p - \theta \cdot PMC_p$.[11] With a central government matching aid at rate m_p (≥ 0), the coalition's effective price of public services is lowered to $(1 - m_p) \cdot PMC_p$; thus the ruling coalition's demand for the public good becomes: $g_p = \delta \cdot D_p - \theta \cdot [(1 - m_p) \cdot PMC_p]$.

If g^* is the minimal standard level government services to be provided in all provinces, then a matching rate of m_p defined as:

$$m_p = 1 - [\delta \cdot D_p - g^*]/[\theta \cdot PMC_p], \qquad (10.6)$$

will be sufficient to induce the leaders in provinces where g_p with no matching aid ($m_p = 0$) is less than g^* to provide the minimal target of g^*. In provinces where g_p at $m_p = 0$ just equals g^*, the matching rate m_p will be equal to zero. In provinces where more than the minimal standard is provided when $m_p = 0$, the matching rate will be constrained $m_p = 0$.[12] The matching rate required for public goods equity rises as the target service level (g^*) rises and as the ruling coalition's costs

(PMC_p) rise. The matching rate falls as the province's own demand for the good (D_p) rises.[13] Plausible candidates for 'merit good' status and matching aid include education, health care, and those goods which contribute to a minimally safe public environment. From most demand specifications, matching rates for merit goods should be lower in richer provinces.

C On Specifying a National Grants Policy

Intergovernmental transfers have a potentially important role to play in the fiscal management of a federalist public economy, but the specification of a nation's grants policies depends crucially upon the wider structure of fiscal institutions. Appropriately designed grants-in-aid can: (1) correct private sector inefficiencies arising from provincial source-based taxation of rents or the provincial provision of pure public goods (E_p); (2) correct public sector inefficiencies because of public good spillovers and mobile provincial tax bases (s_p); (3) save administrative costs when tax bases are shared as well as correct provincial overuse of such shared bases (A_p); (4) ensure horizontal equity in the consumption of provincial public goods (T_p); and (5) guarantee that residents of each province will receive the societal preferred level of provincially provided merit goods (m_p). As specified, each of these five grants policies responds to a 'market failure' in the provincial public goods economy.

The source of these market failures is ultimately the assignment of tax and spending responsibilities between the central and lower tiers of governments. For example, if provinces are given responsibility for only fully congestible ($\alpha = 1$) public services and are not allowed access to source-based taxes on rents, then E_p aid can be set to zero. If all public services with significant geographical spillovers and taxes with mobile bases are assigned to the central government, then s_p aid can be set at zero. If provinces are given taxes which can be equally well administered by the central or provincial levels of government (that is, on activities only within the province), then A_p can be zero. If provincial revenues are restricted to user fees and head taxes, and all merit goods are centrally provided then horizontal equity aid (T_p) and merit good aid (m_p) are no longer needed. In this light, intergovernmental transfers and fiscal assignments are seen as substitute fiscal policies. Altering fiscal assignments in a federalist public economy alters the need for intergovernmental transfers.

This observation suggests committing, perhaps through the constitution, to an assignment of service responsibilities and taxing powers and then using centrally chosen aid policies to correct any resulting economic inefficiencies or inequities.[14] One assignment structure might allocate all clearly pure ($\alpha = 0$) public goods (for example, national defence, domestic competition and trade policies, and research) and goods with significant spillovers (for example, environmental and redistribution policies) to the central government as well as exclusive access to the taxation of capital and rents. Provincial and local governments would be allocated responsibility for fully congestible ($\alpha = 1$) public services and granted user fees and head taxes as revenue sources. Under this assignment structure the provincial economy approximates the institutional structure of a Tiebout public goods economy. There is no need for efficiency (E_p), spillover (s_p), shared revenue (A_p), or equalization (T_p) grants in such an economy.[15] Merit want grants m_p might be useful, however, but only to the extent merit goods are congestible and therefore assigned to the provinces and the merit good standard requires only a minimum level, allowing provincial supplementation. If merit goods are not fully congestible or if full equity is required, then responsibility should be assigned centrally and m_p grants also become unnecessary.

A second assignment structure relaxes the central government's monopoly control over redistributive taxation and allows provinces access to a residential income tax. Provinces whose residents would like a more progressive payment structure for local public goods than that allowed by user fees and head taxes can use a residential income tax instead. Giving provinces access to the residential income tax comes at a cost, however. Administrative duplication and problems of tax coordination may arise with a shared income tax base, and principles of horizontal equity may be violated as rich provinces can purchase provincial goods at lower tax rates. Fortunately, appropriately designed intergovernmental transfers specified as shared revenue grants (A_p) and equalization grants (T_p) can correct these problems. Again, in this assignment structure merit good grants (m_p) may be appropriate too.

A third assignment structure, and perhaps the most common, calls for a full range of central government grants policies. In addition to giving provinces access to residential income taxes, this third structure allows provinces to tax business profits and provincial rents. Allowing rich provinces to tax domestic rents and profits may be a necessary compromise when forming the original federalist union, but such a bargain imposes potentially high efficiency costs on the public and private sectors once the union is in place. But again, grants policies can correct the resulting market failures from this structure of tax assignments. Private sector efficiency aid (E_p) taxing back provincial rents and public sector spillover aid correcting for mobile tax bases (s_p) can offset inefficient provincial source-based taxation.[16] Under this third assignment structure, E_p, s_p, A_p, T_p, and m_p grants all have a role to play.

There is one final role for intergovernmental transfers, applicable in each of the three assignment structures above. Because fiscal assignment is likely to be an inflexible fiscal policy – reallocating assignments will require one legislative and administrative structure to be dismantled and another to be constructed – it is not well suited to managing temporary shifts in public goods technologies and demands. For example, while provinces might be given responsibility for road construction and maintenance in the original fiscal assignment, increased integration of the union's economy or national defense needs may arise over time requiring a truly national road network. Rather than duplicate an already existing provincial administrative structure for roadways, the central government can use matching spillover grants (s_p) and regulations to stimulate provincial construction of a national highway system. Once these roads are built, the matching grant can be adjusted to a smaller highway maintenance subsidy.

Intergovernmental transfers are important complementary policies to the use of tax and expenditure assignment rules to ensure efficiency and equity in a federalist public economy. For each pattern of fiscal assignment and for each economy there is a correspondingly appropriate system of intergovernmental transfers. The grants analysis summarized here provides a template against which to judge the potential economic performance of any country's grants system. Section III applies the analysis to evaluate South Africa's proposed system of intergovernmental transfers for its newly created provincial governments.

III INTERGOVERNMENTAL TRANSFERS AND THE FUNDING OF PROVINCIAL GOVERNMENTS IN THE NEW SOUTH AFRICA

On 18 November 1993 negotiators representing the previous apartheid government and the African National Congress (ANC) agreed to an Interim Constitution creating a non-racial, multi-party, multi-tier, democratic government in South Africa. In December a special session of the South African Parliament approved an Interim Constitution, and in the country's first truly democratic election, Nelson Mandela was elected President on 27 April 1994. A new national Parliament was elected in November 1994 and charged with drafting a permanent Constitution. On 11 October 1996 the new Constitution was adopted by the Constitutional Assembly.

Central to the new Constitution of South Africa is the establishment of nine provinces, each with a democratically elected premier and legislature. Those elections were successfully completed in November 1994 in anticipation of the approval of the new Constitution. Table 10.1 details the basic economic and demographic facts of the nine new provinces of South Africa. All economic data are reported in Rand, exchanged at approximately R4.70 to $1 (1996 prices). As the data make clear, there is a wide disparity in personal incomes across the provinces; Gauteng containing Johannesburg and Pretoria and Western Cape containing Cape Town are the richest provinces. The rural provinces of Eastern Cape, KwaZulu-Natal, North West, and the Northern Province are particularly impoverished.

Table 10.1 The demographics of South Africa's new provinces

Province	Population (000s)	Personal income tax base per resident (Rand)	Percentage rural	Percentage poverty	Percentage 5–17 years
Western Cape	3906.7	5755	14.29	18.40	25.51
Eastern Cape	7296.2	1560	64.85	63.88	31.38
Northern Cape	796.5	3926	26.73	37.77	26.04
KwaZulu–Natal	9264.5	2631	62.99	51.47	31.42
Free State	3023.6	3098	46.45	50.02	25.64
North West	3812.3	2010	72.41	37.21	28.30
Guateng	8305.7	7711	5.62	19.90	23.11
Mpumalanga	2956.8	3491	67.47	48.82	28.97
Northern Province	5553.3	991	91.17	72.42	36.18
All Provinces	44915.7	3524	51.27	45.70	29.04

Source: Financial and Fiscal Commission, *The Allocation of Resources Between the National and Provincial Governments*, Table 1: Basic Data, Draft, March 1996.

The new Constitution specifies explicitly the assignment of fiscal responsibilities between the national and provincial governments. Significant fiscal powers are given to the nine provinces. Provinces are allowed to set spending and regulatory policies for a wide variety of public activities, the most important of which are education (excluding university and technical schools), environment, health services, housing, local governments, sport and recreation, public transport, roads and traffic regulation, trade and industrial promotion, and urban and rural economic development. Importantly, reserved for the central government is responsibility for national defense, police security, foreign policy, and income redistribution. Provinces are granted the right to impose their own taxes other than an income tax, value-added tax, general sales tax or custom duties. These taxes are reserved for the national government. However, provinces may, if granted the right by national legislation, impose a flat-rate surcharge (that is, 'piggy-back') on the national residential (not business) income tax or the national general sales tax.[17] Finally, the new Constitution explicitly requires a scheme of national revenue-sharing with the provinces: 'Local government and each province is entitled to an equitable share of revenue raised nationally to enable it to provide basic services and perform functions allocated to it' (Chapter 13, section 227.1).

Potentially the most innovative feature of the new Constitution's structure for provincial public finance is the specification within the Constitution of a national Financial and Fiscal Commission (FFC) charged with giving advice and making recommendations to the national Parliament, to provincial legislatures, and local and regional authorities regarding fiscal policies. In particular, the FFC is charged with recommending the constitutionally required revenue-sharing formula, the appropriate taxes to be levied by provincial and local governments, the appropriate role for provincial and local borrowing, and criteria for the allocation of fiscal resources generally. The FFC is to consist of 22 members composed of a chair and deputy chair as full-time appointments, one representative from each of the nine provinces, two representatives from local government, and nine additional members 'some of whom must be experts in local government finance.' The Commission is to be a panel of experts, none of whom may hold political or party office during their tenure on the Commission. In June 1996 the FFC submitted to the National Parliament for its approval a detailed intergovernmental grants proposal for the funding of provincial governments in South Africa.

A The FFC Provincial Grants Proposal

The June 1996 FFC proposal for the financing of the nine provincial governments of South Africa recommended that provinces be granted the right to impose a residential income tax surcharge atop the federal income tax and be allocated centrally raised revenues through four separately specified grants-in-aid programs: (1) a revenue-sharing grant (A_p) as required by the new Constitution; (2) a tax capacity equalization grant (T_p); (3) two categorical grants to ensure minimum levels of service provision in education and primary health care (constrained m_p); and (4) a closed-ended matching grant for physician training and tertiary health services (constrained s_p). In addition, through the concept of 'tax room' accounting, the FFC proposal ensures that provincial fiscal choices will not violate national targets for overall tax rates and deficits, two important constraints for any developing economy seeking to attract international private and public sector investments.

1 Revenue-sharing aid

The FFC's proposed revenue-sharing grant is designed to provide each province with a core funding sufficient to undertake the various functions assigned to it by the new Constitution. The basic grant is a per resident grant, adjusted upward for the proportion of the province's population classified as living in rural areas. Each rural person is weighted as an additional 0.25 of a person. The FFC proposal is quite explicit that this additional rural weighting is a value judgement made by the Commission in the absence of reliable cost or needs data, although a micro-analysis by the Commission's staff showed that rural areas are also high poverty areas with markedly inadequate levels of housing, water, electricity, sanitation, and transportation services. Allocation of basic grants revenues to each province follows the formula:

$$A_{pt} = \alpha_{pt} \cdot A_{.t}, \qquad (10.7)$$

where α_{pt} is the share of total basic grants in year t ($A_{.t}$) allocated to province p, and is specified as:

$$\alpha_{pt} = [N_{pt} + 0.25 \cdot n_{pt}^{rural}]/\Sigma_p[N_{pt} + 0.25 \cdot n_{pt}^{rural}],$$

where N_{pt} is the total provincial population, n_{pt}^{rural} is the total rural population in the province, and 0.25 is the additional rural weighting.

In the FFC proposal, total revenue-sharing aid allocated in year t, $A_{.t}$, is set by national budgetary considerations as a residual after allowing for other grants programs and for provincial and national tax rates. There is no special compensation for possible differences in public sector inflation rates across provinces in the FFC revenue-sharing grant. This seems appropriate given that the major component of provincial costs, public sector wages, is set nationally in South Africa. Table 10.2, columns (1) and (2) report the FFC's estimates for the distribution of the basic revenue-sharing grant for fiscal year 1996/97 for the nine new provinces.[18]

2 Tax capacity equalization aid

The FFC's tax capacity equalization aid formula is specified as:

$$T_{pt} = \{Y_{.t}^{*}/Y_{pt}) - 1\}[\tau_{.t}^{*} \cdot Y_{pt}] = Y_{.t}^{*} \cdot \tau_{.t}^{*} - \tau_{.t}^{*} \cdot Y_{pt}, \qquad (10.8)$$

where both $Y_{.t}^{*}$ and $\tau_{.t}^{*}$ are policy parameters chosen by the national government. The provinces are to receive aid sufficient to cover the gap between what they would raise if they used a nationally set target tax rate ($\tau_{.t}^{*}$) on the national target tax base per resident ($Y_{.t}^{*}$) and what they do raise using that target rate ($\tau_{.t}^{*}$) on their own tax bases per resident (Y_{pt}). The personal income tax base is the FFC's preferred tax base for provincial taxation and, therefore, the basis for tax capacity equalization aid. The formula makes no allowances for public service cost differences between the provinces, again, because public sector wages, the main component of public sector costs, are uniform across all provinces.

The FFC's preferred national target tax base ($Y_{.t}^{*}$) is the nation's average personal income tax base. The choice of the national average personal income tax base ensures that the tax capacity equalization grant will be self-financing

Table 10.2 South Africa's provincial grants: the FFC proposal for fiscal year 1996/97 (Rand)

Province	Revenue-sharing aid		Tax capacity equalization aid			Merit good categorical aid				Matching health care aid	Total aid	Total revenues
						Education		Health Care				
	Grant per rural weighted resident	Grant per resident	Surcharge per resident	Grant per resident	Net revenue per resident	Grant per child	Grant per resident	Grant per 'qualified' resident	Grant per resident	Grant per resident	Grant per resident	Grant plus tax surcharge per resident
	(1)	(2)	(3)	(4)	(5)	(6)	(7)	(8)	(9)	(10)	(11)	(12)
Western Cape	690	715	173	(67)	106	2150	571	136	103	130	1452	1625
Eastern Cape	690	802	47	59	106	2150	704	136	130	20	1715	1762
Northern Cape	690	736	118	(12)	106	2150	574	136	118	0	1667*	1785*
KwaZulu–Natal	690	799	79	27	106	2150	703	136	123	43	1695	1774
Free State	690	770	93	13	106	2150	579	136	124	75	1 561	1654
North West	690	815	60	46	106	2150	639	136	125	0	1625	1685
Gauteng	690	700	231	(125)	106	2150	530	136	100	117	1 322	1553
Mpumalanga	690	806	105	1	106	2150	649	136	123	0	1579	1684
Northern Province	690	847	30	76	106	2150	805	136	127	0	1855	1885
All Provinces	690	778	106	0	106	2150	653	136	119	50	1583	1689

Note: * The total grants and total revenues per resident for the Northern Cape include the FFC's proposed supplemental grant of R251/resident for FY 1996/97.

Source: Financial and Fiscal Commission, *The Allocation of Resources Between the National and Provincial Governments*, Second Draft, 28 March 1996.

– that is, $\Sigma T_{pt} \cdot N_{pt} = 0$ – with richer than average provinces contributing revenues to pay for the transfers to the poorer than average provinces.[19] The FFC proposes a national target tax rate of $\tau^*_{.t}$ equal to 0.03, but notes that alternative rates could be used. Target tax rates greater than 0.03 will be more equalizing. Table 10.2, columns (3)–(5), report the FFC's estimates of tax surcharge revenues by province (column 3), tax equalization aid by province (column 4), and net revenues by province (surcharge plus aid, column 5) for financial year 1996/97, assuming a $\tau^*_{.t} = 0.03$. The richer than average provinces of Western Cape, Northern Cape, and Gauteng receive 'negative' equalization aid (reported in $(\cdot)$), while the poorer than average provinces receive positive equalization aid.

The FFC adopted this constrained specification of the capacity equalization aid, rather than the unconstrained specification recommended in equation (10.5) above, for two reasons.[20] First, at the time of the FFC's proposal the provinces had not yet been granted the legal right to apply a tax surcharge on the national personal income tax base in their provinces. (This was still the case in September, 1997.) The FFC equalization policy could therefore only be applied against assumed provincial rates. The FFC's approach was to assume a common tax rate of $\tau_{pt} = \tau^*_{.t}$ for all provinces. Second, it recognized the overall budgetary uncertainty of allowing the new provinces to set their own surcharge rates on the personal income tax base. When taxing powers are granted to the provinces it is likely the FFC will recommend the surcharge be limited to a maximum rate. If all provinces tax at the chosen maximum rate, then again $\tau_{pt} = \tau^*$ is the appropriate specification for tax capacity equalization aid.

3 Merit good categorical aid

The FFC proposed two categorical aid grants for the provinces, one to be used for the financing of a national minimum standard for education and a second grant to fund national minimum standards for primary health care services. The education categorical grant gives each province sufficient funds to meet the national target teacher-to-pupil ratio:

$$M^{ed}_{pt} = (n^{5-17}_{pt}/N_{pt}) \cdot x^{ed.}_{teach}\, W^{ed.}_{teach,t} \cdot (1 + \omega^{ed}_t), \qquad (10.9)$$

where M^{ed}_{pt} is the level of educational aid per resident given to province p in year t, (n^{5-17}_{pt}/N_{pt}) is the percentage of the province's population which is of school age in year t (see Table 10.1), $x^{ed.}_{teach}$ is the weighted average national standard target teacher-to-pupil ratio of 1:38,[21] $W^{ed.}_{teach,t}$ is the nationally negotiated teacher wage in year t, and $(1 + \omega^{ed}_t)$ is an estimated national mark-up on wages in year t ($\omega^{ed}_t = 0.41$ in financial year 1996/97) to ensure each teacher has sufficient instructional resources. While the categorical education grant *per resident* (column 7) will differ across provinces, the categorical education grant *per school-aged child* (column 6) will be identical across provinces.

The FFC's categorical health care grant seeks to give each province sufficient resources to meet a national standard of (on average) 3.5 publicly funded clinic visits per year for each citizen using the public health system and (on average) 0.5 publicly funded clinic visits per year for each citizen using the private (insured) health system. Currently, citizens using the public health system receive 1.82 clinic visits per year. The national target of 3.5 clinic visits is to be reached incrementally over an eight year period. The target of 0.5 public clinic visits for citizens enrolled in the private health system is to remain constant. The resulting categorical health care grants formula is therefore:

$$M_{pt}^{hlth} = (n_{pt}^{priv}/N_{pt}) \cdot x_{priv}^{hlth} \cdot C_t^{clinic} + (n_{pt}^{pub}/N_{pt}) \cdot x_{pub,t}^{hlth} \cdot C_t^{clinic}, \tag{10.10}$$

where M_{pt}^{hlth} is the level of categorical health care aid per resident in province p in year t, (n_{pt}^{priv}/N_{pt}) is the share of residents who have private insurance in province p in year t, x_{priv}^{hlth} is the target level of public clinic visits for the privately insured population (= 0.5 visits on average), C_t^{clinic} is the average annual cost of one clinic visit and subsequent care resulting from that visit in year t, (n_{pt}^{pub}/N_{pt}) is the share of residents who use public health care in province p in year t, $x_{pub,t}^{hlth}$ is the target level of public clinic visits for the publicly insured population in year t (= 1.82 visits, rising incrementally over eight years to 3.5 visits on average), and C_t^{clinic} is again the average annual cost of one clinic visit and subsequent care resulting from that visit. The target number of clinic visits and the annual cost of those visits do not vary across provinces. Table 10.2, column (8) reports the health grant per 'qualified' patient $((n_{pt}^{priv} \cdot x_{priv}^{hlth} + n_{pt}^{pub} \cdot x_{pub,t}^{hlth})/N_{pt}))$ and column (9) reports the health grant per resident in each province.

The FFC proposal makes no explicit allowance for the monitoring of these merit good grants to ensure that each province spends its allotted categorical aid to achieve the national education and health care targets. The FFC's categorical grants are therefore indicative, not conditional. Further, the FFC proposal fully funds the national education and primary health care standards; there are no unfunded mandates.

4 Matching aid for national health care training and service provision

The FFC's proposal recognizes that the academic hospitals in Gauteng, Free State, KwaZulu-Natal, Western Cape, and the Eastern Cape provide significant national benefits in speciality health care services and in training, education, and research. To assist the provinces in funding these activities, the FFC proposed a 'spillover' matching grant for the *n*ational *i*nterest in advanced medical care, *t*raining, *e*ducation, and *r*esearch (NITER). The FFC proposal for financial year 1996/97 matches academic hospital spending in these provinces at the rate of

0.30,[22] up to a maximum allocation equal to 0.30 of the financial year 1995/96 academic hospital budget adjusted for inflation. That is:

$$s_p = 0.30, \qquad (10.11)$$

where total matching aid in Rands is constrained to equal:

$$S_p^{hosp} = \min[s_p \cdot \exp_{pt}^{hosp}; \quad s_p \cdot \exp_{p95/96}^{hosp} \cdot (1 + \pi_{96/97}^{hosp})] \qquad (10.11')$$

Table 10.2, column (10), reports the value of the NITER, closed-ended matching grants per resident under the (reasonable) assumption that all medical centers will spend to the proposed limit for aid.

5 Provincial aid constrained by national tax and deficit targets

The FFC provincial revenue proposal makes an explicit effort to respect national budgetary constraints on the aggregate national deficit and the overall rate of taxation when allocating revenues to provincial governments. First, the FFC proposal only uses nationally raised revenues, not deficits, to pay for intergovernmental grants, consistent with the Government's commitment to the international capital markets to reduce the national deficit to 5 percent or less of GDP. Second, any additional provincial tax revenues raised through the FFC's recommended provincial tax surcharge on the national residential income must be counted against the Government's commitment to taxpayers that aggregate national plus provincial government tax revenues will not exceed 25 percent of GDP. The FFC proposal meets this constraint in two ways. First, it recommends that each province's tax surcharge on personal income earned within the province be less than or equal to a maximum rate. Second, the aggregate provincial budget including national government grants and maximal provincial surcharge revenues must be specified as part of the overall national budget process using an FFC developed budgeting concept called 'tax room.' Tax room budgeting ensures that as provinces use their new surcharge taxing powers – thus raising the national average tax rate on residential income – the effective average tax rate imposed by the national government is reduced equivalently. The fall in the national government average tax rate means either national government service spending must be reduced or national intergovernmental transfers to the provinces must fall. The FFC proposal recommends a reduction in intergovernmental transfers, in particular that the basic, revenue-sharing grant ($A_{.t}$) be reduced with the introduction of provincial tax surcharge powers. This is appropriate. As provinces begin taxing on their own, the need for a basic lump-sum grant declines.[23]

B Evaluating the FFC Proposal

The FFC proposal for intergovernmental transfers to South Africa's new provincial governments is notable in at least two respects. First, it is a concrete and significant step towards the decentralization of fiscal policy in the new South Africa signaling a clear break with the centralized, apartheid past. Second, the proposal itself offers an integrated policy where each grants program is designed to serve a clear policy objective with the grants instrument appropriate to the chosen objective.

1 Economic efficiency

The structure of fiscal assignments in the new Constitution goes a long way towards ensuring the efficient allocation of public and private resources in the newly decentralized public economy of South Africa. The South African Constitution's fiscal assignments deny provinces and localities rental taxation and the taxation of business capital and allocate primary responsibility for pure public goods and income redistribution to the central government. With such an assignment structure, efficiency grants (E_p) are not needed. The Constitution's one assignment 'mistake' is to give provinces continued responsibility for physician training and providing sophisticated tertiary health care, arguably both national public goods. The FFC proposal responds to this mis-assignment with a matching grant ($s_p = 0.30$) to cover the estimated costs of these services,[24] capped to give each province no more total aid than that which they would receive in financial year 1996 adjusted for the *national* rate of hospital cost inflation. Capping the aggregate grant, tying future funding to the pre-aid, financial year 1996 base, and indexing the grant to the national rate of inflation protects the central government budget from exploding health care costs and, further, gives provinces an incentive to be efficient once at the maximal grant.

The South African assignment structure also gives provinces access to a proportional residential income tax based, for administrative reasons, upon income earned by workers within the province.[25] The purpose of this tax assignment is to give provinces access to a broad-based, redistributive revenue instrument, but the administration of this tax, using the workers' place of employment, has potential implications for the efficient location of labor services. With a worksite-based income tax, workers have a fiscal incentive to leave high tax rate (low tax base) provinces and to relocate in the low tax rate (high tax base) provinces; see Inman (1992). With worksite-based income taxes, workers will continue to exit the high tax rate provinces until their after-tax (or for residents, after-fiscal surplus) incomes are equalized across all provinces. Thus pretax wages must rise in the high tax provinces to compensate remaining workers and fall in low tax provinces so as to absorb entering workers. In equilibrium, these differences in pre-tax wages across provinces will equal the difference in provincial tax rates. Importantly, this tax-created difference in pre-tax wages indicates an inefficiency in the location of labor services; workers abandon more productive employment because of relatively high provincial taxes. The more mobile are provincial workers and firms, the larger is the economic inefficiency from differential taxation.

Fortunately, the FFC proposal makes a significant step towards controlling these potential labor market inefficiencies. First, it recommends constraining provincial income tax rates below a maximum rate. The constraint limits the range of final tax differences and hence the extent of labor relocations. Second, the FFC recommends the introduction of a tax base equalization grants program (T_{pt}) as specified in equation (10.8); see Table 10.2, column (4). Though not fully equalizing, the FFC's T_{pt} grant goes a long way towards eliminating the effects of fiscal base on the average tax cost of public services to residents; see Figure 10.1. While workers will still have fiscal incentives to relocate, the FFC proposal is likely to minimize, though not eliminate, their adverse effects on labor market allocations.

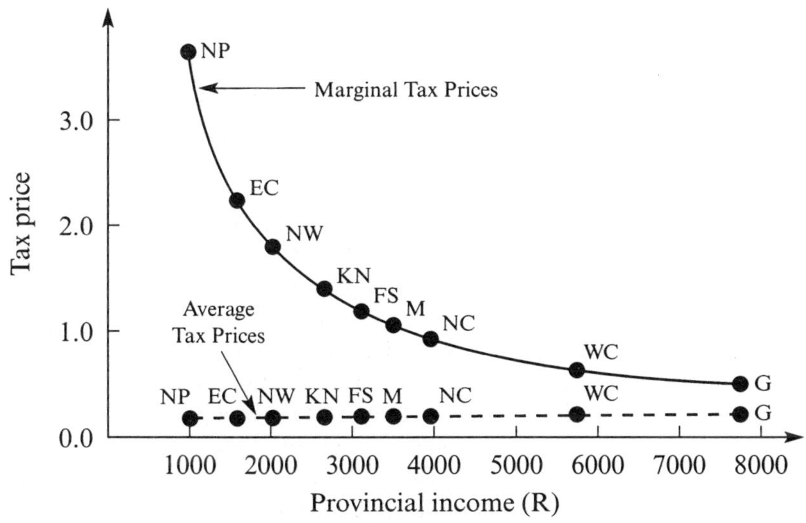

NP =	Northern Province	KN =	KwaZulu–Natal	NC =	Northern Cape
EC =	Eastern Cape	FS =	Free State	WC =	Western Cape
NW =	North West	M =	Mpumalanga	G =	Gauteng

Figure 10.1 Marginal and average tax prices by provincial income

2 Tax equity

The FFC proposal also makes a significant contribution towards horizontal tax equity and merit goods spending equity across provinces. Horizontal tax equity is achieved when the price of purchasing public goods – $(y/Y_p)\ SMC_p$ – for each resident is equalized across provinces. Public employee labor costs, the main component of SMC_p, are uniformly set at the national level. Horizontal tax equity therefore requires tax base equalization. The FFC's proposal specifies the constrained equalization grant in equation (10.8), reported in Table 10.2, column (4). Under constrained equalization, the *marginal* tax price of buying one additional unit of the public good remains equal to $(y/Y_p) \cdot SMC_p$; however, the *average* tax price equal to total taxes paid per unit of public good received is significantly equalized using the FFC formula. When SMC_p is across all provinces and provincial services are fully congestible ($\alpha = 1$), the marginal tax price for a resident equals (y/Y_p) while the average tax price equals total taxes paid by the resident divided by provincial spending per resident. Figure 10.1 plots marginal and average tax prices under the FFC equalization grant for a resident with the average national income (= R3524) living in each of the provinces.[26] The marginal tax price schedule is also the average tax price schedule when there is no FFC proposal. Without FFC policies, an average income resident in the two richest provinces of Western Cape and Gauteng is able to purchase public services at about 1/6th the tax cost for those same services in the poorer provinces. With the FFC proposal average tax prices are nearly identical. Clearly the FFC proposal moves South Africa's public sector a long way towards full horizontal equity, at least, on average.

Merit goods equity is promised with the FFC's commitment to fund the national standards for primary and secondary education and for primary health care visits. Merit good education grants (Table 10.2, columns 6 and 7) are by definition allocated to provinces with more children/resident. As it happens, these are also the provinces with higher rates of poverty and lower rates of literacy.[27] Merit good health care grants, by definition, will be allocated to provinces with more public clinic users/resident. Again these are also the provinces with the greater health care needs as measured by low life expectancy and high rates of infant mortality.[28] Whether the promise of the FFC's merit good allocations is achieved remains to be seen, however. Lump-sum categorical aid is fungible aid, capable of being reallocated to spending categories other than education and primary health care. The FFC proposal makes no explicit allowance for monitoring these merit good grants to ensure that each province spends its allotted aid to achieve the national education and health care targets.

3 Building democratic institutions

The largest single grant in the FFC proposal, almost half of all aid distributed, is a basic revenue-sharing grant (A_{pt}) per resident; see Table 10.2, columns (1) and (2). As specified this grant is a lump-sum transfer to each province, favoring more rural and poorer provinces.[29] Lump-sum aid has no role to play in the economic theory of intergovernmental transfers outlined in section II; as specified each grant program is a price subsidy, either to the public budget as a whole – E_p, A_p, and T_p aid – or to particular public services – s_p or m_p aid.

Is there a rationale for the FFC's large lump-sum transfer? There is, but the motivation lies beyond the economist's usual goals of economic efficiency and equity, a point first emphasized by Oates (1972, pp. 85–94) in his own evaluation of grants policies. The motivation for the FFC's initially large A_{pt} grant is to give each newly elected provincial government resources sufficient to carry out the public service responsibilities assigned to it by the new Constitution. Lower tier governments in federalist hierarchies are typically the most vibrant arenas for citizen political participation.[30] Viewed in this light, the large lump-sum A_{pt} grants are investments in democratic institution building. Under the FFC proposal, the total allocation to provincial governments is estimated to equal 55 percent of all budgeted government spending for financial year 1996/97. As provincial political institutions develop and competitive politics comes to provide effective control over spending allocations – as in holding elected officials accountable for public spending – then provincial responsibilities can be extended to include greater choice over provincial tax revenues. When greater choice over provincial tax rates is allowed, the large, lump-sum portion of the A_{pt} grants can be reduced. In the FFC proposal this is accomplished through tax room budgeting. When provinces are finally granted full control over spending and revenues – presumably when viewed as truly responsible democratic institutions – then the lump-sum component of the revenue-sharing grant can be set at 0, as recommended by the purely economic theory of intergovernmental transfers.

C The Current Status of Intergovernmental Aid in South Africa

The National Parliament has approved with only minor modifications three of the FFC's four recommended intergovernmental aid programs: revenue-sharing, primary education and health care (merit good) categorical aid, and matching aid for tertiary health care services and training. Not yet approved is the FFC's tax capacity equalization grant (T_{pt}); a decision on tax equalization aid awaits a prior decision to grant provinces the right to use a 'piggy-backed' tax surcharge on the national individual income tax base. The FFC has recently proposed to Parliament that provinces be given access to a uniform rate surcharge on the national individual tax base within each province, subject to a maximum provincial rate of 7 percent phased in over the next five fiscal years. As provinces raise their individual tax surcharge rates, the FFC's proposed use of tax room budgeting will reduce the aggregate pool of nationally funded revenue-sharing aid ($A_{.t}$ in equation (10.7)) to ensure that the average combined national plus provincial tax rate does not exceed the national target average tax rate of

0.25. As the average provincial surcharge rises, the average national income tax rate falls identically, with national tax relief paid for through reductions in unconstrained revenue-sharing aid. Under FFC's tax room budgeting, a province's own revenues will gradually replace national revenue-sharing aid, which is consistent with the FFC's objective to establish in each province a politically accountable link between provincial revenues raised and services provided.[31] If provincial powers to set an individual income tax surcharge on provincial incomes is approved, then Parliament will need to consider the need for tax capacity equalization aid as specified in equations (10.5') or (10.8) above.

To date, South Africa has made significant progress towards an economically sensible program of intergovernmental grants. The role of grants in fiscal policy is to correct the problems created by mis-assignments of spending and taxing responsibilities in a country's original fiscal constitution. The fiscal assignments in South Africa's new Constitution created three potential problems: (1) Giving provinces responsibility for physician training and tertiary health care raises the possibility of too little investment in these national public goods; (2) assigning provinces the responsibility for primary education and clinic health services means these 'merit goods' may be inequitably allocated; and (3) allowing provinces a flat-rate personal income tax surcharge which, for administrative reasons, becomes a worksite-based labor tax may lead to inefficient labor market allocations and horizontal tax inequities. The first and second problems are well handled with the recently approved categorical grants for basic education (M_{pt}^{ed}), primary health care (M_{pt}^{hlth}), and tertiary health care (S_p^{hosp}). Problem (3) is just now being addressed by Parliament. If Parliament approves the provincial income tax surcharge, then the FFC's partial equalization grant in equation (10.8) – or better yet, a fully equalizing grant equation (10.5') – becomes an appropriate grants response.

Once approved, holding these good grants policies in place may be difficult, however. If the experiences of other federalist public economies are a guide, there will be significant legislative pressures to neutralize the now targeted nature of South Africa's grants policies; see Inman (1988). Premiers from provinces receiving relatively less assistance will argue through their legislative representatives for 'provincial fairness.' Against this pressure, the equalization aid used to neutralize the inefficiencies and inequities of provincial income taxation and the matching grants used to correct interprovincial spillovers and merit goods inequities may then become equal per resident grants, thereby undoing the economic purpose of the original policies. To offset these legislative pressures, strong executive branch leadership will be required. The independent Financial and Fiscal Commission – assigned by the Constitution the important role as a gatekeeper for fiscal policies – may also come to play an essential role in protecting the integrity of intergovernmental grants policies.

IV A CONCLUDING COMMENT

With the growing interest in federalism as an institutional structure for managing a nation's public finances, new attention is being paid by economists and policy-makers to the important role of service and tax assignment and intergovernmental transfers. For each structure of spending and tax assignments, there is a corresponding structure of intergovernmental grants to correct any resulting economic inefficiencies or inequities. Wallace Oates's treatise *Fiscal Federalism* provided us with the first systematic guide to the optimal design of fiscal assignments and intergovernmental grants. This paper has sought to update Oates's original contribution, providing guidance for when and how to use intergovernmental transfers to facilitate efficient and fair public sector allocations. That these ideas, many first articulated in *Fiscal Federalism*, now guide fiscal policies in emerging democracies is just further testimony to Wally Oates's important contribution to the theory and practice of public finance.

NOTES

1. The comments of Junaid Ahmad, Richard Bird, and Charles McLure on various aspects of this paper are much appreciated.
2. The most common measure of the influence of a scholar is the aggregate number of citations of his or her work, and by this count Wally Oates's *Fiscal Federalism* must surely rank as one of the most important books in public finance in the last twenty-five years. But perhaps a better measure of whether a work is foundational is how widely it is cited. Both Professors Weingast and Beer cite *Fiscal Federalism*. The fact that two leading political scientists – one a political theorist and the other a political philosopher and intellectual historian – rely upon *Fiscal Federalism* at crucial points in their arguments is further testimony to the clarity and strength of Oates's analysis.
3. Since only citizens vote in this model, they clearly prefer the 100 percent taxation of locally earned rents. Following the provincial taxation and redistribution of rents, each individual worker receives a wage equal to his marginal product plus an equal share of rents from the government: $f_p'(L_p) + R_p/L_p$. Total rents earned in the province (R_p) equals total output minus total wages paid, or $R_p = f_p(L_p) - L_p f_p'(L_p)$. Thus, $f_p'(L_p) + R_p/L_p = f_p(L_p)/L_p$, or each worker receives an equal share of total provincial private output.
4. The extra public facility needed to maintain the flow of services g_p will equal (dG_p/dL_p) holding g_p fixed. From the congestion relationship $g_p = G_p/L_p^{\alpha}$:

$$dg_p = dG_p/L_p^{\alpha} - dL_p \cdot (\alpha G_p/L_p^{(\alpha+1)}).$$

To hold the level of public services fixed ($dg_p = 0$) when population increases ($dL_p > 0$) will require an increase in the public facility ($dG_p > 0$) of:

$$dG_p/dL_p = \alpha(G_p/L_p).$$

5. The values of R_p, G_p, and L_p in equation (10.2) must be defined at the efficient population level. To see how this grant program ensures the efficient allocation of families across provinces, note that with the aid program, household consumption in each province is now defined as $x_p = [f(L_p) - G_p]/L_p + E_p$. This definition of x_p gives this alternative specification for MB_p:

$$MB_p = v_x[(1 - \alpha_p)(G_p/L_p) - R_p/L_p - E_p]. \tag{10.1'}$$

Specifying net aid E_p as in equation (10.2) above gives:

$$MB_p = v_x \cdot \beta. \tag{10.1''}$$

As long as the marginal utility of private income is equal across all provinces – that is, no provincial advantages other than income and public services – then location efficiency is achieved. In *Fiscal Federalism* Oates (1972, pp. 82–84) anticipates the Boadway and Flatters argument for the grants formula E_p.

6. With a matching rate of s_p the *net* private marginal costs to the ruling coalition of funding provincial services becomes $(1 - s_p) \cdot PMC_p$. Provincial services are now provided until $PMB_p = (1 - s_p) \cdot PMC_p$, or until $PMB_p = (1/\phi_p \rho_p) \cdot PMC_p$. As $\phi_p \cdot PMB_p = (1/\rho_p) \cdot PMC_p$ implies $SMB_p = SMC_p$, social efficiency is achieved. In his survey of intergovernmental grants, Oates (1972, Appendix A) extends the analysis to allow for joint spillovers between jurisdictions.
7. The precise meaning of horizontal equity in fiscal policy remains a topic of some controversy; see Kaplow (1989) for a survey of the debate and Usher (1995) and Boadway's (1996) review of Usher for an application to grants policy. Article 42 of the Swiss Constitution, Article 107(2) of tine German Constitution, and Section 36(2) of the Constitution of Canada each embrace principles of horizontal equity.
8. See Rawls (1971, Chapter 7) or Besley (1989) for how these constraints might be motivated.
9. A taxpayer's private marginal cost of buying another unit of a provincial public service – often called the 'tax price' of the public service – is defined as $PMC_p = (y_p/Y_p) \cdot SMC_p$. Two taxpayers with identical individual tax bases (y_p) but living in different provinces can have different tax prices if their provincial taxes bases (Y_p) or the provincial costs of public services (SMC_p) differ across the two provinces. Taxpayers in poorer and more expensive provinces will pay more for provincial public services than their counterparts in other provinces.
10. See LeGrand (1975, pp. 534–5) or Ladd and Yinger (1994, p. 215). The specification of *SMC* in the aid formula should be an overall public service price index; see Inman (1979) for one approach.

    Canada uses a variant of this formula as a provincial tax base equalization grant. The Canadian formula ignores cost differences across provinces and sets $\tau_p = \tau^*$. Basing T_p aid on τ^* rather than actual provincial tax rates, τ_p, will not be fully equalizing in tax prices; see note 20 below. For a more general critique of the Canadian formula, see Usher (1995). For a defense of the formula, see Boadway (1996).
11. The argument for the structure of matching aid for merit goods is shown most easily for the linear demand curve, but the results generalize to other specifications.
12. If the merit good is to be provided not just to a minimal standard but equally across all provinces, then for the high spending provinces the matching rate in equation (10.7) is still appropriate, but for these provinces the grant becomes a tax at a rate $m_p < 0$.
13. Implicit in the specification of the grants formula is an assumption that the central government knows the behavior of the ruling coalition in each province, specified by the coefficients δ and θ. If so, then the central government can do better than the matching program specified in equation (10.6). Central government tax dollars can be saved by matching not all provincial spending, but only those units of service beyond the level of g_p purchased when ($m_p = 0$). The calculation of this critical level of g_p is possible only when the demand curve for public services (δ and θ) is known.
14. For one approach to setting fiscal assignments, see Inman and Rubinfeld (1996a) on tax assignment and Inman and Rubinfeld (1996b) on expenditure assignment.
15. It is true that when provinces are large, preference heterogeneity may preclude the attainment of full public goods efficiency. But the fact that this economy does not achieve full efficiency is not an argument for central government grants. For grants to correct this problem, the central government must be able to reveal the preferences of provincial residents more effectively than does the provincial government itself. If provincial governments are truly democratic, this seems

unlikely. Without a preference revelation advantage, there is no role for central government intervention and thus no role for central government grants.

16. The approval of such programs necessarily requires an override of the original constitutional contract which granted provinces unconstrained access to these revenues. While the adoption of the constitution required unanimity – and thus the need to grant rich provinces access to these rents and profits – central government policies in the new union will typically need only simple or 2/3 majority approval.
17. Provincial taxing authority is assigned in Chapter 13, section 228 of the new Constitution.
18. Also included in the basic grant is a temporary, supplemental grant of R251/resident for the new province of the Northern Cape to establish an effective governmental administration in this rural and geographically large province. This interim grant is included as part of the totals in Table 10.2, columns (11) and (12).
19. The sum of all Rands transferred by equalization aid equals $\Sigma T_{pt} \cdot N_{pt}$ where N_{pt} equals provincial population in year t. If $\Sigma T_{pt} \cdot N_{pt} = 0$, then equalization aid will be self-financing. The equalization program moves monies from one province to another, but there is no additional claim by the provincial sector on the private economy in the aggregate. In this special case, $Y^*_{.t}$ must equal the population weighted (by tax rates) national average level of tax capacity.
20. The unconstrained equalization aid formula of equation (10.5) uses the actual provincial tax rate, τ_{pt}, rather than a policy chosen common target rate, $\tau^*_{.t}$, as in the constrained FFC formula. The FFC formula is similar to the Canadian equalization formula; see note 10 above.
21. The FFC uses the national Education Department standards of 1:40 for primary education and 1:35 for secondary education to estimate a weighted average teacher to pupil ratio of 1:38.
22. The FFC choose the rate of 0.30 to approximate the added costs of training doctors plus the additional costs for treating the interprovincial flow of patients to these advanced medicine, tertiary care hospitals.
23. An unpublished Appendix to this paper is available which describes in detail the FFC's 'Tax Room' approach to grants budgeting.
24. As specified in equation (10.3) and note 6 above, s_p also can be defined as the ratio of external (EMB = interprovincial) benefits to total social (SMB = provincial plus interprovincial = $PMB + EMB$) benefits. The FFC proposal is implicitly assuming that for each Rand of benefits provided to residents of the province by the province's major medical center, R0.43 in benefits are provided to non-residents: $s_p = EMB/[PMB + EMB] = 0.43 \cdot PMB/[PMB + 0.43 \cdot PMB]$ when $EMB = 0.43 \cdot PMB$ which implies $s_p = 0.30$.
25. An important practical issue facing the FFC – and fiscal planners in most developing countries – is how to assign the nation's personal income tax base to each province. Four alternatives are possible: (1) place of employer; (2) place of employment; (3) place of taxpayer's personal residence; and (4) place of taxpayer's family's residence. The issue arises because approximately half of all national personal income taxes are collected only by place of employment (called SITE collection). From an administrative point of view it would be easiest to assign tax base by place of employer. This approach, however, creates potentially significant bias in assignment of base as firms with multiple employment sites typically report tax payments only from firm headquarters. From an economic perspective, the best assignment of tax base would be to use the place of taxpayer and family residence, the most plausible point of public service consumption. In an economy with significant migrant labor such as South Africa's, however, this will be very difficult. The FFC proposal strikes a compromise between minimizing administrative costs and best economic practice and recommends the use of the worker's place of employment as the basis for allocating SITE's share of the personal tax base to provinces. Under SITE taxation, therefore, the labor incomes of residents and non-residents will be taxed at the worksite.
26. The marginal tax price is defined as ($R3524/Y_p$) where Y_p is given in Table 10.1. The average tax price is calculated assuming each province adopts the maximum allowed provincial rate of 0.0.3 and provincial spending per resident equals total revenues per resident as reported in Table 10.2, column (12) ($= 0.03 \cdot R3524/\text{Total revenues per resident}_p$). Because each province receives much of its public budget from intergovernmental transfers, the average tax price is very low; the mean average tax price is only R0.062 per Rand of spending.

27. A simple regression of merit good education aid per resident on the rate of poverty in the provinces and on the rate of literacy in the provinces gave these results:

$$(\text{education grant/resident})_p = 1244 - 990.9 \cdot (\text{literacy rate})_p,$$

$$(\text{education grant/resident})_p = 92.65 + 804.2 \cdot (\text{poverty rate})_p.$$

All coefficients are statistically significant at the 0.001 level.

28. A simple regression of merit good health care aid per resident on life expectancy and infant mortality in the provinces shows:

$$(\text{health care grant/resident})_p = 418.3 - 4.72 \cdot (\text{life expectancy})_p;$$

$$(\text{health care grant/resident})_p = 85.25 + 0.797 \cdot (\text{infant mortality})_p,$$

Regressions of health care aid on health care inputs also shows aid going to the more needy provinces:

$$(\text{health care grant/resident})_p = 131.2 - 20.7 \cdot (\text{doctors/resident})_p;$$

$$(\text{health care grant/resident})_p = 145.7 - 6.29 \cdot (\text{nurses/resident})_p,$$

$$(\text{health care grant/resident})_p = 126.2 - 78.8 \cdot (\text{pharmacies/resident})_p,$$

Again, all coefficients are statistically significant at the 0.001 level.

29. A simple regression of revenue-sharing aid per resident on the percent of residents classified as rural or poor in provinces gave these results:

$$(\text{revenue-sharing grant/resident})_p = 577.0 + 416.3 \cdot (\text{rural rate})_p;$$

$$(\text{revenue-sharing grant/resident})_p = 178.8 + 923.4 \cdot (\text{poverty rate})_p;$$

All coefficients are statistically significant at the 0.001 level.

30. There is extensive international evidence on the point; see Inman and Rubinfeld (1997a) for a review of the theoretical and empirical literature on political participation.

31. One should note that tax room budgeting does create a 'second-order' incentive effect which may discourage this substitution of own revenue for central government aid. As each province raises its own revenues through the imposition of a provincial tax surcharge, it will also increase the national average provincial surcharge which in turn will reduce the aggregate pool of revenue-sharing aid ($A_{.t}$) when tax room budgeting applies. The fall in $A_{.t}$ reduces the province's own level of revenue-sharing (A_{pt}). Thus raising own tax revenues reduces own revenue-sharing, creating a disincentive to use own revenues. The magnitude of the disincentive is likely to be very small, however, only increasing the tax price of provincial public services by at most 4 to 5 percent in the largest provinces (KwaZulu-Natal and Gauteng) and by no more than 2 percent in all other provinces. (Author's calculations available upon request.)

REFERENCES

Arnott, Richard and Joseph Stiglitz (1979), 'Aggregate Land Rents, Expenditure on Public Goods, and Optimal City Size', *Quarterly Journal of Economics*, **93**, 471–500.

Beer, Samuel (1993), *To Make a Nation: The Rediscovery of American Federalism*, Cambridge: Harvard University Press.

Besley, Timothy (1989), 'A Simple Model for Merit Good Arguments', *Journal of Public Economics*, **35**, 371–84.

Bewley, Truman (1981), 'A Critique of Tiebout's Theory of Local Public Expenditures', *Econometrica*, **49**, 713–39.

Boadway, Robin (1996), 'Book Review: The Uneasy Case for Equalization Payments', *National Tax Journal*, **49**, 677–86.

Boadway, Robin and Frank Flatters (1982), 'Efficiency and Equalization Payments in a Federal System of Governments: A Synthesis and Extension of Recent Results', *Canadian Journal of Economics*, **15**, 613–33.

Boadway, Robin and Michael Keen (1996), 'Efficiency and the Optimal Direction of Federal-State Transfers,' *International Tax and Public Finance*, **3**, 137–55.

Brown, Charles and Wallace Oates (1987), 'Assistance to the Poor in a Federal System', *Journal of Public Economics*, **32**, 307–30.

Constitutional Assembly (1996), *Constitution of the Republic of South Africa*, Government of South Africa, Department of Constitutional Affairs, Pretoria, South Africa.

Gramlich, Edward M. and Deborah S. Laren (1984), 'Immigration and Income Redistribution Responsibilities', *Journal of Human Resources*, **19** (4), 489–511.

Inman, Robert P. (1979), 'Dissecting the Urban Fiscal Crisis: Facts and Counterfacts', *National Tax Journal*, **32**, 127–42.

Inman, Robert P. (1988), 'Federal Assistance and Local Services in the United States: The Evolution of a New Fiscal Order', in Harvey Rosen (ed.), *Fiscal Federalism: Quantiative Studies*, Chicago: Chicago University Press, pp. 33–74.

Inman, Robert P. (1992), 'Can Philadelphia Escape its Fiscal Crisis with Another Tax Increase?', *Business Review, Federal Reserve Bank of Philadelphia*, September/October, 5–20.

Inman, Robert P. and Daniel L. Rubinfeld (1996a), 'Designing Tax Policies in Federalist Economies: An Overview', *Journal of Public Economics*, **60**, 307–34.

Inman, Robert P. and Daniel L. Rubinfeld (1996b), 'The Political Economy of Federalism', in D. Mueller (ed.), *Developments in Public Choice*, Cambridge: Cambridge University Press, pp. 73–105.

Inman, Robert P. and Daniel L. Rubinfeld (1997a), 'Making Sense of the Antitrust State-Action Doctrine: Balancing Political Participation and Economic Efficiency in Regulatory Federalism', *Texas Law Review*, **75**, 1203–99.

Inman, Robert P. and Daniel L. Rubinfeld (1997b), 'Rethinking Federalism', *Journal of Economic Perspectives*, **11**, 43–64.

Kaplow, Louis (1989), 'Horizontal Equity: Measures in Search of a Principle', *National Tax Journal*, **42**, 139–54.

Ladd, Helen and John Yinger (1994), 'The Case for Equalizing Aid', *National Tax Journal*, **47**, 211–24.

LeGrand, Julian (1975), 'Fiscal Equity and Central Government Grants to Local Authorities', *Economic Journal*, **85**, 531–47.

Oates, Wallace (1972), *Fiscal Federalism*, New York: Harcourt Brace Jovanovich.

Pauly, Mark (1973), 'Income Redistribution as a Local Public Good', *Journal of Public Economics*, **2**, 35–58.

Rawls, John (1971), *A Theory of Justice*, Cambridge: Harvard University Press.

Usher, Daniel (1995), *The Uneasy Case for Equalization Payments*, Vancouver: The Fraser Institute.

Weingast, Barry, R. (1995), 'The Economic Role of Political Institutions: Market-Preserving Federalism and Economic Development', *The Journal of Law, Economics and Organization*, **11**, 1–31.
Wildasin, David (1986), *Urban Public Finance*, New York: Harwood Academic Publishers.
Wildasin, David (1989), 'Interjurisdictional Capital Mobility: Fiscal Externality and a Corrective Subsidy', *Journal of Urban Economics*, **25**, 193–212.
Wilson, John (1986), 'A Theory of Interregional Tax Competition', *Journal of Urban Economics*, **19**, 296–315.
Zodrow, George and Peter Mieszkowski (1986), 'Pigou, Property Taxation and the Under Provision of Local Public Goods', *Journal of Urban Economics*, **19**, 356–70.

11. Public pensions in the EU: migration incentives and impacts*

David E. Wildasin

INTRODUCTION

The allocative and distributional consequences of public policies depend crucially on the behavioral responses to which they give rise. In an economy where factors of production are partially or completely mobile, the possibility of migration provides one margin of behavioral response with potentially far-reaching consequences. The literature of fiscal federalism, which has been heavily influenced by the work of Wallace Oates, has drawn attention to the implications of capital and labor mobility for the analysis of such policies as property, corporate income, and other forms of capital taxation, individual income taxation, education and income maintenance policy, and environmental regulation, among others. Many of the early applications of Oates' ideas were made in the context of local public finance, especially with reference to local public education provision and finance in the United States. The present paper addresses what at first sight might appear to be a completely unrelated set of issues, namely, the provision of social insurance by national governments in Europe. However, powerful analytical insights in economics often have implications that extend well beyond the contexts in which they are initially developed. To motivate and justify the analysis presented in subsequent sections, a brief overview of major developments in the literature will be helpful.

Wallace Oates and Open-Economy Public Economics

Following Samuelson's famous contributions of 1954 and 1955 on the pure theory of public goods, Tiebout (1956) argued that the problem of efficient provision of *local* public goods could effectively be solved through the exercise of locational choice. Households express their demands for local public goods – 'reveal their preferences' – when they choose to live in one locality rather than another. A major milestone in the further development of this provocative idea is Oates's well-known 1969 paper on capitalization effects and local public finance. This article focuses attention on the expression of preferences for locally-provided education in the market for residential housing. Oates argues that preferred combinations of local public education and local taxes should command a premium in the housing market and examines empirically the relationship between local fiscal variables and housing prices. This paper, and the large body of subsequent research that it spawned, has drawn attention to the role of household mobility in achieving more efficient provision of public goods, helping to add both theoretical and empirical content to the somewhat loosely-expressed ideas found in Tiebout's original contribution.

Of course, the distributional effects of public policy can be just as important as their allocative effects. As Oates explains in his 1972 classic *Fiscal Federalism* and elsewhere, however, that the ability of local governments to pursue policies aimed at distributional objectives may be quite limited.[1] As observed also by Stigler (1957), Musgrave (1969), and others, the relative openness of lower-level governments constrains their ability to impose burdens on some individuals in order to transfer resources or to provide services to others. Localities that attempt to transfer resources from one group to another are likely to stimulate inflows of beneficiaries and outflows of contributors, with adverse allocative effects and uncertain distributional impacts. The redistributive interventions of higher-level governments, however, are harder to avoid because their geographical scope is generally larger. Consequently, a standard conclusion from the literature of fiscal federalism is that redistributive policies are best undertaken by central rather than local governments.

These basic conclusions from the literature of fiscal federalism point to a dilemma for policy. On the one hand, fiscal decentralization may promote economic efficiency in the public sector; on the other hand, it may interfere with the pursuit of distributional equity goals. This dilemma is well-illustrated by the case of local public education. The essence of efficient allocation is the adjustment of resource allocation to reflect benefits and costs, and both the benefits and costs of education certainly vary across economic and demographic groups. Uniformity of educational quality is thus certain to conflict with allocative efficiency. Yet variations in educational quality may violate ethical norms. In the US, locational sorting within large and fragmented metropolitan areas has resulted in wide local variations in levels of education spending, peer-group attributes, and other determinants of educational quality. As standard models of local public finance lead us to expect, decentralized public provision of education has produced a distribution of educational resources which reflects the underlying social and economic diversity of American society, an outcome that is no doubt more efficient than the more uniform levels of provision that might be achieved through a more centralized system. However, the economic and social stratification of metropolitan areas in America, which is in itself a vivid manifestation of inequality in American society, may also perpetuate inequality across generations. Perhaps it is not surprising, therefore, to find that state governments have intervened in the financing of education in order to achieve more equal outcomes than would have been achieved by localities acting alone. In particular, the past half-century of American experience in school finance has seen substantial growth in the use of grants from state governments to local school districts, generally designed to mitigate local variation in the level of fiscal resources available to finance schools.[2] As the principles of fiscal federalism would suggest, higher-level governments – in this case, the state governments – appear to be more effective than lower-level governments in achieving equity goals in public policy.

Factor Market Integration and the Welfare State

The mixed roles of state and local governments in education provision and finance in the US exemplify how higher- and lower-level governments may play rather different roles in balancing the sometimes conflicting objectives of equity and efficiency in public policy. A basic lesson to be derived from the work of Oates and others is that governments whose jurisdictional boundaries are relatively open to movements of capital and labor are constrained in their ability to undertake redistributive transfers. This lesson has far-reaching implications, going well beyond the context of local school finance in the United States. The 'intrinsic' or fundamental economic costs of factor movement within and among countries have been declining steadily over time due to technological progress in transportation and communications. Policy impediments to factor mobility, though often very great, have also begun to decline in many regions. The postwar era has seen the global integration of financial markets, the reduction of barriers to trade brought about by successive GATT rounds and the-North American Free Trade Agreement, increased internal migration in countries such as Germany, South Africa, and China in the wake of dramatic political and economic changes, and international migration between and among both more developed and less developed countries. Broader integration of markets for goods and services, capital, and labor has gradually occurred in post-war Europe since the founding of the EEC, marked by milestones such as the Single European Act, the Maastricht Treaty, and the growth of the European Union (EU) through the accession of new member states.

It is especially interesting to consider the implications of open-economy public economics for the highly-developed welfare states of Western Europe, precisely because their programs of redistributive policy are so extensive. These economies seem at first glance to fit the conventional fiscal federalism model, with 'central' (that is, national) governments raising large amounts of revenue to support cash and other transfers to the aged, the sick, the unemployed, children, and other target groups in society. However, the European welfare state developed in an era in which labor and capital were less mobile than they are today. Moreover, looking to the future, the intrinsic barriers to labor and capital movements in Europe are likely to continue to fall, and a recurring policy issue is whether or not to take more steps to lower the policy barriers to factor mobility still further, for instance by expanding membership in the European Union.[3] The basic insight of the traditional fiscal federalism model of centralized redistribution is that the geographical scope of the redistributing authority should encompass the relevant factor markets. In a world where the economic costs of factor mobility are very high, national governments might well meet this criterion. However, as capital and labor are increasingly traded in international markets, national economies gradually become smaller units within large ambient factor markets. Keeping the responsibility for redistributive policies at the level of national governments thus implies that the redistributive functions of the public sector are gradually being shifted to what are effectively 'lower-level' governments. This process may or may not provide a rationale for the development of supra-national institutions for redistribution (see Brennan and Buchanan, 1980 and Padoa-Schioppa et al., 1987), but in any case it provides fertile ground for positive analysis of the economics and political economy of income redistribution in a changing market environment.

The present paper analyses one aspect of income redistribution policy, namely, public pension programs, in the context of an integrated European Union among whose member states workers are potentially mobile.[4] When a household migrates from one EU member state to another, it typically assumes various fiscal obligations and obtains fiscal benefits in the destination country, while reducing or eliminating its fiscal connection to the origin country. In particular, a worker who migrates from one EU country to another ends or, at least, curtails its participation in the public pension program of one country in exchange for participation in that of another. For a destination country, immigration adds new contributors, and eventually new beneficiaries, to the public pension program. Migrant contributions and benefits affect the other residents of the country in the form of changes in their required contribution levels or in the benefits that they eventually receive.

Because of these fiscal externalities, the social benefits and costs of migration do not correspond to its private benefits and costs. Most significant migrations in history antedate the development of the modern welfare state, and most of the benefits and costs of migration in earlier eras could therefore be presumed to accrue to migrants themselves (leaving aside forced migrations and expropriation of indigenous populations). The level of migration in modern Europe is now fairly high (see, for example, Straubhaar and Zimmermann, 1993) and it thus offers an important and unusual example of a situation where social policies may insulate migrants from market signals of the economic consequences of their behavior. A crucial question, however, concerns the magnitude of the divergence between the private and social costs and benefits of migration in general, and, in particular, the magnitude of the net fiscal impacts of migration attributable to public pension programs. *A priori*, these effects could be very large, or they could be trivial. The principal objective of the following empirical analysis is to shed some preliminary light on this quantitative question.

The paper is organized as follows. Section II discusses the fiscal dimension of migration in general terms. Simple theoretical models identify the fiscal contributions and burdens of migrants as crucial determinants of the allocative and distributional impacts of migration. Empirical analysis should in principle take comprehensive account of the total interaction between a migrant and the fiscal system, an interaction that spans many aspects of policy and many time periods. The first part of section III sketches the conventional life-cycle model which is used as the organizing framework for the subsequent calculations of 'net public pension wealth.' The second part of section III presents calculations of net public pension wealth for representative workers in seven European countries, using 1986 public pension contribution and benefit formulae. It also reports estimates of the change in net public pension wealth which these workers would experience in moving from one to another of the seven countries. Section IV illustrates a potential application of the results by estimating the welfare effects of changes in public pension policy under the assumption that some portion of the labor force is internationally mobile. Section V concludes with a brief summary of some of the major results and a discussion of open questions and directions for further research.

II FISCAL ASPECTS OF MIGRATION: A GENERAL CONCEPTUAL FRAMEWORK

Market conditions, fiscal treatment, and environmental and social amenities are all potentially important factors for migrants to take into account when contemplating a move from one country to another. From a life-cycle viewpoint, it is not just the current conditions in each country that matter, but also those expected to obtain over the remainder of the household's planning horizon.[5] Similarly, migration affects market conditions (that is, the prices of non-traded goods and factors, such as wages and housing prices), fiscal conditions, environmental quality, and social conditions, both in the short and the long runs, and in both the origin and destination countries.

Fiscal variables relevant for household locational choice can be either pecuniary or non-pecuniary in nature. Pecuniary variables include cash transfer payments, taxes, and subsidies, and may be lump-sum or non-lump-sum in nature. Fiscal variables may also have pecuniary indirect effects on households;

for instance, harbors, rail freight systems, and other infrastructure for commercial and industrial transportation may raise the productivity of labor and lower production costs, leading to higher real wages for households. Non-pecuniary variables include public goods and services that benefit households directly, such as public safety, defence, or environmental, land-use, health, or other regulations. The boundary between the categories of pecuniary and non-pecuniary public benefits and costs is not clear-cut. Some public in-kind benefits, such as food coupons, are almost identical to cash benefits in their effects on consumer welfare; some, like public health, housing, and education benefits are also very closely substitutable for private consumption; as a practical matter, this means that monetary equivalents for these benefits may be ascertained relatively easily.

The fiscal consequences of migration for the origin and destination countries may also be either pecuniary or non-pecuniary in nature. A household that moves from one country to another may begin paying taxes and receiving subsidies in the new country and cease to do so in the old. Many public services, such as public safety, transportation, education, or health care are 'impure' or congestible, that is, at any given level of service, more resources must be expended to serve larger populations than smaller ones. Immigration generally congests these services and emigration decongests them, an effect which is non-pecuniary in its initial impact but which can be measured in monetary units as the cost of restoring service to the pre-migration level (see however Hobson, 1991).

A simple static general equilibrium model illustrates the principal efficiency and distributional consequences of fiscal policy in the presence of labor mobility. Figure 11.1 depicts the allocation of a fixed amount of labor between two countries, 1 and 2. VMP_i shows the marginal productivity of labor in each country. If migration is costless, goods prices are the same in both countries, and there are no locational amenities and no public sector, workers will migrate until wages are equalized. If labor markets are competitive, the resulting allocation of labor (L_1^*) is efficient. This simple model can be generalized easily; for instance, if there are non-traded goods whose prices differ across countries, one may interpret the VMP_i schedules as regional real income schedules, with no change in the basic conclusions. If there are country-specific amenities which all workers value equally, one can interpret VMP_i as the real income schedule of workers in country i; the efficiency of the competitive equilibrium is unaffected. If there are (positive or negative) attachments to place, the real income obtainable by immigrants in each country must be adjusted accordingly, but once again the efficiency of the equilibrium is undisturbed, provided that the costs of migration are borne by migrants.

To take the public sector into account, suppose that workers in each country pay taxes of T_i and receive benefits of B_i per capita. T_i could include income, earnings, consumption, or other residence-based taxes.[6] The benefits could be family allowances, welfare benefits, public pension benefits, or other cash transfers, as well as the monetized value of any other congestible public services provided on a residence basis, such as education, health, or transportation. Define the *net fiscal benefit* from residing in country *i* as $N_i \equiv B_i - T_i$. The VMP_i curves in Figure 11.1 must be shifted up or down by the amount N_i to show the real incomes of workers in each country, inclusive of fiscal effects. For illustrative purposes, negative values of net fiscal benefits have been assumed in Figure 11.1.[7]

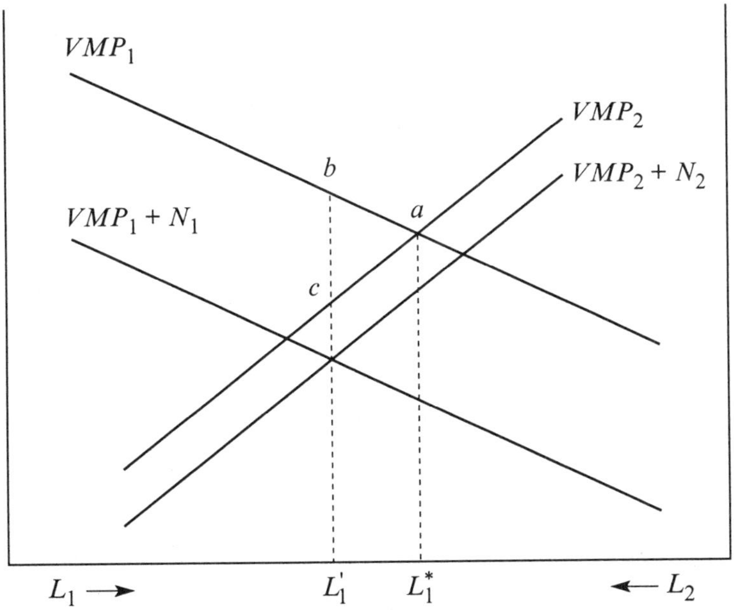

Figure 11.1 The allocation of a fixed amount of labor between two countries

Clearly, the allocation of labor will no longer be efficient if $N_1 \neq N_2$. In the figure, the efficiency loss from fiscal interventions is given by the triangle *abc*, the magnitude of which depends on fiscal differentials $(N_1 - N_2)$ and on the elasticities of demand for labor in each country. Fiscal policies also change equilibrium gross and net factor prices and thus the distribution of income, and, once again, the magnitudes of these effects depend on the demand for labor and the sizes of the net fiscal benefits to workers in each country. A number of theoretical studies discuss the evaluation of fiscal policy and related issues in models of this general form (for example, Wellisch and Wildasin, 1994 and Wildasin, 1991, 1992, 1994, and references therein). They confirm that the elasticities of demand for labor in different countries (the elasticities of the VMP_i

curves) and the net fiscal contributions of workers in different countries (the N_is) are crucial determinants of the allocative and distributional consequences of fiscal policy in a world with mobile labor.

Empirical implementation of a model like that presented in Figure 11.1 is conceptually straightforward. One should measure the slopes or elasticities of the VMP_i curves and the net fiscal benefits accruing to workers in each country. Empirical determination of net fiscal benefits presents several challenges, however. While the benefits and costs of fiscal and other policies can in principle be measured in monetary terms, the actual calculation of the variables N_i can, in practice, be quite difficult. This is especially true on the benefit side – so much so that empirical studies sometimes focus entirely on tax differentials. Omitting the value of the benefits from public expenditure is likely to lead to serious error, however. In fact, as a rough working hypothesis, it is probably reasonable to assume that benefits from public expenditures are of the same order of magnitude as the taxes that finance them.

A second main source of difficulty in taking fiscal variables into account in empirical work on migration is that migration decisions are not costlessly reversible, and are therefore probably made with fairly long planning horizons (Topel, 1986, LaLonde and Topel 1991, and Burda, 1993). The static model of Figure 11.1 can easily be reinterpreted in present-value terms (or in terms of perpetual flows in a stationary equilibrium), in which case the variables N_i represent net fiscal benefits to workers over the relevant horizon – such as a lifetime. This presents a problem for empirical analysis, since the net benefit streams anticipated by potential migrants are not observable. For instance, a 30-year-old Italian who made a permanent move to Germany in 1990 could expect to pay taxes in Germany for a period of several decades. However, neither German taxes in 2020 nor the worker's forecast of those taxes is observable.

The goal of the following empirical analysis is to estimate the net fiscal benefits that accrue to workers who participate in public pension programs in selected EU countries. Public pension policy has been selected for investigation for three main reasons. First, public pensions are quantitatively important in European countries. Social security contributions, a very substantial fraction of which are directed to public pension programs, amounted to about 15–20 percent of GNP in 1986 (the year to which the data analysed here pertain) for most of the countries studied (Eurostat, 1990a). Second, both the benefits from public pensions and the taxes used to support them are mainly pecuniary in nature, substantially obviating the difficulty of determining the subjective evaluation placed by program beneficiaries on program benefits. Third, the impact of these programs on participant households is inherently intertemporal in nature, as are the fiscal impacts of migrants on the programs of both origin and destination countries. This case therefore illustrates how and why an explicit intertemporal accounting for fiscal effects can and should be undertaken.[8]

III PUBLIC PENSIONS AND MIGRATION INCENTIVES AND IMPACTS

Theoretical Framework

To set the stage for the empirical analysis, it is useful to formulate a simple theoretical framework. Suppose that households are life-cycle utility-maximizers who supply labor inelastically and who have utility functions defined over lifetime consumption streams. Retirement occurs with certainty at age R and death occurs with certainty at age D. Assume that every household supplies one unit of labor until retirement, earning the annual wage of w_i if it resides in country i. (For notational simplicity, the present discussion takes this wage as fixed over time; the subsequent empirical analysis allows for time-varying wages.) Assume that the prices of consumption goods are the same in all countries (relative to some common numeraire), let c_t denote the value of consumption in period t of the life cycle, and r denote a fixed market interest rate. In the absence of any government fiscal policy, the household faces a lifetime budget constraint, starting at age 0, of

$$\sum_{t=0}^{D} \frac{c_t}{(1+r)^t} = \sum_{t=0}^{R} \frac{w_i}{(1+r)^t}. \tag{11.1}$$

The budget constraint for an older household is of course identical to (11.1) except that it covers a shorter horizon, beginning at some initial $t_0 > 0$.

To incorporate a public pension program into this framework, suppose that public pensions are financed by proportional payroll taxes, with the tax rate in country i denoted by τ_i. Although a more realistic specification is used in the empirical analysis, assume here for simplicity that the benefit received by a worker in country i is a lump-sum annuity of b_i. Then the budget constraint facing a worker residing in country i becomes

$$\sum_{t=0}^{D} \frac{c_t}{(1+r)^t} = \sum_{t=0}^{R} \frac{(1-\tau_i)w_i}{(1+r)^t} + \sum_{t=R}^{D} \frac{b_i}{(1+r)^t}. \tag{11.2}$$

Public pensions raise lifetime wealth by providing a flow of benefits during retirement, but reduce lifetime wealth by requiring a flow of contributions during the working years. The net effect of the public pension program on lifetime wealth for workers in country i, which (following Feldstein, 1974) is called *net public pension wealth* (*NPPW*), is given by

$$NPPW_i = \sum_{t=R}^{D} \frac{b_i}{(1+r)^t} - \sum_{t=0}^{R} \frac{\tau_i w_i}{(1+r)^t}. \qquad (11.3)$$

Depending on the tax rates and benefit structure of the program, net public pension wealth could be positive or negative.

A household that derives utility only from private good consumption and that faces identical goods prices in all countries will choose to reside in a country where net lifetime wealth is maximal; that is, where the right-hand side of equation (11.2) is as large as possible. Other things the same, higher net public pension wealth makes a country a more desirable place to live. $NPPW_i$ is a measure of the fiscal incentive for a household to reside in country i. This is also a measure of the net fiscal impact, in present-value terms, of having the household reside in the country. If $NPPW_i$ is negative, then (in present-value terms) the country receives more in tax contributions from the household than the benefits that it must pay out, and conversely if $NPPW_i$ is positive.

The next subsection estimates the net public pension wealth for 'representative' workers in several EU member states.

Empirical Findings

Public pension programs in modern societies are large and complex. The public pension benefits and contributions of any one worker or household depend on a wide range of worker and household attributes, including length of life, earnings, marital status, and occupational status. If a worker relocates from one country to another, benefits and contributions will in general depend on all factors relevant for the programs in both countries, and may in addition be subject to special rules that apply to migrants. Thus, there is no one simple measure of the change in net public pension wealth experienced by every worker originating in one country and moving to another. Instead, there are many measures, corresponding to all of the possible circumstances facing every possible kind of worker or household.

The present analysis is limited to some simple central cases, leaving refinements and more comprehensive treatment of the problem for future research. In broad terms, the analysis proceeds by specifying the attributes of the hypothetical worker, then by calculating the present value of lifetime public pension contributions and benefits for this worker conditional on residence in a given country, and finally by calculating how these present values would change if the worker relocated from one country to another.[9]

More specifically, net public pension wealth is calculated for workers whose lifetime average wages are equal to the mean wage in each of the countries analysed.[10] The worker's lifetime earnings are assumed to grow over time in accordance with the estimated effect of experience on the wages of West German workers reported in Krueger and Pischke (1992). (Lifetime earnings streams were also estimated under the alternative assumptions that (a) earnings are constant over the life cycle, and (b) earnings grow at the rates estimated by Mincer (1974) for US workers. The qualitative conclusions are not highly sensitive to these assumptions.) It is assumed that all workers begin working at age 20 and retire at the ages at which they qualify for 'full' retirement benefits. Calculations are presented for workers who migrate either at age 20, that is, at the very beginning of the working lifetime, or at age 40, under the assumption that workers only migrate once during their lifetimes. It is also assumed that each worker lives to an age equal to the conditional life expectancy for the worker's final country of residence (Eurostat, 1989). Workers are assumed either to be single or to be married with a non-working spouse and no children. If married, the spouses are assumed to die at the same age as the worker.

It is necessary to make some assumption about the earnings received by a worker migrating from one country to another. One view would be that the earnings are an attribute of the worker rather than the country, and that (for instance) Italian workers earn less than German workers because they have less human capital. In this view, an Italian worker earning the mean Italian wage who moves to Germany would not be expected to earn the mean German wage, and might instead be assumed to continue to earn the mean Italian wage. An alternative view is that workers have higher earnings in Germany because German firms have more capital or better technology which raise the productivity of labor. In this case, an average Italian worker migrating to Germany would earn the average German wage. Although a case could be made for either of these views, the calculations below assume that workers retain the mean earnings of the country from which they originate. Thus, for example, workers moving from a low-wage to a high-wage country are assumed to continue to receive low wages in the destination country and thus to pay the taxes, and receive the benefits, accruing to a low-wage worker in the destination country.

One difficulty in calculating public pension benefits and contributions arises from the fact that contributions are not, in all countries necessarily specifically earmarked for old-age pensions. Obtaining reasonably comparable data on contribution and benefit rates presents the most formidable data problem for this study, and perforce limits the number of countries investigated to seven: Belgium, Denmark, France, Germany, Italy, Luxembourg, and the Netherlands.[11] Program contribution and benefit formulae are assumed to be time-invariant at their 1986 values.[12]

Consider now a hypothetical worker of age 20 or 40 living initially in one of the seven countries under consideration and following the assumed life-cycle wage profile of a typical manual worker in that country. Using 1986 benefit formulae and contribution rates, it is possible to calculate the present value of this worker's lifetime contributions, pension benefits, and net public pension wealth, contingent on remaining in the country of origin. This net public pension wealth figure is a measure of the fiscal cost to the country of having that worker remain there for the duration of his life, or of the savings that the country would obtain if the worker were to emigrate. (If net public pension wealth is negative, the worker is a net contributor in present-value terms and the country would experience a fiscal loss from the worker's departure.) It is also possible to calculate the present value of contributions, retirement benefits, and net public pension wealth under the assumption that this hypothetical worker relocates to one of the other countries and remains there until death, discounted back either to age 20 or to age 40, as the case may be. For 20-year-old workers, the resulting net public pension wealth figure is both a measure of the benefit to the worker, in present-value terms, of participating in the destination-country public pension program, and the cost, in present-value terms, that an immigrant will impose on the destination country. For 40-year-old workers, the resulting figure shows the net benefit from participating, over the remainder of the life-cycle, in the public pension program of the destination country, taking into account the benefits accrued to the worker from prior participation in the public-pension program of the origin country.

Based on the above calculations, it is finally possible to determine the *change in net public pension wealth resulting from migration*, that is, the difference between net public pension wealth in the destination country of the hypothetical migrant and the net public pension wealth in the origin country. This difference is a measure of the fiscal incentive, in present-value terms, that the public pension program creates for a worker to migrate from one country to another.

The results of these calculations are shown in Tables 11.1 and 11.2. All absolute figures are shown in 1986 ecus, which are approximately equal to 1986 $US; conversion rates between national currencies and the ecu for 1986 are taken from Eurostat (1990b).[13] In addition to showing absolute figures, public pension wealth and wealth changes have been expressed as percentages of the lifetime wealth of the workers being analysed. (For 40-year-old workers, 'lifetime wealth' means the present value of earnings from age 40 to retirement, discounted back to age 40.) Table 11.1 presents the estimated net public pension wealth for workers who remain in their host countries.[14]

The figures in Table 11.1 show how much the hypothetical workers would gain, in present value terms, from continuing to participate in the public pension programs in their origin countries until death. It is not altogether obvious what metric to use in deciding whether these amounts are large or small, and for the main purpose of this paper, the absolute value of *NPPW* in each country is less important than international variations in *NPPW*. Nevertheless, the estimates in Table 11.1 do suggest that the impact of participation in public pension programs on the lifetime wealth of representative may be large and, in most instances, negative. In fact, the public pension programs in many of these countries may lower lifetime wealth by as much as one to five years' worth of earnings. However, there are substantial differences among these countries. The Netherlands stands out as having a strongly negative net public pension wealth. In Denmark and France, the reduction in lifetime wealth from the public pension program is much smaller, and public pension wealth is actually positive for older married workers in Denmark and for all older workers in France and Italy.

Table 11.1 *Net public pension wealth by age and marital status (in ecu and as percentage of lifetime wealth)*

Country	Single age 20	Married age 20	Single age 40	Married age 40
Belgium	–30152	–28224	–20240	–15503
	–13%	–12%	–8%	–6%
Denmark	–11438	–7289	–3707	6701
	–3%	–2%	–1%	2%
Germany	–53059	–53059	–38758	–38758
	–16%	–16%	–11%	–11%
France	–13634	–9652	15558	24786
	–6%	–4%	8%	12%
Italy	–28698	–28698	18173	18173
	–13%	–13%	9%	9%
Luxembourg	–33543	–33543	–15939	–15939
	–11%	–11%	–5%	–5%
Netherlands	–91018	–87810	–84439	–76772
	–31%	–30%	–28%	–25%

Source: Author's calculations

These figures also show the size of the net fiscal burden (generally negative) that each worker imposes on the origin country as a result of continued participation in the public pension program, and thus the size of the fiscal benefit that the country would receive if the worker were to emigrate and sever his links with the host country program. The figures can also be interpreted as showing how much net fiscal burden an immigrant would impose on the given country if he had the same earnings and demographic attributes as a representative native worker in the country. Most countries would experience net fiscal benefits from immigration of workers with average earnings levels, consistent with the pro-immigration policy views of some observers (Straubhaar and Zimmermann, 1993).

One interesting way to describe the magnitude of a worker's net public pension wealth is to relate it to the present value of a worker's earnings, and the figures in Table 11.1 show that net public pension wealth for 20-year-old workers range from –2 percent in Denmark to –31 percent in the Netherlands. This means that participation in the public pension programs in these countries affect the lifetime welfare of young workers in the same way as a 2 percent to 31 percent reduction in earnings. Equivalently, participation in these programs has the same effect on lifetime wealth as a proportional earnings tax at rates ranging from 2 percent to 31 percent. For most countries, this earnings-tax equivalent is greater than 10 percent.

Since the calculations in Table 11.1 just show *NPPW* for a representative worker in each country, they cannot be used directly to compare the position of workers in different countries. Nevertheless, the results in Table 11.1 do suggest that public pension programs affect the lifetime budget constraints of workers in different countries in rather different ways, and that workers could therefore experience gains or losses in public pension wealth by moving from one of these countries to another. They also suggest that the fiscal impact of migration may be significant. Remembering of course that this analysis looks only at the public pension impact of migration, it appears that most countries would reap some fiscal benefit from increased migration of workers with average earnings potential.

Table 11.2 addresses these issues more directly. For each of the seven countries, it shows how *NPPW* changes for a resident worker who migrates to one of the other six countries.[15] To interpret the figures in the table, take first the case of a single Belgian worker age 20. This worker would enjoy an increase in *NPPW* from moving to Denmark, France, Italy, or Luxembourg. The size of this benefit varies by destination country. A young single Belgian worker obtains comparatively little benefit by moving to Italy or Luxembourg, although even 2400 ecu, the change in *NPPW* for a worker moving to Italy, is not negligible, amounting to about 1/3 of the annual earnings of a 20-year-old worker. This worker stands to gain quite a lot (approximately the equivalent of several years' worth of earnings) in moving to France or Denmark. A single young Belgian worker moving to Germany or the Netherlands, on the other hand, is estimated to suffer a loss in lifetime wealth in exiting from the Belgian public pension program and participating in that of one of these countries. The loss is particularly great in the case of a move to the Netherlands, which entails a loss of about 15 percent of lifetime wealth. This is approximately equal to 6 times the initial annual earnings of a 20-year-old worker.

Table 11.2 Changes in net public pension wealth for migrants, by age and marital status (in ecu and as percentage of lifetime wealth)

Migrant from Belgium to:	Single age 20	Married age 20	Single age 40	Married age 40
Denmark	23801	26022	23067	25847
	10%	11%	10%	11%
Germany	–6270	–8198	–5681	–8093
	–3%	–3%	–2%	–3%
France	16653	18706	31718	36126
	7%	8%	13%	15%
Italy	2400	472	22849	22131
	1%	0%	10%	9%
Luxembourg	3896	1968	5044	2412
	2%	1%	2%	1%
Netherlands	–40167	–38887	–40287	–38228
	–17%	–16%	–17%	–16%

Migrant from Denmark to:	Single age 20	Married age 20	Single age 40	Married age 40
Belgium	–37142	–38186	–35397	–35952
	–10%	–10%	–9%	–9%
Germany	–47245	–51394	–45228	–49438
	–12%	–13%	–11%	–12%
France	–10311	–10479	9807	15239
	–3%	–3%	2%	4%
Italy	–33275	–37424	–4483	–4177
	–9%	–10%	–1%	–1%
Luxembourg	–31795	–35944	–28538	–33334
	–8%	–9%	–7%	–8%
Netherlands	–106265	–107206	–107485	–106872
	–28%	–28%	–26%	–26%

Table 11.2 continued

Migrant from Germany to:	Single age 20	Married age 20	Single age 40	Married age 40
Belgium	9134	11942	8371	12205
	3%	3%	2%	3%
Denmark	42906	47055	39957	45740
	12%	14%	11%	13%
France	33394	37375	53756	58883
	10%	11%	15%	17%
Italy	12631	12631	40835	40835
	4%	4%	12%	12%
Luxembourg	14115	14115	14770	14770
	4%	4%	4%	4%
Netherlands	–52672	–49464	–54874	–50615
	–15%	–14%	16%	–15%

Migrant from France to:	Single age 20	Married age 20	Single age 40	Married age 40
Belgium	–16818	–18854	–33923	–38344
	–7%	–8%	–17%	–19%
Denmark	7200	7367	–11038	–12713
	3%	3%	–5%	–6%
Germany	–23152	–27134	–39445	–46300
	–10%	–11%	–19%	–23%
Italy	–14395	–18377	–8958	–14085
	–6%	–8%	–4%	–7%
Luxembourg	–12900	–16882	–28849	–35928
	–5%	–7%	–14%	–18%
Netherlands	–57460	–58234	–74283	–76663
	–24%	–24%	–37%	–38%

Table 11.2 continued

Migrant from Italy to:	Single age 20	Married age 20	Single age 40	Married age 40
Belgium	–2482	–489	–30995	–28274
	–1%	–0%	–15%	–14%
Denmark	22063	26212	–8731	–2948
	9%	11%	–4%	–1%
Germany	–8967	–8967	–36025	–36025
	–4%	–4%	–17%	–17%
France	14739	18721	9171	14298
	6%	8%	4%	7%
Luxembourg	1494	1494	–25851	–25851
	1%	1%	–12%	–12%
Netherlands	–44265	–41057	–71323	–67064
	–18%	–17%	–34%	–32%

Migrant from Luxembourg to:	Single age 20	Married age 20	Single age 40	Married age 40
Belgium	–4519	–2087	–5822	–2500
	–2%	–1%	–2%	–1%
Denmark	25008	29157	21381	27163
	8%	10%	7%	9%
Germany	–12435	–12435	–12599	–12599
	–4%	–4%	–4%	–4%
France	16503	20484	37659	42786
	5%	7%	12%	14%
Italy	–1489	–1489	26463	26463
	–0%	–0%	9%	9%
Netherlands	–57114	–53906	–58413	–54154
	–19%	–18%	–19%	–18%

Table 11.2 continued

Migrant from Netherlands to:	Single age 20	Married age 20	Single age 40	Married age 40
Belgium	52 817	52 050	54 482	52 977
	18%	17%	18%	17%
Denmark	82 445	83 386	83 194	83 641
	27%	28%	27%	28%
Germany	44 871	41 663	46 833	42 289
	15%	14%	15%	14%
France	73 915	74 689	90 748	93 607
	25%	25%	30%	31%
Italy	55 857	52 649	79 511	77 243
	19%	17%	26%	25%
Luxembourg	57 346	54 138	60 317	55 479
	19%	18%	20%	18%

Source: Author's calculations

The sign and magnitude of the change in public pension wealth differ by age, marital status, and origin/destination country pairs. Certain patterns are fairly clear from the calculations. First, *NPPW* is low in the Netherlands and workers generally experience a fiscal benefit from leaving there and are harmed if they move there. This seems to be due mainly to the high contribution rates in the Netherlands. Young workers can generally raise their *NPPW* by moving to Denmark, typically experiencing increases in lifetime wealth of 10 percent or more in doing so; young Danish workers are estimated to sacrifice around 10 percent or so of lifetime wealth in moving to most of the other countries analysed. These changes in *NPPW* are generally on the order of 3–5 years' worth of earnings at the beginning of the life-cycle. The differentials in *NPPW* for young workers moving among France, Germany, and Italy are somewhat smaller; these differentials typically amount to less than 10 percent of lifetime wealth.

The calculations in Table 11.2 also show how much a 40-year-old worker would gain or lose upon moving from one country to another, under the assumption that public pension contributions and benefits are determined in accordance with EU rules.[16] The changes in *NPPW* are expressed both in absolute terms (ecu) and as a percentage of lifetime wealth as of age 40 (that is, as a percentage of the present value of earnings from age 40 to retirement). In most cases, the results are quite similar to those for 20-year-old workers. However, pension benefits in both France and Italy are more closely tied to earnings in the immediate preretirement period than in the other countries considered. As a result, a move to France or Italy is generally more attractive (or less unattractive) for older workers than for younger ones. For instance, while a move to Italy raises the lifetime wealth of a young single Belgian worker by 2400 ecu, a 40-year-old single Belgian worker's lifetime wealth rises by almost 23 000 ecu upon moving to Italy. Differences of this magnitude for old vs. young migrants to France or Italy are typical in the calculations presented in Table 11.2.

IV EVALUATING CHANGES IN PUBLIC PENSION POLICY

The estimates in Tables 11.1 and 11.2 suggest that public pension programs can create large fiscal incentives for intra-EU migration and that intra-EU migration can have large fiscal and welfare impacts. Those estimates could, in principle, be used for a variety of econometric and policy applications. As an illustration of one of several possible applications, this section shows how these estimates can be used to evaluate the welfare impact of changes in public pension policy undertaken by a single country. The exercise is only illustrative since, as might be expected and as will be made clear, such policy changes are likely to involve intergenerational transfers that are best analysed in an explicitly dynamic setting, an exercise for which estimates like those presented here are necessary but which also requires the development of a model that goes beyond the scope of the present paper.[17] The more modest objective here is to show how estimates of net public pension wealth presented above can be used for one type of policy analysis and to get some sense of the potential quantitative importance of such estimates for policy evaluation. This can usefully be done within the framework of a simple static general equilibrium model.

Suppose that an EU country is considering some change in its public pension policy. A change in policy will make the country more or less attractive to potential migrants and thus will change the international allocation of labor. How should this effect be taken into account in assessing the impact of the policy on national welfare? An answer to this question clearly presupposes some measure of economic welfare. This concept is intrinsically ambiguous when population is subject to change, either by migration or through fertility and mortality, since it is difficult to know whose welfare is to be taken into account. Although other alternatives might be of interest, I assume for the present analysis that there is some initial population of workers and owners of other factors of production in country i, and that it is the real incomes of these individuals that 'matter' for economic welfare. To use this concept of welfare to evaluate public pension policy, it is convenient to make several simplifying assumptions.

Let L_{it} be the number of workers employed in country i of age t, where $t = y$ corresponds to 'young' workers and $t > y$ represents older workers. Assume that the supply of young workers to country i is perfectly elastic at an externally given net lifetime income of $\overline{w}_y$. (Note that this assumption does not require migration costs to be zero.) All other workers are completely immobile. Let L_{it}^0 be the number of workers of age t initially employed in country i. Assume that there is no unemployment or that the amount of unemployment is invariant to public pension policy, so that $L_{it} \equiv L_{it}^0$ for all $t > y$. Assume that national output is an increasing concave function $F_i(L_i)$ of total employment $L_i = \Sigma_t L_{it}$, implying that workers of all ages are equally productive and that labor is the only variable input in the production process. Since net public pension wealth is estimated generally to be negative, participation in the public pension system is on net like a tax on workers. Thus, let τ_{it} be the *negative* of net public pension wealth for workers of age t expressed as a proportion of lifetime earnings, corresponding to the percentage estimates that appear in Table 11.1. Assuming no distortions in the labor market other than those created by the public pension system, the (lifetime) net income of a worker of age t is (the present value of) $(1 - \tau_{it})F_i'(L_i)$ and the (present value of) net income to owners of other factors of production is (the present value of) $F_i(L_i) - L_iF_i'(L_i) + \Sigma_t\tau_{it}F_i'(L_i)L_{it}$, where the latter expression incorporates the government budget constraint. National welfare is the sum of net incomes across all initial workers and owners of other factors of production, which adds up to

$$W_i = F_i(L_i) + (1 - \tau_{iy})F_i'(L_i)(L_{iy}^0 - L_{iy}), \tag{11.4}$$

making use of the assumption that only the young are mobile. Note from (11.4) that changes in the net public pension wealth of older workers through changes in the policy parameters $\tau_{it}, t > y$, has no effect on national welfare, though of course it would affect the distribution of income.[18] Suppose that there is a change in the public pension program that affects the net public pension wealth of young workers and thus τ_{iy}. Using the equilibrium condition for mobile workers,

$$(1 - \tau_{iy})F_i'(L_i) = \overline{w}_y, \tag{11.5}$$

one can solve for L_i as a decreasing function of τ_{iy}. It is straightforward to calculate the change in W_i per unit change in τ_{iy} from (11.4) and (11.5). However, the resulting expression involves absolute magnitudes that depend, for instance, on the size of the work force. This is unsurprising, since W_i itself depends on the size of the economy. A more useful way to express the impact of changes in public pension policy is to compare the welfare change with the size of policy change measured in revenue terms. Define $R_{iy} \equiv \tau_{iy}F_i'L_{iy}$ to be the net fiscal burden that the public pension system imposes on each young worker. A change in τ_{iy} will affect both W_i and R_{iy}, and one can then calculate the impact of a change in policy on welfare relative to the size of the change in net fiscal contributions. This normalizes the absolute size of the welfare change, showing the change in welfare, expressed in ecu, per l-ecu change in the net fiscal contributions of the young. It is easily shown (see Appendix) that

$$\frac{dW_i}{dR_{iy}} = \frac{\tau_{iy}\varepsilon_i}{\sigma_i + \tau_{iy}\varepsilon_i} \tag{11.6}$$

where $\varepsilon_i < 0$ is the demand elasticity for labor and σ_i is the proportion of young workers in the labor force. For this expression to make sense, it is important that the fiscal burden on mobile workers not be so high that an increase in the burden per worker would actually decrease total contributions. Provided that this is the case, $sgn\{dW_i/dR_{iy}\} = -sgn\{\tau_{iy}\} = -sgn\{R_{iy}\}$, that is, moving the net public pension contribution of mobile workers closer to zero is always welfare-improving. (This result is well-known in the literature on tax competition and, fundamentally, is just a restatement of the standard optimal tariff argument in the context of a small jurisdiction trading in inputs rather than outputs.) In particular, if mobile workers are net fiscal contributors, national welfare can be increased by lowering their fiscal burden.

With values of τ_{iy} drawn from the Table 11.1 estimates for 20-year-old workers, it is only necessary to add estimates of the demand elasticity of labor and the proportion of young in the population to use (11.6) in calculating the impact on national welfare of a l-ecu increase in the fiscal contributions of young workers. Suppose, for example, that a change in pension policy increases the fiscal contribution of 50 percent of the work force, so that $\sigma_i = 0.5$. The appropriate value for the demand elasticity, ε_i, depends on the production technology, particularly the substitutability between the mobile and immobile factors of production. For example, if the production function exhibits unitary elasticity of substitution between labor and other inputs and overall constant returns to scale, the elasticity of demand for mobile labor is $-1/(1 - \alpha_i)$ where α_i is the income share of mobile labor in country *i*.[19] If labor accounts for two-thirds of national income and the elasticity of substitution between labor and other inputs is equal to 1, the demand elasticity ε_i would be –3. If either the substitution elasticity or the income share of labor is lower, the demand elasticity ε_i is also lower.

Table 11.3 presents calculations of the welfare change per ecu increase in fiscal contributions by 'young' workers, for both low and high values of the demand elasticity of labor (–1 and –3, respectively) and for values of τ_{iy} based on Table 11.1's estimates of *NPPW* as a percentage of lifetime wealth for workers of different ages and marital status. To take an illustrative entry, the figure of –0.35 in the first row of the 'Single, Age 20' column for Belgium means that if the initial contribution rate of young workers is equal to the figure of –0.13 shown in the corresponding entry of Table 11.1, then an increase in this contribution rate sufficient to raise an extra 1 ecu of net contributions from all young workers would lower national welfare by 0.35 ecu, assuming that the demand elasticity of labor were –1. The figure of –3.58 in the second row of the same column shows that the welfare loss would be much higher if the demand elasticity of labor were –3.

Table 11.3 Marginal welfare cost of increase in fiscal burden on young workers (per ecu)

		Worker type used to estimate public pension burden					
Country	Elasticity of labor demand	Single age 20	Married age 20	Single age 40	Married age 40	Mean Single	Mean Married
Belgium	–1	–0.35	–0.32	–0.20	–0.15	–0.27	–0.23
	–3	–3.58	–2.73	– 1.03	–0.63	– 1.81	– 1.27
Denmark	–1	–0.06	–0.04	–0.02	0.03	–0.04	–0.00
	–3	–0.22	–0.13	–0.06	0.09	–0.13	–0.01
Germany	–1	–0.46	–0.46	–0.29	–0.29	–0.37	–0.37
	–3	–16.96	– 16.96	–2.00	–2.00	–4.14	–4.14
France	–1	–0.14	–0.10	0.13	0.20	0.01	0.07
	–3	–0.61	–0.37	0.31	0.42	0.04	0.19
Italy	–1	–0.35	–0.35	0.15	0.15	–0.04	–0.04
	–3	–3.51	–3.51	0.34	0.34	–0.15	–0.15
Luxembourg	–1	–0.30	–0.30	–0.12	–0.12	–0.20	–0.20
	–3	–2.21	–2.21	–0.46	–0.46	–1.01	–1.01
Netherlands	–1	–1.64	– 1.49	– 1.25	–1.02	–1.43	– 1.23
	–3	na	na	na	na	na	na

Source: Author's calculations.

Moving across the columns for Belgium in Table 11.3 corresponds to using different values for the initial fiscal burden of the public pension program. Since all countries are assumed to have identical shares of young workers in the workforce, moving across rows for different countries for a common value of the labor demand elasticity also corresponds to using different values for the initial fiscal burden. In general, the lower the initial burden, the lower the marginal welfare impact of a change in public pension policy, as standard principles of second-best welfare economics would lead one to expect. Since one-half of the work force is assumed to be 'young' for the purposes of this calculation, neither the contribution rates for 20-year-olds nor those for 40-year-olds represent the contribution rate for 'average' young workers. In principle, *NPPW* could be calculated for each age cohort, and the resulting contribution rates could then be weighted by the proportion of workers in each age cohort. For simplicity, the last columns of Table 11.3 illustrate what happens when the fiscal contribution rates are the simple arithmetic average of the figures for 20- and 40-year-olds. The estimates in these columns show that the assumed marital status of workers is not very important for estimating the welfare cost of changes in public pension policy.

There are two major conclusions to draw from the figures in Table 11.3. First, the estimated welfare cost of increases in the public pension contributions of young workers may vary quite a bit among countries because their initial burdens differ significantly. Focusing on the last two columns of the table, it appears that the marginal welfare cost of an increase in contributions by young workers is relatively high in Belgium, Germany, Luxembourg, and especially the Netherlands.[20] For France, Italy, and Denmark, the welfare impact of an increase in contributions is relatively small, and in the case of France, it is positive, implying that 'average young immigrants' receive a net subsidy from participation in the public pension system and that national welfare would be increased by an increase in pension contributions. Second, the welfare effect of changes in public pension policy is sensitive to the assumed value of the labor demand elasticity. Particularly in countries where there is a substantial loss associated with increases in pension contributions, the magnitude of the loss can be much higher when the demand elasticity is high. Since long-run elasticities can greatly exceed short-run elasticities, these findings raise interesting issues about myopic and far-sighted policy evaluation and time consistency of policy. A proper analysis of these issues, however, requires a model with explicit dynamics.

The calculations in Table 11.3 are only illustrative but they demonstrate convincingly that public pension policy may well cause significant distortions in labor allocations and that there may be substantial international differences in the magnitudes of these distortions.

V CONCLUSION

Differentials in the net benefits from public pensions, along with other policies such as income taxes and public service provision, alter the pay-off to migration and can influence the international allocation of labor. These tax/transfer/public service 'wedges' can cause inefficient locational choices, create deadweight welfare losses, and alter the distribution of income through changes in equilibrium factor prices. The prospect of such effects may constrain countries in their policy choices. In particular, they may find it advantageous to limit the redistributive dimensions of their policies in order to reduce the extent of fiscally-induced migration and to limit the fiscal impact of such migration as does occur. Alternatively, they may choose to tailor their fiscal policies in order to select for immigrants with favorable attributes and to encourage emigration of households with unfavorable attributes.

An essential first step in empirical application of standard theoretical models is the identification of the net fiscal benefits and costs facing households who move from one jurisdiction to another. The empirical analysis in section III suggests that public pension programs in EU member states can have significant effects on the lifetime wealth of representative workers, perhaps reducing lifetime wealth by 10–15 percent or even more in typical cases. It also suggests that public pension programs create fiscal differentials in the treatment of workers in different countries, some of non-negligible size. These differentials imply that potential migrants can often raise or lower their lifetime net wealth by 5–15 percent or even more by moving between certain countries. These differentials create fiscal incentives for inefficient labor allocation and give rise to significant fiscal impacts from migration. The calculations in section IV suggest that welfare in several countries would be increased by reductions in the public pension burdens on young workers. This of course raises a policy dilemma since most public pension programs are underfunded and there are therefore pressures to *raise* fiscal burdens on workers rather than *lower* them.[21] The results in section IV also indicate that the welfare effects of changes in public pension policy differ substantially among countries. Efforts toward harmonization of public pension systems that would lower fiscal burdens in countries where these burdens are high while raising those in countries with low burdens are low might generate overall welfare gains, but would not necessarily be pareto-improving, unless accompanied by appropriate international compensatory transfers.

Empirical research on migration commonly assumes that migration decisions are heavily influenced by earnings differentials. Since the public sector accounts for about half of GDP in Western Europe, however, one should presume that fiscal variables may also play a crucial role in determining the magnitude and direction of migration. If the estimates of *NPPW* presented above are even approximately correct, participation in public pension programs is an important determinant of the net benefits or costs of migration among EU countries. One might therefore wish to include international differences in *NPPW* as explanatory variables in econometric analyses of migration. Indeed, according to the simple life-cycle hypothesis (ignoring liquidity constraints and other complications), *NPPW* should have the same effect on migration choices as differences in gross lifetime wealth. This is a testable hypothesis.

It must be noted, however, that a regression model that uses only *NPPW* would ignore all other fiscal variables that might influence migration; these other variables might or might not be well proxied by *NPPW*. The present investigation should be viewed as a sort of pilot study. Further research is clearly needed to provide a better empirical basis for the analysis of policy issues relating to migration and fiscal policy in the EU. Part of the agenda is to consider the implications for migration of other fiscal policies – income taxes, VAT, family allowances, or quality of public service provision – that have been ignored here. Empirical analysis of other fiscal policies could be combined with the present results to provide more satisfactory estimates of the net fiscal benefits accruing to migrants among EU countries.

The estimates of net public pension wealth in the seven countries analysed here provide, at best, a reasonable comparison of public pension benefits and costs for a subset of worker types, namely those who are young or middle-aged and who have average earnings. A valuable extension of the present analysis would be to investigate the public pension implications of migration for other worker types: those who are nearing retirement, those who are some distance away from the mean of the wage distribution, or those who may be unemployed, disabled, or sick. A more complete evaluation of public pension programs, and of social insurance programs more generally, remains to be undertaken.

Perhaps the most interesting extension of the present study would be to expand the number of countries analysed to include some of the poorer members of the EU, such as Spain, Portugal, and Greece. In view of the current controversies surrounding immigration from Eastern Europe and the possible membership of East European countries in the EU, inclusion of these countries would also be very valuable, though of course the fiscal systems of these countries are in such flux that calculations based on them must at best be viewed as provisional.

APPENDIX

This Appendix details the derivation of equation (11.6) in the text. First, substitute from (11.5) into (11.6). Then

$$\frac{dW_i}{d\tau_{iy}} = \left(F_i' - \overline{w}_y\right)\frac{dL_i}{d\tau_{iy}}. \tag{11.1A}$$

Solving (11.5) implicitly for L_i in terms of τ_{iy},

$$\frac{dL_i}{d\tau_{iy}} = \frac{F_i'}{\left(1-\tau_{iy}\right)F_i''}, \tag{11.2A}$$

and hence, using (11.5) in (11.1A),

$$\frac{dW_i}{d\tau_{iy}} = \frac{\tau_{iy}\left(F_i'\right)^2}{\left(1-\tau_{iy}\right)F_i''}. \tag{11.3A}$$

Next, note that

$$\frac{dR_{iy}}{d\tau_{iy}} = F_i' L_{iy} + \tau_{iy}\left(L_{iy}F_i'' + F_i'\right)\frac{dL_i}{d\tau_{iy}}. \tag{11.4A}$$

Substituting from (11.2A) into (11.4A) and using (11.3A),

$$\frac{dW_i}{dR_{iy}} \equiv \frac{dW_i / d\tau_{iy}}{dR_{iy} / d\tau_{iy}}$$

$$= \frac{\tau_{iy}\left(F_i'\right)^2}{\left(1-\tau_{iy}\right)F_i''F_i' L_{iy} + \tau_{iy}\left(L_{iy}F_i'' + F_i'\right)F_i'}$$

$$= \frac{\tau_{iy}F_i'}{F_i'' L_{iy} + \tau_{iy}F_i'}$$

$$= \frac{\tau_{iy}\left(F_i' / L_i F_i''\right)}{L_{iy} / L_i + \tau_{iy}\left(F_i' / L_i F_i''\right)}$$

$$= \frac{\tau_{iy}\varepsilon_i}{\alpha_i + \tau_{iy}\varepsilon_i}$$

which is (11.6). The last step uses the fact that

$$\varepsilon_i = \frac{F_i'}{L_i F_i''}.$$

NOTES

* Earlier versions were presented at the University of Illinois, Chicago and at the meetings of the Regional Science Association and of the European Society for Population Economics. I

am grateful to participants for comments, and to D. Dudley and to H.S. Brown III for assistance in carrying out the calculations. I am also grateful to A. Panagariya and R. Schwab for helpful comments. I retain responsibility for errors.

1. Oates (1968) discusses local distribution and returns to this issue in Brown and Oates (1987). Mobility of capital as well of households limits the ability of local government to redistribute income. Similarly, mobility of capital, as well as of households, can drive local governments to pursue policies that promote allocative efficiency, an idea developed, for example in Oates and Schwab (1988).
2. State grants to local school districts have emerged partly as a response to litigation aimed at equalizing the level of local finance for education. Inman and Rubinfeld (1979) survey many of the key economic and legal issues in the local school finance debate in the US. The allocative and distributional impacts of various forms of equalizing transfers from higher- to lower-level governments have been the focus of sustained attention in the literature of school finance and fiscal federalism. See Ladd and Yinger (1994), 0akland (1994), and Reschovsky (1994) for a recent symposium discussion and references to relevant literature. It is worth noting that the analysis of equalizing transfers has long been of interest to scholars in Canada (see, for example, Boadway and Flatters, 1982 and Boadway and Hobson, 1993), no doubt because of their importance in a country where interprovincial transfers are a major and controversial component of the overall fiscal system.
3. The EU countries face a number of policy issues that affect labor and capital mobility. These include not only the accession of new member states, but liberalization of labor market regulations, control of illegal immigration, and refugee policy.
4. The empirical relevance of labor mobility, in Europe and elsewhere, is a topic of debate. Several points deserve brief mention. (1) Labor mobility alters the allocative and distributional consequences of redistributive policy even if migration is costly. (2) What matters for policy is whether *some* labor is mobile at the margin, not whether all labor is mobile. (3) Labor is more mobile over long than short periods. In the present context, the time horizon of the analysis is on the order of a lifetime or generation. (4) The observed level of migration is not a reliable indicator of the extent of potential labor mobility, both because the level of observed migration is an equilibrium-adjustment phenomenon and because governments can, and do, pursue policies that artificially limit migration. Indeed, concerns about migration may well explain why the EU acted quickly to allow rich nations like Austria or the Nordic countries to become members but refused membership to Turkey. In such circumstances, it would be more accurate to say that policies are selected in order to limit migration than to say that labor is immobile. See Wildasin (1998) for more detailed discussion of empirical aspects of labor mobility.
5. In principle, this could be quite brief or it could extend beyond a single generation; the focus in the present discussion will be on permanent moves by households who do not take into account the welfare of future generations.
6. Note that personal income taxation of *capital* income (such as, capital gains taxation) affects the attractiveness of different tax homes and thus the allocation of *labor* (Wildasin, 1993).
7. Models of this type appear repeatedly in the literature of fiscal federalism. See Flatters et al. (1974) for one important example, and Mieszkowski and Zodrow (1989) and Wildasin (1986) for further discussion and many additional references.
8. Simon (1989, ch. 6), Borjas (1990, ch. 9), and references therein discuss the fiscal impact of immigration in the US. In the US context, attention has tended to focus on the extent to which low-income immigrants take advantage of cash transfers and other direct subsidies for the poor (see also Borjas and Hilton, 1996). The OECD (1987) reports on the annual income tax and social insurance contributions of a typical worker in 23 countries and makes allowance for some cash benefits in the form of family allowances. Very few studies have attempted to quantify the fiscal impact of immigration over a multi-year horizon, although the importance of analysing fiscal policy from such a perspective is widely appreciated (for example, Kotlikoff, 1992).
9. For the sake of brevity, the following paragraphs outline only the essentials of the empirical methodology. Additional details are presented in a longer version of this paper, available on request from the author.

10. Annual earnings are derived from Eurostat (1986, Table 3.6.3) United Nations Statistical Office (1990, p. 16).
11. The principle source for these calculations is the Commission of the European Communities (1988). Contribution rates are those given in Table II-1 for old-age, survivors, and invalidity contributions for Denmark, Germany, Italy, Luxembourg, and the Netherlands. (For Belgium and France, invalidity contribution rates are not separately available and so only the contribution rates for old-age and survivors are used.) Benefit formulae are given in Table VII-1.
12. There are many plausible hypotheses that one could make about expectation formation for public pension policy (Leimer and Lesnoy [1982]), and calculations of net social security wealth, including those presented here, can be quite sensitive to these assumptions.
13. The ecu was worth US $1.07 in 1986.
14. Present values are calculated using a (real) discount rate of 4 percent.
15. Recall that migration is assumed not to affect a worker's lifetime earnings stream. Thus, *NPPW* for a Belgian worker who migrates to Luxembourg will differ from that shown in Table 11.1 for a native worker in Luxembourg because the earnings of a Belgian worker in Luxembourg differ from that of the native worker. Hence, one cannot determine the change in *NPPW* for migrant workers simply by calculating differences in *NPPW* directly from Table 11.1.
16. See Secretariat of the Administrative Commission of the European Communities on Social Security for Migrant Workers (1989). Essentially, for a worker who is employed in more than one EU public pension system, benefits are determined by the rules of the public pension programs in all of the countries involved. The worker then receives a fraction of benefits from each country, in proportion to the time employed in each country.
17. Homburg and Richter (1993) analyse the efficiency implications of public pensions in an overlapping generations model with mobile labor. Although the basic insights of the simple static model sketched below are fundamentally consistent with the results of the Homburg-Richter analysis, they are able to explore the interactions between migration and feasible pay-as-you-go public pension systems that cannot be captured in a static model.
18. See, for example, von Weizsäcker (1994) for a discussion of the impact of public pension policy on the intergenerational distribution of income, a topic that goes beyond the scope of the present analysis.
19. Let $F_i(L_i) = \mathrm{A}_i L_i^{\alpha_i}$, corresponding to a Cobb–Douglas production function with an income share for labor of α_i. Equilibrium factor pricing implies that the gross wage is equal to $F_i' = \alpha_i A_i L_i^{\alpha_i - 1}$ and the elasticity of demand for labor can then be computed from $\varepsilon_i^{-1} \equiv d \ln F_i' / d \ln L_i = \alpha_i - 1$.
20. The denominator of (11.6) is negative for the Netherlands when the demand elasticity of labor is high; taken literally, this means that a *reduction* in the contribution rate would lead to an increase in total contributions, as well as a welfare gain.
21. For discussion of public pension funding issues in Europe with some reference to migration, see, for example, Marchand and Pestieau (1991).

REFERENCES

Boadway, R.W. and F. Flatters (1982), 'Efficiency and Equalization Payment in a Federal System of Government: A Synthesis and Extension of Recent Results', *Canadian Journal of Economics*, **15**, 613–33.

Boadway, R.W. and P.A.R. Hobson (1993), *Intergovernmental Fiscal Relations in Canada*, Toronto: Canadian Tax Foundation.

Borjas, G. (1990) *Friends or Strangers: The Impact of Immigrants on the U.S. Economy*, New York: Basic Books.

Borjas, G.J. and L. Hilton (1996), 'Immigration and the Welfare State: Immigrant Participation in Means-Tested Entitlement Programs,' *Quarterly Journal of Economics*, **111**, 575–604.

Brennan, G. and J.M. Buchanan (1980), *The Power to Tax: Analytical Foundations of a Fiscal Constitution*, New York: Cambridge University Press.
Brown, C.C. and W.E. Oates (1987), 'Assistance to the Poor in a Federal System', *Journal of Public Economics*, **32**, 307–30.
Burda, M.C. (1993), 'The Determinants of East–West German Migration: Some First Results', *European Economic Review*, **37**, 452–61.
Commission of the European Communities (1988), *Comparative Tables of the Social Security Schemes in the Member States of the European Communities*, 14th edn, Luxembourg: Office for Official Publications of the European Communities.
Eurostat (1986), *Eurostat Review, 1977/86* (Luxembourg).
Eurostat (1989), *Demographic Statistics*, (Luxembourg).
Eurostat (1990a), *General Government Accounts and Statistics, 1970–1987* (Luxembourg).
Eurostat (1990b), *Eurostatistics*, No. 5 (Luxembourg).
Feldstein, M.S. (1974), 'Social Security, Induced Retirement, and Aggregate Capital Accumulation', *Journal of Political Economy*, **82**, 905–26.
Flatters, F., V. Henderson and P. Mieszkowslci (1974), 'Public Goods, Efficiency, and Regional Fiscal Equalization', *Journal of Public Economics*, **3**, 99–112.
Hobson, P.A.R. (1991), 'On the Form of the Locational Efficiency Condition in Local Public Goods Models', *Canadian Journal of Economics*, **24**, 705–9.
Homburg, S. and W. Richter (1993), 'Harmonizing Public Debt and Public Pension Schemes in the European Community', in B. Felderer (ed.), *Public Pension Economics*, Supplementum 7 to *Journal of Economics/Zeitschrift für Nationalökonomie*, Vienna: Springer Verlag, pp. 51–65.
Inman, R.P. and D.L. Rubinfield (1979), 'The Judicial Pursuit of Local Fiscal Equity', *Harvard Law Review*, **92**, 1662–1750.
Kotlikoff, L.J. (1992), *Generational Accounting*, New York: Free Press.
Krueger, A.B. and J.-S. Pischke (1992), 'A Comparative Analysis of East and West German Labor Markets Before and After Unification,' Zentrum für Europäische Wirtschaftsforschung Discussion Paper No. 92-11.
Ladd, H.F. and J. Yinger (1994), 'The Case for Equalizing Aid', *National Tax Journal*, **47**, 211–24.
LaLonde, R.J. and R.H. Topel (1991), 'Labor Market Adjustments to Increased Immigration', in J.M. Abowd and R.B. Freeman (eds), *Immigration, Trade, and the Labor Market*, Chicago: University of Chicago Press, pp. 167–99.
Leimer, D. and S. Lesnoy (1982), 'Social Security and Private Saving: New Time-Series Evidence', *Journal of Political Economy*, **90**, 606–29.
Marchand, M. and P. Pestieau (1991), 'Public Pensions: Choices for the Future', *European Economic Review*, **35**, 441–53.
Mieszkowski, P. and G. Zodrow (1989), 'Taxation and the Tiebout Model', *Journal of Economic Literature*, **27**, 1098–146.
Mincer, J. (1974), *Schooling, Experience, and Earnings*, New York: Columbia University Press.
Musgrave, R.A. (1969), *Fiscal Systems*, New Haven: Yale University Press.
Oakland, W.H. (1994), 'Fiscal Equalization: An Empty Box?' *National Tax Journal*, **47**, 199–210.
Oates, W.E. (1968), 'The Theory of Public Finance in a Federal System', *Canadian Journal of Economics*, **1**, 37–54.
Oates, W.E. (1969), 'The Effects of Property Taxes and Local Public Spending on Property Values: An Empirical Study of Tax Capitalization and the Tiebout Hypothesis', *Journal of Political Economy*, **77**, 957–71.

Oates, W.E. (1972), *Fiscal Federalism*, New York: Harcourt Brace Jovanovich.
Oates, W.E. and R. Schwab (1988), 'Economic Competition Among Jurisdictions: Efficiency Enhancing or Distortion Reducing?', *Journal of Public Economics*, **35**, 333–54.
OECD (1987), *The Tax-Benefit Position of Production Workers*, Paris.
Padoa-Schioppa, T., M. Emerson, M. King, J.-C. Milleron, J. Paelinck, L. Papademos, A. Pastor and F. Scharpf (1987), *Efficiency, Stability, and Equity: A Strategy for the Evolution of the Economic System of the European Community*, New York: Oxford University Press.
Reschovsky, A. (1994), 'Fiscal Equalization and School Finance', *National Tax Journal*, **47**, 185–98.
Samuelson, P.A. (1954), 'The Pure Theory of Public Expenditure', *Review of Economics and Statistics*, **36**, 387–9.
Samuelson, P.A. (1955), 'Diagrammatic Exposition of a Theory of Public Expenditure', *Review of Economics and Statistics*, **37**, 350–56.
Secretariat of the Administrative Commission of the European Communities on Social Security for Migrant Workers (1989), *Guide Concerning the Community Regulations on Social Security*, Brussels.
Simon, J.L. (1989), *The Economic Consequences of Immigration*, Oxford: Basil Blackwell.
Stigler, G.J. (1957), 'The Tenable Range of Functions of Local Government', Joint Economic Committee, *Federal Expenditure Policy for Economic Growth and Stability*, reprinted in E.S. Phelps (ed.) *Private Wants and Public Needs*, Revised edn 1965, New York: Norton, pp. 167–76.
Straubhaar, T. and K.F. Zimmermann (1993), 'Towards a European Migration Policy', *Population Research and Policy Review*, **12**, 225–41.
Tiebout, C.M. (1956), 'A Pure Theory of Local Expenditures', *Journal of Political Economy*, **64**, 416–24.
Topel, R.H. (1986), 'Local Labor Markets', *Journal of Political Economy*, **94** (Part 2), 111–43.
United Nations Statistical Office (1990), *Monthly Bulletin of Statistics*, **44**, No. 6.
von Weizsäcker, R.K. (1994), 'Public Pension Reform, Demographics, and Inequality', Centre for Economic Policy Analysis Discussion Paper No. 978.
Wellisch, D. and D.E. Wildasin (1994), 'Asylum Policy with a Common Labor Market', Vanderbilt University working paper 94-W03.
Wildasin, D.E. (1986), *Urban Public Finance*, New York: Harwood Academic Publishers.
Wildasin, D.E.(1991), 'Income Redistribution in a Common Labor Market', *American Economic Review*, **81**, 757–74.
Wildasin, D.E.(1992), 'Relaxation of Barriers to Factor Mobility and Income Redistribution', in P. Pestieau (ed.), *Public Finance in a World of Transition*, a Supplement to *Public Finance/Finances Publiques*, **47**, 216–30.
Wildasin, D.E. (1993), 'State Income Taxation of Mobile Labor', *Journal of Policy Analysis and Management*, **12**, 51–75.
Wildasin, D.E. (1994), 'Income Redistribution and Migration,' *Canadian Journal of Economics*, **27**, 637–56.
Wildasin, D.E. (1998), 'Factor Mobility and Redistributive Policy: Local and International Perspectives', in P.B. Sorenson (ed.), *Public Finance in a Changing World*, London: MacMillan Press, 151–92.

12. Early American federalism and economic development, 1790–1840

John Joseph Wallis

It is both a pleasure and an honor to contribute to this volume in recognition of Wallace Oates. One of Wally's many contributions to economics is a deeper understanding of how federal governments, governments with several interdependent levels of authority, should and do function. Perhaps at no time in American history were questions about federalism more pressing than in the early nineteenth century. Relations between the national and state government, loosely specified in the Constitution, were in continuous flux and, ultimately, broke down in the Civil War. It was also an era when the appropriate role of the government in promoting economic growth and insuring equality of economic and political opportunity were central political issues at both the national and state level. From independence to the Civil War, state governments had the biggest impact on the course of economic development. In 1840, the states by themselves had incurred debts of roughly $190 million, over 90 percent for investments in canals, railroads, and banks. The federal government had invested $1 885 000 in four canal projects, slightly more than $2 000 000 in stock subscriptions to the National Road, land grants of some 2 500 000 acres, and $7 000 000 in stock in the Second Bank of the United States. Allowing a generous $2 an acre for the National Road lands, federal investment came to only $15 885 000, less than 10 percent of state investment.[1] This is a particularly interesting historical case, since the relative importance of state investment does not appear to be the result of a deliberate decision on the part of politicians to concede the initiative to state governments. Politicians and voters at every level of American government felt that economic development was a good thing and, within reason, pursued policies that promoted development. Why state governments were so active in the early nineteenth century appears to be the result of social and economic influences on the political system, rather than a conscious policy decision.

Why didn't a national, rather than a state system of internal improvement investments develop in the early nineteenth century? It is a natural question for a theory of fiscal federalism to address, a question of assigning functions to different levels of government – a topic that Wally has often written about. Several key elements in a fiscal federalism explanation were operating after 1800.

There were differences in the kind of revenue instruments used by the national and state governments, and these produced differential costs of raising revenues at each level. There were co-ordination problems, since at least part of the gains in building a transportation network were external to the state that built the road, canal, or railroad. These kind of co-ordination problems may be better solved at higher levels of government. Differences in the costs of raising revenues and the benefits of spending money at each level of government did lead to larger state programs, although not always in a simple and direct manner.

In the sections that follow I consider the nature of economic development before the Civil War. One view emphasizes the importance of manufacturing and the development of a national market. This perspective highlights the importance of co-ordination and planning, and suggests that a national system of investments might have been a more efficient choice than the state investments that were actually made. A second perspective emphasizes the importance of agriculture in the early nineteenth century and the impact of investments in transportation and finance on the wealth of farmers through higher land prices and growing markets. This perspective highlights the importance of local initiative in promoting investment projects. Taken together, these two ways of thinking about development show the potential benefits that voters and politicians would receive from building canals and banks. There is no doubt that politicians at both the national and state levels expected that the net benefits from investment would be positive. But the political situation was different in Washington from that in the states. The use of publicly chartered corporations to carry out the investments created much more political opposition at the national than at the state levels.

These political issues were complicated. That Americans hate taxes and do not trust their governments is a fact of political life in the United States. At no time was that more true than after the revolution to gain independence from Great Britain. 'No Taxation without Representation' was an effective rallying cry, and Americans, whatever the causes of the revolution, were worried about the specter of higher taxation raised by British policies after 1763.[2] Anti-tax sentiments were a mixture of ideological and economic interests, as were the strong passions over issues of privilege that dominated the early nineteenth century. The revolution was not only an independence movement; it was a statement about the appropriate role of government in men's lives. A critical element in this was a revolution against privilege, namely, the old kind of privileges the lord of the manor had enjoyed, the privileges that large landowners continued to enjoy, and privileged access to government enjoyed by the wealthy (particularly in an era of substantial property, wealth, or income requirements for voting). Not least of these privileges were those profitable ones that the government conferred on specific groups of individuals through the granting of corporate charters, favorable treatment of claims and land grants, and manipulation of the laws and judicial system. These antagonisms ran deep in early

America, and economic interests were entwined with people's feelings about justice, equity, and community.

Opposition to taxation and privilege were two powerful political forces at work among the American population. The early century's most successful politicians, Jefferson and Jackson, were able to tap directly into that force. But when it came to economic development, the two forces were in conflict. If a state chartered a bank, it could tax the bank or own stock in the bank and receive dividends. This type of 'asset finance' was very attractive, since direct property taxes could be eliminated if a state could produce enough asset income. At the same time, chartering a bank created an obvious grant of privilege to a select group of individuals not shared throughout the community. Weighing the fiscal benefits of chartering a corporation against the political costs of creating identifiable privileges for a select few was a balancing act more readily accomplished at the state than the national level.

I

Economic development produces sustained increases in per capita income, but the process itself is more than income growth. In the nineteenth century it involved the transformation of an agrarian-based economy into one based on a combination of agriculture, manufacturing, transportation, commerce, and finance. Development is a matter of quality as much as quantity, a change in the pattern and texture of everyday life. By 1900, close to half the population lived in urban areas and the cities grew rapidly. Far fewer workers were their own bosses in 1900 than in 1800; wage labor had become the rule. Independent yeomen farmers were becoming a smaller share of the population and labor force. Cities and factories were linked together by an integrated transportation network and a system of production and distribution dominated by a small number of very large corporations. A sophisticated capital market had developed to finance government debt, the debt and equity issues of railroads, and a growing number of manufacturing firms.

Looking back over the nineteenth century from the country's position in 1900, it appears that productivity growth, technological change, and the growth of the manufacturing sector were the central driving forces in the process of development. Opening national markets through improvements in transportation and finance played an instrumental role in releasing these forces, but the creation of an integrated national market faced several obstacles. It was in transportation and finance that government contributed most to the process of development.[3] Many of the most successful new technologies were in industries where products were standardized and mass-produced what became known as the American System of Manufacturing. These products were produced in factories of ever-growing size. Capturing economies of scale required wider markets and lower transportation costs, and investment in more costly plant and equipment required more sophisticated financing.[4] The cost of moving bulky, low-value agricultural products over the mountains was prohibitive, and moving them by water down the Ohio, Mississippi, and through the Caribbean was costly and risky.[5] Commercial credit was essential for moving crops to markets in the land-rich, cash-poor west, for moving manufactured goods from the north-east to the west and south, and moving the cotton crop from the south to Britain and New England. The questions were: who would pay for these canals, railroads, and banks? Who would decide when and where they were built? Who would reap the profits, if any, from these enterprises? Would it be public or private enterprise, and if public, at the national, state, or local level?

The importance of transportation and finance for the development of agriculture has not been overlooked by economic historians.[6] Yet, one can argue that, over time, manufacturers were the major beneficiaries of lower transportation costs and national markets, and that growing specialization and division of labor led to a relative decrease in the importance of agriculture and the number of farmers. Can we assume, therefore, that manufacturing and commercial groups pushed for internal improvement investment and that they played the key role in stimulating investment?[7] Had manufacturing and financial interests been the primary movers behind internal improvements, the geographic concentration of manufacturing and finance in the north-east would have required a complicated interregional compromise to build roads, canals, railroads, and banks in the west and south. Only the national government could have brokered such a deal. North-eastern manufacturers would have had to convince southerners and westerners to build the improvements wanted by the north-easterners. Manufacturers could have agreed to finance these projects by higher national taxes on their products. For example, a constitutional national excise tax on manufactured goods in return for federal transportation projects in the west and south.

This was not an implausible scenario. The Federalist program called for a stronger national government. George Washington argued that a better system of internal transportation would create a more integrated society and work against the centrifugal forces that would pull the union apart. Western states, in particular, courted federal aid for transportation projects. (Banks were more complicated, as I will discuss shortly.) The Congressional act admitting Ohio to the Union reserved 5 percent of the revenues from land sales in Ohio for internal improvements in that state. The money was to be spent under the direction of Congress, not of Ohio.[8] Alexander Hamilton argued for a national system in his *Report on Manufactures* and Albert Gallatin, under Jefferson's direction, produced a plan for an integrated national system in his *Report on Roads and Canals* in 1808. Henry Clay's 'American System' was built around a protective tariff for manufacturing, internal improvements directed by the national government and funded by land sales, and maintenance of the Bank of the United States.[9] Every President from Jefferson to Jackson came out in favor of internal improvements at some point (Jefferson in his second inaugural address in 1805). Those same Presidents occasionally vetoed internal improvement bills, most notably Andrew Jackson, but they continued to sign laws allowing for federal government investment and land grants for banks, canals, and railroads, or in support of state investments in those enterprises.

In the language of fiscal federalism, a national system is a solution to the problems of co-ordination and spillovers. A co-ordinated approach would avoid duplication of facilities and ensure that investments followed the best, or most informed, engineering estimates of cost and productivity. Spillovers occur, for example, because the benefits of roads and canals in Ohio accrue to residents of both Ohio and Pennsylvania, and the level of roads provided by the voters of Ohio would, in general, be lower than the socially optimal level of roads since the Ohio voters were unlikely to tax themselves for the benefits of Pennsylvanians.[10] In short, the argument is that the national government would provide a more efficient system because of co-ordinated planning and a higher level of service because externalities would be internalized.[11]

But a national system did not develop. Despite the presence of a well-articulated plan for national promotion of economic development and a succession of political parties (the Federalists, National Republicans, and the Whigs) who professed support for a national system as one of their stated goals, the United States ended up with a transportation and financial system constructed and operated by small units, chartered, organized, and financed by state governments.

II

Rather than looking back on the nineteenth century from the 1900 position, we can instead look ahead to the prospects for economic development from 1800. Roughly 75 percent of the labor force was directly engaged in agriculture in 1800 (Weiss, 1992, p. 22). It is unlikely that even 10 percent of the labor force was in manufacturing. Most of the non-agricultural labor force was engaged in servicing the agricultural sector directly in transportation, construction, and finance. If the ratio of agricultural to manufacturing employment was 10/1, a 1 percentage increase in the productivity of the average farmer would raise the rate of economic growth as much as a 10 percent increase in the productivity of the average manufacturing worker. Relatively modest increases in farm productivity would prove more important for the growth of the economy than manufacturing improvements well into the nineteenth century. Even though the logic of Jefferson's agrarian empire is not usually put in these quantitative terms, the numbers are consistent with his notion that America was a nation of farmers, and the way the farmers went so went the nation.

Given the relative importance of agriculture, it was by no means clear that improvements in manufacturing alone would determine the direction economic growth would or should take in the early nineteenth century. Indeed, there was every hope that agriculture would enjoy productivity growth as farmers moved over the Appalachians into what was reported, and would ultimately prove to be, some of the best farm land in the world.[12] Not only was the land in the Ohio river valley and the plains beyond more fertile than much of the eastern farm lands, there was a great deal more of it. Output per farmer would rise steadily through the nineteenth century as farmers moved on to more productive land and increased the amount of land per farmer.[13]

Not only were there good reasons for believing that agriculture could play a leading role in economic growth, there were even stronger reasons why farmers, particularly in the west, wanted internal improvements. As an example, suppose that a bushel of wheat sells for $1 in Philadelphia and a pair of shoes sells for $ 1 on the farm. A bushel of wheat weighs 60 pounds and a pair of shoes weighs 2 pounds.[14] If the cost of shipping a ton of wheat and a ton of shoes is $0.20 a mile (roughly the cost of overland hauling by wagon), the cost of shipping a bushel of wheat is $0.006 per mile and a pair of shoes is $0.0002 per mile. If it costs $0.80 to produce a bushel of wheat, the farm can be no further than 33.3 miles from Philadelphia before shipping costs exhaust the profits from moving the wheat. If it costs $0.80 to produce the shoes, on the other hand, they can be shipped up to 500 miles before profits are eliminated. Even at the wagon rates prevailing before canals and railroads were built, eastern manufacturers had access to interior markets for many of their products.

Transportation costs fell rapidly when wagons were replaced by canals and railroads. The most often quoted figure is the decline in the cost of shipping a ton of wheat from Buffalo to New York from $100 a ton to $10 a ton after the opening of the Erie canal. This may understate the overall fall in transportation costs. Wagon rates were typically between $0.15 and $0.20 a mile, while canal and railroad rates were $0.01 or less. Fogel's back of the envelope calculation for 1890 concluded that if a comparison between wagon and railroad costs were used, assuming that wagons costs $0.17 and railroads $0.005 per ton mile, then the cost savings of moving the 1890 crop to market by rail rather than wagon would have saved $2.1 billion, and if other omitted charges were factored into the wagon costs, the savings would be roughly $3 billion, or 25 percent of 1890 GNP.[15]

Going back to the example, if transportation costs fell from $0.20 per ton mile to $0.01 per ton mile, wheat could be profitably shipped 666 miles and shoes 10 000 miles. East/west price gradients for wheat and other grain crops were steeper than those used in the example. In 1859–60 wheat farmers received $0.90

a bushel in Illinois, $1.15 in Ohio, and $1.25 in New York (Atack and Bateman, 1987, p. 233). If the price difference between the farm and city were $0.40 a bushel, then wheat could be shipped 1600 miles by rail or canal, far enough to bring almost all of the west Mississippi within range of eastern cities. At $0.01 per ton mile there would be no measurable east/west price gradient for shoes due to transportation costs: a pair of shoes could be shipped 1000 miles for $0.01, well within any detectable variation in shoe prices.

Not all manufacturers made light commodities like shoes, and some, like ironmasters were as constrained by transportation costs as farmers were. But in general, farmers stood to gain much more from transportation improvements than did manufacturing firms. The effect was magnified by the capitalization of lower transportation costs into land values. Although lower transportation costs would raise the value of a manufacturing firm, the lack of a well developed market for equity in firms would make it difficult for a manufacturer to realize the increase in value. Farmers, on the other hand, were major players in a very active market for land. There is every evidence that transportation improvements were capitalized into land values.[16]

The relationship between farmers and banks was more complicated. Banks were one of the most divisive political issues of the early nineteenth century. Unlike the legions of theorists, economic and otherwise, who favored or opposed the banking system in the United States for macroeconomic and other reasons, popular opposition to banks in the early nineteenth century was grounded in the fact that banks were created by government charters which endowed bankers with privileges denied to other citizens – limited liability and the right to issue bank notes being the most important. Opposition to banks was sociological as much as economic; it was an expression of the popular antagonism to privileges of any kind. Farmers, in general, were not opposed to banks because of what they did. In this regard, the fact that agriculture is a more capital intensive activity than manufacturing is often overlooked. Not only were farmers interested in obtaining loans to acquire and improve farms, they were engaged in a production process with long lead times. Access to credit on favorable terms was important to farmers, particularly to farmers further west who needed (directly or indirectly) access to commercial credit to market their crops.[17]

In short, there were good reasons why farmers supported investments in both transportation and finance. Unlike manufacturers, farmers were not geographically concentrated. There was an agrarian interest in every section of the country that wanted better transportation and finance. The failure of a national political group to put together the concurrent interests of farmers, bankers, merchants and manufacturers into a national coalition producing a national system of internal improvement investments is puzzling. Anticipating the argument that follows in a later section, the lack was due, in part, to the complications of early nineteenth century politics. With the exception of slavery and, perhaps, the tariff, there were no major political issues that produced clear cut divisions within the voting public. There were, however, clear differences in society: urban/rural, manufacturing/agricultural, east/west, north/south, pro-bank/anti-bank, elitist/common man, and republican/democratic (referring to political systems, not political parties). These regional, sectoral, and class differences overlapped sufficiently to preclude stable coalitions of interests. National politics was an exercise in balancing competing interests long enough to put together a winning coalition. No clear and persistent configuration of political parties emerged until the 1830s. Even then the alignment of Whigs and Democrats shifted again in the 1850s when the Whigs were replaced by the Republicans. The coming to power of a purely northern political party, the Republicans, pushed the nation into Civil War.

Support for internal improvements in transportation and finance transcended the more obvious divisions within society; both farmers and manufacturers in different parts of the country were interested. In order to understand why a state system evolved, we need to go back to the Revolution and recall the aversion to taxation that animated the revolution and early American politics. Then we will examine the fiscal implications of banks and transportation improvements. Combined with the chaotic state of national politics, the evolution of a state system of transportation and finance can be explained.

III

During the colonial period Americans were among the most lightly taxed people in the world.[18] The British Empire undertook to provide the colonies with military protection, and because of the threat that French and Spanish influence might diminish loyalty to Britain, the colonists were not asked to pay directly for their own defence. Domestic, or internal, taxation lay largely within the control of the colonial legislatures, subject to the oversight of governors appointed by the Crown and the Board of Trade in London. After 1763, when the British removed the French from Canada (in the process giving substance to their fears that other American colonies might have gone to the French earlier), the British faced a large war debt and for the first time asked the colonies to share part of the cost of their own defense.

Over the next thirteen years the British tried three times to impose higher taxes on the colonies. Each attempt to raise colonial taxation was successfully resisted, and the third resulted in the Revolution. The way in which the British 'bungled' their attempt to raise colonial taxes contributed to the Revolution and the fiscal environment that followed independence.[19] Colonial resistance to the Sugar and Stamp Acts from 1764 to 1766 created a network of contacts and organizations that would successfully resist the Townsend Acts from 1767 to 1770 and the Intolerable Acts after 1774. Had the British not repealed the Stamp Act, later organized resistance might have been less effective. Whatever its causes, the Revolution bequeathed the new United States a legacy of legitimate and successful political organization to oppose taxation.[20]

The colonial attitude toward taxation was reflected in the Articles of Confederation, which forbade the national government from collecting internal taxes. Congress had to requisition funds from the states, an arrangement that proved unwieldy at best. The Revolution was financed largely through debt and currency issues at the national level, leading to a rapid inflation and depreciation of the national currency. The Revolution ended with a weak and poorly organized national government, no effective way for the national government to raise revenues, and a large debt, at both national and state levels.[21]

The Constitution provided solutions to these problems.[22] The Federalists proposed a stronger, but limited, national government with the power to tax, raise armies, regulate foreign affairs, and manage the currency. The national government could not tax exports. Tariffs on imports and indirect taxes (such as excises) would become the main source of federal revenues. Direct taxes (which at the time were primarily poll and property taxes, but included income taxes) could only be apportioned among the states according to population. This meant that any direct taxes the national government levied would be administered and collected by the states, which occurred between 1798 to 1800 and again during the war of 1812.[23] The reserved powers clause and the election of senators by state legislatures (rather than the popular vote) gave states a further check on the national government.

When Congress approved Hamilton's financial program, existing national and state government debt was refunded with new national bonds, and tariff duties were imposed. Bond interest would be the largest single item in the federal budget until 1809 when the threat of hostilities with Britain and France increased War Department expenditures.[24] Tariff revenues would be the mainstay of federal revenues until the Civil War, indeed up until 1917 and implementation of the income tax. One result of Hamilton's plan was to reimburse those states with small debts, which would not benefit from having their existing debt assumed by the federal government, by issuing them federal bonds. A number of states began the national period with a tidy nest-egg.

The nest-eggs were important in several states, and almost every state began accumulating other revenue-producing assets. As unrealistic as it may seem today, the idea that a state might support its expenditures with a combination of investment income and indirect taxes was plausible in the early 1800s. Investment income came primarily from dividends on bank stock, interest on national bonds, land sales, and tolls or dividends from transportation projects such as roads or canals. Indirect taxes included taxes on businesses, fees, and licenses.[25] Voters preferred investment income to indirect taxes and preferred both, by a wide margin, to direct taxes. Ideally, a state could live completely off its capital. This model of 'asset finance' was very attractive politically, for obvious reasons. The hope that federal land sales would provide a steady and lucrative source of federal revenue was based on the same fiscal model.

In practice, asset finance meant living off investment income *and* indirect tax revenue, with no direct taxes. With the exception of wars, the federal government was able to do this throughout the nineteenth century. States were willing to go to great lengths to avoid property and poll taxes, substituting investment income and indirect taxes wherever possible. Maryland and Pennsylvania did not have regular property taxes until the 1840s. New York, Massachusetts, Rhode Island, Delaware, Alabama, Georgia, and South Carolina would all abolish their state property taxes by the mid-1830s (New Jersey would follow in the 1840s.)[26]

The preference for investment income was matched by growing opportunities for states to invest in enterprises. Since states possessed the power to charter corporations, they attracted investment opportunities in prospective enterprises. Banks were the first businesses to seek incorporation in large numbers, and states were interested in promoting the banking industry. In the late eighteenth and early nineteenth centuries Virginia, Maryland, Pennsylvania, New York, Delaware, and Massachusetts all chartered banks and, in the process, acquired significant blocks of bank stock; other states soon followed. Dividends from bank stock formed a small, but significant, part of state revenues. States also charged charter fees to the banks; in some cases the 'bonuses' became a substantial source of revenue as well.[27] Massachusetts, and later Rhode Island, began taxing bank capital. By the 1830s over half of Massachusetts' revenues came from the bank tax. Not surprisingly, Massachusetts encouraged entry into the banking industry and was very liberal in granting charters.[28]

As states began chartering banks, they created the groundwork for popular opposition to banks that would become so prominent by the 1830s. Bank charters were grants of privilege: the right to issue bank notes and some form of limited liability (although often not complete limitations) literally gave bankers the right to print money. The privileges were valuable, as shown by the substantial amounts bankers were willing to pay for charters. Charters were usually issued to wealthy and powerful groups with the capital to start the bank and the political pull to obtain a charter. As Naomi Lamoreaux has shown, once early New England Banks were chartered, the banks were likely to serve the larger commercial community by discounting commercial paper, but they focused their longer term investments in enterprises controlled by the board of directors.[29] This 'insider lending' raised the ire of businessmen, small and not so small, who were on the outside such as farmers. They naturally, and correctly, claimed that the bank charters conferred privileges on the bankers which were not available to everyone. When these middle-class groups were agitated about banks, it was relatively easy to convince landless laborers, either urban or rural, that banks were monsters of privilege which controlled the economy and their livelihoods in mysterious ways. Such was the popular discontent that Jackson tapped into in his campaign against the Second Bank of the United States.

The national government had chartered the (First) Bank of the United States in 1791. The bank acted as the depository for Treasury funds and, with branches throughout the country, accumulated large amounts of state bank notes in the course of its daily business. The bank, while not conceived as a central bank, did regulate the currency by design or inadvertence through its policy of holding or redeeming state bank notes. Jeffersonian Republican opposition to the bank resulted in its charter not being renewed in 1811, although Jefferson's Treasury Secretary, Gallatin, had argued for its renewal. The country entered the war of 1812 without a federal bank and the government experienced extreme difficulties in financing the war. These problems were exacerbated by regional tensions. New Englanders and New England banks were unwilling to subscribe to federal bond issues because of their opposition to the war. Shortly after the end of the war, in 1817, the Republicans chartered the (Second) Bank of the United States. After a rocky start, the Second Bank became the dominant financial institution in the country. The campaign to renew its charter in 1832 (the charter expired in 1836) and its aftermath played a central role in the politics of the early 1830s. Jackson vehemently opposed the Bank and vetoed the charter renewal (the 'Bank War.') In 1836 the Bank of the United States was dissolved and reformed under a Pennsylvania state charter.

The importance of banks to state revenues is often forgotten in this history.[30] States chartered and regulated banks, partly because it served powerful interest groups which owned the banks, partly because of popular demands for a larger currency circulation, and partly because it brought money into state coffers without raising taxes. These effects operated in all parts of the country. When Florida, Mississippi, Louisiana, and Arkansas defaulted on their state debts in 1841 and 1842, it was on debts incurred in purchasing bank stock (Alabama narrowly averted default). Indiana and Missouri had monopoly state banks by the 1830s. State chartered banks in Ohio held so much state debt that they, along with Barings Bank in London, continued to loan the state funds in the early 1840s to protect their investments, while other states were defaulting. Indeed, almost every state had some relationship with banking, although few states derived revenues as substantial as Massachusetts and Rhode Island.[31]

The relationship between transportation improvements and state finances has been studied in more detail.[32] The fiscal success of the Erie Canal, undertaken completely by the state of New York, begun in 1817 and completed in 1825, was matched by its economic and geographic importance in opening up a water route to the west. Tolls on the Erie began flowing into the Canal Fund accounts years before the canal was completed, as produce from farms in upstate new York began flowing through Albany down the Hudson to New York. Ohio began its canal network in 1825, and within a few years it too was returning a handsome dividend to the state treasury.[33] The next two states to launch transportation improvements were not so lucky. Pennsylvania began its canal in 1826 and Maryland in 1828; both canals proved to be financial disasters. Virginia substantially expanded its public works projects in 1831. Massachusetts began a successful investment in the Western Railroad in 1830. Illinois, Indiana, Michigan, Georgia, North Carolina, South Carolina, Tennessee, and Kentucky would all begin more or less ambitious rail and/or canal projects between 1835 and 1837.[34] Some projects would fail spectacularly, others would scrape by, and some would prove to be profitable investments.

It may be noted that of the 26 states in the Union by 1840, only Connecticut, New Hampshire, Maine, Vermont, and New Jersey have not been mentioned as having significant connections either with transportation or banking improvements. In Connecticut, the cities of New Haven, Hartford, Bridgeport, and Norwich were involved in railroad promotion (Goodrich, 1960, pp. 130–31). New Jersey tapped related sources of revenue such as corporate charters and railroads (Cadman, 1949). Vermont made an abortive try to run a state bank in 1806 (Hammond, 1957, p. 166). Maine established a Board of Internal Improvement in 1834, but it took no action and, in 1848 the state constitutionally bound itself to undertake no internal improvements. But in 1845 the city of Portland invested $1 000 000 in the Atlantic and St Lawrence Railroad, and the investment was later doubled (Goodrich, 1960, pp. 132–3). With the exception of the remote reaches of New England, there was not a part of the country where banks, railroads, or canals were not being provided by eager state governments. Perhaps the enthusiasm was overdone – by 1841 eight states and the territory of Florida were in default on their debts – but it was not lacking. The lure of asset financing was a strong one, particularly to states in the west who lacked the level of business activity to support indirect taxation. For them it was investment income or property taxation. This may be the simplest reason why a national system of transportation and finance did not develop – states were already developing it – but there are more reasons.

IV

American politics is always complicated, but in no period was it more complicated than the era between the Revolution and the Civil War. The list of antagonistic interests that could serve as salient organizing issues was long: urban versus rural, slave states versus free states, manufacturing versus agriculture, pro-tariff versus free traders, pro-national government versus pro-state government, and public land states versus non-public land states. Some issues divided the country east and west, others divided the country north and south, and some were not geographic. It was a classic example of multiple voters with multiple preferences over multiple issues. What resulted was cycling: transitory coalitions supporting a mix of policies, policies that changed marginally and continuously as the losing coalition tried to lure away enough of the majority coalition to gain power. The outcome was a mélange of Federalists, Republicans, National Republicans, Democratic Republicans, and Whigs together with an assortment of Antimasonics, Locofocos, and Know Nothings. Although stable national parties emerged at the end of the 1 830s in the form of the Whigs and Democrats, political coalitions would be in flux up until the Civil War.

The 'new political historians' have made this point with a different emphasis. They stress the inability of simple sectional or economic interests to explain much of the pattern of voting in the early nineteenth century, be it voting for political office or the voting of legislators at the state and federal level.[35] Political party affiliation seems to explain a much larger portion of the variance across individual voters and legislators than any other identifiable interests. By the 1840s, at the latest, parties had become the central organizing force in American politics, but even then their configuration was still changing. No party alignments lasted more than twenty-five years before the Civil War. In part, this was the result of attempts by national leaders to prevent the division of parties along straightforward, geographical, and sectional division between the north and the south. Such a division would prove mortally dangerous to the union when it finally appeared in 1860.

One of the organizing principles for the parties and coalitions that did emerge was the ongoing debate over the proper role of the national and state governments. The conflict was often over the proper role of each level of government in promoting economic development, for in no area of national/state relations were the issues of jurisdiction and responsibility more apparent than in banking and transportation. In *McCulloch v Maryland* (1819) the issue was whether the state of Maryland had the right to tax the Second Bank of the United States.[36] The Supreme Court decided it did not. In *Gibbons v. Ogden* (1824), the issue was steamboats and whether the states of New York and New Jersey could grant monopoly privileges to steamboat companies operating within and between the states, or whether any vessel with a national coasting license could carry passengers between states. The Supreme Court decided that the states did not have the power to restrict interstate trade in that way.

As I have emphasized already, politicians on both sides of the political divide supported internal improvements. Jefferson suggested a national plan of public works and a constitutional amendment to insure its constitutionality. Jefferson, Madison, and Monroe were all supporters of internal improvements, although Madison (in 1817) and Monroe (in 1822) both vetoed internal improvement bills because of constitutional scruples. Yet, in those administrations, work on the national Road was initiated and continued, the federal government bought a large block of stock in the Chesapeake and Ohio Canal and made smaller investments in several other canal projects, and 'rivers and harbors' appropriations became a regular part of the Congressional calendar in 1824. Jackson supported internal improvements as a senator, but his veto of the Maysville Road appropriation in May of 1830, followed by another veto of a stock subscription in the Washington Turnpike Company and a pocket veto of a bill for improving lighthouses and harbors, seemed to indicate that the possibility of nationally supported internal improvements had ended: 'the Era of National Projects may be thought of as ending in his administration.'[37] In the 1840s, the Democratic party made opposition to nationally funded internal improvement projects part of its national platform.

Of course, it was not the end of national support for internal improvements. In 1841, the public land states would each receive up to 500000 acres of land in support of transportation improvements and, in the 1850s, the federal government would embark on a series of land grant projects that culminated in the transcontinental railroads.[38] The federal government would continue to support rivers and harbors improvements through the entire period. What Jackson had killed, at least for a time, was the idea of a nationally planned and integrated system along the lines of the Gallatin plan. What remained was federal government support for individual projects initiated by individual states.

One possibility for the demise of co-ordinated national action was 'constitutional scruples.' Van Duesen (1959, p. 52) felt that Jackson's veto had nothing to do with constitutional scruples at all, but was merely an operation for short term political gain:

> The veto was largely political, for Jackson signed some internal improvement bills fully as local as the Maysville Road. It was a slap at Clay, who had energetically pushed the Maysville Road, and at the American system. It was also a canny slap. The Maysville Road was primarily a local project, and therefore the veto would, as Van Buren observed, displease the smallest number of voters. More positively, the veto pleased New York and Pennsylvania, which were financing their own internal improvements and saw no reason why they should help finance developments in other states.

It is difficult to venture a concrete opinion on what was and was not constitutional in the early nineteenth century. If we read Jackson's veto message carefully, he considered the Maysville road unconstitutional only because it was a national project contained completely within the boundaries of one state. Presumably a truly national project, like the National Road, which stretched from state to state would be constitutional. Since the federal government was already involved in internal improvements, for example the various canals in which it invested before the 1830s, and none of them were declared unconstitutional, it seems reasonable to conclude provisionally that a truly national plan of internal improvements would have been constitutional; and that, while constitutional scruples were often raised by Presidents when vetoing some internal improvement bills, they were not an insurmountable obstacle to a national system.[39]

States' rights and the proper relationship between the national and state governments was a burning issue in the politics of the time, but it isn't clear exactly how this affected national investments in transportation and finance. Proponents of states' rights favored a limited national government and state improvements, but they often acted precisely as if they believed the opposite. Jefferson proposed a national system of investments to be financed from surplus revenues and Gallatin produced a workable, national plan that would have cost $20 million. The Republicans killed the First Bank of the United States, but they chartered the Second Bank of the United States. Presidents made repeated references to the potential unconstitutionality of internal improvement investments in their veto messages, but continued to sign bills that made similar investments. And the Supreme Court, rather than being a staunch advocate of states' rights and a limited national government, was ready, in several landmark decisions, to assert the full rights of the national government.

There was a second salient issue over which the various parties tended to divide. The issue was privilege. As already discussed, early bank charters were clearly grants of privilege to a small number of people. These privileges, with some risk, earned their owners substantial profits and preferential access to capital.[40] The same would be true of later charters for railroads. Agitation over these grants of privilege had its class component; the poorest in society could be roused to opposition against the privileged few. Complaints over privilege ran in deeper and more complicated ways than simple class divisions, however. In New York, for example, the 'Albany Regency,' a group of politicians led by Martin Van Buren, controlled the state in the 1820s and 1830s, and clearly used bank charters to reward their political friends. There were many middle and upper class groups opposed to this particular use of privilege.[41]

Privileges were originally granted in corporate charters in return for a service to the community. The corporation would provide a needed public service – for example, currency, a bridge, a river ferry – and in return received the right, sometimes a monopoly right, to charge for the service. As a growing number of charters went to industrial concerns, and as traditional corporate enterprises, like banks, became more privately oriented, questions were raised about the propriety of granting a public privilege to serve a purely private interest. States had always granted charters by legislative act and in some states charters became increasingly harder to obtain. It took some time for voters to appreciate the paradox that limiting charters only made more valuable the smaller number issued. Ultimately, popular pressure found its outlet in laws which made it much easier to incorporate and, as a result, reduced the value of the privilege. In banking this was accomplished by the various free banking laws, which made a bank charter available to all those with a minimum of capital. Other sectors of the economy were served by general incorporation laws. These laws would take effect in the late 1830s, and in most states not until the 1850s or later.[42]

There was a strong ideological commitment to the idea that the government should serve all the people, an idea articulated in the Revolution that played an important role in mobilizing support among all levels of colonial society. The Revolution was against part of American society, the privileged, as well as against British rule.[43] Conflicts over privilege were not settled with Independence. The new federal constitution was written and supported by those who felt that loss of privilege had gone far enough. The common man could not vote directly for either the President or senators under the Constitution. Suffrage in national elections was controlled by the states, and many states were still very far from enjoying free, white, male suffrage even by the 1840s.[44]

The cause of the common man was taken up successfully by the Jeffersonian Republicans and opposed, delicately, by the Federalists. The parties and coalitions that followed had no choice. In New York, '... the Democrats as well as the Whigs stood committed to equal rights and antimonopoly. Neither party advocated the Federalist ideal of a highly centralized economic system, tightly controlled, administered, and operated by a relatively small elite group.'[45] Debates over privilege had ceased to be partisan by the 1830s. Those siding with the common man had a distinct electoral advantage. Since most of the original thirteen states did not have free, white, male suffrage, politicians who supported the extension of the franchise could not only win over existing voters, but could win a large share of new voters created when suffrage qualifications were relaxed. This conflict goes some way to understanding why the South remained so resolutely a two-party system with aristocratic, slave holding, eastern interests and common, western interests.[46] Conflicts over privilege were intense and went right to the heart of the debate over what America was and was to become. Debates over privilege had their systematic national component, like the Bank War, but conflict most often involved local interests and conflict between propertied groups – for example, groups with and without bank charters, and up-stream and down-stream mill owners – rather than class conflict between wealthy elite and the laboring poor.

Privilege was central to the relationship between national and state governments. These privileges were worth fighting over because they were valuable and, because they were valuable, they could be used to generate revenues for the level of government that granted the privileges. As we have already seen, this was important in several states in the early nineteenth century, including the politically critical states of New York and Pennsylvania, both of which used the sale of bank charters for revenue and political purposes. (They supported Jackson's Maysville Road veto because of their own transportation projects.) But even larger implications would have arisen if the federal government began creating its own corporations on a large scale. In *McCulloch v. Maryland*, Chief Justice Marshal not only held 'that the power to tax is the power to destroy,' but the Court also ruled that the State of Maryland could not tax the Second Bank of the United States. The principle of reciprocity, the 'immunity of federal and state instrumentalities from federal and state taxation,' would continue in force until the early twentieth century. It was not until 1939 that state government employees became subject to federal income taxation, and the reverse for federal employees, in *Graves v. New York*. Interest on state and local bonds is still exempt from federal taxation. Had the national government chartered a national transportation and banking system, those corporations would have been beyond the fiscal reach of state governments.[47]

V

We are now ready to consider why a national system of internal improvements in finance and transportation did not emerge in the early nineteenth century. Most of the points have already been developed, but some require more discussion.

First, given the preference for asset financing, states were rapidly developing their own systems of finance and transportation. A national system was redundant and threatening to state fiscal interests. Two of the largest and most politically important states were New York and Pennsylvania. Both states had banking and transportation projects that competed, either directly or in prospect, with national banks and transportation projects. Hammond argues that a primary element in the success of the Jacksonians in vetoing the charter renewal of the Second Bank was the opposition of New York bankers to the 'Philadelphia Bank.'[48] New York bankers would have been glad to support a national bank if it had been in New York. One of the proposals in the air in the 1830s was to create a branch of the national bank in each state, with local bank directors. This may sound familiar; in 1914 the Federal Reserve System was created with 12 independent regional banks, each with its own directors. A national system of transportation improvements would have faced the same opposition.

Second, the intense political conflict over the creation of privileges through corporate charter and other means, would have involved any national system of internal improvement investment in charges that it created extensive privilege for a few. This was one of the strongest arguments against the First and Second Banks of the United States and contributed to the downfall of both. Jackson's veto of the Maysville Road criticized the policy of public investment in private corporations. National politicians were much more susceptible to this kind of public outrage than state governments and politicians. At the state level, venal privileges were tied to local improvements that earned state taxpayers a fiscal dividend and brought desired financial or transportation services into the state. Localized benefits could be spread widely enough to garner support within a state, but localized benefits created problems at the national level. Any party that created privileged interests in banks or transportation enterprises would be held accountable by public opinion for creating a privileged interest that appeared to serve some other region or state.

Third, while the opportunity to earn fiscal returns was a strong element in state support for internal improvements, any such 'fiscal dividend' would have created difficulties at the national level. National revenues came primarily from the tariff. Proponents of internal improvement investments on revenue grounds would be caught in the long standing conflict over protection and international trade. Manufacturers supported internal improvements, but would have strongly opposed any fiscal dividend that reduced tariffs. Support for national investments in internal improvements was weakened considerably by the difficulty of using the potential fiscal dividends that would flow to the federal Treasury as an argument for federal investment.

Fourth, there were no technological reasons why an integrated system would be more efficient than an aggregation of state systems. In its early stages, transportation technology was unable to operate railroad lines that were longer than roughly 50 miles. It was not until the 1850s that railroads reached over the Appalachians, and just before the Civil War that managerial techniques became sophisticated enough to co-ordinate even a regional railroad, much less a national system. There would be little penalty to pay if transportation systems were somewhat balkanized, with the obvious exception of standardization of equipment; canals would have benefited even less from national standards. The potential gains from co-ordination were small.

The technical arguments for a national bank included both convenience for the federal Treasury and benefits from a more stable currency. The first benefits were real, the second may have been. The establishment of national banks during the Civil War and the Federal Reserve System in 1914 did not eliminate either inflation or instability. Banking panics and financial collapse were still the periodic norm, rather than the exception. The conclusion of recent nineteenth-century banking history is that the state banking systems did not deserve the opprobrium heaped on them by banking historians in the first sixty years of the twentieth century. The presence of a strong national bank created unpleasant competition for the state banks, whose profits went to pay dividends on state holdings of bank stock, or boosted the charter fees paid by banks, or attracted more capital investment in banks which could be taxed.

Fifth, throughout the late eighteenth and early nineteenth century there was always doubt over the stability of the Union. Whether it was western Pennsylvania in the Whiskey Rebellion agitating against the federal excise tax in the 1790s, or New England in the War of 1812 and the Hartford Convention contemplating succession, or South Carolina attempting to nullify the collection of tariffs in its harbors, or the ultimate breakdown that occurred in 1861, the threat that neighboring states would no longer be part of the Union at some point in the future was real. Under those uncertain circumstances it is difficult to see how the national government could have worked out a national plan that would have satisfied everybody. Why pay for some one else's improvements today if they might be out of the Union when your turn comes?

Those internal improvement investments the national government did undertake are illuminating in this regard. With the exception of the National Road and support for a few canals, the national government invested in river and harbors improvements: building light houses, dredging harbors, and clearing rivers. Finances for these projects were authorized each year in a 'rivers and harbors' bill, the original 'pork-barrel' legislation. It worked because the projects were small, easily completed, and every state and almost every congressman could bring home a piece of the bacon. Such a deal could not be worked out for internal improvements, like the Erie canal, that would cost millions of dollars and take close to a decade to complete.

The only politically viable way to build a national system of improvements would have been to plan and build the system everywhere at the same time,[49] but that would have been an expensive proposition. It was one thing for Jefferson to advocate a program of internal improvements out of surplus revenues, which were primarily tariff revenues that could not be easily reduced; it was quite another to advocate a national system financed by a national excise tax, or a national direct tax administered by the states. This would have conflicted with the anti-tax sentiments of the voters as well as the asset-financing approach that the national and state governments were trying, with some success, to implement

VI

I have tried to identify several key developments in the public finances of early nineteenth-century America that shaped the structure of American federalism and the role of the state in supporting economic development through investment in finance and transportation.

The starting point is the intense anti-tax sentiments, inherited from the Revolution, that severely constrained the national and state governments. Their response was to seek alternative sources of income; the most attractive was to acquire income-earning assets. For the national government, asset finance came readily in the form of land sale revenues and tariffs. For the states, early asset income came from national Treasury bonds and bank stock, and grew to include stock in other corporations or direct operation of canals and other transportation improvements. Some states even established their own banking monopolies. At both the state and national level, asset financing relied on indirect taxes and investment income in order to avoid politically costly direct taxes.

The Constitution prevented states from taxing interstate or international trade. The national government was able to raise indirect taxes with relative ease; indeed, raising tariff rates was seen as a positive good by a substantial part of the population. Ample tariff revenues enabled the national government to avoid pressure to develop new sources of investment income, despite the unfulfilled expectation about public land sale revenues. States, on the other hand, were faced with fiscal pressures and sought out new investment opportunities. Often these opportunities arose in conjunction with the state's power to charter corporations. As a result, states made the first moves into transportation improvements, and made investments in banking at the same time that the national government invested in the First and Second Banks of the United States.

Investment in improvement projects, particularly when it was accomplished by chartering a private corporation, ran hard against another dominant element in early American politics: the revolt against privilege. The idea that the government should provide equal opportunity for all, and not privileges for a wealthy and influential few, was widespread. State legislatures had to weigh the conflicting political benefits of asset finance for internal improvements against the political costs of creating visible vested interests. In a few cases, like New York and the Erie canal, the state avoided the privilege problem by undertaking the investment itself. But direct public ownership and operation raised other difficulties with efficiency and privilege. Monopoly state banks could not make a profit if they loaned money to every citizen, and who would decide who got the loans?

Again, the dynamics worked against national investments. There would be no political gain at the national level from substituting tolls or dividends from investments for tariff revenues, since there were strong interests groups which wanted higher tariffs regardless of the revenue consequences. The fiscal dividend that states hoped would come from their investments had little weight at the national level. States, as we have seen, continued to pursue those investments more actively than the national government.

As time went on and technological innovations in steam power began to open up new opportunities in transportation, states moved forward vigorously. The same forces acted on the national government, but national attempts in transportation now had to overcome competition with existing or planned state systems. Not that this opposition was decisive; many states would have welcomed a $2 or $3 million national transportation investment in their state if they could have had some say over where it went. But such a national system would have required essentially simultaneous construction in all parts of the country. A piecemeal national system would not have been viable after the late 1820s. Only a nationally planned and integrated system could have worked, but it would have been very expensive. The lack of fiscal incentives at the national level and growing state competition effectively thwarted national projects.

The political forces at work cannot be characterized in any simple way. This was not just a battle between the farmers and the manufacturers, between the countryside and the city, between the east and the west, between the north and the south, between the poor and the rich, between freetraders and protectionists, or between anti-bankers and pro-bankers. Battles over banks were most often fights between bankers rather than between pro- and anti-bank groups. Battles over canals and railroads were between groups of farmers who wanted the route nearer to them, or commercial interests in different cities who wanted to be the terminus of the route. The battles were not between farmers, merchants, and manufacturers as identifiable groups.

The struggles between bankers or between merchants or between farmers could, however, easily be translated into a language which reflected the widespread concern over the use of privilege. New Yorkers could argue, as Van Buren did, that the Second Bank of the United States created an unconstitutional privilege. It was a simple argument that people could accept, and it was the issue at the heart of the public debate. It was of little importance to the public debate that the privileges of bankers in Philadelphia versus the privileges of bankers in New York were really at stake. The Bank War was a conflict between New York and Philadelphia and between share holders of state chartered banks and the Second Bank, not between the poor and the rich.

I have placed little weight on constitutional scruples or the issue of states' rights. It is not at all clear that a national system of improvements would have been unconstitutional; the Supreme Court did not declare the Maysville Road unconstitutional – Jackson did. Abstract and ideological concerns about state and national rights abounded in the early nineteenth century, but states were continually petitioning Congress to aid specific projects. New York undertook the Erie canal only after its appeal for national aid had been rejected.

Relatively strong incentives were at work under the surface – fiscal federalism incentives. The economic benefits from a nationally co-ordinated system were negligible, perhaps zero. The political benefits were even smaller. Both the national and state governments had a fiscal interest in developing income-producing assets, but the relative net benefits were much higher for the states. The state's fiscal dividend could be applied directly to a politically popular reduction in direct taxes. A national fiscal dividend could not be applied to a reduction in tariff revenues without raising a host of troublesome political questions. Once the process had been set in motion and states had made investments in banks and transportation, any national system would, perhaps adversely, effect state revenues.

In the end, the federal system that developed in the early nineteenth century was, in a fiscal sense, efficient. Revenues were raised and expenditures were made by the level of government with the lowest cost of collecting the revenues and the ability to place expenditures to receive the highest return. This is the result that Dr. Oates, fiscal federalist, would prescribe. Had the national government assumed a larger role in providing internal improvement investments, it is quite likely that the overall level of investment would have been lower. For example, suppose the Constitution had prohibited states from chartering any corporations, effectively preventing states from entering banking or transportation. Would the national government have built a financial and transportation system that was larger than the one the states had built by 1840? The same political obstacles would have been in the national government's way, with the one exception that the states would not have their own projects to protect. I suspect that state-led investment produced a larger investment in infrastructure than would have occurred under a national system, and that the nation was better off as a result.

The system began to break down in the 1840s, but not because it was inefficient. Asset financing had provided a powerful incentive for states to enter the investment field, but its promise had proved to be illusory. The notion that states could live off their investments would not stand the test of time, but that is another story. Asset financing didn't work for the national government either; land sales were never an important source of national revenues. Experience would change people's opinions in the 1830s and 1840s, but the economics of asset finance were clear and the incentives it held out drove the evolution of the federal system for the nation's first fifty years.

NOTES

1. The state debt figure is taken from Ratchford, 1941. Federal investments in transportation are from Goodrich, 1960, p. 41, and in the Second Bank of the United States from Hammond (1957), p. 244.
2. The causes of the American Revolution will be debated as long as there is an America. For authoritative, but not conclusive, histories see Wood, 1991 and Bailyn, 1967. The economic history of the causes of the Revolution has revolved around the economic burden of membershiip in the British Empire, which is now widely thought to have been small, but not zero.
3. The third way in which the government contributed to economic development were changes in the legal system. See Horowitz, 1977 and Hurst, 1956 and 1970.
4. See Alfred Chandler, 1977, 'The Visible Hand' for a detailed history of how large firms developed over the nineteenth century and the role of an integrated national economy in that process.
5. This is a classic story told in Taylor, 1951.

6. The debate about the importance of the railroads revolves around the shipment of agricultural products to market. See Fogel, 1964 and Fishlow, 1965.
7. One of the great paradoxes of American history is that economic development fostered by the growth of an integrated national market which many farmers felt would produce more income for farmers, ended up producing a more rapidly growing urban manufacturing economy which led in turn to a decline in the relative number of farmers from the beginning of the nineteenth century and absolute declines in the number of farmers in the twentieth century.
8. See Paul Wallace Gates, 1968. States admitted later were able to get control of these transportation and education funds and spend them at their own discretion.
9. 'As Clay himself used the term, his American system was the opposite of what he was wont to refer to as the "colonial" or "foreign" system of free trade. It meant, basically, the use of a protective tariff to build up American industry. This industrial development would serve as a source of national wealth and as a constant nourishment for an urban population that, in turn, would furnish a steady and reliable home market for the nation's agriculture ... Certain other major policies to which Clay was devoted were often identified as part of his American system These were internal improvements at national expense, the use of public land revenues for such improvements, the maintenance of the Bank of the United States as essential to a stable and uniform currency.' Van Duesen, 1959, p. 51.
10. If Ohio voters were able to charge tolls on their roads, they may have been able to capture some of the external benefits.
11. The argument that a national system would have been more efficient is implicit throughout Goodrich, 1960.
12. There were doubts about how fertile the prairies would be: after all, they did not grow trees. As a result the optimistic guesses about western fertility were not optimistic enough. See Atack and Bateman, 1987, for examples of expectations about western land.
13. Movement into the west in the early nineteenth century would have limited impact on cultivated land per farmer, since farm size in the north and on free farms in the south was limited by a labor constraint. But western farms would have more uncultivated acres per farm and a corresponding increase hunting and pasturage. The tremendous growth in the productivity of farm labor can be seen in the continuously declining number of man hours required to produce 100 bushels of wheat which fell from 373 hours in 1800, to 233 hours in 1840 to 108 hours in 1900; corn which fell from 344 to 276 to 147 in the same years; and per bale of cotton which fell from 601 to 438 to 284 (U.S. Department of Commerce, 1975, p. 500, series K 449, 454, and 459).
14. These figures are roughly correct. In 1860 wheat sold for \$1.00 to \$1.30 a bushel in eastern cities, and between \$0.60 and \$0.80 in western states.
15. See Fogel, 1964, p. 23 and 57 for a discussion of wagon, canal, and rail rates and the example cited. Of course, the small social savings that Fogel found for the railroads was the result of comparing railroads with canals. Canals actually had lower costs per ton mile shipped than railroads.
16. See Fogel, 1964, Fishlow, 1965, Atack and Bateman, 1987, Heckelman and Wallis, 1997, Atack 1998, Coffman and Gregson, 1998, and Craig, Palmquist, and Weiss, 1998.
17. Hammond devotes a considerable amount of argument to the notion that farmers were antibank in the early nineteenth century. But by anti-bank he really means anti-inflation; he is arguing against the impression, given by many late nineteenth century reformers, that agrarian populists had always wanted inflation and more banks, which they clearly were not pressing for in the early nineteenth century.
18. Walton and Sheppard, 1979 and Davis and Huttenback, 1988.
19. Walton and Sheppard, 1979 discuss these points in their chapter on 'British Bungling.'
20. There is a long and multifaceted literature on the causes of the American Revolution, see Bailyn, 1967 and Wood, 1991.
21. For the financial history of the national government during the Revolution see Dewey, 1968 and Studenski and Krooss, 1963.
22. There is a large literature on the economic origins of the Constitution. Beard, 1935 made a forceful statement of how economic interests were served by the Constitution, particularly

bondholders who held debt of the Continental Congress. The Beard hypothesis is making something of a comeback see McGuire and Ohsfelt, 1984 and MacDonald, 1958.

23. The direct tax clause in the Constitution is somewhat difficult to understand. Dewey (1968 p. 65) writing in 1934, noted that 'The definition of the term "direct tax" has proved troublesome; it is probable that the makers of the Constitution intended to limit its application to polls and land; yet, though the Supreme Court has had occasion to deliver several important decisions bearing on this subject, no satisfactory interpretation has been reached.' In order to understand its intent, note that property taxes in the states were often levied in the following manner. An estimate was made of the state's revenue needs for the upcoming year. That amount was divided by the assessed value of property in the state to determine the state tax rate. The revenue total was then allocated between counties (or townships), each county responsible for collecting its share of the 'state tax.' When the federal government levied a direct tax in 1798, or later to finance the War of 1812, it aimed to raise a certain amount of revenue. That amount was divided among the states on the basis of population. Each state was then responsible for raising its own taxes to pay for its share. By apportioning direct taxes by population, the Constitution effectively continued the Articles of Confederation policy of allowing the states to collect their own revenues, but only for this particular type of tax.
24. Taken from US Department of Commerce, 1975, Series Y 457–63, p. 1115. In only three years from 1789 to 1808 were combined War and Navy Department expenditures greater than interest payments, 1798–1800.
25. Like a direct tax, an indirect tax was hard to define. In *United States v. Hylton* in 1796 the Supreme Court was asked to rule whether the federal excise tax on carriages was a direct tax, and if so must be levied according to population. Dewey (1968, p. 107) summarizes the Court's decision: 'A tax on expense was regarded by the court as an indirect tax; and inasmuch as a carriage was a consumable commodity, and a tax on it was a tax on the expense of the owner, an annual tax on carriages was to be properly classified as an indirect tax. Furthermore, a tax on carriages could not be a direct tax, because apportionment would tend to gross and arbitrary differences in the contribution of each State. The court, without giving a judicial opinion on the exact distinction between direct and indirect taxes, was inclined to believe that the direct taxes contemplated by the Constitution were only two – a capitation or poll tax, without regard to property, profession, or any other circumstance; and a tax on land.' Carriages, however, were usually taxed as personal property by the states and counties.
26. Evidence on state property taxes is provided in Grinath, Wallis, and Sylla, 1997.
27. The biggest charter fee was paid to Pennsylvania by the Bank of the United States in 1836. It was $2 million, plus obligations to support internal improvements in the state. Estimates of state revenues from bank sources before 1860 are presented in Sylla, Legler, and Wallis, 1987.
28. There was a strong correlation between how a state taxed banks and the number of banks in the state. On one extreme, states that taxed bank capital, like Massachusetts and Rhode Island, had large numbers of banks and easy entry policies. On the other extreme, states like Alabama, Indiana, and Missouri had only one bank, chartered and owned by the state. Dividends from the bank were a substantial revenue source in each of those states. In the middle were states like Virginia, which had substantial dividend income, and was fairly restrictive on entry to protect its dividends; and Pennsylvania, which derived much of its income from charters and, as a result, had more banks than Virginia, but not as many banks as Massachusetts, since issuing too many charters would drive down their value. These issues are explored in Wallis, Sylla, and Legler, 1994.
29. Lamoreaux (1994, pp. 7–9), also discusses the evidence that insider lending predominated in other regions of the United States and in England.
30. There is a long and rich history of early nineteenth century banking. See Hammond, 1957, Redlich, 1968, Schweikart, 1987, Sylla, 1966, Rockoff, 1974 and 1975, for an introduction.
31. The debt crisis of 1841 and 1842 is analysed in Grinath, Wallis, and Sylla, 1997.
32. The classic source on transportation improvements is Goodrich, 1960. For the Erie specifically see Miller, 1962.
33. For Ohio canals see Scheiber, 1969.
34. Goodrich (1960, chapter 3), 'Appalachian Competition' provides a compilation and description of each state's involvement.

35. One of the leading members of this group is Joel Silbey (1967, 1985, 1991), who has written extensively on the relative unimportance of section and economics. Several important papers are collected in *The Partisan Imperative* (1985), particularly relevant is 'Delegates Fresh from the People: American Congressional and Legislative Behavior' which originally appeared in the *Journal of Interdisciplinary History*. For a discussion of the period before 1838, which he characterizes as 'anti-Party, elite-factional' see chapter One in *The American Political Nation, 1838–1893*.
36. Actually the 'Maryland Assembly had enacted a statute which gave the Baltimore office of the Bank the hard choice of buying stamped paper from the state, on which the notes issued by the office were to be printed, of paying the state $15,000 a year, or of going out of business.' Hammond, 1966, p. 30.
37. Goodrich, 1960, p. 42.
38. These activities are documented in Goodrich (1960, chapter 5), 'An Era of National Subsidy.'
39. Goodrich, 1960, p. 44; 'Yet it is difficult for a modern student to believe that the constitutional issue, for all the passion with which it was contested, was in fact the decisive one.'
40. For example, see the profits on bank stock reported by Lamoreaux, 1994 (p. 72 and 91 and the references cited there).
41. For the Albany Regency and Van Buren's role in Jackson's veto of the Second Bank of the United States charter renewal and state banking in New York, see Hammond, 1957.
42. See Hurst 1970, for a general discussion of incorporation laws. See Horowitz, 1977 for a specific example of water mills and the way in which the courts and the legislatures had to modify their existing corporate concepts to adjust to industrialization.
43. This is developed in much greater detail in Wood, 1991.
44. For a discussion of these issues in terms of constitutional structures at the state level, including suffrage restrictions, see Green, 1966.
45. Benson, 1961, p. 105.
46. The issues of privilege extended beyond suffrage. There were also property requirements for holding office and the geographic apportionment of representation in state legislatures (and, as a result, in the election of US senators and Presidential electors). Geographical apportionment was a particular thorny issue in the south. Slaves were counted as 3/5 of a person, giving aristocratic areas more representation with fewer qualified voters. Representation was, in some states, allocated on the basis of wealth, giving low country aristocrats more representation. Finally, representation was often allocated to counties, and legislatures controlled by slave-owning, aristocratic low-country interests created large upland counties with correspondingly smaller proportional representation in the state legislature. See Green for a description of the conflicts these constitutional structures created.
47. I am not clear exactly how far the reciprocity arrangement went in the early nineteenth century, nor exactly how it would have affected national transportation improvements. During the Civil War, the National Banking Act imposed a note tax on state chartered banks, but these banks were not 'instrumentalities' of the state.
48. Hammond, 1957, pp. 353–68. 'Yet, in the federal Bank Philadelphia retained an impressive stronghold of her former primacy [over New York City in commercial matters]. It was the Bank in Philadelphia in whose Wall Street office the revenues of the port of New York were received on deposit. Those revenues, paid by New York business men, were larger than those of all other American ports together, but they passed into the control of directors who were mostly Philadelphians. New York's jealousy in this matter was no empty question of first place in an honorific sense but a lively question of whose pockets the profits were going into.' (p. 353).
49. Evidence of the pressure to build something for everybody at the same time can be seen in Ohio and New York. Both states built a small network of large, successful canals. Popular pressure then forced both states in the 1830s to embark on a much larger investment in a large system of small canals that would hook every region of the state into the canal network. Maryland and Pennsylvania pursued multiple projects from the beginning, to their ultimate dismay.

REFERENCES

Atack, Jeremy (1998), 'Introduction', *Journal of Real Estate Finance and Economics*, **16** (2), 131–4.

Atack, Jeremy and Fred Bateman (1987), *To Their Own Soil: Agriculture in the Antebellum North*, Ames: Iowa State University Press.

Bailyn, Bernard (1967), *The Ideological Origins of the American Revolution*, Cambridge: Harvard University Press.

Beard, Charles A. (1935), *An Economic Interpretation of the American Constitution*, New York: Free Press.

Benson, Lee, (1961), *The Concept of Jacksonian Democracy. New York as a Test Case*, Princeton: Princeton University Press.

Cadman, John W. (1949), *The Corporation in New Jersey, Business and Politics 1791–1875*, Cambridge: Harvard University Press.

Chandler, Alfred (1977), *The Visible Hand*, Cambridge: Belknap.

Coffman, Chad and Mary Eschelbach Gregson (1998), 'Railroad Development and Land Values', *Journal of Real Estate Finance and Economics*, **16** (2), 191–205.

Craig, Lee, Raymond D. Palmquist and Thomas Weiss (1998), 'Transportation Improvements and Land Values in the Antebellum United States: A Hedonic Approach', *The Journal of Real Estate Finance and Economics*, **16** (2), 173–90.

Davis, Lance E. and Robert A. Huttenback (1988), *Mammon and the Pursuit of Empire. The Economics of British Imperialism*, New York: Cambridge University Press.

Dewey, Davis R. [1934] (1968), *Financial History of the United States*, 12th edn, New York: Augustus Kelley.

Fishlow, Albert (1965), *American Railroads and the Transformation of the Ante-Bellum Economy*, Cambridge: Harvard University Press.

Fogel, Robert William (1964), *Railroads and American Economic Growth: Essays in Econometric History*, Baltimore: The Johns Hopkins Press.

Gates, Paul Wallace (1968), *History of Public Land Law Development*, Washington, DC: GPO.

Goodrich, Carter (1960), *Government Promotion of American Canals and Railroads, 1800–1890*, New York: Columbia University Press.

Green, Fletcher M. (1966), *Constitutional Development in the South Atlantic States, 1776–1860. A Study in the Evolution of Democracy*, Norton: New York.

Grinath, Arthur, John Joseph Wallis and Richard E. Sylla (1997), 'Debt, Default, and Revenue Structure: The American State Debt Crisis in the 1840s', NBER working paper, Historical Series, no. 96.

Hammond, Bray (1957), *Banks and Politics in America from the Revolution to the Civil War*, Princeton: Princeton University Press.

Hammond, Bray (1966), 'The Bank Cases', in John A. Garrity (ed.), *Quarrels that Have Shaped the Constitution*, New York: Harper and Row.

Heckelman, Jac and John Joseph Wallis (1997), 'Railroads and Property Taxes', *Explorations in Economic History*, **34**, 77–99.

Horowitz, Morton J. (1977), *The Transformation of American Law, 1780–1860*, Cambridge: Harvard University Press.

Hurst, James Willard (1956), *Law and the Conditions of Freedom*, Madison: University of Wisconsin Press.

Hurst, James Willard (1970), *The Legitimacy of the Business Corporation in the Law of the United States. 1780–1970*, Charlottesville: The University Press of Virginia.

Lamoreaux, Naomi, R (1994), *Insider Lending: Banks, Personal Connections, and Economic Development in Industrial New England*, New York: Cambridge University Press.

McDonald, Forrest (1958), *We the People: The Economic Origins of the Constitution*, Chicago: University of Chicago Press.

McGuire, Robert A. and Robert L. Ohsfelt (1984), 'Economic Interests and the American Constitution: A Quantitative Rehabilitation of Charles A. Beard', *Journal of Economic History*, **XLIV** (2) 509–19.

Miller, Nathan (1962), *The Enterprise of a Free People: Aspects of Economic Development in New York State during the Canal Period, 1792–1838*, Ithaca, New York: Cornell University Press.

Ratchford, B.U. (1941), *American State Debts*, Durham: Duke University Press.

Redlich, Fritz (1968), *The Molding of American Banking*, New York: Johnson Reprint Corporation.

Rockoff, Hugh (1975), 'Varieties of Banking and Regional Economic Development in the United States, 1840–1860', *Journal of Economic History*, **XXXV** (1): 160–81.

Rockoff, Hugh (1974), 'The Free Banking Era: A Reexamination', *Journal of Money, Credit, and Banking*: 141–67.

Scheiber, Harry N. (1969), *Ohio Canal Era: A Case Study of Government and the Economy, 1820–1861*, Athens, Ohio.

Schweikart, Larry (1987), *Banking in the American South from the Age of Jackson to Reconstruction*, Baton Rouge: Louisiana State University Press.

Silbey, Joel H. (1991), *The American Political Nation, 1838–1893*, Stanford: Stanford University Press.

Silbey, Joel H. (1985), *The Partisan Imperative. The Dynamics of American Politics Before the Civil War*, New York: Oxford University Press.

Silbey, Joel H. (1967), *The Shrine of Party. Congressional Voting Behavior, 1841–1852*, Pittsburgh: University of Pittsburgh Press.

Studenski, Paul and Herman E. Krooss (1963), *Financial History of the United States*, New York: McGraw-Hill.

Sylla, Richard (1966), 'American Banking and Growth in the Nineteenth Century: A Partial View of the Terrain', *Explorations in Economic History*, **9** (2): 197–227.

Sylla, Richard, John B. Legler and John Joseph Wallis (1987), 'Banks and State Public Finance in the New Republic', *Journal of Economic History*, **XLVII**: 391–403.

Taylor, George Rogers (1951), *The Transportation Revolution, 1815–1860*, New York: Harper and Row.

United States, Department of Commerce, Bureau of the Census (1975), *Historical Statistics of the United States, 1790–1970*, Washington: GPO.

Van Duesen, Glydon G. (1959), *The Jacksonian Era, 1828–1848*, New York: Harper and Row.

Wallis, John Joseph, Richard E. Sylla and John B. Legler (1994), 'The Relationship between Taxation and Regulation of Banks in Early Nineteenth Century America', in C. Goldin and G. Libecap (eds), *The Regulated Economy*, Chicago: University of Chicago Press.

Walton, Gary and Sheppard, W. (1979), *The Economic Rise of Early America*, New York: Cambridge University Press.

Weiss, Thomas (1992), 'U.S. Labor Force Estimates and Economic Growth, 1800–1860', in Robert E. Gallman and John Joseph Wallis (eds), *American Economic Growth and Standards of Living Before the Civil War*, Chicago: University of Chicago Press.

Wood, Gordon (1991), *The Radicalism of the American Revolution*, New York: Vintage Books.

13. Capitalization and efficiency

John Yinger*

Throughout his career, Wallace Oates has demonstrated a knack for identifying and contributing to key issues in local public finance. Among his better known contributions are his articles on capitalization, which is the impact of property taxes and public service quality on house values, and his articles on inefficiency in the provision of local public services, even with many jurisdictions. This chapter brings those two strands together by showing that capitalization itself has implications for efficiency.[1]

A REVIEW OF OATES'S CONTRIBUTIONS

Capitalization

Oates's justly famous article on capitalization (1969) opened the gates to a flood of empirical work. His was not the first empirical study of capitalization,[2] but it was the first to link capitalization to positive and normative questions of wide interest, namely the questions raised by Tiebout (1956). Thanks to this connection, capitalization studies have become one of the central empirical tools of local public finance. Oates, of course, made other contributions to this topic, including Oates (1973) and Heinberg and Oates (1970).

Oates's 1969 article used a simple methodology and widely available data, two characteristics that undoubtedly contributed to its appeal. For a sample of 53 residential communities in northern New Jersey in 1960, he regressed the median house value on the log of the effective tax rate, the log of school spending per pupil, and several control variables. These control variables, designed to capture the impact on house values of factors outside the public sector, include the log of the linear distance from downtown Manhattan, the median number of rooms, the percentage of houses built in the last 10 years, median family income, and the percentage of families with a low annual income. The regression employed two-stage least squares to account for the possible endogeneity of the tax rate and of public spending. All the variables were statistically significant, with a negative sign for the tax variable and a positive sign for the spending variable.

In a well known comment on the Oates's article, Pollakowski (1973) argued that small changes in Oates's specification could eliminate his results. In particular, Pollakowski argued that the Oates specification incorrectly omitted non-school spending, improperly included median household income and poverty (which he claimed were endogenous), and used instruments that were themselves endogenous.[3] When he deleted the control variables and instruments he believed to be endogenous, Pollakowski found that the tax and spending variables were no longer statistically significant. Oates responded (1973) by including the log of municipal spending per capita, which also proved to be statistically significant, but he rejected Pollakowski's other criticisms.

The choice of control variables and instruments is, of course, central to empirical work of this type, and the Pollakowski/Oates debate undoubtedly helped researchers focus on these issues. Most following researchers have tended to side with Pollakowski, at least implicitly, by emphasizing control variables that reflect housing characteristics, not resident characteristics, and by limiting themselves to instruments that are clearly exogenous. Somewhat ironically, however, virtually all of the subsequent literature supports Oates's conclusion that significant capitalization exists. For reviews, see Yinger et al. (1988) and Ross and Yinger (1999).

Subsequent literature (including Yinger et al., 1988) has identified additional limitations of Oates's equation, including misspecification, particularly of the tax term (discussed below); the use of public spending instead of public service outcomes, such as test scores; and the limited number of control variables. These limitations are shared by many of the subsequent studies, particularly those based on aggregate data. However, these are relatively minor limitations, and by the most widely used standard for successful research, that is, whether it stimulates more research, Oates's article was a resounding success.

Inefficiency

Oates makes a clear statement of the distortion from a property tax in his well-known book (1972, p. 136):

> [S]ince the price an individual pays for the local public good depends on the rental price of the dwelling he selects, there exists an extra pecuniary incentive to economize on the expenditures for dwellings. To purchase an extra unit of housing services, an individual must pay more than the marginal cost of the unit: he must also make an additional contribution to the public treasury. As a result residents of the community will tend to purchase less than efficient levels of housing.[4]

Oates also hints at the connection between capitalization and efficiency in his 1969 article, which appears to suggest that the presence of capitalization can be seen as a test of Tiebout's hypothesis that local public services are provided at the efficient level. According to Oates (pp. 957–8), Tiebout

> suggested that at least at a theoretical level we can envision a system in which we get something resembling a market solution to the production and consumption of local public goods. Very simply, Tiebout's world is one in which the consumer 'shops' among different communities offering varying packages of local public services and selects as a residence the community which offers the tax expenditure program best suited to his tastes.... [I]ndividuals working in a central city frequently have a wide choice of suburban communities in which to reside, and the quality of the local public schools, for instance, may be of real importance in the choice of a community of residence. If this is true, the outputs of public services (as well as taxes) should influence the attraction of a community and thereby affect local property values.

For the most part, this discussion (and the article's conclusions) emphasize Tiebout's behavioral hypothesis that people select communities in part on the basis of expenditure-tax packages, not his normative hypothesis that the resulting levels of local public services are efficient. However, the phrase 'market solution' makes it appear as if Oates does not distinguish between these two hypotheses and leaves the reader with the impression that capitalization provides a test for the normative as well as for the positive hypothesis.

Oates returns to this issue in a later article (1994), in which he argues that only the positive hypothesis can be tested.

> [C]apitalization can legitimately be taken as evidence that individuals shop among communities and pay more for houses in fiscally advantaged jurisdictions – but it does not tell us anything about whether the 'supply side' of the Tiebout world is functioning as envisioned in the model. Some capitalization is, in fact, consistent with both the benefit view [which claims no inefficiency] and the new view of local property taxation [which supports inefficiency], so that this finding does not help us to distinguish between these two basic hypotheses (p. 141).[5]

After reviewing some other types of evidence, he concludes that 'it is impossible to reject either the new view or the benefits view in favor of the other' (p. 142). Apparently, therefore, Oates is no longer so sure that the property tax is a source of distortion. I will return to this issue below.

AN ANALYSIS OF EFFICIENCY WITH CAPITALIZATION

This section provides a formal analysis of efficiency in the provision of local services and explores whether the efficiency conditions are met in a world with capitalization. To highlight the role of capitalization, this analysis does not consider several issues that have been extensively studied in the efficiency literature, including the behavior of public officials, heterogeneous populations, and the impact of a community's demographic characteristics on the cost of its public services.[6] Oates has made important contributions to some of these topics, particularly the latter. See Oates (1981) and Schwab and Oates (1991).

The Efficiency Problem

Consider a planner's problem for a community containing N identical households.[7] Following the standard approach, the planner's objective is to maximize the utility of a representative household, subject to the constraints imposed by both resource availability and production technology.[8] Let Z be a composite good, H be housing services, and S be public services, which are assumed to have the characteristics of a private good, not a public good. All three outputs are produced with capital, K and land, L. The production function for firm (or government) j is written in implicit form, $F^j(Z, S, H; K, L) = 0$, and the planner has a fixed amount of K and L to allocate. Thus the planner's problem is to[9]

$$\begin{aligned}
&\text{Maximize} \quad U(Z, H, S) \\
&\text{Subject to } F^j(Z, S, H; K, L) = 0 \quad \text{for all } j \\
&\qquad \sum_j K^J = \bar{K} \\
&\qquad \sum_j L^j = \bar{L} \\
&\qquad \sum_j Z^j = NZ \\
&\qquad \sum_j H^j = NH \\
&\qquad \sum_j S^j = NS,
\end{aligned} \tag{13.1}$$

where the superscripts indicate firms (or a government).

The first-order conditions of this problem imply that for any firm j that produces Z and any firm j' that produces H,

$$\frac{U_H}{U_Z} = \frac{F_H^{j'} F_K^j}{F_Z^j F_K^{j'}}, \tag{13.2}$$

where the subscripts indicate partial derivatives. This result indicates, of course, that the marginal rate of substitution must equal the marginal rate of product transformation.[10] Similar results apply when one considers any government j'' that produces S. To be specific,

$$\frac{U_S}{U_Z} = \frac{F_S^{j''} F_K^{j'}}{F_Z^{j'} F_K^{j''}}, \tag{13.3}$$

and

$$1 = -\frac{rF_Z^j}{F_K^j}, \tag{13.4}$$

The Problem Facing Firms and Governments

Do competitive markets satisfy these efficiency conditions? This section explores the behavior of firms and governments, the next one turns to households.

A firm's problem is to maximize profits, subject to its production technology and the cost of inputs. Let r be the price of K and R be the price of L. Consider first a firm j that only produces Z, which has a price of one. This firm's objective is to

$$\text{Maximize} \quad \pi = Z - rK - RL + \eta^j F^j(Z; K, L), \tag{13.5}$$

where η is a Lagrangian multiplier. The first-order conditions of this problem imply, as usual, that the firm sets the value of the marginal product of K equal to r, or, after rearranging,

$$1 = -\frac{rF_Z^j}{F_K^j}, \tag{13.6}$$

where the left side represents the price of Z. The problem for a firm j' that only produces H is analogous and results in an expression equivalent to (13.6) with P on the left side and F_H replacing F_Z on the right side. Combining these two results yields

$$\frac{P}{1} = \frac{F_H^{j'} F_K^j}{F_Z^j F_K^{j'}}, \tag{13.7}$$

where, as before, the 1 represents the price of Z. If market prices equal the true shadow prices from the planner's problem, the normal case with competition, then (13.7) implies that inefficiency does not arise on the firm side of the trade-off between H and Z.

The final good, S is produced by a government, j''. To avoid introducing any new sources of inefficiency, I assume that this government minimizes cost, so that its problem is to

$$\text{Minimize} \quad rK + RL + \eta^{j''} F^{j''}(S, K, L) + \delta^{j''}(S^0 - S) \tag{13.8}$$

where δ is another Lagrangian multiplier and S^0 is the level of service the government selects. Since δ can be interpreted as the impact of another unit of S on total costs, that is, as marginal cost, it serves as the price concept here. The first-order conditions of this problem lead to an equation analogous to (13.6), with δ in the place of the output price. It follows directly that

$$\frac{\delta^{j''}}{1} = \frac{F_S^{j''} F_K^{j}}{F_Z^{j} F_K^{j''}} \text{ and } \frac{\delta^{j''}}{P_H} = \frac{F_S^{j''} F_K^{j'}}{F_H^{j'} F_K^{j''}}. \tag{13.9}$$

So long as δ equals the true shadow price of S, these conditions also satisfy the requirements of efficiency, so again inefficiency does not arise on the production side.

The Household Problem

Now let us turn to the behavior of household/voters.[11] Even in a community with identical homeowners, the voter problem is more complicated than the firm problem, largely because it involves many unresolved issues concerning voters' perceptions of capitalization. In fact, the problem cannot be specified without making assumptions, implicitly or explicitly, about five different type of perceptions:

1. Do voters perceive that changes in P caused by changes in S and t can result in capital gains or losses on their houses?
2. Do voters perceive that the opportunity cost of their housing services, P, changes when S or t changes?
3. Do voters perceive that changes in the value of their property caused by changes in S and t will result (assuming, as we will, accurate assessment practices) in an increase in their property taxes?
4. Do voters perceive that changes in P caused by changes in S and t can result in changes in the value of other property in the community and hence in the property tax base?
5. Do voters perceive that change in P caused by changes in S and t can result in changes in the amount of housing consumed by other voters and hence result in a change in the property tax base?

To model the voter problem, let us define five perceptions parameters, ρ_1 through ρ_5, corresponding to these five types of perception. Each parameter takes a value of zero if the answer to the corresponding above question is negative and a value of one if the answer to this question is affirmative and the perception is complete, in the sense that the full extent of the adjustment is recognized.

A voter wants to maximize its utility subject to both its own budget constraint and the budget constraint of its community.[12] The first two types of perception affect the first constraint and the second two types affect the second. The annualized value of capital gains due to capitalization, for example, is a form of income, and the opportunity cost of housing is its current price. Now let $\bar{H}'$ be the current level of housing services in the community, S' be the current public service level, and t' be the current property tax rate. Then the household problem can be written as follows:

$$\text{Maximize} \quad U(Z, H, S)$$
$$\text{Subject to } Y + \rho_1[P(S,t) - P(S',t')]H = Z + (P(S',t') + \rho_2[P(S,t) - P(S',t')])H$$
$$+ \frac{t\left(P(S',t') + \rho_3\left[P(S,t) - P(S',t')\right]\right)H}{r}$$
$$E(S) = (t/r)(P(S',t') + \rho_4[P(S,t) - P(S',t')]) \times (\bar{H}' + \rho_5[\bar{H}(P(S,t)) - \bar{H}']) \quad (13.10)$$

If $\rho_2 = 0$, for example, the opportunity cost of housing is perceived to be $P(S', t')$, the price that applied when the household bought its house, whereas the perceived opportunity cost shifts to the current price, $P(S,t)$, when $\rho_2 = 1$.

Following Yinger (1982), I make the assumption that this community is in long-run equilibrium, which implies that the people moving in bid the same amount for housing as the people who already live there [$P(S,t) = P(S',t')$] and also consume the same amount of housing as existing residents [$H(P(S,t)) = H'$].[13] (Although the focus here is on a homogeneous community, I retain the 'bar' to indicate community average $\bar{H}$.) Voters are assumed not to be aware of these equilibrium conditions. With these assumptions, the first-order conditions of this problem reduce to:

$$U_Z - \lambda = 0$$
$$U_H - \lambda[P(1 + t^*)] = 0$$
$$U_s + \lambda[P_S H(\rho_1 - \rho_2) - \rho_3 t^* P_S H] + \eta[\rho_4 t^* P_S \bar{H} + \rho_5 t^* \bar{H}_P P_S - E_S] = 0$$
$$\lambda[P_t H(\rho_1 - \rho_2) - \rho_3 t^* P_t H - PH/r] + \eta[P\bar{H}/r + \rho_4 t^* P_t \bar{H} + \rho_5 t^* \bar{H}_P P_t] = 0 \quad (13.11)$$

where λ and η are the Lagrangian multipliers for the two constraints and $t^* = t/r$.

One possible set of assumptions about preferences is that $\rho_1 = \rho_2$, $\rho_3 = \rho_4$, and $\rho_5 = 0$. This set corresponds to a case in which voters have the same perceptions about the opportunity cost of housing and about capital gains, the same perceptions about the direct impact of capitalization on both the taxes they pay and the taxes other people pay, and no awareness at all of the indirect impact of capitalization on the tax base through changes in housing consumption. Somewhat ironically, this case covers both the models in Epple et al. (1983, 1984, 1993) in which voters are completely ignorant about capitalization (all ρs equal zero), and Yinger's (1982, 1985) in which voters are very aware of capitalization (ρ_1 through ρ_4 equal one).[14]

In this case, all terms containing a ρ cancel out. Perceptions about capital gains exactly offset perceptions about the opportunity cost of housing, and perceptions about the community tax base exactly offset perceptions about one's own taxes. The first-order conditions reduce to:

$$\frac{U_H}{U_Z} = P\left(1+t^*\right)$$

$$\frac{U_S}{U_Z} = E_S$$

$$\frac{U_S}{U_H} = \frac{E_S}{P\left(1+t^*\right)}. \tag{13.12}$$

With P as the shadow price of H and the marginal cost term, E_S, as the shadow price of S, these conditions reveal that the property tax is a source of distortion in the household's choice between H and Z and between S and H. This is, of course, the distortion emphasized by Oates (1972, 1977a). Somewhat ironically, capitalization ensures that the housing price households respond to, namely $P(1 + t^*)$, does not vary across communities (see Yinger, 1985; Yinger et al., 1988), so it may appear at first glance that capitalization eliminates distortion from the property tax. The problem is that the housing price firms respond to, namely P, does vary across communities with capitalization, so household decisions do not line up with those of firms as required for efficiency.

Recall that Oates has backed away from the conclusion that the property tax causes inefficiency. This change of heart is based on the well known work of Hamilton (1975, 1976, 1979, 1983), who builds a model in which a local property tax is not a source of distortion. The first key assumption in the Hamilton model is that communities can be created costlessly, so that everyone lives in a homogeneous community that provides exactly the public services they prefer at the least possible cost. The second key assumption is that a community sets a zoning ordinance exactly equal to the housing demand of its identical residents. In selecting its own housing consumption, a household also is selecting the community tax base – and knows it is doing so. Thus the level of housing services selected by the household, H, also becomes the housing services variable in the community budget constraint in (13.10). In this case, the second condition in (13.11) becomes $U_H - \lambda = 0$. It follows that $U_H/U_Z = P$, which, when combined with firms' behavior, satisfies the necessary conditions for efficiency.[15]

Oates (1994) and Fischel (1992) argue that some evidence supports this model, such as the tendency for communities to be more homogeneous than urban areas. As Oates puts it (p. 141), 'There are some bits of evidence that one can take as favorable to the Hamilton–Fischel position.' Even on the surface, however, the central assumptions of the model are extreme. Communities may be more homogeneous than urban areas, but often they are very heterogeneous. Moreover, actual zoning tools, such as lot-size restrictions, are far too blunt to control H in the way required by the theory, and current residents have an incentive to set zoning barriers above their own level of H so that they will be subsidized by future residents (see Miceli, 1991, 1992).[16]

More importantly, the tidbits of evidence that might support the Hamilton model are far outweighed by the evidence that contradicts it. In particular, the Hamilton assumptions imply no capitalization of public services and taxes into house values. No one would pay a relatively high price for housing in a community with relatively good public services if another community with the same services could be costlessly created. Thus the extensive literature documenting public service and tax capitalization explicitly contradicts the Hamilton model.[17]

The Hamilton model also assumes that the marginal cost of public services is not a function of income or concentrated disadvantage (see Ross and Yinger, 1999). If it were, then a household might outbid existing residents in a community with a higher average income than its own, even with zoning barriers, to take advantage of the lower cost of public services there. Thus, it is somewhat ironic that Oates would come close to embracing the Hamilton model, because his work (Bradford et al., 1969; Oates, 1977a, 1981) has been instrumental in convincing people that this assumption is not correct. Indeed, dozens of studies show that the cost of public services is higher in communities with more concentrated poverty or disadvantage.[18]

In short, I conclude that Oates's original position was correct: the local property tax is a source of distortion in housing consumption.

Capitalization and Efficiency

The second equation in (13.12) reveals that there is no distortion in the choice between S and Z; combined with (13.9), this equation shows that the relevant efficiency condition, (13.3), is satisfied. Some authors (see for example Brueckner, 1979, 1982, 1983) have concluded on the basis of a comparable result that the choice of S is efficient. As I have pointed out elsewhere (1985), this is not correct: according to the theory of the second best (Lipsey and Lancaster,

1956), if one of the first-order conditions is not met (in this case the condition for H relative to Z) then the others are no longer valid guides to optimality.[19] However, this result does suggest that if local governments were funded by a non-distortionary tax, capitalization would not be a source of inefficiency, at least, not under this set of assumptions about perceptions.[20]

The question is whether this result holds for other sets of perceptions. To answer this question, let us bring in expressions for capitalization, namely, P_t and P_S. These derivatives have been extensively studied (see Henderson, 1977; Wheaton, 1993; Yinger, 1982, 1995; Yinger et al., 1988). Let β be the degree of property tax capitalization. Then the well-known expression for the capitalization of property taxes is[21]

$$\frac{P_t}{P} = \frac{-\beta}{r + \beta t}. \tag{13.13}$$

In theory, β should be equal to unity, but may not be in practice.[22] In the current context, we are concerned with voters' perceptions about capitalization, so we will interpret β as the perceived degree of capitalization.[23]

The expression for $P_S H$ is also well known. Adding α to indicate the degree of public service capitalization, this expression is:

$$P_S H = \alpha \frac{U_S^*}{U_Z^*} \frac{r}{r + \beta t}, \tag{13.14}$$

where the asterisk is included to indicate that the relevant utility function is that of people moving into the community, not of people who already live there. As before, α is interpreted as the (accurate) degree of capitalization perceived by voters. In addition, I assume that the people at the margin of moving into the community have the same marginal benefit from local services as voters. This assumption is not the same as the long-run equilibrium assumption made earlier. Long-run equilibrium requires that the people in the community want services just the way they are and that everyone in the community pays the same price of housing. But this assumption is about the derivative of willingness to pay; even in equilibrium, it might be true that an increase in S would be more valued by people living elsewhere (but who are just indifferent between their community and the voters' community) than by the voters.[24] I assume this case away.

These assumptions make it possible to substitute (13.14) and (13.13) into (13.11). The result is:

$$\frac{U_S}{U_Z} = E_S\left(\frac{V}{\overline{V}}\right)\left(\frac{r + \beta t + \beta r(\rho_1 - \rho_2) - \beta t\rho_3}{r + \beta t + \alpha r(\rho_1 - \rho_2) - \beta t\rho_4 + (\alpha - \beta)t\dfrac{\overline{H}_P}{\overline{H}}\rho_5}\right) \tag{13.15}$$

In two important cases, (13.15) reduces to the second equation in (13.12) – the result that indicates no distortion from capitalization itself. (Recall that we are examining a homogeneous community, where $V/\overline{V} = 1$.) The first case is the one already considered, namely $\rho_1 = \rho_2$, $\rho_3 = \rho_4$, and $\rho_5 = 0$. The second case is defined by $\alpha = \beta$ and $\rho_3 = \rho_4$. In an expansion of the irony mentioned earlier, this case includes, but is not limited to, the full-information case in which α, β, and all the ρs equal unity and the no-awareness case in which all these parameters equal zero. If the degree of capitalization is perceived to be the same for services and taxes, then a budget increase (from the optimal level) will be perceived to have no impact on housing bids. With no change in housing bids, community-wide housing consumption responses to price change are irrelevant and drop out, regardless of the value of ρ_5. However, ρ_3 must still equal ρ_4; otherwise, the capitalization effects in the individual and community budget constraints do not offset each other.

These two cases define sufficient conditions, not necessary ones. In fact, (13.15) reduces to the second condition in (13.12) in an infinite number of other cases. However, all these other cases could be described as coincidental in the sense that unrelated terms happen to add up in such a way that the numerator and denominator of (13.15) are equal to each other.

These results can be summarised by the following *capitalization/perceptions neutrality theorem*: if voters' perceptions are such that either (a) $\rho_1 = \rho_2$, $\rho_3 = \rho_4$, and $\rho_5 = 0$ or (b) $\alpha = \beta > 0$ and $\rho_3 = \rho_4$, then the second condition of (13.12) is satisfied and capitalization can be said to make no independent contribution to inefficiency in public service provision. With any other set of perceptions, capitalization will be neutral in this sense only by coincidence. For example, capitalization may not be neutral if voters are aware of property tax capitalization, perhaps because wide variation in assessment practices, and hence in effective tax rates within their community, can be observed to affect house values, but are not aware that house values increase with public service quality improvements.[25]

The problem, of course, is that we have essentially no evidence on voters' perceptions, concerning either the five ρ parameters or the two types of capitalization. We can state the conditions under which capitalization will not be a source of inefficiency, but we do not know whether these conditions hold or the direction of the inefficiency if they do not.

Possible Empirical Tests

In principle, we could gain insight into voter preferences through an empirical investigation either of the demand for public services or the determinants of house value. Consider first public service demand. Equation (13.11) indicates that a voter sets the marginal benefit from public services equal to the perceived tax price. In traditional models, the tax price consists of the tax share, $V/\bar{V}$, and the marginal resource cost, E_S.[26] In a log-linear model, which is often used in this context, the log of each of these variables enters as a separate variable. These studies are reviewed in Rubinfeld (1987). See Duncombe and Yinger (1997) for a recent example. Voter perceptions result in a third term, the one in large parentheses in (13.15). The importance of perceptions could be examined by including this term in an empirical analysis of public service demand.

This step appears to be difficult, however, if not impossible. In the first place, the key parameters in this term, namely the ρs, enter in a non-linear fashion, and indeed ρ_1 and ρ_2 cannot be distinguished. Moreover, this term requires either that the researcher estimate α and β, which also enter non-linearly, or come up with outside estimates of them. Finally, one of the variables in the term, namely $\bar{H}_p$, cannot be measured without a complex estimating procedure of its own.

The second potential empirical test, based on house values, does not appear any more promising. Many studies have estimated β (see Yinger et al., 1988), and, following Oates's (1969) lead, several studies have included both public service variables and tax rates in a house-value regression. Some studies, including Oates's, use public spending and others use outcome measures, such as school test scores. For a review, see Ross and Yinger (1999). However, the degree of capitalization in (13.14), α, applies to the marginal benefit from public services, not to either spending or outcomes. In fact, α cannot be estimated without obtaining a measure of this marginal benefit, presumably by estimating the demand function for public services, as in Duncombe and Yinger (1997), and then inverting it.[27] The estimated value of α is the coefficient of this marginal benefit measure in a house value regression. No study of public service capitalization has included such a measure, so no study has provided an estimate of α.

Moreover, a house value regression can provide only one piece of information relevant to equation (13.15), namely whether $\alpha = \beta$ in the market housing price function. It cannot determine whether voters' perceptions about these parameters are accurate and it cannot provide direct evidence on the efficiency of public services. As shown earlier, capitalization can be a source of inefficiency even when $\alpha = \beta$ if $\rho_3 \neq \rho_4$, and capitalization may not be a source of inefficiency when this condition is violated if $\rho_1 = \rho_2$, $\rho_3 = \rho_4$, and $\rho_5 = 0$. Thus, an estimate of a would be valuable, but would provide only partial information about voters' perceptions – and about the efficiency consequences of capitalization.

Overall, therefore, it seems unlikely that clear answers about voters' perceptions or about capitalization and efficiency will be forthcoming in the near future. Given the apparent importance of voters' perceptions in determining public service outcomes, and given the need for clearer insight into the efficiency of our system of local governments, I hope that some clever researcher(s) will undermine this prediction.

CONCLUSIONS

Oates's contributions have profoundly affected the development of local public finance over the last few decades. His initial statements on the inefficiency caused by a local property tax helped enrich the debate on the efficiency of local governments and to remind scholars that even Tiebout or Tiebout-like assumptions may not remove all the obstacles to efficient levels of local public services. His empirical work on capitalization inspired dozens of scholars, including myself, and started one of the principal branches of empirical work in local public finance.

The analysis presented here brings these two elements of Oates's work together. It shows that, except under extreme assumptions, the local property tax does distort housing decisions, regardless of voters' perceptions about capitalization. This distortion implies that local public service levels also are not efficient. Moreover, this analysis shows that the capitalization of taxes and public services into house values can be a source of efficiency in local public service levels even with non-distortionary taxes, although both the existence and sign of this inefficiency depend on perceptions concerning capitalization about which we have no direct evidence. It appears that existing methods for studying both public service demand and house value determination are ill-suited to measuring these perceptions. As a result, new methods will be required to study these important issues, and Oates's legacy will undoubtedly remain central to both conceptual and empirical research in local public finance for many more years.

NOTES

* It has been a great pleasure to prepare this paper for a volume honoring Wally Oates. My interest in local public finance was sparked in his public finance class at Princeton twenty-five years ago (for which, I recall, I wrote my first paper on capitalization), and I have been an admirer of his work ever since. This paper has been enriched by conversations with Stephen Ross and the comments of Arvind Panagariya and Bob Schwab.

1. This connection was first made, I believe, in Yinger (1985), but that paper did not quite have it right and was incomplete.

2. For example, Wicks, Little, and Beck (1968) estimate property tax capitalization and Orr (1968) estimates the impact of property taxes and education spending on rents. Even earlier studies of property tax capitalization, which are not sophisticated methodologically, go back as far as 1931. See Bloom, Ladd, and Yinger (1983).
3. The instruments used by Oates were median schooling of adult males, population density, percentage of dwellings owner-occupied, percentage change in the population over the last decade, percentage of population enrolled in public school, a dummy variable for Hudson County, and the value of commercial and industrial property per resident. Pollakowski argued that the first three instruments describe the characteristics of the people who choose a community, choices that are, in principle, endogenous. Neither Oates nor Pollakowski provides any evidence about which variables actually are endogenous.
4. Oates also mentions a second type of inefficiency that arises because with a property tax, compared with a non-distortionary head tax: 'the relatively wealthy, who typically occupy the residences of higher value, will find that their tax-price at the new rent levels exceeds the head tax they paid previously.... Conversely, those living in relatively low-value dwellings will find, for a time, that their position is improved, since their tax-price is less than under the head tax' (p. 136). I do not find this analysis to be compelling. A distortion is caused by the introduction of a connection between housing consumption decisions and property taxes, not by a change in amount of tax paid. This connection is introduced for all residents, regardless of their wealth. There may be equity issues here (as Oates also says), but I do not see a second type of inefficiency.
5. As discussed below, I disagree with Oates's statement that capitalization is consistent with the benefits view. Apparently, he used to disagree with it himself: '[S]everal authors have pointed out that *full*-Tiebout equilibrium would imply an absence of any capitalization' (1981, p. 94)
6. The efficiency implications of the behavior of public officials are explored in Inman (1987) and the other two efficiency topics are reviewed in Ross and Yinger (1999). All these efficiency topics, and several others, also are reviewed in Wildasin (1986).
7. This approach requires the assumption that households and firms are efficiently allocated to communities; otherwise, by the theory of the second-best, the first-order conditions of this problem are not valid guides to optimality. See Ross and Yinger (1999). For an analysis of the efficient allocation of households to communities, see Wildason (1986).
8. Although the notation is different, the formulation of the planner's problem presented here is identical to the one in Henderson and Quandt (1980), except for two simplifications: individual consumption or sale of inputs is not considered and all individuals are assumed to be alike (so that the utility of other individuals need not be held at a fixed level). Neither of these simplifications affects the results of interest here.
9. This formulation improves on the formulation offered in Yinger (1985). Second-order conditions are not considered here.
10. Henderson and Quandt (1980) use the term rate of commodity substitution instead of marginal rate of substitution. Note that the more familiar form of the rate of product transformation does not contain the derivatives with respect to K (or *L*, which could also be used) and has the same firm in the numerator and denominator. Both forms can be derived from equation (13.1).
11. Although not relevant to the formulation presented here, Oates also has contributed to our understanding of the behavior of household/voters, particularly their responses to intergovernmental aid, Oates (1972), and the extent to which their choices are influenced by decentralization, Oates (1985, 1989).
12. In some of my earlier work (1982, 1985), I analyse a household's housing and voting decisions separately. Here I combine them. As my earlier work emphasizes, these two approaches lead to the same answers.
13. I make no attempt to prove that an equilibrium exists. For a full discussion of this issue, see Epple et al. (1983, 1984, 1993).
14. A few other sets of assumptions have been considered. For example, Crane (1988, 1990). Sets $\rho_2 = 1$ and all the other ρs equal to zero.
15. In this case, *t* also drops out of the third condition in (13.11).
16. Oates (1977b) discusses assumptions about zoning himself.
17. For a more formal treatment of these issues, see Ross and Yinger (1999).

18. For a review, see Ross and Yinger (1999). Also, ironically, this work of Oates has implications for the Oates/Pollakowski debate of 1973. If, to some degree, income and poverty measure the cost of providing public services, then Oates's regression clearly does not untangle public service variables from exogenous control variables. The best way to handle this issue, it seems to me, is to switch from public spending to public outcome variables and not to use public service costs as control variables in the capitalization equation.
19. For one attempt to derive second-best efficiency conditions with a local property tax, see Yinger (1985).
20. Here the joke is on me; in an earlier paper (1985) I argued, incorrectly I now believe, that capitalization can be a source of inefficiency even with these assumptions.
21. This equation gives the exact form for estimating property tax capitalization (see Yinger et al., 1988). It is not the form used by Oates (1969). At least approximately, the theoretically correct form is log(*V*) regressed on *t*, not, as in Oates, *V* regressed on log(*t*).
22. For a review of the evidence, see Yinger et al. (1988) or Ross and Yinger (1999).
23. An equilibrium may not exist if the perceived degree of capitalization (of taxes or services) differs from the actual degree of capitalization. We do not consider this issue here and assume that voter perceptions are accurate.
24. These concepts are discussed at length in Epple et al. (1983, 1984, 1993).
25 In the case considered by Crane (1988, 1990), capitalization is not neutral unless $\alpha = \beta$. See note 14.
26. As first pointed out by Bradford et al. (1969), the resource cost of public services reflects both input costs and environmental factors. For recent work on public service costs, see Ladd and Yinger (1991), Downs and Pogue (1994) and Duncombe and Yinger (1997).
27. Oates's (1969) article compares the impact on house values of increased spending on schools with the impact of the taxes that spending would require. However, this calculation sheds no light on the value of α.

REFERENCES

Bloom, Howard S, Helen F. Ladd and John Yinger (1983), 'Are Property Taxes Capitalized into House Values', in G.R. Zodrow (ed.) *Local Provision of Public Services: The Tiebout Model After Twenty-Five Years*, New York: Academic Press, pp. 145–64.

Bradford, D., R. Malt and W.E. Oates (1969), 'The Rising Cost of Local Public Services: Some Evidence and Reflections', *National Tax Journal*, **22**, 185–202.

Brueckner, Jan K. (1979), 'Property Values, Local Public Expenditure, and Economic Efficiency', *Journal of Urban Economics*, **11**, 223–46.

Brueckner, Jan K. (1982), 'A Test for Allocative Efficiency in the Local Public Sector', *Journal of Public Economics*, **14**, 311–32.

Brueckner, Jan K. (1983), 'Property Value Maximization and Public Sector Efficiency', *Journal of Urban Economics*, **14**, 1–16.

Crane, Randall (1988), 'Second-Best Property Value Capitalization', *Economic Letters*, **26**, 175–8.

Crane, Randall (1990), 'Price Specification and the Demand for Public Goods', *Journal of Public Economics*, **43**, 93–106.

Downes, Thomas A. and Thomas F. Pogue (1994), 'Adjusting School Aid Formulas for the Higher Cost of Educating Disadvantaged Students', *National Tax Journal*, **67**, 89–110.

Duncombe, William and John Yinger (1997), 'Why Is It So Hard to Help Central City Schools?', *Journal of Policy Analysis and Management*, **16**, 85–113.

Epple, Dennis, Radu Filimon and Thomas Romer (1983), 'Housing, Voting, and Moving: Equilibrium in a Model of Local Public Goods with Multiple Jurisdictions', in J.V. Henderson (ed.), *Research in Urban Economics*, Vol. III, Greenwich, CT: JAI Press, pp. 59–90.

Epple, Dennis, Radu Filimon and Thomas Romer (1984), 'Equilibrium Among Local Jurisdictions: Toward an Integrated Treatment of Voting and Residential Choice', *Journal of Public Economics*, **24**, 281–308.

Epple, Dennis, Radu Filimon and Thomas Romer (1993), 'Existence of Voting and Housing Equilibrium in a System of Communities with Property Taxes', *Regional Science and Urban Economics*, **23**, November, 585–610.

Fischel, William A. (1992), 'Property Taxation and the Tiebout Model: Evidence for the Benefit View from Voting and Zoning', *Journal of Economic Literature*, **30**, 171–7.

Hamilton, Bruce W. (1975), 'Zoning and Property Taxation in a System of Local Governments', *Urban Studies*, **12**, 205–11.

Hamilton, Bruce W. (1976), 'Capitalization of Intrajurisdictional Differences in Local Tax Prices', *American Economic Review*, **22**, December, 743–53.

Hamilton, Bruce W. (1979), 'Capitalization and the Regressivity of the Property Tax: Empirical Evidence', *National Tax Journal*, **32**, Supplement (June), 169–80.

Hamilton, Bruce W. (1983), 'A Review: Is the Property Tax a Benefit Tax?' in G.R. Zodrow (ed.), *Local Provisions of Public Services: The Tiebout Model after Twenty-Five Years*, New York: Academic Press, pp. 85–108.

Heinberg, J. and W.E. Oates (1970), 'The Incidence of Differential Property Taxes on Urban Housing: A Comment and Some Further Evidence', *National Tax Journal*, **23**, 92–8.

Henderson, James M. and Richard B. Quandt (1971), *Microeconomic Theory: A Mathematical Approach*, second edition, New York: McGraw-Hill.

Henderson, J. Vernon (1977), *Economic Theory and the Cities*, New York: Academic Press.

Inman, Robert (1987), 'Markets, Governments, and the "New" Political Economy', in A.J. Auerbach and M. Feldstein (eds), *Handbook of Public Finance*, Vol. 2, New York: North-Holland, pp. 647–778.

Ladd, Helen F. and John Yinger (1991), *America's Ailing Cities: Fiscal Health and the Design of Urban Policy*, updated edition, Baltimore: Johns Hopkins University Press.

Lipsey, Richard G. and Kevin Lancaster (1956), 'The General Theory of the Second Best', *Review of Economic Studies*, **24**, 11–32.

Miceli, Thomas J. (1991), 'Free Riders and Distortionary Zoning by Local Communities', *Journal of Urban Economics*, **30**, 112–22.

Miceli, Thomas J. (1992), 'Optimal Fiscal Zoning when the Local Government is a Discriminating Monopolist', *Regional Science and Urban Economics*, **22**, 579–96.

Oates, W.E. (1969), 'The Effects of Property Taxes and Local Public Services on Property Values: An Empirical Study of Tax Capitalization and the Tiebout Hypothesis', *Journal of Political Economy*, **77**, 957–71.

Oates, W.E. (1972), *Fiscal Federalism*, New York: Harcourt Brace.

Oates, W.E. (1973), 'The Effects of Property Taxes and Local Spending on Property Values: A Reply and Yet Further Results', *Journal of Political Economy*, **81**, 1004–8.

Oates, W.E. (1977a), 'An Economist's Perspective on Fiscal Federalism', in W.E. Oates (ed.), *The Political Economy of Fiscal Federalism*, Lexington: Lexington Books.

Oates, W.E. (1977b), 'The Use of Local Zoning Ordinances to Regulate Population Flows and the Quality of Local Services', in O.C. Ashenfelter and W.E. Oates (eds), *Essays in Labor Market Analysis*, New York: John Wiley & Sons, pp. 201–20.

Oates, W.E. (1981), 'On Local Finance and the Tiebout Model', *American Economic Review*, **71**, May, 93–8.
Oates, W.E. (1985), 'Searching for Leviathan: An Empirical Study', *American Economic Review*, **75**, September, 748–57.
Oates, W.E. (1989), 'Searching for Leviathan: A Reply and Some Further Reflections', *American Economic Review*, **79**, June, 748–57.
Oates, W.E. (1994), 'Federalism and Government Finance', in J.S. Quigley and E. Smolensky (eds), *Modern Public Finance*, Cambridge, MA: Harvard University Press, pp. 126–61.
Orr, Larry L. (1968), 'The Incidence of Differential Property Taxes on Urban Housing', *National Tax Journal*, **21**, 253–62.
Pollakowski, Henry O. (1973), 'The Effects of Property Taxes and Local Public Spending on Property Values: A Comment and Further Results', *Journal of Political Economy*, **5**, 119–29.
Ross, Stephen, and John Yinger (1999), 'Sorting and Voting: A Review of the Literature on Urban Public Finance', in Paul Cheshire and Edwin S. Mills (eds), *Handbook of Urban and Regional Economics, volume 3, Applied Urban Economics*, Amsterdam: North-Holland, pp. 2001–60.
Rubinfeld, Daniel L. (1987), 'The Economics of the Local Public Sector', in A.J. Auerbach and M. Feldstein (eds), *Handbook of Public Economics*, Vol II, New York: North-Holland, pp. 571–646.
Schwab, Robert and Wallace E. Oates (1991), 'Community Composition and the Provision of Local Public Goods: A Normative Analysis', *Journal of Public Economics*, **44**, 217–37.
Tiebout, Charles M. (1956), 'A Pure Theory of Local Expenditures', *Journal of Political Economy*, **64**, 416–24.
Wheaton, William C. (1993), 'Land Capitalization, Tiebout Mobility, and the Role of Zoning Regulations', *Journal of Urban Economics*, **34**, 102–17.
Wicks, J.H., R.A. Little and R.A. Beck (1968), 'A Note on Capitalization of Property Tax Changes', *National Tax Journal*, **21**, 263–5.
Wildasin, David E. (1986), *Urban Public Finance*, London: Harwood Academic Publishers.
Yinger, John (1982), 'Capitalization and the Theory of Local Public Finance', *Journal of Political Economy*, **90**, 917–43.
Yinger, John (1985), 'Inefficiency and the Median Voter: Property Taxes, Capitalization, Heterogeneity, and the Theory of the Second Best', in J.M. Quigley (ed.), *Perspectives on Local Public Finance and Public Policy*, Vol 2, Greenwich, CT: JAI Press, pp. 3–30.
Yinger, John (1995), 'Capitalization and Sorting: A Revision', *Public Finance Quarterly*, **23**, April, 217–25.
Yinger, John, Howard S. Bloom, Axel Boersch-Supan and Helen F. Ladd (1988), *Property Taxes and House Values: The Theory and Estimation of Intrajurisdictional Property Tax Capitalization*, New York: Academic Press.

Wallace E. Oates: published books and papers

BOOKS

1972, *Fiscal Federalism* (NY: Harcourt Brace Jovanovich); translated into Spanish: *Federalismo Fiscal* (Madrid: Instituto de Estudios de Administracion Local, 1977). Chapter 1 translated into German as 'Ein okonomischer Ansatz zum Foderalismusproblem', in G. Kirsch (ed.), *Foderalismus* (Stuttgart: Gustav Fisher Verlag, 1977), pp. 15–26. Chapter 1 reprinted in S. Baker and C. Elliott (eds), *Readings in Public Sector Economics* (Lexington, MA: Heath, 1990), pp. 554–65. Reissued by Gregg Revivals (Aldershot, UK, 1993). Chapter 1 translated into Spanish as 'Un enfoque economico del Federalismo', in J. Corona (ed.), *Lecturas de Hacienda Publica* (Madrid: Minerva, 1994), pp. 403–18. Japanese translation, Tokyo, 1997.

1974, *An Introduction to Econometrics: Principles and Applications*, with H. Kelejian (NY: Harper and Row); revised edition, 1981. Portuguese translation: *Introducao a Econometrica* (Rio de Janeiro; Elsevier/North-Holland, 1978). Third edition (1989).

1975, *The Theory of Environmental Policy*, with W. Baumol (Englewood Cliffs, NJ: Prentice-Hall). Translated into Spanish: *La Teoria de la Politica Economica del Medio Ambiente* (Barcelona: St. Pere Claver, 1982). Second edition (Cambridge, MA: Cambridge University Press, 1988).

1975, edited jointly with E. Mills, *Fiscal Zoning and Land Use Controls* (Lexington, MA: Heath-Lexington).

1975, editor, *Financing the New Federalism: Revenue Sharing. Conditional Grants, and Taxation* (Baltimore, MD: Johns Hopkins Press).

1977, editor, *The Political Economy of Fiscal Federalism* (Lexington, MA: Heath-Lexington).

1977, edited jointly with O. Ashenfelter, *Essays in Labor Market Analysis* (NY: Wiley).

1979, *Economics. Environmental Policy. and the Quality of Life*, with W. Baumol (Englewood Cliffs, NJ: Prentice-Hall). Chapter 2 reprinted as 'Long Run Trends in Environmental Quality', in J. Simon and H. Kahn (eds), *The Resourceful Earth* (Oxford: Basil Blackwell, 1984), Ch. 16, pp. 439–75;

reprinted in J. Simon (ed.), *The State of Humanity* (Oxford: Blackwells 1995), pp. 449–69. Reissued by Gregg Revivals (Aldershot, UK, 1993).

1991, *Studies in Fiscal Federalism* (Aldershot, UK: Edward Elgar).

1992, editor, *The Economics of the Environment* (Aldershot, UK: Edward Elgar).

1996, *The Economics of Environmental Regulation* (Aldershot, UK: Edward Elgar).

1998, editor, *The Economics of Fiscal Federalism and Local Finance* (Cheltenham, UK: Edward Elgar).

MONOGRAPHS, JOURNAL ARTICLES, AND CHAPTERS IN BOOKS

1966, *The Implications of International Economic Integration for Monetary, Fiscal, and Exchange-Rate Policy*, with R. McKinnon (Princeton, NJ: Princeton Studies in International Finance, No. 16.)

1966, 'Budget Balance and Equilibrium Income: A Comment on the Efficacy of Fiscal and Monetary Policy in an Open Economy', *Journal of Finance* (September), **21**: 489–98.

1968, 'The Theory of Public Finance in a Federal System', *Canadian Journal of Economics* (February), **1**: 37–54.

1968, 'The Dual Impact of Federal Aid on State and Local Government Expenditures: A Comment', *National Tax Journal* (June), **21**: 220–23.

1969, 'The Rising Cost of Local Public Services: Some Evidence and Reflections', with D. Bradford and R. Malt, *National Tax Journal* (June), **22**: 185–202; reprinted in *Bobbs-Merrill Reprint Series in Economics*, Econ-49; reprinted in W. Patrick Beaton (ed.), *Municipal Needs, Services, and Financing* (New Brunswick, NJ: Center for Urban Policy Research, Rutgers University, 1974), pp. 223–40.

1969, 'The Effects of Property Taxes and Local Public Spending on Property Values: An Empirical Study of Tax Capitalization and the Tiebout Hypothesis', *Journal of Political Economy* (November/December), **77**: 957–71; reprinted in A. Atkinson(ed.), *Modern Public Finance* (Aldershot, UK: Edward Elgar, 1991), pp. 344–58.

1970, 'The Incidence of Differential Property Taxes on Urban Housing: A Comment and Some Further Evidence', with J. Heinberg, *National Tax Journal* (March), **23**: 92–8.

1970, 'The Effectiveness of Graduate Students as Teachers of the Principles of Economics', with R. Quandt, *Journal of Economic Education* (Spring), **1**: 131–8.

1970, 'Group Size and the Output of Public Goods: Theory and an Application to State-Local Finance in the United States', with J. Litvack, *Public Finance*, **25** (1): 42–62.

1971, 'The Analysis of Public Policy in Dynamic Urban Models', with W. Baumol and E. Howrey, *Journal of Political Economy* (January/February), **79**: 142–53.

1971, 'Towards a Predictive Theory of Intergovernmental Grants', with D. Bradford, *American Economic Review* (May), **61**: 440–48; reprinted in Spanish translation, 'Hacia una teoria predictiva de las subvencciones intergubernamentales', in A. Gimenez, (ed.), *Financiacion de las Autonomias* (Madrid: H. Blume Ediciones, 1979), pp. 143–62; reprinted in B. Grewal, R. Mathews, and G. Brennan (eds), *The Economics of Federalism* (Canberra: Australian National University Press, 1980), pp. 321–33.

1971, 'The Analysis of Revenue Sharing in a New Approach to Collective Fiscal Decisions', with D. Bradford, *Quarterly Journal of Economics* (August), **85**: 416–39; reprinted in Spanish translation, 'El analysis de la participacion impositiva en el marco de las decisiones fiscales colectivas', in A. Gimenez (ed.), *Financiacion de las Autonomias* (Madrid: H. Blume Ediciones, 1979), pp. 163–88.

1971, 'The Use of Standards and Prices for Protection of the Environment', with W. Baumol, *Swedish Journal of Economics* (March), **73**: 42–54; reprinted in P. Bohm and A. Kneese (eds), *The Economics of the Environment: Papers from Four Nations* (NY: St. Martin's Press, 1972); reprinted in Italian translation in P. Bohm and A. Kneese (eds), *L'Economia Dell'Ambiente* (Milano: Fra Angeli; editore, 1974), pp. 101–19; reprinted in German translation in H. Siebert (ed.), *Umwelt und Wirtschaftliche Entwicklung* (Darmstadt: Wissenschaftliche Buchgesellschaft, 1979), pp. 169–88; reprinted in German translation in H. Moller et al. (eds), *Umweltokonomik: Beitrage zur Theorie und Politik* (Verlagsgruppe, Athenaum, 1982), pp. 254–66; reprinted in W. Oates (ed.) *The Economics of the Environment* (Aldershot, UK: Edward Elgar, 1992), pp. 161–73; reprinted in Czech translation in P. Sauer and M. Livingston (eds), *Ekonomic Zivotniho Prostredi a Ekologicka Politica* (Praha, 1996), pp. 121–33.

1972, 'The Cost Disease of the Personal Services and the Quality of Life', with W. Baumol, *Skandinaviska Enskilda Banken, Quarterly Review* (No. 2): 43–54; reprinted in H. Hochman (ed.), *The Urban Economy* (NY: Norton, 1976), pp. 41–56; reprinted in Spanish translation, 'La Enfermedad de Costes de los Servicios del Sector Publico', in A. Vinardell (ed.), *Teoria de la Democracia, una Approximacion Economica* (Madrid: Instituto de Estudios Fiscales, 1980), pp. 461–84.

1972, 'The Incidence of Differential Property Taxes on Rental Housing: An Addendum', with J. Heinberg, *National Tax Journal* (June), **25**: 221–2.

1973, 'The Effects of Property Taxes and Local Public Spending on Property Values: A Reply and Yet Further Results', *Journal of Political Economy* (July/August), **81**: 1004–8.

1974, 'Suburban Exploitation of Central Cities and Governmental Structure', with D. Bradford, in H. Hochman and G. Peterson (eds), *Redistribution Through Public Choice* (NY: Columbia University Press), pp. 43–90.

1975, 'The Instruments for Environmental Policy', with W. Baumol, in E. Mills (ed.), *Economic Analysis of Environmental Problems* (NY: Columbia University Press), pp. 95–128.

1975, 'Automatic Increases in Tax Revenues: Their Effect on the Size of the Public Budget', in W. Oates (ed.), *Financing the New Federalism: Revenue Sharing, Conditional Grants, and Taxation* (Baltimore, MD: Johns Hopkins Press), pp. 139–60.

1976, 'Conservation of Resources and the Price System', with W. Baumol, in R. Leiter and S. Friedlander (eds), *Economics of Resources* (NY: Cyrco Press), pp. 15–35.

1976, 'The Uncertain Search for Environmental Quality', *University of Pennsylvania Law Review* (January): 864–91.

1977, 'An Economist's Perspective on Fiscal Federalism', in W. Oates (ed.), *The Political Economy of Fiscal Federalism* (Lexington, MA: Heath-Lexington), pp. 3–20; reprinted in Edward C. Kienzle, *Study Guide and Readings for Stiglitz's Economics of the Public Sector*, Second edition (NY: Norton, 1989), pp. 331–9.

1977, 'The Use of Local Zoning Ordinances to Regulate Population Flows and the Quality of Local Services' in O. Ashenfelter and W. Oates (eds), *Essays in Labor Market Analysis* (NY: Wiley), pp. 201–19.

1978, 'The Changing Structure of Intergovernmental Fiscal Relations', in H. Recktenwald (ed.), *Secular Trends of the Public Sector* (Paris: Editions Cujas), pp. 151–60.

1978, 'The Use of Effluent Fees to Regulate Public-Sector Sources of Pollution: An Application of the Niskanen Model', with D. Strassmann, *Journal of Environmental Economics and Management* (September), **5**: 283–91.

1979, 'Lump-Sum Intergovernmental Grants Have Price Effects', in P. Mieszkowski and W. Oakland (eds), *Fiscal Federalism and Grants-in-Aid* (Washington, DC: The Urban Institute), pp. 23–30.

1980, 'The Role of Intergovernmental Grants in the U.S. Economy with Special Attention to Countercyclical Policy', in Joint Economic Committee, US Congress, *Special Study on Economic Change, Volume 6, Federal Finance: The Pursuit of American Goals* (Washington, DC: US Government Printing Office, 23 December), pp. 331–57.

1981, 'Fiscal Structure in the Federal System', in J. Aronson and E. Schwartz (eds), *Management Policies in Local Government Finance*, Second edition

(Washington, DC: International City Management Association), Ch. 11, pp. 234–54. Third edition (1987), pp. 51-73. Fourth edition (1996), pp. 58–76.

1981, 'On Local Finance and the Tiebout Model', *American Economic Review* (May), **71**: 93–8.

1981, 'Corrective Taxes and Auctions of Rights in the Control of Externalities: Some Further Thoughts', *Public Finance Quarterly* (October), **2**: 471–78.

1982, 'Efficiency in Pollution Control in the Short and Long Runs: A System of Rental Emission Permits', with R. Collinge, *Canadian Journal of Economics* (May), **15**: 346–54.

1982, 'The New Federalism: An Economist's View', *The Cato Journal* (Fall), **2**: 473–88.

1983, 'On Marketable Air-Pollution Permits: The Case for a System of Pollution Offsets', with A. Krupnick and E. Van De Verg, *Journal of Environmental Economics and Management* (September), **10**: 233–47. An earlier draft of this paper appeared in E. Joeres and M. David (eds), *Buying a Better Environment*, Land Economic Monograph No. 6 (Madison, WI: University of Wisconsin Press, 1983), pp. 7–23.

1983, 'The Regulation of Externalities: Efficient Behavior by Sources and Victims', *Public Finance*, **38** (3): 362–75.

1984, 'Effluent Fees and Market Structure', with D. Strassmann, *Journal of Public Economics* (June), **24**: 29–46; reprinted in W. Oates (ed.), *The Economics of the Environment* (Aldershot, UK: Edward Elgar, 1992), pp. 261–78.

1984, 'Economic Incentives for Environmental Management: The Recent U.S. Experience', in H. Schneider and R. Sprenger (eds), *Mehr Umweltschutz fur Weniger Geld* (Munich: Ifo-Institut fur Wirtschaftsforschung), pp. 459–91.

1985, 'The Public Sector in Economics: An Analytical Chameleon', in H. Hanusch, et al. (eds), *Public Sector and Political Economy Today* (Stuttgart: Gustav Fischer Verlag), pp. 45–58.

1985, 'The Environment and the Economy: Environmental Policy at the Crossroads', in J. Quigley and D. Rubinfeld (eds), *American Domestic Priorities: An Economic Appraisal* (Berkeley, CA: University of California Press), pp. 311–45.

1985, 'Marketable Pollution Permits and Acid Rain Externalities: A Comment and Some Further Evidence', with A. McGartland, *Canadian Journal of Economics* (August), **18**: 668–75.

1985, 'Searching for Leviathan: An Empirical Study', *American Economic Review* (September), **75**: 748–57.

1985, 'Marketable Permits for the Prevention of Environmental Deterioration', with A. McGartland, *Journal of Environmental Economics and Management* (September), **12**: 207–28.

1985, 'Fiscal Limitations: An Assessment of the U.S. Experience', in E. Gramlich and B. Ysander (eds), *Control of Local Government* (Stockholm: The Industrial Institute for Economic and Social Research), pp. 91–136.

1986, 'Market Incentives for Environmental Protection: A Survey of Some Recent Developments', in M. Peston and R. Quandt (eds), *Prices. Competition. and Equilibrium* (London: Philip Allen), pp. 251–67.

1987, 'Assistance to the Poor in a Federal System', with C. Brown, *Journal of Public Economics* (April), **32**: 307–30.

1988, 'On the Nature and Measurement of Fiscal Illusion: A Survey', in G. Brennan et al. (eds), *Taxation and Fiscal Federalism: Essays in Honour of Russell Mathews* (Sydney: Australian National University Press), pp. 65–82.

1988, 'Decentralization in the Public Sector: An Empirical Study of State and Local Government', with J. Wallis, in H. Rosen (ed.), *Fiscal Federalism: Quantitative Studies* (Chicago IL: University of Chicago Press), pp. 5–28.

1988, 'A Pollution Tax Makes Sense', in H. Stein (ed.), *Tax Policy in the Twenty-First Century* (NY: Wiley), pp. 253–65.

1988, 'Economic Competition Among Jurisdictions: Efficiency-Enhancing or Distortion-Inducing?', with R. Schwab, *Journal of Public Economics* (April), **35**: 333–54.

1988, 'On the Measurement of Congestion in the Provision of Local Public Goods', *Journal of Urban Economics* (July): **24**, 85–94.

1988, 'Does Economic Sclerosis Set in with Age? An Empirical Study of the Olson Hypothesis', with J. Wallis, *Kyklos*, **41** (3): 397–417.

1989, 'Searching for Leviathan: A Reply and Some Further Reflections', *American Economic Review* (June), **79**: 578–83.

1989, 'The Net Benefits of Incentive-Based Regulation: A Case Study of Environmental Standard Setting', with P. Portney and A. McGartland, *American Economic Review* (December), **72**: 1233–42.

1990, 'Decentralization of the Public Sector: An Overview', in R. Bennett (ed.), *Decentralisation, Local Governments, and Markets* (Oxford: Oxford University Press), pp. 43–58.

1990, 'Economics, Economists, and Environmental Policy', (Presidential Address to the Eastern Economic Association), *Eastern Economic Journal* (October/December), **16**: 289–96.

1991, 'Community Composition and the Provision of Local Public Goods: A Normative Analysis', with R. Schwab, *Journal of Public Economics* (March), **44**: 217–37.

1991, 'The Allocative and Distributive Implications of Local Fiscal Competition', with R. Schwab, in D. Kenyon and J. Kincaid (eds), *Competition Among States and Local Governments* (Washington, DC: The Urban Institute), pp. 127–45.

1991, 'The Theory and Rationale of Local Property Taxation', in T. McGuire and D. Naimark (eds), *State and Local Finance for the 1990s: A Case Study of Arizona* (Tempe, AZ: School of Public Affairs, Arizona State University), pp. 407–24.

1991, 'Fiscal Federalism: An Overview', in R. Prud'homme (ed.), *Public Finance with Several Levels of Government* (The Hague: Foundation Journal of Public Finance), pp. 1–18.

1992, 'Economic Incentives and the Containment of Global Warming', with P. Portney, *Eastern Economic Journal* (Winter), **18**: 85–98.

1992, 'Environmental Economics: A Survey', with M. Cropper, *Journal of Economic Literature* (June), **30**: 675–740.

1992, 'Global Environmental Management: Towards an Open Economy Environmental Economics', in *Environment, Ethics, Economics and Institutions* (Milan: Cariplo), pp. 144–60.

1992, 'Measuring Peer Group Effects: A Study of Teenage Behavior', with W. Evans and R. Schwab, *Journal of Political Economy* (October), **100**: 966–91.

1993, 'Pollution Charges as a Source of Public Revenues', in H. Giersch (ed.), *Economic Progress and Environmental Concerns* (Berlin: Springer-Verlag), pp. 135–52.

1993, 'Fiscal Decentralization and Economic Development', *National Tax Journal* (June), **46**: 231–37.

1994, 'Federalism and Government Finance', in J. Quigley and E. Smolensky (eds), *Modern Public Finance* (Cambridge, MA.: Harvard University Press), pp. 126–51.

1994, 'Environment and Taxation: The Case of the United States', in *Environment and Taxation: The Cases of the Netherlands, Sweden, and the United States* (Paris: OECD), pp. 103–43.

1995, 'Green Taxes: Can We Protect the Environment and Improve the Tax System at the Same Time?', (Presidential Address to the Southern Economic Association), *Southern Economic Journal* (April), **61**: 915–22.

1995, 'Tightening Environmental Standards: The Benefit–Cost or the No-Cost Paradigm?', with K. Palmer and P. Portney, *Journal of Economic Perspectives* (Fall), **2**: 119–32.

1996, 'The Theory of Regulatory Federalism: The Case of Environmental Management', with R. Schwab, in W. Oates (ed.), *The Economics of Environmental Regulation* (Cheltenham, UK: Edward Elgar), pp. 319–31.

1996, 'Estimating the Demand for Public Goods: The Collective Choice and Contingent Valuation Approaches', in D. Bjornstad and J. Kahn (eds), *The Contingent Valuation of Environmental Resources* (Aldershot, UK: Edward Elgar), pp. 211–32.

1996, 'Taxation in a Federal System: The Tax-Assignment Problem', *Public Economics Review* (June), **1**: 35–60.

1996, 'Asymmetries in the Response to Increases and Decreases in Intergovernmental Grants: Some Empirical Findings', with S. Gamkhar, *National Tax Journal* (December), **49**: 501–12.

1997, 'The Impact of Urban Land Taxation: The Pittsburgh Experience', with R. Schwab, *National Tax Journal* (March), **50**: 1–21.

1997, 'On Environmental Federalism', *University of Virginia Law Review* (October), **83**: 1321–9.

1998, 'The Impact of the New Deal on American Federalism', with J. Wallis, in Michael Bordo et al. (eds), *The Defining Moment: The Great Depression and the American Economy in the 20th Century* (Chicago: University of Chicago Press for the National Bureau of Economic Research), pp. 155–80.

1998, 'The Pittsburgh Experience with Land Value Taxation', with R. Schwab, in H. Ladd (ed.), *Local Government Tax and Land Use Policies in the United States* (Aldershot, UK: Edward Elgar), pp. 133–43.

1998, (forthcoming) 'Environmental Policy in the European Community: Harmonization or National Standards?', *Empirica*.

Index